AN
EXEMPLARY
LIFE

AN EXEMPLARY LIFE

Siegfried Lenz

Translated by Douglas Parmée

 **HILL** AND **WANG**

NEW YORK

A division of Farrar, Straus and Giroux

First published in German as *Das Vorbild*
© Hoffmann und Campe Verlag, Hamburg 1973

English translation © 1976 by Farrar, Straus and Giroux, Inc.
All rights reserved
Published simultaneously in Canada by
McGraw-Hill Ryerson Ltd., Toronto
Printed in the United States of America
First edition, 1976

Library of Congress Cataloging in Publication Data

Lenz, Siegfried.
  An exemplary life.

  Translation of Das Vorbild.
  I. Title.
PZ4.L575Ex3 [PT2623.E583] 833'.9'14 76–23113

AN
EXEMPLARY
LIFE

1

Easy does it; they aren't going to appear suddenly out of the blue. They can't arrive as though by chance on a misty railway platform in November or turn up unexpectedly in the gloomy, scaffold-encased hotel like parcels through the mail. No, we can't spare them all the effort it takes to get together; we can't simply push them into the conference room, its walls heavily bedecked with all sorts of weapons, and then exhibit them in the cut and thrust of their judgments in a town such as this, which itself passes judgment on everyone who spends any time here. And once having entered Hamburg's gravitational field, they can't be presented in a vacuum as if they and their task were the only things around, because anyone who arrives in this city all set up with assignments and plans is, despite himself, evaluated, exposed, and compared—and that includes this man, Valentin Pundt, this stiff, burly man with his unparted hair brushed straight back, who is being carried up into the main hall of the central railway station on an escalator.

Let us put you in the picture straightway: this man standing hesitantly in the wan light of the hall and about to head for the wrong exit—with a leather suitcase in one hand and a weighty, travel-stained briefcase in the other, Valentin Pundt himself, who in his youth had met Beckmann and had been painted by him: "A North German Schoolmaster"—Pundt is one of the three experts who have been commissioned by a study group of the Ministry of Education and Cultural Affairs to produce a

3

prose anthology of material on Germany; they're meeting in Hamburg this time, in the damp month of November, which covers everything with grime.

Uncertainly, and unnoticed, eyeing a group of tired, blank-faced men who are promenading their cardboard boxes like grumbling, protesting children, he makes for the wrong exit and even on this short stretch becomes aware of all that this town has to offer and of its habit of accumulating events. For during their discussions, in appropriate privacy, of the third section of an entirely new reader on Germany, the port of Hamburg will, among other things, be celebrating its anniversary—more than seven hundred years of existence—and the Navy will be holding an Open House as part of a recruiting program. So flags and pennants will be flying briskly from halyards and masts, you'll be allowed onto the gundeck to let off a salvo in the direction of the cold-storage warehouses in Altona. A cook will play at being cook and distribute outsize portions of stew.

"No, you've made a mistake, this is the Glockengiesserwall exit, the Kirchenallee is on the other side," says a railway police-man; and so Valentin Pundt goes back again through the dreary, drafty hall, taken aback by the lack of consideration shown by two female sweepers, who are pushing their formidable brooms against the shoes of people standing nearby. Briskly they wield their brooms, the bristles swish over the dirty stone floor, raising clouds of dust which swirl up to the grime-darkened glass roof where scruffy pigeons eke out a living in permanent confine-ment. Valentin Pundt knows that he is expected at the Kirchenal-lee exit beside a mailbox, a mailbox impossible to miss, as Frau Dr. Süssfeldt had put it; others might thus have been tempted to speed up their pace and press on toward the meeting place more boldly, more eagerly and impetuously, perhaps even making a private wager with themselves: will she? won't she? But this man, coarse-skinned and unapproachable, apparently unwilling to ad-mit how heavy his luggage is, merely plods with a stiff and even stride through the gloom of the hall in his long, shaggy overcoat, which seems to have absorbed a lot of damp, perhaps the damp of a clump of autumnal fir trees, and we can easily understand why at the sight of Valentin Pundt groups of stocky Turks, Greeks, and Yugoslavs cut short their hearty conversations, nudge one another, exchange meaningful nods, and grin as they watch him struggling on toward the exit, successfully slicing through a formation of schoolchildren coming the other way. Those who continue to follow him with their eyes will see that he is hardly out of the station before he turns his inscrutable face to the left and—since he doesn't look to the right—presumably discovers the mailbox that is "impossible to miss" and, indeed, the mailbox and nothing else, although this neither perturbs nor discourages him but merely prompts him to scan the immediate vicinity from beneath his bristling eyebrows, relentlessly, as he slowly swivels from the hips. Nothing there; there's no one waiting for him even though he has now found the right exit. The train was not late. The date is indisputably correct. The outsize mailbox has no rivals in sight; and yet there is no one waiting for him.

Valentin Pundt decides to telephone. He goes diagonally across the hall, ponders whether to step on one of the brooms that are swishing toward him, but merely rivets the two shapeless women with a glance and, without setting down his luggage, joins the line in front of the telephone booths.

What is it that makes his luggage so heavy? It can't be the shriveled-up dried fruit which he has been passing around from time to time during their work sessions and will continue to pass around this time; similarly, it can't be the bundle of cats' skins which he uses to keep his rheumatism at bay; it must be the bottles of homemade schnapps, distilled by himself, which he never leaves behind on his travels, a brand of his own which he takes a slug of before breakfast as he sits dozing in bed and, as he says, "gets a kind of message from"—if you know what I mean. And last but by no means least, his baggage is of course weighed down by the mass of index cards and notes, periodicals and books which he has unmercifully, but not indiscriminately, stuffed into various compartments and subcompartments, as well as by the manuscript, in two parts, of his *The Invention of the Alphabet*, which he has been working on for some fourteen years and on which he is hoping, vainly of course, to do further work between sessions.

But now we can cut short the straggling line and allot Valentin Pundt a booth, although he is not yet in a position to enter it, for through the glass door there can be seen a performance which seems likely to continue for some time, the traditional dumb show put on by a young man with plastered-down hair and luxuriant sideburns: Pundt, always tempted to find a name for everything, baptizes it the "unsuccessful reconciliation scene"; in this case the actor begins with a vapid laugh, a beseeching gesture, the head meanwhile being held to one side; then he becomes more tense and incredulous, without, however, sinking to anxious supplication, for timid appeals for tolerance and understanding continue to be voiced, manifestly unsuccessful, though, so that after a preliminary pursing of the lips there follows a petulant outburst of reproach, reinforced by a toe kicked against the wall of the booth and a hand imperiously tapping a coin against the instrument itself, all of which is equally fruitless, whereupon the dumb-show performer stops breathing, draws his head back as though about to butt somebody, and, with a face expressing unadulterated and impenetrable ill humor, slams down the receiver, rushes out of the booth, and dashes off to some predetermined destination.

And now it's Valentin Pundt's turn. He heaves his baggage into the booth, puts the suitcase against the wall, places his briefcase on top, wedges his knee against it, and in this posture feels for the letter which has the number in it; how hot the receiver is, how damp and misted up.

"This is Pundt speaking, Rektor Pundt, the headmaster from Lüneburg, I've an appointment with Frau Dr. Süssfeldt."

"Not here," replies a strained male voice, and hangs up.

Valentin Pundt dials again, hears the same male voice, and says, "May I speak to Dr. Rita Süssfeldt?"

"You rang a moment ago," says the male voice.

6

Pundt says, "This is Pundt speaking, Pundt from Lüneburg. Dr. Süssfeldt was to have picked me up at the station. We may have missed each other."

"She left for the station an hour ago," says the male voice, "and if nothing's happened, if she hasn't run over some old-age pensioner or a policeman, she'll be along to pick you up."

Valentin Pundt is about to reply, but he can hear a female voice peevishly objecting in the background: "Don't say that sort of thing, Heino, you're not to answer the phone. Who are you talking to, anyway?"

"Lüneburg, someone from Lüneburg wants to speak to Rita."

"Are you there? Süssfeldt speaking," says the woman's voice.

Valentin Pundt repeats: "This is Pundt speaking, Rektor Pundt from Lüneburg. Dr. Süssfeldt was to have picked me up at the station. We've obviously missed each other. Could you perhaps take a message, please, to say that I'll go straight to the hotel, the one where we'll be holding our meetings?"

"Don't do that," says the female voice. "My sister's on her way to meet you. She left at least an hour ago; she's often driven to the station."

"Thank you," Valentin Pundt says, and hangs up the receiver, lugs his baggage out of the booth, and, leaving the hall by a side exit this time, steers his way toward the "impossible to miss" mailbox.

He stands beside the mailbox and waits, and through the prism of his anticipation everything expands and proliferates to disturbing proportions: the solemn façades of these Hamburg hotels move closer together, threatening the theater; the big stores conspire to block the way for everybody; the long procession of vehicles, seemingly composed of nothing but dry cleaners' delivery vans and purveyors of office furniture, forbids any attempt to cross the road. A news vendor tries to attract customers with an unusual bankruptcy case. Norway's traditional Christmas present, a fir tree, all tied together, rides by on a special truck. Over there, groups of pedestrians are lining up in front of the traffic lights, while here men with numb fingers are gloomily unloading coils of cable. And over all that the light is struggling against this misty November.

Valentin Pundt stands waiting beside the mailbox at the central railway station. This time they will be deciding on the third section of the new German reader, the chapter entitled "Exemplary Lives," while in the south colleagues will be working on a counterpart of the same project. The first two chapters have already been compiled, checked, and completed: agreement on "Work and Leisure" had been reached swiftly, almost without argument; on the other hand, "At Home and Abroad" was produced with greater effort and less pleasure; there were irritable queries and sarcastic retorts, and even though the result is regarded as the final version, some doubts still remain—although not on his part, not in the mind of Valentin Pundt. He recalls the difficult, halfhearted agreement reached at the end of the last session. What a strain it is convincing people and how comfortless to let oneself be convinced! On that occasion he had come carefully prepared. . . . Where on earth can the woman be?

An ungainly frog-green automobile executes a sprightly slalom between the waiting taxis and stops in front of him. Behind the grime-caked windows, a hand waves. "Quick, quick, I'm not allowed to stop here." The hand taps against the glass, urging Valentin Pundt to hurry, he's ready, he hasn't put his luggage down for one second, he's already making his way around the car, and when the door opens, he can see the seat back nodding forward inviting him to dump his bag and briefcase—"Careful, there are bottles in that one"—on the back seat and then the seat immediately springs back, he squeezes himself in and slams the door shut, unaware that his long overcoat is caught in it. "How are you . . . ?"

Rita Süssfeldt drives off. As far as she is concerned, there's no point in having rearview or side mirrors. She drives off with her usual sigh of satisfaction at proving to a traffic sign how superfluous it is, as the man in the passenger seat turns toward her with a brief word of thanks. Rita Süssfeldt directs her gaze at the only windshield wiper still functioning, albeit halfheartedly. "I've been driving around the station in the same direction for the last twenty minutes. I've given up trying to park here, after all we were certain to meet sooner or later, we couldn't help it. In any case, you were right to wait by the mailbox as we'd agreed." And Rita Süssfeldt drives on, as already stated, steering the lively little car past the gas station, along the one-way street, a cigarette dangling from her painted lips, not, however, painted right up to the corners of her mouth, this was predictable, just as the bright color of her lipstick and the gray specks on her coat and dress were predictable, specks of cigarette ash which she brushes off, shrugging her shoulders, often with a smile of feigned concern whenever the crooked gray worm of ash drops off and scatters itself all over her clothes. How simple she makes it for you to recognize her every time you meet; there's always, thinks Valentin Pundt, as he openly looks her up and down, there's always this same impression of having left in a rush, dashed off to dress with a cry of dismay and holding a sandwich in one hand: always, in everything she does, this unfinished, rough sketch of herself. Her coat isn't buttoned, the transparent scarf is loosely tied, the headband which is intended to keep her unruly reddish-brown hair under control is all askew; at the hotel, the headmaster will also discover that Rita Süssfeldt is wearing only one earring. Everything about her shows signs of reflection and planning and preliminary preparation; she has started to do everything that's necessary but then some unexpected idea, some diversion, or simply some overriding weakening of interest has prevented her from finishing what she has begun.

Smoke is curling up from her dangling cigarette and blowing across her smooth freckled face, over the even dome of her childlike forehead, she's forced to close her eyes, which are watering and which she wipes with one hand as she drives along; in a second the other hand will let go of the steering wheel, but this will not worry Valentin Pundt or make him in any way anxious, for the worthy teacher, the newly retired headmaster, is, in his own words, an "enlightened non-driver." Has he made the same terrifyingly careful preparations as before? Yes, he has come

9

reasonably well prepared. In addition to the agreed-upon texts, has he brought any other books along with him? He has—the schoolmasterly hand makes a ponderous gesture toward the suitcase—he has brought along an adequate supply of texts. And how about the dried fruit? In moments of crisis will he still be able to pass around the dried fruit? He will be able to do so.

Rita Süssfeldt smiles and, smiling, pursues her forward progress, frequently with the help of energetic and rather exaggerated gestures of thanks, and when other drivers try to indicate that there is a coat caught in the door, that a sizable corner of material is hanging out, that, in any case, there is some soft object dragging along the road—she completely misunderstands their signals and takes them to be cheerful, if not indeed admiring, greetings.

She tries to go over the Kennedy Bridge, but without success, for the approach road has apparently been moved somewhere else overnight; now, however, they're heading in the right direction, down to the Lombard Bridge, past the Art Gallery, which this morning—a morning seemingly ripe for snow or rain but more probably for the usual local brand of sleet—has assumed a gloomy mood, the seasonal gloom which regularly descends upon the brickwork every November.

Wouldn't Valentin Pundt like to see the exhibition which had just opened? Well worth a visit: "Child Portraits by European Painters." He would go if he found time. In general—she takes her hand off the steering wheel to rub a spot of fallen ash into her navy-blue woolen dress—Hamburg had a lot to offer, especially in November, and you'd have to organize yourself very drastically to find time even to see just the main things. For instance, there was the anniversary celebration for the port of Hamburg. In the Plants and Flowers Hall, there was the traditional Scandinavian Food Exhibition. The "Get to Know Your Police" recruiting week was featuring various entertainments. And there was the Bach week. And the international Puppeteers' Congress. He would certainly be able to find time to visit something; in any case, Dr. Dunkhase was away and wouldn't be back for a few days.

After the Lombard Bridge, Rita Süssfeldt swings right without catastrophe and drives along the Alster, now deserted and slate gray: no sails are mustered for their ballet; glass-fronted insurance offices, where local disasters are silently dealt with, vainly seek their shimmering mirror image; the wooden landing stages are no longer defended by hissing short-assed swans. Now, at the end of November, the Alster belongs entirely to the wild ducks, drifting motionless in long lines on the water, all round, like dark glass balls attached to a moored net. In front of the nimble calligraphy of the weeping willows, on the so-called Wanderer's Path, blurred less by fog than by smog, young people in amazingly scanty clothes are acting out parts expected of the loving couples of Hamburg. They catch each other in playful throttle holds, single and double nelsons, they attempt lifts and headlocks, and all the time their heads are pressed together beneath long manes of hair. The worthy schoolmaster Valentin Pundt looks at the woman in the driver's seat and thinks of one of those glass balls in which an artificial flurry of snow conceals a tiny log house in a clump of firs.

The traffic light at the Alte Rabenstrasse suddenly turns red, and Pundt reads the name on the street sign to himself and then asks aloud: "Is this the Alte Rabenstrasse?" And when the woman says yes, he runs his hand over his gray, unparted hair and over his forehead, as if reminded of or forcing himself to recall something which he had not in fact forgotten but had set aside until some indefinite time in the future.

"So this is the Alte Rabenstrasse?"

"Yes."

"I must stop in here to pick up something that's been waiting for six weeks. It won't take a second."

The woman notices the changed expression on his face, a hard composure and sudden withdrawal, which must be some sort of reaction to something, and so she asks, "Right away? Shall we do it now?"

"If it's feasible," says Valentin Pundt.

As the left-turn indicator ceases to function every autumn without fail, never later than the first fall of snow, Dr. Süssfeldt

II

winds down the window, sticks out her left hand, and snaps her fingers to indicate to the driver behind that as soon as the lights turn green she will be turning left into the Alte Rabenstrasse.

It's a short, steep street. "Slowly, can we go a little more slowly? There's an older house with a front garden about the size of a pocket handkerchief, it must be there. Are we allowed to stop here?" Rita Süssfeldt can't see any sign either in front or behind, so she stops, offers to help, but ex-headmaster Pundt shakes his head: he can carry everything himself, they've only been keeping a cardboard box and a suitcase for him, it's all been ready for weeks, thanks very much. And he worms his way out of the cramped but cozy car, heaves one shoulder forward, makes a thirty-degree turn, bends his neck, then lifts one leg and his back out of the car and, stooping forward, finally extracts his whole body. The bottom of his coat, the right-hand hem, is darker and thicker than the rest and seems to have shrunk somewhat, leaving the impression that the coat is hanging unevenly—later on in the hotel, Valentin Pundt will be examining all this more closely. But for the moment the burly, bareheaded man walks across the poky little front garden, presses the doorbell, pushes open the door, and, without looking around, goes in.

Rita Süssfeldt, a free-lance publisher's reader and editor of anthologies, is surprised how quickly Pundt comes back; in any case, he has been true to his word, for here he is carrying a suitcase and a cardboard box tied with string; few words, if any, could have been exchanged, his face is still tense and hard and he is wearing an almost bitter expression of rejection; there must be a special relationship between him and the two pieces of baggage, for he is carrying them with great care, dangling them from his fingers as he stows them away on the rear seat.

"Not any fresh material, I hope," says Rita Süssfeldt.

Looking straight ahead, Pundt says flatly, "Something my son bequeathed me."

They turn around and drive back down to the Alster and then the woman asks whether the expression "bequeathed" doesn't refer to a death and the man replies: yes. And then she asks if this was true in this case and the man says that was so. And she goes on to ask whether it was an accident and the man says: he committed suicide in a house where he had friendly people all around him, just as he had completed his studies, which he had always taken in his stride without any difficulty. And then the woman asks, speaking now with greater urgency, whether the sad event had occurred just before the exams and the man says: no, they'd been able to verify the exact time of the suicide and it was two days after he had passed his examinations, not only without difficulty, but with distinction. And cautiously the woman asks what the reasons could have been for such an act and the man says that for the moment he doesn't know of any. And the woman gently asks what Valentin Pundt's son had been studying and the man says he had been studying history and education.

We may certainly assume that the woman would have liked to continue asking questions and that she would have been able to come closer to the heart of the matter until something of it, although obviously not all, had been clarified—but they've reached the hotel, you have to turn left although a solid yellow line forbids you to do so, you have to concentrate on the narrow entrance flanked by weather-beaten posts—the iron gates are open—and then take a quick run up the steep asphalt drive leading to the Hotel-Pension Klöver (proprietress: Ida Klöver) and ending in front of the covered porch. Imprisoned in scaffolding —it's impossible to say whether the work is already over or just beginning—from the very first glimpse the hotel reveals that in its youth, at least before the First World War, it wanted nothing better than to be a private house, a thoroughly typical Hamburg villa, that is to say, solid, melancholy, and taking up a great deal of space. It stands back, but not overlooked by any other structure, on a much-sought-after hillside site, a cream-colored box with narrow windows and turrets pierced by loopholes. And it is so situated that, especially in summer, the Alster looks like a bay or gulf, shimmering with light, a gulf on which your eager gaze falls not dreamily but sharply, for busy schooners might well be sailing in to carry away pepper and coffee and profitable sandalwood from the warehouses. Memory has settled here in its old age.

However, the time has come for them to arrive. They must go into the house that Rita has discovered for their meetings—central and amazingly quiet, she described it in her letter—and they have to bring the luggage into the gloomy walnut-paneled vestibule.

Janpeter Heller is there: the third of the experts, he's standing expectantly in front of the fireplace that is never used; he arrived yesterday and has already been in touch with Rita Süssfeldt; now he pulls away from the marble slab and propels himself toward Valentin Pundt, his face contorted in mock grief; their hands meet and clasp each other, not to express their normal pleasure at meeting, but instead moving gently, almost reverently, up and down, exactly as if the two men were exchanging condolences.

What is Janpeter Heller's intention? What is he hoping for? The chief hope of this young expert, who is wearing a faded burgundy pullover and who has allowed his receding chin to be overgrown with a beard which he wears brushed sharply forward, his chief hope—and he says it as soon as they shake hands —is that they can come to a speedy understanding in the course of this session. Yes, he'd like to set a new record in reaching agreement, not, indeed, because the third section of the anthology is particularly amenable or suitable for such agreement, but rather because it's Hamburg, a city that has so much to offer, which encourages them to be expeditious. We shall have only ourselves to blame, he says, if we can't find time for the discussion on the theater—"What's Happening behind Our Scenes?" We shall be missing something, he says, if we don't take in the "Modern Photography" exhibition. And "Beat, Words, and Music in the Waiting Room." And the demonstration of inflatable furniture. And the concert given by the Monkeys. In fact, everything that he had fished out of the calendar of events in *What's On in Hamburg* and which he could never hope to see in his home town of Diepholz. He thinks he has made his point. He looks at his colleagues. "Well now, 'Exemplary Lives,' who hasn't felt himself a really changed person because of them, who hasn't realized that he was preordained to follow them ever since he was a toddler?—each of us has had such a varied experience of them that we really only need to cut them out of their frames as they hang above our heads, so to speak." No one supports him; his colleagues merely nod noncommittally, their minds elsewhere, they are still taking in the unfamiliar vestibule, unwilling or unable to tie themselves down, and when Valentin Pundt speaks, it's merely to say, "You've lost an earring." Rita Süssfeldt knows she has, she makes a deprecatory gesture, and informs him resignedly that she'll certainly never manage to have two earrings at the same time, one of them is always playing hide-and-seek; yes, she knows she has. Janpeter Heller can already see that it is going to be difficult to fix an earlier starting date for their sessions or to arrange specifically for a speedier treatment of the third section, so he tries another tack: "Have we all done our homework? Because if we have, this job of ours, these 'Exemplary Lives,' can be over with in no time; as a matter of fact, I've got some private business to attend to."

They really won't be left standing unnoticed for very long in the gloomy vestibule of the Hotel-Pension Klöver, for anyone who comes in needs neither to ring nor to call out in order to make his presence known; merely standing there without saying a word leads very soon to a door's being opened on the second floor, followed by a bad-tempered voice addressing itself and then heavy breathing approaching, so that involuntarily you look upward, and anyone who understands the meaning of the puffing and blowing which reaches him from the staircase immediately regrets having come here or at least starts quickly looking around for an excuse.

The proprietress, Ida Klöver, is obviously used to such apologetic excuses, because even before she has emerged from the staircase her heavily beringed hand can be seen flapping limply in the air, that's all right, don't worry, and she climbs laboriously downstairs propelled by some ancient mechanism, perhaps already worn out but still effective, which she finds it impossible to resist: a woman in a black suit with ponderous tread and flabby cheeks. Her face shows what she thinks of herself, her open, mobile face which can never disguise its look of annoyance and disgust.

She shakes hands with her guests and as she covers the short distance to the reception desk she gives out unsolicited information about her problems: with no husband and inadequate staff, at her age it's no longer any pleasure running a hotel. She pushes an opened notebook toward Pundt and asks him to sign. She goes on talking over his bent back: "Yes, we had a hotel in South-West Africa; twenty-eight years we spent there, my husband and I." She unconcernedly closes the book, puts it on the windowsill, and hands Pundt a key, saying, "It can't go on like this much longer, not much longer." She pauses, there was something else, yes, someone had phoned, a call for Herr Heller, would he please not call to see his wife this evening. Then she asks them to follow her, just up these stairs here, through the swinging doors: "There's our conference room, full of memories as you can see, you won't be disturbed here—if you want anything, you need only ring, and now I must leave you to yourselves."

So it's here, in this room with its brightly papered walls— depicting cheerful scenes of work through the centuries, principally cheerful men carrying sacks—that their meetings will be taking place, under these photographs framed in glass, all looking thoroughly sickly and somewhat overexposed, and all portraying the same melancholy giant kneeling, standing, or, in one case, lying on his elbow beside his slaughtered prey. Crossed spears on the walls, spears with wooden and iron shafts adorned with copper or leather. Bows hang facing each other, waiting for someone to place an arrow in their strings and pull. Arrows in quivers, arrows loosely tied in sheaves, arrows with heads of bone and iron and stone. Deformed but handy axes offer their services; a blowpipe is asking to be tried out.

This is where the meetings will take place. The wicker chairs are standing there creaking as if continuing a conversation that has just been held in them. The wide rosewood table offers a most suitable place for depositing things, as does a tea cart. Here it is that these "Exemplary Lives" will be spread out and turned over, here they'll be tested and assessed and sorted out until there emerges from this joint sitting the single, longed-for "Life" on which everyone can agree. Yes, this is where they'll meet and hold their sessions.

Unlike Rita Süssfeldt, Valentin Pundt does not sit down to try out a chair, but peers suspiciously at the tall windows, holds his hand against the windowsill, immediately ascertains that there's a draft, and, not content with this discovery, similarly detects that the pipes of the radiator are also causing a draft, and since his suspicions are aroused by the keyhole—certainly an immense one—and by the blowpipe, he is mulling over how he can plug the pair of them, the keyhole and the blowpipe; the windows and radiator pipes will no doubt be dealt with later. "I've no objection to the room," he says, "no objection, provided we can stop the drafts."

Drafts have never worried Janpeter Heller, nor do they now. The young expert tests the sharpness of the weapons for himself by gently pressing the ball of his finger against the tips of the spears, the arrowheads, and the points of the two-edged hunting knives, just enough to cause a little pain. "They're still quite serviceable," he says. "If we can't agree, these things are perfectly serviceable." He doesn't expect anyone to smile at his remark, which is rather an obvious one. There seems to be plenty of confidence on Dr. Süssfeldt's part when, as she once more strides casually round the room, she points out how much experience and knowledge they have gained in the course of their first two sessions. Hadn't they come almost spontaneously to an agreement over the "Work and Leisure" chapter? And hadn't they come closer to each other's views in their discussion of "At Home and Abroad"? So how can anyone talk about not having good omens? In addition, she had already gathered that this time everyone had come prepared.

So all that remains is to assemble beneath the dull glow of an antelope's antlers and after a few brief inquiries fix the time of the first meeting, shall we say this afternoon, shall we say three o'clock? Everyone is in agreement and signifies so in his own particular way: with a nod or, in Pundt's case, a grunt of acquiescence. And then everyone calculates to himself how much time is left, divides it up, and allocates it in advance: till three o'clock then; then I can, then I shall have to, then I might, in any case we ought to be off now so that we can start on our allotted task at the time agreed, well equipped, in a good mood, armed with knowledge, firm in our convictions but ready to make concessions if we must. They take their leave of each other in the foyer.

Here we could switch off the spotlights and could let these three dissimilar experts leave the scene, relegate them to some trivial interval to help them in their preparations or their agreement, and, in their own words, I could also say: three o'clock then, see you at three o'clock, when the decisive action, so to speak, can start. However, we insist on keeping our eye on them. So we'll encourage Rita Süssfeldt to filter boldly but with impunity into the traffic on the Harvestehuder Weg; she goes over the Mittelweg crossing—on amber—drives straight on to the Kloster traffic circle, not because she needs to but simply because she forgot to turn left, drives up the Rothenbaumchaussee as far as Oberstrasse, bears right down the Hochallee and right again into Innocentiastrasse—only natives of the town will realize how far she has gone out of her way.

It's certain that Janpeter Heller helps Pundt carry his luggage up to his room—"Careful, there are bottles in the large case"— puts the luggage down in the middle of the room, casts a glance out the window and verifies that Pundt has a view of almost the same section of the Alster as he does; then retreats hastily backward to the door as if afraid that the old man might engage him in conversation: "See you later."

And how about Valentin Pundt? He locks the door before heaving the big suitcase onto the luggage rack, hangs his overcoat on a coat hanger, milks some drops of dirty water out of its swollen hem (which he then mops up with a handkerchief), suddenly hesitates, and then with one tug lifts the suitcase and the cardboard box onto the table.

18

And Rita Süssfeldt dashes past her elder sister, Margarethe, pursing her lips in a kiss and, with a suppliant gesture of her hands, rejecting any attempt to give her any news: "Not now, Mareth, and none of Heino's antics either, for God's sake hold him off for the next few hours, I've got work to do, I've still got some things to prepare; but I wouldn't mind a cup of tea and a couple of slices of toast."

And Janpeter swings his leg over the back of the chair, deposits himself on the seat, and slumps down in front of the different-colored files, buries his face in his hands and offers the spectator the sight of a man immersed in laborious though not hopeless meditation, until he suddenly sits up, lifts the telephone, dials a number, and although nobody explicitly answers at the other end, says, "It's my right, I suppose I have the right to see my daughter, even if you don't want me to, so will you answer, I can hear you breathing, and anyway you said you were ready for us to meet any time when I was in town; so why shouldn't I come around and see you?"

And the old schoolmaster untangles the knots, raises the lid of the cardboard box, and bends down to view the contents but without touching or unpacking anything; he just stands staring at the small bundles of letters and photographs, note-books fastened with rubber bands, his eye slides over the empty loose-leaf files, the bundles of pencils, and the Meer-schaum pipe with its cracked mouthpiece, and now he shuts the box, puts it under the table, hesitates, and finally drags it toward the wardrobe.

And Dr. Süssfeldt runs a pointed forefinger over the array of large brown envelopes sticking up like pay envelopes on a book-shelf, fishes one or two of them out, and sits down at the danger-ously overcrowded desk where her work space has been reduced to a miniature size, lights a cigarette, and reads what she has written in her own hand on the brown envelopes: "III. Exem-plary Lives."

And after his third attempt to phone—each time the receiver was lifted but no voice answered—Heller opens the pale-green file, pulls out a handwritten sheet of paper, and without taking them in, reads his own words: "Put yourself in the place of everyone who needs models to copy."

And after a swig of his homemade schnapps Pundt extracts the necessary manuscripts from the main compartment of his leather briefcase and is immediately brought up short by a sentence, written in his stiff, upright handwriting, which he had himself used as an objection to one of the suggestions: "Unsuitable as an example because of its ambiguity."

And Rita Süssfeldt nods as if in repeated recognition of the truth of the note which she has jotted down in her own private shorthand: "An example must be two things: a commitment and a challenge"; this note she now underlines.

Now the distances are narrowing, they're coming closer and closer together as they make their preparations, they can already see each other move clearly and hear each other's voices—voices raised in defense or persuasion but also in doubt and rejection— and now, as they sift and read and reread, none of them feels isolated any more but rather surrounded by the others, under their constant supervision: they know that everything has now begun.

2

"A LITTLE closer together, lean slightly forward, leave the papers where they are: before we start, let's take a photo in the Hotel Klöver's conference room to commemorate our meetings, there's a time release, I'm nearly there." Janpeter Heller looks up from his viewfinder, checks and rechecks the group he has arranged, stations himself beside Rita Süssfeldt, and, wrinkling his nose, goes once again to the camera and carefully squints through the viewfinder toward the corner—there's something wrong. There's something wrong with Valentin Pundt, who is sitting there stiffly with his smoking jacket pulled up to his ears, fixing the camera with a reproachful stare as though trying to intimidate the little bird; and there's something wrong with Rita Süssfeldt, whose freckled hands seem to have increased in number and seem to be playing a game of catch on the rosewood table with her remaining earring. But what is wrong exactly? This isn't just a triviality, it means something, thinks Heller, and suddenly he walks up to the so-called memorial wall, looks around triumphantly, and carefully pulls down some weapons— a very thin hunting knife for Dr. Süssfeldt, a spear for Valentin Pundt, and for himself an arrow with an extremely jagged head of whitish shark's teeth: "That's better, it's visible evidence that we've not met unarmed." But if that's the case Rita Süssfeldt would prefer the blowpipe. Heller puts back the hunting knife and passes her the blowpipe.

There we are and now the apparatus of the camera itself comes into play: this moment of time must be held with everything that comes into its field of vision, which means the papers, notes, and books, and perhaps, if the picture is sharp enough, it will bear witness that at the first session one exemplary life was X-rayed and assessed—it's been proposed by Heller and is to be found in a story by O. H. Peters. Three manuscript copies are lying on top: it's entitled "The Renunciation." They've been passing it around among themselves for some time now, reading it, tapping it all over, applying the stethoscope, and garnishing it with little notes detailing their diagnoses: Can it be certified as suitable? Completely satisfactory? Partly satisfactory? Really worth being explored?

Now Janpeter Heller need not worry any more about his commemorative photograph, which, if not strikingly eloquent, is at least ready to bear witness that this is and remains his proposal, his contribution, which after long and disappointing research, not unmixed with doubts, he would like to offer to the others: "The Renunciation" by O. H. Peters. Here we go:

The office hours were over. Only one patient was still waiting outside, his file was lying on the desk, but before my father asked him to come in he went to the medicine cabinet again and poured himself a glass. And, as he always did, he offered me one as well, but I declined. The glasses were very small.

He gulped it down and then stood in silence for a moment with his mouth open. He wiped his lips with the fleshy part of his hand. He gave me a wink. He put his hand on my shoulder and remarked how well the white coat fit me; it was one of his own white coats. We wouldn't even need to change that, my father said: I could take over his job with the pension board and his white coats as well, just for the asking. I ought to give up these long voyages, quit being a ship's doctor, and take over what he had built up over the years: a small but respectable private practice and this official post with the pension board. Five years at sea are enough, he said. There's nothing for a doctor to do on board, he said. Between Brest and Cape Town, all you'll ever get are appendectomies and squashed fingers.

I was following his movements with my eyes: they were neat and economical, not the movements of an old man. I listened to his voice, which still sounded as I remembered it, gentle and unctuous, a parson's voice. And he still had this evasive look, as if he couldn't bear being looked at directly in the face. He was friendly. He was humorous. In his fifties, he could have played the family doctor in any German film. "Why can't you make up your mind?" he asked. "Isn't this good enough for you?"

I shrugged my shoulders. I said, "There's still someone waiting to see you," and my father went to the door and asked for the patient to be sent in, while I remained sitting on my chair by the window.

My father was reading this last patient's record, meanwhile sucking on a peppermint. He was using the file card as a fan to cool himself when the patient came in, and my father walked toward him and greeted him with friendly familiarity as though offering him an alliance against illness. The patient was old and surly and walked with a stick, which he propped up against the desk, hanging his cap over the handle. As he sat down, his hair, sparse but long, spread over the collar of his jacket. He looked challengingly at my father. His name was Boysen and he worked on the docks. As he usually did with his patients, my father addressed him familiarly in the plural: "Now what's wrong with us? What can we do about it?" Boysen took off his orthopedic shoe with its domed toepiece. Without a word he undid his bandages and removed a dirty white dressing. My father brought over a stool and Boysen lifted his foot onto it. The foot was suffused with blue, the instep streaked with yellow, while the joints of the deformed, deeply scarred foot were red and raw. The scars were from shell wounds. In a surly voice he invited my father to "take a look at that": the old wound and now where his foot had been crushed by a hatch cover. He was in pain. He looked at my father through cold, narrow eyes and asked why it was that his disability pension was being reduced all the time. After the war he was granted a twenty-five percent pension and now it was only fifteen percent. And he could see the day coming when it would be even less. He wanted his old percentage back and he wanted my father to help him.

My father examined the foot. He carefully ran his hand down over the instep to the ends of the toes. He asked Boysen to put his weight on the foot and take a step; as he did so the patient turned his face toward me with a suspicious, hostile look. My father examined the X rays which the patient had brought along with him and then tapped the foot with his forefinger and massaged it to discover how sensitive it was. Without looking at the man, he told him he was sure that the swelling would soon subside. There was no trace of inflammation. Boysen replied that that was no use to him, he wanted a fair percentage, he knew for himself what was wrong with his foot, he could feel it when he was walking or standing. I could tell from my father's attitude that for him the examination was over, he knew what his report would be; all the same, he was reluctant to send the patient away. He was always like this. By prolonging the examination he was proving that he was willing to take everything into consideration that might be favorable to the patient. In the end he asked me to examine Boysen's foot. I did so and was about to walk back to my chair when Boysen stopped me with an outstretched hand. "Well, what do you think about it? Isn't this foot worth more than fifteen percent? Shouldn't they add something to that?"

"It looks nasty," I said.

"Nasty," he said scornfully. "You can't buy anything with the word 'nasty.'"

My father asked him to put the dressing and the bandages back on. He himself sat down at his desk and wrote some letters and figures on Boysen's card.

"Well," asked Boysen, "how much can I expect?"

"I don't know," said my father. "They'll let you know by letter of their final decision; they'll be writing to you."

"More than this measly fifteen percent?" asked Boysen.

"We've received new directives," said my father. "We have to make all our decisions in accordance with our directives."

"What a pity," said Boysen, "what a pity we never get a chance to see the people who work out those directives."

"I can understand your feelings," said my father.

"I bet," Boysen went on, "I bet none of them depends on a pension. Directives: they're just to cover up."

My father impassively handed the patient a long-handled shoehorn. He supported him while he used it. He handed him his stick and cap and accompanied him to the door.

"How long will it take?" asked Boysen as he went out.

"It doesn't depend entirely on me," said my father.

We took off our white coats and hung them up in the closet. I looked at the record card and tried to decipher what my father had written.

"You won't understand that," he said, "not yet anyway." And he added, "We have to be rather tough, my boy. There are too many people trying to cash in on that racket. He ought to be glad to get his fifteen percent."

"Won't you give him any more?" I asked.

"More?" he said. "Do you think he ought to receive more money?"

"Yes," I said.

He took the card out of my hand and slipped it into a box. He placed his hand on my shoulder. Gently he pushed me toward the window. Boysen was standing in the street below waving his stick threateningly in the direction of a departing cyclist. "So you haven't resigned yet," my father said.

"No," I said, "we've gone into dock and I've merely taken some leave."

"But you will resign," he said, "you will do it now, won't you?"

"Why?" I inquired.

"You're needed here," he said.

He was in a hurry. He'd been elected to a committee which was organizing a congress. He had to go to the first meeting. He wanted to take me with him in his car, but I declined. We went down in the rickety elevator together and parted at the door. I walked off into a thin drizzle in the same direction as Boysen. In the gardens a young lad was carving his name in the back of a bench: "Paul was here." From where I was, I could see my ship at the dock. Its afterpart towered light gray over the rust-colored

25

dock walls. A trickle of smoke hung over the funnel. I asked the lad the way to Karolinen Strasse. He pointed up toward the town with the handle of his knife and I walked on in that direction. Twice more I had to ask the way and then I found Karolinen Strasse.

An empty baby carriage was standing in the hall and a bicycle was blocking the door to the cellar. Although it was a new house, the hall floor was cracked all over and the whitewashed walls were scraped and scratched. The paint was peeling off the iron banisters. I looked at the list of tenants. A boy appeared silently, watched me while I read through the list, went upstairs with me, floor by floor, and didn't take his eyes off me until I found the name I wanted and twirled the knob of the old-fashioned bell.

His wife opened the door. She looked me up and down, crossly rather than suspiciously. She was narrow-shouldered and flat-chested; there were dark shadows under her eyes and her lips were twitching. I asked if it was possible to speak to her husband, and she said angrily that nobody could do that, not even herself. She tried to shut the door.

I said, "I'd only like to give your husband a piece of advice, nothing else, a piece of advice that he might find useful."

She let me in and shut the door behind me. I went ahead of her along the gloomy corridor and past a closet which had nothing but caps hanging in it.

"He's lying down," she said.

Boysen was lying on a sofa in the kitchen. Beside the sofa there was a yellow plastic bowl; a kettle of water was singing on the stove: presumably he was preparing a footbath. He recognized me straightway. He was not greatly surprised, or if he was, his surprise quickly vanished. His wife checked the temperature of the water in the kettle. Neither of them offered me a seat or inquired why I was there.

"May I say something?" I said. "I was there while your foot was being examined."

"Then you know all about it," he said. "And now leave me alone, or do I owe you anything?"

"I'd like to give you some advice," I said. "I've only come to give you a word of advice."

"Me?" he said suspiciously, massaging his foot.

"I know your case," I said, "and I know how important it is for you to hang on to your fifteen percent pension. And it's not even certain that you'll get that and that's why I came to see you."

"You can keep what you know to yourself," he said, "and leave me alone. I've gotten used to not expecting anything."

"We've gotten used to it," said his wife. "The two of us. They wouldn't accept my heart trouble and one of these days his foot isn't even going to be worth five percent. We've gotten used to not expecting anything more."

She poured the water into the bowl and stirred the water with her hand. She looked at him reproachfully and put the kettle back on the stove.

"Go to Number 12 Bromberger Strasse—it's a private practice —put on your best clothes and get yourself examined by the same doctor."

"Why?" asked his wife. "Why should he do that?"

"You can keep that sort of advice to yourself," said Boysen, "and now leave me alone."

"You'll get more favorable treatment," I said. "If you really want to get something for your foot, do what I say. You may even be able to get a better percentage."

"Get lost," said Boysen. "I didn't ask you to come."

"Can't you hear?" said his wife. "Who are you, anyway?"

"One of those pension merchants," said Boysen. "He was there while I was being examined."

"Let's get going," said his wife, crossly pointing to the bowl. "Get going or the water will get cold."

They didn't even reply when I said goodbye. They let me go and I opened the door of the flat and left. I drove to my hotel on the Dammtor. There were telephone messages for me: an old friend from medical school had invited me to dinner and my shipping company had left a message to call them. I lay down on my bed and looked at the picture of a North German market. It was an old photograph showing fishermen selling sturgeon from a cart. After sleeping for a few hours, I telephoned the company. They had a job for me. They needed a surgeon for the *Frisia*, which was going to sail to the West Indies. The *Frisia* was a new acquisition and this was to be its maiden voyage after its refitting. I didn't accept but promised to consider the offer. I also promised to let them know my decision the following day.

My father phoned before breakfast. He expressed surprise that I'd spent almost the whole of my second day's leave in my hotel. Once again he tried to convince me that I really ought to move in with him at home. I said no. As long as Mother was in the sanatorium I didn't want to live in that big house with him. He invited me to his private office. He was eager to show me all the changes he had introduced. I could hardly say no and after breakfast I drove over to Bromberger Strasse. His office was on the ground floor of a private residence, a brick house surrounded by tall copper beeches. As I walked through the garden he waved to me through the window; I was able to go straight in through his private door. He had had some coffee made for us and with it he once again offered me a sticky liquid in a small glass. I took just the coffee and let him do the talking: he spoke of growing old, of all that he'd achieved and of the need for someone to take over and continue his work. "There's the desk, my boy," he said. "All you have to do is sit down at it. Who else is there to take over?"

Each time he had a patient I went into the next room and contemplated the fish in an aquarium. I gave them some fish food. I cleaned out the weeds and ran the suction hose over the bottom of the tank. Then he called me back in and went on from where he had stopped: "It's not a proper job, on board ship, for a doctor; give up this ship's doctor stuff and take over what I've managed to build up here." He kept on repeating himself. He never stopped expatiating on all the advantages. But he still couldn't bring himself to ask the decisive question. A new patient was announced and I went back into the other room. What an odd way the fish had of going after their food. At first it seemed as if they meant to swim past. They approached unconcernedly and quite casually and then, suddenly, with a swish of the tail they twisted their bodies and with a vigorous swoop snapped up their bits of food. I was bending over the aquarium and prodding an almost transparent fish with the suction hose when the door leading to the corridor opened. I turned around, but it had already been closed again and then, for some strange reason, it reopened.

Boysen's wife was standing in the doorway. She was wearing a suit and carrying a shiny black bag. She apologized. "I couldn't find the way out," she said. I showed her the right direction and instinctively went toward her. "What are you doing here?" she asked.

"Visiting," I said, "just on a visit."

She gave a cautious smile. She looked as if she had hopes of something.

"Have you already been in?" I asked, nodding my head toward the doctor's office.

"This time it looks okay," she said. "They've confirmed what needed confirming and now all I've got to do is have an X ray. This is my last try." She pulled the door shut and walked toward the exit.

My father was waiting for me behind his desk. He offered me a seat. He stood up as I took my raincoat out of the closet.

"Aren't you staying?" he asked.

"They've got a job for me," I said. "They need a doctor for the *Frisia*, which is making a trip to the West Indies."

"But surely not today," he said.

"Tonight," I said, "but I must go back to my hotel first."

So there we have "The Renunciation," which was and still is Janpeter Heller's suggestion for the third section of the anthology, a contribution which he had unearthed in an omnibus edition and now finds himself defending against Pundt's cautious objections and Dr. Süssfeldt's obstinate interrogation, while outside the Alster becomes unrecognizable beneath the long-expected sleet, and Magda, the gloomy hotel maid, appears with a pot of tea with rum, a cup of coffee, and an apple juice. The weapons which Heller had selected for the commemorative photo are now back on the wall, except for the arrow with the jagged shark's-tooth head, which he is balancing in his hand, pointing it aimlessly in all directions, while at the same time using it to beat time to his own words. Is there a light on? No, there's no light on. True, Magda switched it on when she came in; but Heller had switched it off again because the dusk and twilight, the permanent November gloom, is not only adequate but even seems appropriate to their task.

Now this anonymous ship's doctor: the ex-headmaster, holding his heavy schoolmasterly hands placidly clasped in front of him on the table, is anxious to know a little more about him because, according to his present reading of O. H. Peters' tale, he didn't quite understand what was supposed to be exemplary in this ship's doctor's behavior. Perhaps he might just run through it; and please stop him if necessary.

"So we have a young ship's doctor whose father offers him his private practice and also his post as official doctor for the pension board—what you might call a nice, cozy, comfortable job. Before deciding, he discovers that his father uses a double standard in his judgment, that in his official position he methodically rejects what he is quite happy to accept as a private G.P., and this revelation is enough to make the ship's doctor decide to turn down the offer. He goes back to his ship. So here we have rejection, refusal, renunciation: but is that sufficient to make his behavior exemplary?" Pundt could see quite well that, by tipping Boysen off, this ship's doctor did, in a way, show that you can redress an injustice by using guile, but the whole thing was inadequate, it was too thin, it left too many questions unanswered. It was too special a situation to be a model. A unique dilemma. A challenging decision. Should a moral example really consist of a decision to opt out? Just to say "no" and go off with your kit bag to the nearest ship? He hoped Janpeter Heller wouldn't take offense, but the Navy hardly had all that much room for recruits at the moment.

30

Rita Süssfeldt, never really relaxed, always restless even when she seems entirely placid, takes a fresh cigarette from the open pack lying in front of her, lights it from the butt of the last one, and smooths her dress over her firm, fleshy thighs. Now she would like to say a word. She would like to know what duty was being advocated, what kind of model was being set up, what did it stand for exactly? This ship's doctor eventually decides to leave, to make a planned escape. All right. But is that sufficient? She invites them to imagine what would happen if everybody after some unpleasant experience offered no other solution than to pick up his hat and leave. Wasn't leaving the typical action of people who were lukewarm or sulking, or at least of those people who wanted to enjoy the luxury of a clear conscience by refusing to take sides? Dr. Süssfeldt was not impressed by this ship's doctor. But suppose he had stayed? Suppose he had accepted his father's offer? And having done so, had tried at all costs, whatever the risk, to change things! Staying on: that would have been the bolder thing to do, as well as offering greater possibilities. An exemplary person who can leave any time he wants? No, that is inconceivable, at least for Rita Süssfeldt, who now shrugs her shoulders apologetically as she smiles at Heller and ends rather more gently by making the point that surely you couldn't serve up that sort of example to schoolchildren in the seventh, eighth, and ninth grades.

Now it's Heller's turn—first it's his basket chair in which he is jerking back and forth, producing creaking and crackling sounds like a small fire darting through thin brushwood—and now he sits up, displeased but calm, and taps his arrowhead on the pages of his contribution. He was not surprised, he had even expected such a misinterpretation, for wasn't it always the case that when three very different people read exactly the same story and then retell it, when it's retold you have the impression that they're talking about three different stories? That was as it should be; quite in order. All the same, he could not help feeling surprised at the way the whole point of the story, its central theme, had been lost; what he would like to call its straightforward but challenging symbol. The title of the story was "The Renunciation," wasn't it? With equal justification it could have been called "Giving Notice." What the young ship's doctor is really being offered is nothing less than a comfortable, carefree, blissful existence; providence has laid on everything for him, but he must shut his eyes, stop seeking and stop asking questions: this is the price he must pay. He already has one foot in this Garden of Eden which his father has arranged for him, but then knowledge creeps up on him in such a way as to leave him no choice: he opts for uncertainty and risk, and above all for independence. He hands in his notice. How was it possible not to see that? Valentin Pundt says drily that O. H. Peters might even be responsible for that, and thinking of the capabilities of her eighth-grade pupils, Rita Süssfeldt wonders whether Paradise is necessarily such an incriminating address and whether an exemplary character is required to leave it under all circumstances.

Janpeter throws the arrow down onto the manuscripts, stands up, and slowly moves around the table, taking a sip of coffee as he goes and then setting the cup down with a bang. Is he collecting his thoughts? Preparing to return to the attack? In any case, he looks like a man collecting himself and preparing to deliver himself of something he has long been deliberating and anticipating. He tugs on his burgundy pullover, convincing the wool of its elasticity; he then goes back to his seat and points out to the others what should have been pointed out at the very beginning: the arrogance of the idea of discovering exemplary lives, putting them into an anthology and serving them up to adolescents—here's your Leonidas, your Dr. Schweitzer, now see what you can do. "If you ask me, examples are really only a sort of educational cod-liver oil which nobody likes swallowing and can only manage to get down by closing his eyes. They cramp a child, they destroy his confidence, irritate him, and offer him the wrong kind of challenge. In the traditional meaning of the word, examples are merely magnificent irrelevancies, clarion calls of a bungled educational system which makes you want to cover your ears. All that larger-than-life stuff, from Thermopylae to Lambaréné, is

just a complete scandal and has nothing to do with everyday life."
Superman types, if he might use the expression. And if he might
make his position quite plain: anyone concerned with a chapter
on "Exemplary Lives" today ought not to start from exemplary
situations but from ordinary, everyday happenings, from exemplary behavior in everyday situations. No shattering decisions,
but modest, reasonable, quiet actions which are nonetheless worthy and useful: this was the kind of thing that needed advertising
if one had to put together an anthology of that sort, and this was
why he had put forward "The Renunciation." He hoped that
he'd made himself quite clear.

Valentin Pundt has understood him, in his fashion; he replies
with a gesture which, starting at chest level, moves diagonally
downward, signifying that he forthwith intends to put a stop to
any thought and remove any impression that, for example, there
was anything personal involved or that should a text be rejected,
it might be considered a defeat for the person who proposed it.
"We're here," Pundt says, "to inquire what examples are of value
today and eventually to agree on which of the acceptable proposals we shall put into our anthology."

"Perhaps we can manage to produce something jointly," Rita
Süssfeldt says.

"In any case," says Valentin Pundt, "it can be stated that the
youth of today are asking for examples and our job is to provide
them with examples which are appropriate to the times."

"And which automatically involve a duty and a challenge,"
says Dr. Süssfeldt.

"Or which encourage the possibility of being put into practice," says Valentin Pundt.

"So that the example itself must be definitely a problem and
thus human," says Rita Süssfeldt.

"I'm thinking of standards for use in moments of doubt," says
Pundt, "to help people with their decisions, and I'm thinking,
too, of forcing people to draw comparisons; an outstanding example should invite people to make comparisons."

"Being outstanding is asocial," says Heller, "it's counterproductive; no one can feel a sense of solidarity with something outstanding."

At that Rita Süssfeldt inquires, with some justification: "What else can we use as an example?" and Pundt's long, regular nodding of the head shows his own instinctive agreement.

Now Janpeter Heller shows not only that he's prepared but also what he's prepared for; standing motionless, with his head thrown back against the memorial wall, he repeats what he has been thinking, and in the gloomy conference room he cites a few examples which he would like to dismiss from the start, all too familiar in any potboiler you can mention, and which he would like to denounce, once and for all, as completely useless.

So he brings up the proverbial captain who in accordance with a dreary custom goes down with his ship without ever having done anything to try to save it: Heller awards him a certificate of blind and stupid devotion to duty and dismisses him in the harshest possible terms. He then mentions the well-known commander of a fortress who stays at his post with all his men until the last shot has been fired, in order to enable the civilian population to make their escape: that kind of man, says Heller, must be looked upon merely as a disaster because he will never see that one life cannot be balanced against another. He quickly dispatches the mountaineer who feels it incumbent on himself to prove, despite all warnings to the contrary, that you can climb the north face of the Eiger alone and in winter: Heller lets him crash without a word, with a dismissive gesture of his hand. The successful research scientist entirely unconcerned with the results of his discoveries; the familiar case of the ruler who offers an amnesty to a highwayman while sending his own dissident brother into exile; the sapper who sets off the explosive charge on his back in order to breach an enemy position: all the current varieties of exemplary persons are given their brief turn on the stage by Heller, ironically appraised, examined, and then dismissed as white elephants for any educational system that pretends to be educational. "We mustn't put people like this in our shopwindow," he says. "We must shut them away in the poison

34

cabinet," he says. "If we're going to have models, then let's have those we can learn something from; but you can learn nothing from such people, not even by using them cautiously."

Valentin Pundt now circulates his bag of dried fruit, offering wrinkled prunes, apricots, dried apple rings, and with his quiet, dogged insistence he even manages to ensure that each of them digs into the bag, pulls something out, and under his challenging gaze actually starts to eat it. While Heller evinces annoyance as he chews, forcing his two rows of teeth vigorously apart as they become gummed on the fruit, and already keeping an eye open for an arrow quiver in which to deposit his prune pits, Dr. Süssfeldt extracts a slice of apricot from her mouth which she has already bitten into, looks at it not merely with surprise but with consternation, and then chews dismally on as if in fearful expectation of a sudden explosion. And how about Pundt? He chews on resignedly, phlegmatically, without pleasure, rather like a lethargic koala bear doggedly gnawing at his eucalyptus.

The old schoolmaster whom Beckmann painted in green on a rusty-red background nods his head. He agrees that when they no longer correspond to any cogent experience, even exemplary actions must be dispatched to limbo. He was all in favor of a pitiless scrutiny that would send all the old-fashioned heroes packing. Of course, it's part of the educator's job to question things and he proves his worth by his ability to inspire reasonable doubt in others. But is he not always required to offer something as well, to make positive recommendations and suggestions? "Destroying reputations, exposing and toppling people from their pedestals, hunting them down: yes, we're trained to do all that. But what have we got to offer afterward? Let's see what you've still got in your hand, Heller. Any example tells us as much about the man who chose it as it tells us about itself. Perhaps you'd like to open your bag of samples and show us your wares."

Is Janpeter Heller ready to do that, too? He takes a prune pit out of his mouth. He holds it firmly clamped between thumb and forefinger. He aims at the window, changes his mind, and pops

35

the pit into the blowpipe hanging horizontally on the wall. He sits down again at the table. "Exemplary Lives," he says; the very notion has become ambiguous and misleading nowadays; he would like to put something else in its place, give the whole chapter a different heading, something like: "Common Decency." Whenever he heard the word "exemplary" he was tempted to raise his eyes and adopt a sort of admonitory attitude. What was needed was a more horizontal approach and that meant being more down-to-earth. An example? You need only think of the social worker who discovers that his work is useless but nonetheless refuses to give up; the East and West German representatives on the commission in charge of canal traffic who despite being tied down by regulations still make every effort to further negotiations to make internal navigation between the two countries easier; the town archivist who is promised various advantages if he puts certain documents under lock and key and yet nevertheless persuades his son to write his doctoral thesis on "the part played by prominent persons in O. in the period from 1933 to 1945"; the police officer who when confronted with a photograph admits that he knows the name of the colleague who is putting his boot in the face of a prostrate student. You were talking about offering something positive: aren't these positive?

Valentin Pundt is reluctant to express agreement, he can't really quite see what general obligation is implied in these examples, and he slowly turns toward Dr. Süssfeldt, who gives an involuntary shrug of her shoulders and says that there's something she really must know: she hopes it's not yet half past five? "It's a quarter to six," says Heller. She must fly, she should have left earlier in order not to be late for the meeting of the jury panel in the Winterhuder Fährhaus, where they will be voting on the Züllenkoop prize. The Züllenkoop prize? It's awarded every year for the best work by a journalist on the theme "Hamburg's Traditions." Rita Süssfeldt apologizes for her sudden departure but they'll be meeting again to continue their search for an acceptable exemplary life. However, in order to make progress rather more rapidly or at least with a greater prospect of success, she would like to suggest that they keep much closer to the texts that are put forward, so that next time Pundt's proposal should be discussed: "It's called 'The Trap,' isn't it? I thought so."

Heller switches on the light and notices in her hand a small shiny object, her car key, which is attached to a little chain and which is swinging around on her forefinger like a propeller. Heller hands her her scarf. She stuffs it into her leather briefcase with her papers. There's no room for her coat in there, so she lets Pundt put it over her shoulders, then she shakes hands with the two men, her hand is cool and very smooth, asks the time once again, dashes toward the door with a squeal of dismay pitched in the middle register, denoting conjecture rather than fear, and rushes through the vestibule. The two men remain listening, both obviously expecting her to return; there's a long pause before they relax, look at each other, moodily go up to the table, and simultaneously, almost as though by mutual agreement, gather up their scattered papers and gently shuffle them into a neat pile.

3

Opinion here in Hamburg is unanimous: anyone who leaves the Hotel-Pension Klöver, who then follows the Alster in the direction of the town, who disregards the briefly dissolving lights on the water but carefully counts the streets on the way, and who eventually makes a sharp right turn on reaching a white jetty, won't need to look up at the sign under the streetlamp, he's found his way to the Alte Rabenstrasse all by himself.

Pundt has done just that. In his bulky wet coat he walks across the pocket handkerchief of a garden, rings at the outside door, and sees a light suddenly come on in the hall. Then there's a crackling noise in front of his face, a nibbling, crawling sound like crabs scurrying about in a tin box: it's the intercom. Is he supposed to speak now? *Must* he indeed speak now? "This is Pundt again, the headmaster from Lüneburg." He pulls the empty photograph frame out of his overcoat pocket, pushes open the door, goes into the hall—without, however, immediately responding to the friendly but stiff welcoming gesture of the man who is waiting for him dressed in a blue dressing gown, preferring first to wipe his lace-up boots on a coconut doormat, carefully and with relish. The very way in which he approaches them —head held at an angle, one hand holding out the empty frame, the other at hip level in a frankly appealing gesture—provides Pundt with sufficient excuse for troubling them again. "We're always glad to see you, Herr Pundt, do come in."

Hans Meister, who must be roughly his own age, helps him out

38

of his coat and gives him a gentle, encouraging smile—the same kind of smile which Herr Meister is displaying on all the posters plastered on both walls of the corridor as far as the door at the end: Herr Meister as a patient newly released from the hospital who is smiling at you with the cast-iron confidence afforded by the policy insuring him against any blow of fate; while on this other poster Herr Meister offers comfort to all those nearsighted or farsighted people who have acquired their spectacles from a professional optometrist; and on that one a gardening apron and a pair of shears represent the promise of owning your own home; whether as someone suffering from bad feet or as a vacationer, as the owner of a bank account or as a gourmet, Herr Meister can find good reasons for smiling, and on every poster he confirms that even old age has its compensations.

"My wife hung them there," Herr Meister explains.

Down there, behind the door with the pane of frosted glass, at the end of the corridor—that was where Harald lived, that was where he did it. Pundt quickly glances at the door as he turns aside. He did not want to take his coat off, but now he has done so and, still holding the frame in his hand, he follows the doggedly smiling Herr Meister into the sitting room. "Good evening, Frau Meister." The lady in question is sitting at an oval table in front of a pile of illustrated color catalogues of Dutch bulbs; her husband had presumably been sitting opposite her taking down the numbers of the items on a pad of notepaper. Pundt gratefully accepts a chair but refuses any other offer; he even turns down the glass of schnapps, despite Herr Meister's assurance that anyone who drinks it immediately feels like pouring out the story of his life.

How can he explain in a few words the reason for his visit at this hour, how can he introduce the question without ruining the pleasure that the Meisters were obviously looking forward to, of spending their evening choosing bulbs? "The names are enough to drive you mad," says Frau Meister, "the names of all the tulips. Queen Sirikit is not too bad and Lady of Leicester is quite credible, but some of them are called Sunkissed or Erhardt's Triumph,

39

these you have to get used to slowly, but how about this one here: Light of Aurich, just imagine, Aurich, where I went to school."

Pundt isn't attracted by flowers, he says, not really strongly attracted. But he would like to apologize once again for disturbing them, he would like to explain that he had something particular in mind that he hoped they might be able to clarify for him. He shifts the empty photograph frame between his fingers, turns it around, and holds it at a slight angle as though he were looking for a source of light which he could pick up and reflect onto some object as yet undetermined. He puts the frame on the table and turns its dull gray surface toward Frau Meister: "I found this frame among his belongings, with nothing in it and no apparently suitable picture to go in it, but there are signs that it must have been used, particularly the fact that the clips have been bent back"—and he was hoping that Herr or Frau Meister might be able to remember where the frame was standing and whose face was in the photograph. Pundt is grateful for any guidance, he says; any kind of clue can help him in his investigation, and he picks up the frame again and holds it out to Frau Meister and then to her husband, not pressing or urging them in any way but merely being helpful, he wants to help them in their attempt to remember, because something is stirring in them, he can feel it in the tense silence and the strained expression on their faces, he can see that they're trying hard to recall what picture the frame contained.

The husband is the first to give up: "No," he says, "I can't remember," and he pulls his collar up and draws the sleeves of his dressing gown together as if he were feeling chilly. He is sorry. He gives his gentle, encouraging Herr Meister smile, the one that people like and that earns him money.

Meanwhile his wife is still sitting there motionless and stiff-necked, a dumpy woman with a horny skin; she's biting her lips, massaging her temple with two fingers, she takes on a pained expression as she searches her memory, and then, standing up, she precedes the two men into the corridor and then into the room in which Harald lived. "This is where it was," she says, patting her hand on the corner of the bare desk top, scarred with burn marks. "That's where the frame stood and the picture was of a man with very long fair hair and a guitar. This is where it stood. It was a man with a guitar, now I remember."

Valentin Pundt looks inquiringly at the iron bedstead, the windowsill, the half-open closet; but they give nothing away. He pulls open the drawer of the old-fashioned little bedside table; it's empty. He peers over the desk into the wastepaper basket; there's nothing there. There's no trace anywhere, no clue, nothing left, and he slowly echoes her words: "With a guitar."

They ease themselves slowly out of the room, in single file they go down the corridor on their way toward the clothes closet, when the doorbell suddenly goes mad; it must be an attack, a state of emergency, but while Pundt listens appalled, holding his wet overcoat in his hand, the woman goes with a quiet sigh to the door, opens it, and stands waiting with an expression of placid resignation.

"For goodness' sake, Tom, why do you ring the bell like a madman? Why can't you ring like a grownup?"

"Ulli's waiting!"

So that's the reason. Ulli's waiting, and Tom tries to squeeze by with a friendly grin, a skinny overgrown lad with a triangular face like a hare which gives him a lively expression.

"I need my parka."

He needs his parka. He doesn't worry about them as they watch him pull his parka over his pullover; the garment comes right down to his ankles, yellow with age—who knows, it may already have spent some time on the snowy Russian steppes or camouflaged a soldier during a Karelian winter—and on its white front Tom pins an Iron Cross which he has fished out of his satchel and has thus presumably swapped for something at school.

"Tom," says Herr Meister, "this is Harald's father," and Tom shakes hands without showing any surprise or paying particular attention, without even stopping what he's doing, all he wants to do is to be off and get back to Ulli, who's waiting outside in the sleet.

Perhaps Tom knows the man with the guitar? Pundt shows

him the empty frame and says, "This stood on the desk, do you possibly remember it?"

Tom in his parka has no need to think, without hesitation he says, "That was Mike, Mike Mitchner, who else could it be? Harald was a fan of Mike's." You could hear a slight amazement in his voice, you could make out that he was asking another question in return: Mike—have you really forgotten? Mike in his early days, that is, when he was a protest singer, not like he is today, grand and successful, the Mike, in fact, whom Tom is on his way to see and in whose honor he's donned the parka. Harald wouldn't have put that Mike on his desk, unfortunately. He was going to appear today for the first time in Ernst Merck Hall, a really dazzling show, "Light, Movement, and Music."

"An American?" inquires Pundt.

"Not at all," says Tom. "He went to our school, Mike Mitchner is only his stage name, up to the time of his final exams he answered to the name of Neidhart Zoch." And with mock formality Tom says to Herr Meister, "My dear parents, it may be late before I return, be not alarmed at your independent-minded son."

"Take a key with you," his mother says.

"Dream of your youth, mother mine," says Tom.

"Be careful," says Herr Meister, "watch your tongue."

"My tongue speaks only with words of angels, father mine, didn't you know?"

Tom in his voluminous parka, Tom the snow hare, puts his hand behind his back, takes hold of the door latch, and, drawing himself up, is about to bow low in an exaggerated gesture of respect, when Pundt, carefully pushing the empty frame into his overcoat pocket, says to him, "If you've no objection, I'd like to come along with you; it might help me in my search."

Herr and Frau Meister give him a friendly nod. Tom's bow breaks off, his eyes peer upward, he is not surprised, indeed seems never to have been surprised by anything. "If you have permission," he says, "if you want to go ahead with your investigation, you can come along with us, as far as I'm concerned."

Ulli has no objection either, although his grim silence might

42

be interpreted otherwise; weighed down by his youth, with his head hanging, he slouches crossly along in the sleet beside Valentin Pundt, and if he's listening at all, it would seem to be to the clink of the metal chain which he's wearing under his fringed Afghan coat. The schoolmaster walks between them, bareheaded, the snow briefly settles and then quickly melts on his hair, his face is wet and shining. He's already starting to assign marks to his present experiences.

Over there is the Moorweide with its brick-red tower and behind is the Dammtor railway station, which is beginning to suck in its evening procession of pedestrians through its wide, divided entrance; they struggle toward it, bunching and lining up, laden with briefcases, toys, animals, rugs, rucksacks, blown-up air mattresses; have they all decided to set up house in the railway station? "We've got to get through there, too," says Tom, and calmly says hello, as cool as ice, to a group of young men carrying an iron bedstead on their shoulders, a bedstead festooned in green and pink from which dangles the long, booted leg of a reclining girl. Pundt notices that other people are stopping to look, just as he would have done, at this motley yet purposeful procession, all these high-spirited modern adolescents who think it so natural to parade in their sheepskin coats or their angora shawls, shaking the snow off their tall Afro hairstyles or their shiny shoulder-length curls, who have equipped themselves with necklaces and talismans and heavy rings on their fingers as though to protect themselves from evil spells. Pundt is sucked through the station by the procession, a foreign body incorporated in a piece of flotsam led astray by a current, and carried up to the exhibition site, the big hall, into the separate garden enclosure full of "Light, Movement, and Music."

"You're different from what I expected," says Tom suddenly.

"Different?"

"Harald often called you the signpost because you pointed only one way, you led in only one direction, you know, like a road sign. This doesn't seem to me to be your true direction and yet you're coming along with us."

"Harald?" says Pundt inquiringly.

"Unless I've got it wrong, every day he had to write down on a sort of calendar the time when he left school and when he got home. You used to check what he'd written."

"What a caper," Ulli says darkly.

"Because you object to people not taking the shortest way," Tom says, "he wasn't supposed to go out of his way, and if I understood him right he had to account for every spare minute. That's why I think it's super that you want to see Mike."

There are blockages, various currents are intermingling. The procession is being held back, cut through and infiltrated by groups of visitors, covered with catalogues and laden with samples, who are trickling out of the Scandinavian Food Exhibition, where you can really get your teeth into the frozen North, a tasty, hospitable North which makes no secret of its weakness for mayonnaise and daubs it artistically over its every offering. Voices, flatulent reminders, queries: What was that white gooey stuff called? *Ködboller* are meat dumplings, aren't they? I found the reindeer ham ... the beer's quite ... *Smörbröd* one really ought to. . . . the pastries are simply . . . People are explaining to each other the things they've seen. They're going over the things they've been tasting. Decisions are being taken.

Now the procession is under way again and moving toward the large hall, a nonviolent yet restless caravan which makes the policemen sprinkled here and there seem superfluous, especially in the peaceful atmosphere created by the objects the youths are bringing along with them: in the open briefcases, Pundt can glimpse checkerboards and games such as Keep Your Temper; he sees a pile of Mickey Mouse cartoons and even knitting materials. Pundt finds it impossible to stop making judgments. What sort of a revolt has he let himself in for? Is this some kind of farewell party, a kind of renunciation? Are they about to found a new realm of adolescence? A distant, insubstantial dream world sheltered from grownups? Perhaps they'll keep him out as an enemy, a gray-haired old man? At the entrance, it looks like a crowd scene, not because the procession has become undisciplined but because the owners of the beds, mattresses, and rugs can't extract

44

their tickets from their pockets quickly enough. Now they're swinging their loads up and carrying them on their heads and shoulders.

"I'll take over now," says Tom, "keep close to me and you won't get lost." Pundt is given a ticket and without any checking over or suspicious looks, he's allowed in, overcoat and all, he can go into this arena where for two days and two nights light has been transformed into music and music has discovered its movement. The beams of two violet spotlights are swinging and dancing and jerking around the room and now they both fall on Pundt, focus on him, and hold him in their grip as if they had discovered the adversary, the outsider who has wormed his way in; he closes his eyes and then the lights release him and swing, jerking and swooping in circles, around the room and back to the stage to form a bell-shaped canopy over the two bands. The ex-headmaster opens his eyes and finds himself standing in front of a human zoo extending as far as the eye can see: There are caves under a mountain of chairs, there are paths and tunnels; over there someone has carelessly erected a platform and someone else cautiously built a den of woolen blankets. With their paws interlocked, two dormice are reclining on an air mattress while a spotted hamster wearing sunglasses and being intermittently fed with showers of popcorn seems to be watching over them as they sleep. Jerboas in the shortest of skirts are scurrying off together to the toilet, past exhausted armadillos, still dancing, whose long, long lips are sucking tightly at each other. Pundt stands up. Pundt concentrates: He wants to be sure that what he sees he is seeing in his own way. Underneath the stage, two guinea pigs are playing chess, one sitting down, the other lying smoking, while a black girl in tight white panties is clapping her hands and swinging her head from side to side. Panting heavily, some salamanders are just leaving the dance floor to find a place to rest under a window; Pundt thinks he recognizes one of them from another world: his pupil Eckelkamp. And, over the whole sleeping, dancing, playing, and in any case satisfied gathering, violet and yellow lights are darting, competing with the sickly

45

clouds of smoke rising from the floor of the hall right up to the ceiling.

Pundt finds a folding chair and observes the two exhausted orchestras, who seem quite unaware of each other and whose musical offerings are miles apart from each other's: the understandable melancholy of the cotton picker and the no less understandable sorrow of a Latin-American guerrilla. They're playing with restraint, introspectively, they're not issuing any appeal or any sort of challenge, but rather producing images of lamentation from the depths of their absorption, fruitless lamentation, as you might imagine. Pundt would like to smoke but doesn't dare light up, although many people have. He removes his overcoat and puts it on his lap. Down below, at the foot of the stairs, Tom suddenly emerges, no longer alone under his camouflage jacket but sharing it with a girl who at this moment is pushing her head out through its wide neck, shaking her hair and raising a cheerful face in expectation of the deserved applause for this successful metamorphosis into a double creature. Will they stumble? Are they going to fall over each other? They remain standing propped up against a wall. The material of the parka comes to life, disclosing that their hands are beginning to enjoy themselves. Ulli makes a beeline across the room toward a group of absorbed youngsters squatting on their haunches. They've formed a circle and around it travels a smoking pipe, handed on with mock solemnity from one to the other, a pipe of peace, a pipe offering joy and oblivion, and now it has reached Ulli as he squats down without saying a word, waiting. They gaze longingly into the distance, soon they'll be seeing their comets or the tails of their comets which will offer them consolation for all the injustices they've suffered for their Physics, Math, and Latin. Tired applause for the two bands. That is to say, for their decision to stop playing and leave the platform. All the same, they move off with a wave of their hands and leave the stage free for a bird of paradise who makes his appearance in a glittering silk shirt, fishes for the microphone with a knowing smile, and, after a quick routine to dispose of the wire, stands there for a moment, concen-

46

trating, as if he were about to proclaim not something, but every-thing, a new epoch at least. And it's true; his appearance has been announced, his incarnate presence. HE will appear and be among us, he will give new expression to all our longings: MIKE MITCHNER. The bird of paradise turns around, stuffs the silk shirt hanging over his bottom into his trousers, stares motionless into the wings, and here we go: up HE climbs with his guitar, spread-ing his arms and giving the signal for a piercing awakening.

Pundt is startled. People are jerking and yelling and leaping to their feet, shooting to the surface. They dash forward, stamp, casting aside all their sleepiness and gentle inertia, and give the blond, hollow-cheeked young man a resounding welcome. Pundt can hear circular saws, police whistles, metal drills, rotating grinding stones, plate shears, and, though he is an "enlightened non-driver," the shrill hiss of deflating car tires. Outstretched fingers reach up toward the stage. Screaming and clapping and even tearing their hair, they bunch together under the stage and are on the point of taking it by storm and, in their holy frenzy, tearing this young man to pieces with his long mane of hair and reddish beard, gleaming as if it had been greased, and consuming him, or something like it, on the spot, with no condiments re-quired; but now he moves, abandons his attitude which could be described as one of submission and benediction, and with a smile rests his foot on a chair, exhibiting the length of his thigh sheathed in the suede trousers. The bird of paradise hangs the microphone on a stand and retreats backward, suddenly snap-ping his fingers in the air, whereupon many-colored lights blaze up and swirl around the hall until, having found him, they stop and fasten onto him: MIKE MITCHNER. He strikes a tentative chord, drops his head, hoping for silence but without success, he's used to this, he's prepared for anything, and suddenly he straightens up and remains stockstill. He's discovered something, no, all he's done is to find a point in the hall to fasten his gaze on—can it be Pundt?—and then he begins with "Midnight Letter." Mike Mitchner moans. Mike Mitchner sobs. Reporters, notoriously cold-blooded, have remarked on the trouble that he has always had, continues to have, and always will have with his "Midnight Letter," because this letter, written in the middle of the night, is supposed to tell Katy everything, but everything, and above all relieve his loneliness and put an end to the coldness between them, but although it seems to have succeeded and sounds all right at midnight, it is found to be inadequate in the cold light of day and seems superficial, lame and inappropriate, and so the writer of the letter, who is switched on to inspiration by night but to destructive analysis the following morning, is prevented from ever sending it. The listeners are caught up in the rhythm of the waves of sorrow, they can understand Mike, they obviously have the same linguistic problems as he does, and they moan with him and they sob with him and a very young girl with short, shapeless calves flings herself on the ground and starts crawling around. She flings her head back and forth, her hair brushes over the floor like a mop which has taken leave of its senses: is she looking for the Word, the word which will bring peace to Mike Mitchner?

Ex-headmaster Pundt sees it like that; everything that is happening here he would like to see and experience and assess in his own fashion, and as Mike Mitchner contorts his body into a question mark and, striking a chord on his guitar, gently inquires, "Who can take my heat away?" the schoolmaster gets to his feet, happy not to have to squeeze through the throng, and pushes his way to the door.

He is the only person leaving the hall at this precise moment, and as he knows that his withdrawal can be interpreted as a rejection or a protest, he holds his head down and bends his body forward at a sharp angle: in this way he reaches the entrance, where he runs into an usher so mesmerized by Mike Mitchner that anything could happen under his very eyes. The usher comes up to him, raises his arm, and threatens him with his elbow: "Look, man, he says, you can dust off the food samples over there in the exhibition, you've come to the wrong address here." Pundt apologizes, stops, and ventures to ask for some information: how does one get to the dressing rooms, Herr Mitchner's dressing room? "Well," the usher says, "if you want an autograph, man, write to him, that's my advice, write to him because all hell is going to break loose in front of his door any minute now, if you know what I mean. Anyway, the dressing rooms are over there, but steer clear of them, man, steer clear of them."

Pundt ignores the warning and, getting directions from other ushers, quickly finds out where the dressing rooms are—make-shift ones—but on his way he sees a small sash window at eye level which looks out over the hall, or rather part of the hall. Far below, picked out in the semi-darkness by the swooping, swirling lights, Mike Mitchner is still choking out his troubles in front of a monstrous battery of microphones, complaining of the pitiless heat which is scorching him to death, obviously a heat to which he has been doomed by fate and from which he can only be rescued by someone else, someone long awaited, some secret, chosen angel, and as his gaze wanders outward to the fringe of imaginary horizons, many of his listeners cannot bear to watch his sufferings any longer. Gestures of recognition. Screaming offers. Bodies writhing like leaves in a fire. Explosions of sympathy. "Me," a girl calls out, "me, Mike, me, me!" Hands are waving. A youth in a white crash helmet climbs onto the stage and tries to embrace Mike, kidnap him, carry him off to form a bliss-ful and certainly beautifully undisturbed partnership in some cellar—two ushers drag him away. Mike continues to sing, the young man doesn't seem to be the right sort of offering, nor does he stop singing when a very young girl—fifth grade, thinks Pundt to himself, fifth grade at most—peels off her check blouse and promises to cool Mike down with her torso, naked indeed, but flat as a pancake.

Pundt checks to see if he, the old man, the gate-crasher, is being watched. He moves away from the window and continues to-ward the dressing rooms; he doesn't need to ask the way now; that pile of humanity over there, that surging mass lurching to and fro under its own pressure and counterpressure, confirms that he's reached his goal. He's been mistaken: for the moment

49

there are no personal remarks, no ironical comments—hiya, Granddad, you want an autograph too?—in fact, they seem to be devoting all their attention to clinging to the place they have succeeded in obtaining by depriving themselves of Mike Mitchner's performance. Pundt forces his way into the moving wall of bodies, his arms held in front of his chest ready to fend people off, concentrating on finding space to move and breathe, and by gently leaning and swaying backward and forward with judicious application of his weight at the right moment, he succeeds in pushing through the crowd and working his way toward the door. And now that he is managing to move forward, he does hear remarks and warnings and sarcastic comments addressed to him: "Hey Grandpa, take it easy." "Sure you haven't lost your way, Grandpa?" He's been discovered, they're calling attention to him; nevertheless, they don't expel him from their midst, for the fear of being themselves pushed by an eddy out to the edge of the crowd is stronger than the desire to get rid of him. Should he beat a retreat and give up his plan?

Pundt, who is watching the door intently all the time, suddenly realizes that the door is being opened from the inside; there's a jerk and a push and gradually a gap is forced open and in the gap there emerges a man, greeted with yells and screams, who looks like Janpeter Heller—no, it is Janpeter Heller, who, standing upright in his burgundy pullover, waves his arms in a broad placatory gesture to get the throng to quiet down so he can make an announcement. "Okay, it'll be any minute now. No one's going to be disappointed. But would you please move back a bit and get in line so that you can come forward in an orderly fashion, it'll be to everyone's advantage." They don't believe him, perhaps they don't even understand what he's saying; in any case, the crowd fails to disperse into a long thin line, and with a shrug of his shoulders, Heller says, "Well, if you won't, you won't."

That's that; and now he discovers Pundt's face beneath its unparted brushed-back hair, he hesitates, his expression shows inevitable perplexity at this recognition, but he is forced to believe that it really is Pundt and nobody else, because who else would be making such surprised signs to him, asking for help? And since he no longer has any doubts, Heller opens the door roughly fifteen degrees more and asks the people to let him through—please stand back—and even reaches out a helping hand into the throng, which, though noisily protesting this preferential treatment, nevertheless reluctantly stands back, and Pundt manages to catch hold of Heller's outstretched hand and pulls himself toward the gap in the doorway and into the dressing room.

Breathing heavily, they look at each other in bewilderment: What are you doing here? What are you doing here?

"As you can see, Neidhart was a pupil of mine," says Heller, "back in the days when I was in Hamburg. I can let you have a free ticket."

"Thanks, I only need a piece of private information," Pundt says.

"Didn't you hear him at all?"

"Oh yes," Pundt says, "I was in the hall and heard Herr Mitchner and Herr Mitchner's community too, a community of young people who'd just been roused into activity and were celebrating a mystical union." Pundt had, however, not been unimpressed.

Heller offers him a wooden stool and introduces him to a young athletic-looking Christ wearing a lime-green sweater over his trousers and over the sweater a wide patent-leather belt with an extra-large buckle: "Jürgen Klepatsch, who looks after Neidhart." Klepatsch, an extravagantly long towel tied around his neck, looks up from his crossword puzzle, which is in large print, raises his forefinger in greeting and holds it obliquely in the air for a second, before returning to his meditation on "a type of parrot in three letters."

"And there was I thinking, look at that, Herr Pundt is an admirer of Neidhart's music or perhaps even an expert," says Heller.

"No, not at all, only a private matter."

"All the same, my dear colleague, I'm delighted to meet you

here in this hall, at this performance. Can you see over there, on the windowsill?" Pundt turns his head and looks at the windowsill, on which there are bundles of letters, postcards, and autograph albums and a separate bundle of photographs. "Eighteen thousand a month," says Heller, and then repeats softly, "Eighteen thousand people writing to him every month, probably more than write to our President."

Pundt could well have commented at length on this fact but he confines himself merely to one word: "Enormous."

Chanting? Are they chanting in chorus outside the door? Heller puts his ear to the door, listens, presses his cheek against the wood, and, raising his shoulders and bending forward from the hips with his feet placed as if to run or even take flight, he assumes the posture of an eavesdropper. "They're getting impatient outside, can you hear them?"

"Mike, we've been waiting long enough. Open up or we'll get tough!"

Pundt moves toward the door and can hear the chanting quite plainly; he can even hear the voice of one man yelling new words to fit the chant.

"Do you know Neidhart personally?" asks Heller.

"No, he was a friend of my son, he may be able to tell me something to help me in my inquiries."

Just then Jürgen Klepatsch flings his pencil down onto the crossword puzzle as though to indicate that no type of parrot can ever be in three letters, it must be in at least five and possibly six. Mike's attendant goes to the sink. He turns on the tap. Out of a leather case he takes a washcloth, the kind you can slip on your hand like a glove. The washcloth goes dark as he holds it under the stream of water from the tap. He places the wet cloth over the edge of the basin. What else? The bottle of eau de cologne. He puts the bottle on the windowsill, beside the head of the couch, places the tips of his fingers together and presses and flexes them in preparation for their customary task. He opens the narrow door leading onto the stage.

"Isn't he coming?"

"He's on his way."

In the wake of the bird of paradise, long-legged Mike is on his way, leaning forward as he comes up the slope from down below, alone in his exhaustion or in any case heedless of the compliments which the bird of paradise is showering on him: "Wonderful, Mike. A record, Mike. Only you can do it." His shirt is dark with sweat from the armpits to the waist, as Pundt realizes when Mike stretches out his arms and steadies himself on the sides of the corridor; he is literally swaying with his eyes closed, not disappointed or upset, but pleased with himself, exhausted though he is, because once again he's remained true to his principle: never to spare himself but to demand everything from himself, to give his all.

They drag him into the dressing room, turn him toward the light, hold his arms above his head, and as he stands there submissively, still with his eyes closed, they roll his shirt up to his shoulders and finally lead him over to the couch, where Jürgen Klepatsch pulls his shirt over his head and skillfully presses him down onto the cool, shimmering, silky material. Mike Mitchner is lying on his stomach, his face toward the wall, breathing heavily. Under Heller's endlessly questioning glance, Pundt would like to say something, he would like to say that he hadn't realized "what an exhausting job of work" this involved, but at this moment all eyes are drawn toward Klepatsch as he slips his hand into the washcloth and rubs it all over Mike's lean but pimply back, dabbing it first here, then there, tracing lines on it, drawing curves and writing bold, wet initials which he immediately wipes away with his extravagantly long towel. In silence Pundt observes how Klepatsch carefully turns his bearded charge onto his back, moistens the washcloth again and wipes it gently over his face and then pats it over his hairless chest and almost devotedly rubs down his wrists and armpits: *Who can take my heat away?* Klepatsch pours eau de cologne over the couch in unbelievable profusion, at least Pundt has never seen anything like it, he just slops it vigorously out of the bottle. It spurts over Mike's back, his tight suede trousers, and the couch; a shower like that should bring anyone to life, thinks Pundt, and he feels no surprise at the enthusiastic way Klepatsch sets about combing Mike's hair; Mike is now, of course, no longer recumbent but is sitting up with his legs apart, his hands resting on his thighs, like some peasant woman relaxing after work.

"He's done in after every performance," Heller whispers, "he's completely done in."

Pundt replies, equally softly, "I imagine you need more than strength."

Now Klepatsch holds up a fresh pink shirt over Mike's head and slowly lowers it, making sure that his hands go into the sleeves and that his head comes out through the neck, and at that moment, since the ritual demands it, Mike feels for a cigarette hovering somewhere in the air but without finding it—no, Klepatsch has lit it some time ago and pushes it between the two expectant fingers, which close around it like a pair of scissors and put the glowing tube into his mouth.

"What was I like?" Mike suddenly asks. "Come on, what was I like?"

"You were you," the bird of paradise says, "and nobody else."

"As long as that's good enough," says Mike, standing up and seeing Pundt for the first time in the background in front of the door; he looks at him without expecting him to provide any information or explanation himself, but Janpeter Heller, beckoning to the old headmaster, introduces them: "Herr Pundt, Herr Zoch."

That seems to satisfy Mike and he's about to turn away when Heller says, "There's a private matter Herr Pundt would like to ask you about, that's why I let him in," whereupon Mike turns around to look at Pundt, and stands very upright, his thumbs stuck in his patch pockets.

"A private matter?"

Valentin Pundt says, "Harald, my son Harald. You used to know him? Harald Pundt, a student."

"Has anything happened to him?" asks Mike.

"He's dead," says Pundt.

54

Mike Mitchner turns away, pushes the heap of letters, auto-graph albums, and photographs to one side, and, drawing in his chin, looks down at them as he slowly says that yes, he can remember Harald, although it was a long time ago—when Mike was a protest singer—he can remember him and the cellar bar and the goulash. The bar was called August 4th, he didn't even know why—perhaps it was the landlord's wedding day—anyway that's where the whole bunch of them used to eat. The goulash was very tasty and cheap and while they were eating that really good goulash the group of them used to discuss the things that were happening in the world, it was really more or less a group of friends who thought it was their duty to prevent gross injus-tice, why not use the proper word, any out-and-out shit's trick, from being too easily shelved and forgotten. So the group used to write reams and reams of letters to the newspapers; they'd debate the various matters, arrange them in some order of prior-ity, and then swamp the editors with waves of correspondence. Harald? What else could he say about him? He ate his goulash like everyone else, wrote his letters like everyone else. Anything spe-cial? Possibly his enthusiasm, yes, he could certainly recall Ha-rald's bursts of enthusiasm, which you had to get used to, he seemed to have them automatically at almost every suggestion that came up, an enthusiasm which occasionally seemed hard to justify, something he felt for all their plans. He couldn't say anything more. Nothing more.

And Mike Mitchner turns toward Pundt again with an apolo-getic shrug of his shoulders. "It isn't much, I know."

"Not at all," says Pundt, "you've been very helpful. I'm grate-ful to you and please excuse me for having intruded."

The singer is standing up and looking at Janpeter Heller, who waves to Pundt and says, "We'll be seeing each other soon, won't we?"

4

H<small>E IS</small> not one of the policemen Rita Süssfeldt knows. It's true that he's told her he is assigned to the nearby Oberstrasse district, he even says that his beat has taken him through Innocentiastrasse over the last eighteen months, but she really has never seen him before, either on his own or in the company of any of the other officers whom she not only knows but with whom she has established, in different ways, a sort of connection. As soon as she sets eyes on his embarrassed, humorless face she realizes that this man has never received a bottle of brandy from her and she also realizes that she has never needed to explain to him her particular form of participation in the traffic problem. So he can't have come on her account and he has indeed not come on her account, as he informs her while still standing at the door. "Can you tell me if someone called Merkel lives here? Dr. Heino Merkel?" Rita Süssfeldt chooses to give an indirect answer and points silently to the half-open sliding door leading into the living room, or rather into what at first sight seems a grandly organized furniture store containing heirloom corner chairs, cupboards, coffers, chests of drawers, grandfather clocks, and tables. There is an abundance of walnut and cherrywood; an Italian sideboard jostles a monstrous Gothic cupboard, a Renaissance table supported by carved unicorns, a Biedermeier table, and a fauteuil covered in Beauvais tapestry. The unknown policeman hesitates, just as we might be reluctant to take a seat on an exhibit in a museum —but Rita Süssfeldt points toward the inherited furniture store,

56

encouraging him: "Please take a seat if you can find something suitable." The policeman sits down and props his cap on a silver-backed brush into which a silver-mounted comb has sunk its teeth. All over the tables there are silver boxes, mirrors, apothecaries' scales, and small mortars.

"Will you have a cigarette?"

The policeman doesn't smoke or drink, at least not on duty; he sits there like an object on loan and raises his eyes to look at the pictures, the family portraits in their oval frames, which, without exception, display pale-faced aristocratic-looking men with narrow, harelike heads, who are costumed as Hanseatic senators but who, despite the slight veil through which they are peering, still show something of their strict preference for cash on the barrelhead. Rita Süssfeldt is watching his eyes, but the unknown policeman will never learn from her lips that her family has produced six senators and one mayor; certainly not from her.

"I'm afraid you may have to wait a while," she says, "my cousin has been detained."

The policeman nods and, resting his arms on the carved chair arms, settles down to wait, an exercise in which he appears to be well trained. "In any case, there are a few questions we want to ask," says the policeman.

"Questions?"

"Yes, someone has been opening the cages in the zoo again during the night and letting the animals out."

"Oh, I see."

Rita leaves the room. No, she merely goes for a moment into her study, reaches up to a top shelf, pulls down a book, comes back, and obligingly puts it down beside the policeman's cap. "Just in case you'd like to have a look at it, a book written by my cousin in his younger days, he's an archaeologist."

The policeman thanks her, before he has even read the title of the book, and once again assures her that he doesn't mind waiting, stands up, and remains on his feet until the lady has gone upstairs to the second floor—on stairs covered with coconut matting—opened a door, and shut it again.

The title of the book is . . . *And the Ark Floated,* a history of boatbuilding before the Flood. Now the policeman settles down again. The steps he can hear overhead (the ceiling is twelve feet three inches high) must belong to the lady, they are vigorous, almost impetuous, and now she goes click-clack, presumably on the tiles of a bathroom floor, and then everything is suddenly quiet. No sound of voices, no noise. Upstairs in the study a telephone rings four times but no one lifts the receiver. With mild interest the policeman listens to the numerous clocks striking, reaches lazily out, and, picking up the book, starts reading, paying no more attention to what he is reading than any other reader does.

Upstairs Rita Süssfeldt pushes open the matte-white door. The curtains are drawn. Light is coming from the ceiling lamp, the bedside lamp, and a desk lamp with a curved black foot. On the floor there are books, pillows, newspaper clippings, and articles of clothing, not tidily arranged but thrown violently about and scattered as if there had been a quarrel, as can be seen particularly from the books which are lying around with pages torn out or bindings wrenched apart. But something which no one can fail to see and which distinguishes this from other rooms is the tall chair firmly anchored not only to the floor but to the wall, a somber colossus, albeit perfect in style, standing by itself all ready for some pitiless task. This harsh monstrosity, as tall as a man, inevitably arouses the certainty that it is not there for any peaceful purpose, indeed we are more likely to imagine that anyone sitting in it will be interrogated, accused, or operated on.

At the moment, Heino Merkel, the former archaeologist, is sitting in the chair. He is bound down. Leather straps, holding his wrists firmly against the arms of the chair, cross diagonally over his chest: they are stiff, creaking straps attached to the chair with staples. The slight, emaciated body has slipped sideways, twisted by some overwhelming force, his head is hanging forward, revealing a plate where he has been trepanned; there are weals on his forearms from struggling against his bonds. The man stirs, his head begins to sway gently, his fingers flex, clawing

58

and bending. He lifts his face, full of astonishment, on which can be seen a permanent willingness to apologize, and gives a helpless smile while Margarethe Süssfeldt continues to massage the nape of his neck as she recites the litany of reproaches to which he is regularly subjected.

Hardly has the soothing massage begun to take effect when his face reveals once again his renewed sense of guilt, he would have liked to catch hold of the woman's hand, he would like to make a sign to her to bend her face down to his so that he could whisper something in her ear, upset as he is over this unrelenting affliction, but the straps which he has himself attached to the chair jerk him back. He utters a slight moan, less from pain than because he has failed to make the contact which might have offered him relief.

"Mareth," he says, "Mareth, I tried everything but it came too quickly."

And the woman, looking past him while she speaks: "You've let us down again, you don't get into the chair quickly enough. You didn't call us soon enough."

"But I did keep quiet. I didn't cause you any trouble."

And the woman, in the same stern, monotonous voice: "You've hurt Rita and you've turned your room upside down. If you go on like this, Heino, we won't be able to keep you here any longer."

And then the man again, in a sudden panic: "Not in an institution, Mareth, please not in an institution. I'll change my ways. I'll call you."

"How often have you promised to do that?"

"But I've been good for a long time. The last time was a long while ago. Do you remember how long I've been good?"

And the woman, ceasing her massage: "This time we had to get you into the chair. We had to strap you in. You hurt Rita's shoulder."

And the man, now sitting up in the chair, in an eager, persuasive voice: "They make automatic snap locks, Mareth. I'll get one and fasten it to the straps myself."

Standing in front of the chair, the sisters exchange glances and then, with a word of encouragement and admonition, Rita loosens the straps, but the man doesn't stand up, he remains seated, gently rubbing his wrists, breathing noisily in and out as if for a medical examination; then he buttons his shirt and straightens the tips of his shirt collar: he knows what they want him to do. And he knows all the traces he must remove. While pulling up his socks, brushing the dust off his trousers, and tying an elegant knot in his tie, he keeps repeating his promises; but the women have heard them before and they're not interested, for, by tacit agreement, they are already tidying up the room, putting it into some kind of order to make it easier for them to forget; and Rita now makes a placating, if somewhat absentminded and perfunctory gesture, meaning that she is short of time. "What is the time by the way?"

She must be off. Rita Süssfeldt is due for a session at the Hotel Klöver at which Pundt's proposal is to be voted on. "Sorry, Mareth, but I must read it over again beforehand, if I can lay my hands on the manuscript, that is."

"What sort of a man is Pundt?" Mareth asks, chewing at the corner of her handkerchief; and taken by surprise, her sister gives thought to Valentin Pundt and realizes that she could very easily hold two or three views about him.

"Pundt? What's Pundt like? Well, first of all he's gray-haired and comes from Lüneburg. He often seems to me like a watchtower on Lüneburg heath, dominating and overlooking everything but making it difficult for anyone else to check what there is to be seen. Why is that? It's as if he hasn't got a balustrade or a staircase, no way to get up to him. He's a retired headmaster who swears by dried fruit as a kind of tranquilizer for any situation, you know. Beckmann did a portrait of him as a young man. And since you want to know: whenever you ask Pundt for the time, he first looks at his pocket watch and then, as if this were something quite normal, he looks at his wristwatch, works out the average between the two, and tells you, with reservations, what the time is. There's a son who I think killed himself. But

I must look for the manuscript of the story he's proposing. We've reached the chapter on 'heroes' or, to be more accurate, 'exemplary lives.' "

"Read it to us," Mareth says.

"All of it?"

"Yes, please read it. Heino'd like to hear it too, at least it'll do him good, won't it, Heino?"

"Yes, Mareth, I love listening to Rita reading out loud, and as for the manuscript, it may be in the brown envelope that Rita had in her hand a moment ago. It's on my desk. Take a look. . . . Yes, there it is."

So the story will be read aloud. They settle themselves properly, they focus their attention, their bodies are already appropriately tense, showing that they are all ready, and their hands, too, resting relaxed on their thighs, express expectation or even concentration.

"As I said, this is Pundt's proposal, the story he's selected for our reader," says Rita Süssfeldt as she wets her finger and counts the number of pages, following her own train of thought as she does so. "Perhaps it's useful for people like you to hear it, because you're not involved. We've got to agree on *one* exemplary life anyway. Here goes! The author's name is Kai Köster—presumably a pseudonym—and the story is called 'The Trap.' All set? Well, here we are."

Yes, whatever the risk, I should have ordered him to keep ahead of me, to go on in front through the long, well-trodden corridors of the old fortifications, between the rails now empty of ammunition trucks, and in that way I could have kept my eye on him, silhouetted against the arch-shaped exit and the reflection of the snow. I'd have been safe, I'd have done my bit, whatever else might have happened to him afterward, outside on the snowbound farm and on the frozen beach. If only he had kept in front of me, this little runt of a man, this flyweight with his tinny, perpetually whining voice, I would have been able to keep my eye on him. But perhaps I should have sent him back that night on the dunes near the fortifications, perhaps he would have been let off with a punishment if he'd given himself up to the camp guard, I really don't know. I just can't decide, especially because shortly after we withdrew, the camp was evacuated and the slow boat that was going to bring them back to the West was sunk. And I don't even know what I would do if the same thing were to happen again on a night like that, with a bitter east wind coming off the sea, if a similar encounter were to occur again or, I really should say, were to come at me out of the blue during the middle watch. If another man were to call out to me as he cowered in a hollow in the snow, freezing in his thin striped denims, if another man unhesitatingly, completely confident that he would not be appealing for help in vain, called out of the dark: "Hey, mate! Can you hear me, mate? Help me, mate!" Wouldn't I still, as we have always been taught to do, lift him up and carry him away, first to somewhere warm and then to safety, some kind of safety? Once again I was seized by that ugly desire to look for principles, principles which paralyze us, which simplify everything—here's the debit side and here's the credit side—they provide us with a protective covering, these principles do, you're impregnated, impermeable, dismissive, especially on a night such as this when you're on the middle watch on the dunes over which an east wind is driving flurries of snow and then suddenly a man calls out who is certainly afraid and therefore ought to keep quiet. Where can he have found the sheer courage to address me as "mate," a man so completely cut off from me, who was dependent on me from the very first moment, what could he see in me to make him address me in such a way as I was clambering out of the underground fortifications onto the dunes and unexpectedly found him lying in front of me in the hollow in the snow, having broken through the frozen surface, and obviously too weak to stand up on his own. Although he must have known that I was on guard duty, for he saw me climbing out of the fortifications which, at that time, were being used as an ammunition dump; they were old fortifications, cowering at ground level, and stocked with shelf after shelf of naval mines and torpedoes, obsolete types which they now didn't expect much from but which they could not bring themselves to destroy; so they were stored and this was the second winter that we were keeping guard over them. He must also have seen that I was armed and anyone carrying a gun must surely be an enemy, yet instead of lying low and letting me go by—and I would have gone by without noticing him—he called out to me, lifting both his arms toward me, very thin bony arms which I could have encircled with one hand: "Hey, mate! Help me, mate!" There he lay in his flimsy striped denims, bareheaded, with cropped hair, in this speckled darkness still just bright enough for me to pick out his foxy-looking, arrogant, self-satisfied face—no, I didn't notice that right away, I learned to recognize those qualities in him later on, after my dealings with him, but one thing I did notice was that he was entirely fearless. This man who had succeeded in escaping from the guarded camp, who was being tracked by dogs which only had to follow his footsteps in the snow, felt no fear at all and did not even seem very worried as he kept listening for sounds inland, where the camp was situated, well beyond the dunes and a thick pine forest. "Get me out of here, mate," he said, as he rose laboriously to his feet and pointed impatiently at the dark fortifications as though he knew that he would find safety down there. "Come on, let's get going." But I hesitated and unslung the gun from my shoulder, an obsolescent captured carbine, and stood looking at him, while in the distance behind him, in the night beyond the horizon, bright bursts of light showed where the front was coming nearer.

We stood face to face, I in my superior position and he, strangely enough, in no way dejected or ready to surrender, giving no indication that he'd come to the end of the road; in fact, he seemed unquestioningly certain that I, whom he called his mate, would not hand him over; and this air of certainty filled me with astonishment and made me unsure of myself and it was then that I perhaps first realized that I was no match for him.

He didn't tell me his name, to this day I still don't know what he was called; his plight and his actions were sufficient evidence or confession of what he was, or at least his clothes were, which showed where he came from or at any rate his last place of residence and no doubt this was why he thought it was unnecessary to admit anything more. And then he walked past me, paying no attention to my silent warning, carefully pushing the barrel of my carbine to one side and looking for my footsteps in the snow to help him find his way down the dune, but my stride was too long for him, weak as he was, and I found myself reluctantly supporting him to prevent him from falling down or collapsing into a snowdrift; my rifle had long since found its way back to my shoulder. I followed him down toward the fortifications, warned him of the snow-covered trench, forced him down into the shadow of the rampart, and as we both remained kneeling side by side next to a snow-capped ventilation shaft emerging from the ground, I tried to persuade him that he couldn't remain here at this underground ammunition dump which was constantly patrolled and could well turn out to be a trap for him; he'd do better to make his way eastward along the beach to the small harbor, which was full of wrecked ships, where he could find a hideout and wait until it was all over.

He thrust his unshaven face with its dark eyes horribly near; and as he clung to my arm and stared so closely at me I saw that at the back of his eyes there was a gleam, a desire, a wild confidence. "I'll be best off here, mate, get me in." I refused and wrenched myself free, perhaps too vigorously, for he fell flat on his face and remained lying in the snow beside the ventilation shaft. Some way out to sea they were firing flares into the sky, presumably from a sinking ship, red and yellow flares which flickered in the sky before they curved earthward and were extinguished over the gray sea and no doubt over drifting life rafts and screams and cries for help. I could hear them and yet not hear them as I walked indecisively along the rampart alone up to the iron stairs which led to the emergency exit, the second main exit as we used to call it, and here I opened the two steel doors and just listened, listened to the dimly lit labyrinth and looked over the gleaming array of obsolete mines and torpedoes, over which

64

pulley blocks were uselessly dangling; then I went back to the place where he was still lying, just as I had left him, with his face in the snow. First I gave him a push with my foot and then I lifted him up and angrily dragged him toward the iron staircase.

Just for tonight, I thought to myself, a little warmth and some sleep, just one night, then he'll have to realize where he is and after that no more help from me; and the others mustn't know anything about it, least of all the guard commander. He was light, but stiff and weak; however, I managed to get him down the steps, there was nobody to see us; just one night, then, I said as I led him through the second main exit into the fortifications. He showed no interest in the torpedoes or the mines or any of the other objects around him, he didn't even seem to hear me say he could stay only one night. I pushed him forward underneath the pulley blocks and overhead tackle, he left everything to me as I kept listening and checking, but I got him into the cable room unobserved, shut the fireproof door behind us, and switched on the electric light. I pointed silently to the rolls of cable and to a wide shelf at the top where he could sleep, there was nothing except an electric motor humming away on the other side of the wall; he accepted the suggestion of the shelf, shoved some toolboxes to one side, and I helped him up, once again too vigorously, I had failed to take his lightness into account.

I can see myself glumly helping him up into his sleeping place, just as if I were stowing a piece of equipment away, for there was no contact between us, we had nothing in common; on the contrary, I was all the more reluctant and annoyed because he had intruded, uninvited, into the even tenor of my life and was forcing me to do things which troubled my conscience and even if not exactly that, at least were causing me anxiety which I could easily do without. He rolled over on his side, propped up his head, and stared at me with his large dark eyes, not with any gratitude, it seemed to me, but meditatively and thoughtfully, and then he pointed to my scarf, my dark-blue naval scarf, and I suddenly understood what he needed: "Lend me your scarf, mate, it'll help me. I've always had trouble with my chest since

I was a boy. Come on, mate, you'll be doing me a good turn." I shook my head, but I was already unwinding my scarf and handing it to him as he lay on the shelf. I didn't say good night, I didn't even nod to him, so enraged was I by his barefaced request. I just turned out the light without saying a word and in the dark I said: "Only tonight, do you hear, just this one night." He made no reply. I left him.

I could hardly wait for the end of my watch, which I spent on the well-trodden rampart, not on the dunes or, as I normally did, on the frozen beach, where every step produced a crack or a bang and where I often used to examine the driftwood, planks for example or battered rafts, all the flotsam and jetsam of which the sea at that time contained more than enough.

After being relieved, I went to the guardroom, nothing unusual to report except that something must have happened out at sea, they were firing flares, but nothing special apart from that, and the guard commander dismissed me for the rest of the night, but I was unable to sleep because I realized that now that I had brought him to safety I faced another worry: I couldn't let him lie there without bringing him something to eat and drink. As I would have only my own breakfast to share with him, I decided to divide my bread and margarine into two parts and wait for a suitable time to take it to him, during my off-duty period in the middle of the night or perhaps even earlier, during a cigarette break; but before breakfast we were assembled in formation down in the fortifications, quite close to the cable room, to answer some embarrassing questions, for someone had taken a crap underneath the mines and torpedoes during either my watch or the following one and we had to line up in front of the innocent heap of shit and clear ourselves one after the other. I wasn't free for a single second and so wasn't able to visit him in his hideout or trap until noon that day. But he didn't reproach me, he only stretched out his hand impatiently, for he was hungry; but above all thirsty, he said that the cables gave you a terrific thirst and he didn't hide his disappointment that I'd not brought him anything to drink. To calm him down, I tried to tell him about the morning formation and what had happened, but I couldn't, I really

66

couldn't manage it as I watched him eating, seated on a roll of cable, and saw the trouble he had chewing the hard bread with his bad teeth. "Fluid, mate," he said, "fluid's more important than bread. Next time make sure you bring something to drink, even if it's only water or, better still, tea, what with my stomach."

He'd wound my scarf around his neck and stuffed the ends into his denim tunic, pulling them down almost as far as his belt; he'd apparently forgotten that it was my scarf and that I needed it when I was on guard duty outside, because it was freezing throughout the day, a constant dry frost against which the watery sun moving low on the horizon had no strength. So I let him keep my scarf while making a mental note that I must get it back the following evening as soon as I'd taken him down to the beach or back to the dunes where I'd found him; and to remind him of our arrangement—but was it an arrangement?—or at least to make it plain that I had made a decision and was not going to change it, I said, "This evening, you understand, tonight, you must get out of here."

He answered me with tiny, fluttering gestures, trying to fob me off. "Yes, okay, but just wait till I've got some of my strength back and can walk as far as that harbor you mentioned." The way he looked at me after he had finished eating gave me the impression that he was looking for some pretext, trying to see how he could launch into some important revelation which he perhaps felt he owed me out of gratitude, for after all the only thing he had was his experiences and I could feel those unsolicited experiences heading toward me, the episodes from his biography which he was going to offer me in exchange for my help, which might perhaps put me under some obligation to him once I knew about them; and I was thoroughly relieved at being spared having to listen to what I feared was concealed behind his silence. He was giving nothing away, least of all his name; that suited me fine; the more he concealed from me, the less I felt concerned about him, and I didn't want to become involved by learning about things I didn't want to know, especially as I was going to get rid of him during the coming night.

And with this thought in mind I poured a third of the rum

ration issued to me when I came off duty into my canteen, added some tea, sweetened the mixture with some brown sugar, and took it to him later that evening along with a mess plate half full of noodles cooked in fat.

This time he did complain, in a quiet, intense voice: didn't I see how irresponsible it was of me to offer him spirits, knowing what his stomach and his constitution were like and especially what his situation here was, and he handed back my canteen disapprovingly after barely sniffing at it. "If you want to do me in, mate, then try something else, but not spirits." He said this with a suspiciousness that was quite unfounded but nevertheless made me feel guilty when I left him, so I slipped into the mess kitchen and filled my canteen with tepid but unadulterated tea, and after a cautious preliminary sip, he began to drink it, almost reverently it seemed to me, but with not a word of thanks. He then asked for some tobacco and cigarette paper and I gave it to him; I myself would never have dared to smoke in the cable room, nor would anyone else, but he didn't mind; in fact, in his case I even approved of it, perhaps because I was going to send him packing the following night; yes, it must have been the fact that I had told him how long he could stay and thus made him aware of the hold I had over him that made me feel magnanimous and grant him certain concessions.

My fellow guards paid no attention to me, they were all older men, fathers and family men with no particular illusions, who would write letters, play cards, or sleep when they were off duty; no one worried about anyone else, we all knew that this particular guard duty made no real sense and that when everything was all over we would part company and never meet again. But even though we weren't suspicious of one another, I dared not be too careless. I couldn't confide in anyone and I took every precaution whenever I went to the cable room, particularly on the night when I was going to turn him out.

That night seemed milder and less unpleasant; it seemed, for some reason, a better night to escape than the night when I had found him up there on the dunes, which were now casting purple shadows under the heavy sky. The sea was breaking gently, almost noiselessly, on the beach.

Since everything had been discussed and agreed upon, I hoped to find him waiting by the door, all ready to leave, and so when I opened up, I called in the dark: "Come on, off we go"; but nothing stirred, he made no sign, and so I had to go into the room and turn on the light and there he lay on his shelf blinking at me. I gave him a push and beckoned to him urgently to come along, whereupon he seized my hand, opened my fingers, and with an apologetic expression placed them on his jaw, a swollen jaw, as I ascertained by passing my fingers over it and feeling the inflammation and the throbbing. That was his explanation; he made me feel the swelling and when I again demanded that he come on down—but less firmly, halfheartedly this time—he produced his unbearable toothache, his high temperature, and even claimed that he was suffering from a loss of his sense of balance, surely I could feel and see that—and of course I could see and feel it, he didn't need to persuade me that he was suffering, but how long would it go on? In my annoyance and fury I did in fact ask him how long his pain would be likely to last, not only because of my position but because of his own, for after all he must expect to be discovered one day or other. "When I can, mate," he said. "As soon as I can you'll be rid of me, but you can't turn me out like this, just feel the swelling and the inflammation, I wouldn't get very far in this state."

He asked me for wet compresses, he asked me for some painkilling tablets, apparently without any thought whether it was possible to do what he wanted, in fact I could see that he would have liked to ask me to hurry up.

Today when I think about it all and recall our meetings, first in the cable room and later in the room where the electric motor kept humming away, when I remember him, now that time has softened my memories and dispelled the danger, then I must admit that, even if he didn't dominate me, his plight did form a bond between us and his demands restricted my freedom of action, giving me the feeling in everything I did that I

69

hadn't done enough; I don't know, maybe I'm just imagining it.

In any event, I used to bring him what he wanted, at great risk for both of us; on one occasion he even asked for a newspaper and, having read it, complained to me of the unbearable optimism which saturated it from the first page to the last, and he craftily tried to discover how far I myself had been taken in by this optimism. Meanwhile he was wearing one of my pullovers, he had my socks on his feet, and so that he wouldn't be wearing my scarf all the time, night and day, I had brought him a towel which I'd been sent from home, and just as all these objects had drifted in his direction, so, invariably and constantly, did my thoughts, too; even when I was on duty I kept thinking of him, not just in passing but as if he had become a permanent part of my job, a kind of endurance test.

After he had spent four days and nights in hiding, I stopped thinking about when he would be leaving and I endured him and his demands, even the ones he didn't express—in fact, those especially—just as I endured all the rest—the monotony, the watches, the news—and yet I should have been anxious to get rid of him, because the guard commander seemed to have noticed something, he seemed to be looking at me in a curious way, he would come up behind me unexpectedly as I was walking about, and once he even stopped me as I was coming out of the ammunition dump with an empty mess plate. I was leaving it up to him to decide when he wanted to leave; it was his getaway and it would be his hunger and his fear that would go with him on his journey; but above all, he must be free from pain.

Did I hate him? Many times when he demanded something— "I need your shaving kit, mate"—when he made fun of the food, when he refused to listen whenever I said anything about my own difficulties, yes, at such moments I certainly hated him or at least I regretted having let myself in for all this trouble. During my night watches, when he was asleep down below, I would stand on the dunes looking at the skyline behind the pine woods and see the flickering reflections of firing, a sporadic glow coming nearer and nearer, and hear the sound of the guns as the front approached, and then I would go down to see him, hoping that my account would speed him to a decision; but each time I was amazed at his equanimity, his sang-froid. "Who knows, mate, he would say, who knows whether it won't be all over when the end comes?"

When he talked like that in such dismissive terms, in spite of all my principles I felt a desire to discover more about him, to ask him why he was in the camp, what he did for a living, but I suppressed my curiosity and contented myself with imagining what he had been and inventing reasons for his internment.

On the sixth evening, before hurling himself onto his food, he seized my hand and excitedly, with his mouth open, placed my fingers on his jaw. "Can you feel anything, mate? The swelling's gone down and I haven't got a temperature." He looked at me, he sensed what I was thinking and he didn't hesitate to refer to it, with a crafty smile, as if he were offering me a present, the only present I wanted: he'd decided to move on and escape eastward, as I'd advised, and since, despite my relief, I merely nodded and in any case showed greater calmness than he had anticipated, he was disappointed, he wanted me to appear really pleased. "How about being pleased, mate? I'm off, I'm not going to be a burden to you any more. Isn't that enough to make you pleased?"

I made him a present of my scarf. I suggested that he take my towel with him as well and keep my socks and I promised to bring him some provisions on the following day—not big quantities, he mustn't expect that, but a two-day supply of bread, some margarine, and a piece of smoked sausage: I could let him have that. He barely heard my offer, he listened to it without any show of emotion. When I left he shook my hand but with no particular meaning, not as though he wanted to express his thanks for what I'd done, but almost by accident, casually, and then I left him to himself so that, in his words, he could spend his last night laying in a provision of sleep, curled up on his tarpaulin to the hum of the electric motor.

The nearest inhabited place was some five kilometers away and this was where we had our supply depot. They sent me over there in the morning with the large sledge and, as usual, I hoped to pick up a little more that day, some extra bread or tobacco to take to him, so I went off alone through the dunes in the dazzling bright winter morning. There were aircraft about. In the distance, comfortingly far away, the heavy guns were conducting their dialogue. The frisky sledge was swinging and swaying behind me, overtaking me on one side or the other on the frozen snow when I was going downhill, and I frequently gave such a jerk on the towrope that the sledge reared up perpendicularly. So on I went westward, sliding along parallel to the beach; the members of our guard post had prepared the track themselves; it was a winding track, hard to follow and thus not boring, which suddenly left the dunes and shot off into snow-covered fields up to the edge of the village and to the requisitioned barn from which we took turns fetching our supplies.

Something was happening in the yard in front of the barn. Trucks were parked there and from some distance away I could see that a move was being organized, not a panic move but still a speedy one: crates and boxes and buckets were being passed in a human chain from the barn to the loading area and I recognized the storekeeper in charge standing in front of the door of the barn telling people what to do.

I dragged my sledge into the yard, past the trucks, released the chain, and struggled up to the barn to present my requisition sheet to the storekeeper. He hardly had time to spare me a glance. "We're being moved out, for God's sake," he said, "we're no longer responsible for you." Then he seemed to recognize me, my appearance reminded him of something he'd been asked to do, and he told me that we were to be moved out too, they'd already phoned about me and I was to get back to the fortifications as quickly as possible. I left the sledge in the fields because it was hindering my progress and preventing me from running as fast as my fear would have liked; I was afraid for him, he might already have been discovered and possibly interrogated, but even worse than by fear I was plagued by the thought that they couldn't take the mines and torpedoes away with them, all those outmoded weapons would have to be left behind, but as they

72

were still serviceable they would have to be blown up. Hadn't all the plans for a withdrawal already been worked out?

Over the dunes I went and down onto the beach, where running was easier even though the ground was softer, for once you'd broken through the slight covering of frost it was solid underneath; and so I ran on, accompanied by my long shadow beside the wintry sea whose long watery tongues were licking at the beach. Out there a convoy was slowly beating westward, well dispersed, perhaps it had only just been formed, some fifteen or twenty vessels with torpedo boats and minesweepers on each side. Over there were dark apertures, like so many faces with slits in them, they were the fortifications and the specks which were running away from them and struggling up the dunes were my fellow guards. So the withdrawal had already begun and they were on the move, although possibly they were only looking for cover in some hollow, protection against the sudden upheaval when the camouflaged bunkers were blown up. Without looking underfoot I kept on running, keeping my eyes fixed on the ramparts and the flattened mounds, always expecting them to be blown to pieces, their massive blocks shot sky high, leaving white rubble surrounded by columns of smoke and flame, and then someone called out to me from the top of the dunes and ordered me to fall flat. I pretended not to understand him and ignored his warning, ignored the frantic signals, now that I was running I kept on, urged on by my fear and deaf to the shrill whistle of the guard commander.

The steel doors were open. The lights were on in the corridor. I endeavored to shout but couldn't manage it, so I had to make my way to him through the maze of corridors echoing with the sound of my footsteps, I had to find him where he was lying on his tarpaulin unaware of the decision which was shortly going to be put into effect. He looked up at me disapprovingly, rubbed his neck, and said, "How about food, mate, haven't you brought anything for me to eat on my last day?" But I'd already caught hold of him and jerked him upright. "Come on," I shouted, "get moving!"

My face and my fear and my peremptory order made him

realize there was no time for questions, his nose for danger warned him straightway and spurred him into instant activity such as I would never have thought him capable of: "Quick, out we go." My boots thudded as I made off at full speed past the rows of black-bellied weapons toward the main exit, unaware of anything except my gasping breath and the throbbing in my head. It started and stopped and then started up again as I stumbled along between the rails, and I thought he was following me because neither the thudding of feet nor the heavy gasping seemed to stop and this couldn't be coming from me alone, not just me, and once I felt a slight touch and assumed that he must have touched me as he ran along behind me.

We reached the exit and then we ran down onto the beach, stooping as we made for the dunes, not to where my fellow guards were lying but rather toward the dunes on the eastern side; and then, before we could reach them, I was spun around by the blast of the explosion. I pressed myself down hard against the sand and felt the ground shake and shift sideways, first once and then a second time; and then, when everything seemed to have settled down, there came a shock that flung me in the air, the earth trembled and heaved as if it were about to explode. I found myself lying with my feet in the water. I crawled slowly on all fours back to dry land, leaving an uneven trail in the sand. I got up on my knees, and peered all over the beach, as far as the foot of the dunes.

Hadn't we reached the exit together? Hadn't we both been running toward the dunes until we were knocked over by the blast? Wasn't he lying beside me? I couldn't find him.

Rita Süssfeldt places the sheets of paper on the floor, lights a cigarette, inhales lazily, puffs out rings of smoke, and watches them contemplatively until suddenly and silently she gulps them deep into her lungs. She looks up: what is the reaction of her audience? Mareth, obviously still lost on the wintry beach, has just finished eating or chewing up, at a rough guess, her sixth paper handkerchief; she is sitting with her eyelids half closed,

74

swaying slightly and somewhat tense. Heino Merkel, on the other hand, seems, as it were, to have met the story halfway. He's sitting on the very edge of the colossal chair, resting his chin on his hand and pursing his lips. "So that's Pundt's proposal," says Rita Süssfeldt, "that's the story he wants to put in our anthology as an example of model conduct. If you ask me, the whole thing looks too much like a climbing pole that's too smooth for any pupil to shin up. The thing that troubles me is the unquestioning way in which Pundt's hero plays his part, his purely automatic reaction. He picks up this escaped internee, doesn't he, he hides him without any attempt to gain more information about him, he provides him with food and drink without asking him his name, and finally he's ready to sacrifice himself without knowing who it is he is sacrificing himself for. Even if we bear in mind, specifically, that the guard doesn't know who the escaping prisoner is and assess his action accordingly, it seems to me that the good deed is rather too mechanical. And the only lesson that comes out of the whole story is surely: ask no questions and follow my example. But is that human? Or normal? What's your view, Mareth?"

Mareth isn't quite ready yet, she seems to need to free her mind from the images which are making judgment difficult, but to start with she would simply like to know what sort of example the guard's action is supposed to offer for other people. Doesn't he seem to represent a reluctant willingness to help? A joyless sympathy? That is, if she reads the story correctly. But something like this will never lead her to accept Pundt's story, for what's exemplary about helping someone against your will and standing by someone when your heart's full of anger?

To Mareth's astonishment, Heino Merkel takes a different view: he is impressed precisely because the help was offered reluctantly and because of the guard's unwillingness to add to his responsibilities by learning more about the man. The guard is prepared to help even though he realizes that by doing so he is going to land himself in difficulties and will be forced to abandon the pleasant inertia which up to now has enabled him to put up with the whole stupid business. So any help he offered was bound to be reluctant and Heino can easily understand this.

Rita Süssfeldt gathers up the loose sheets, she must be off, they'll certainly be waiting for her in the Hotel Klöver. "Good heavens, you must excuse me."

There's a knock at the door, and then another one, timid and inquiring, as though someone was trying discreetly to bring himself to their notice.

"Oh yes, the policeman. That'll be the policeman."

"Here?" Mareth asks.

"He wants to ask a few questions, so I took him into the living room."

"And he's been sitting there the whole time? By himself?"

"I gave him something to read," says Rita, in a voice suggesting that there was nothing more to be done for a policeman, and she moves toward the door.

"Wait a second," Mareth says, and walks over to the chair into which the puny little man has retreated in shocked defense, ready, as so often, to confess and retract. She looks sternly down at him and he has no further need to confess, for without a word being spoken she is able to learn everything she needs to know. "I'll talk to the police," says Mareth. "For the last time I'll tell them all about you and perhaps that'll help you."

"It's a new policeman," says Rita, "or at least I don't know him. Unfortunately I must be going now."

"All right, you be off, and I'll cope," says her sister, opening the door.

5

WHENEVER Magda, the Hotel Klöver's morose maid, brings in refreshments, standing for a moment at the conference-room door, tray in hand and listening before knocking, it seems to her that it's not really a conference taking place around the rosewood table amid the panoply of weapons—not like a session of the fish-processing industry, say, or the Hamburg florists or the garbage-incineration experts, which she's seen here before—but more as if they are indulging in funeral speeches or graveside orations interspersed with occasional vexed rebukes. No applause or roars of laughter or enthusiastic "hear, hear's" come resounding through the hall. And always they break off as soon as she comes into the room, and either doggedly read while she's serving them or else take the opportunity to stretch their legs; except that the woman regularly asks her for a fresh ashtray.

The man wearing a comfortable old smoking jacket once surprised Magda by asking her if there was anyone she particularly admired, and when, after some thought, she mentioned Caterina Valente, it was apparent that he had never heard the name. She wastes no time in serving them, unenthusiastically because they pay no attention to her, indeed hardly seem to notice her with her little white maid's cap perched on her knobby forehead, although her stubby bitten fingernails arouse the interest of the redhead.

That was one coffee, one tea, and one apple juice. She collects the money, leaves the room, and as soon as the door closes, she hears the man in the smoking jacket slowly begin to speak, not really asking for anything but drawing the attention of the other two to the hopes and wishes of the committee and its members, the people who had commissioned them. These wishes are quite accurately known, they have been spelled out and laid down in numerous conferences, and since the ministries attach particular importance to the "Exemplary Lives" chapter, it can't merely be dropped because Herr Heller has just discovered that the search for a model is begging the question and is merely paying homage to the idea of a leader of the pack. Heller could have realized this earlier and given up his commission. But now everything had been agreed upon with the officials responsible for setting up the commission, as well as with the publisher; the contents of the anthology had been settled and now they must stick to it—even if they themselves preferred a counterproposal.

Even Magda's inquisitiveness is insufficient to make her stay and listen, so she goes off, while in Pundt's peculiar way of showing excitement he drops his voice, speaks more and more quietly, rubbing the balls of his thumbs together, and reels out longer and longer sentences as if, for the time being, he was not anxious for anyone else to talk or as if talking uninterruptedly was his only way of relieving his feelings after these arguments and the rejection of his proposal. He was not offended because his proposal had not been accepted, indeed not; he could appreciate that in an undertaking like this there was bound to be a tussle, but that after all their preliminary work, after all their voting and even some agreements, Heller should suddenly throw the whole thing back into the melting pot, such behavior he found very odd. It seemed to him unfair and absurd. In order to discover how wrong he was, Heller need only listen to any discussion among young people; at a given point they would always ask for suitable suggestions from their elders—what have you really got to offer us?—and everyone would be happy to see a couple of exemplary lives come in through the door with something to offer and put an end to their indecisiveness. It was an innate and deep-seated desire to look out for signposts when the terrain was difficult;

Pundt had needed it himself in his youth, and the youth of today, torn between so many possibilities, needed it just as much and indeed showed its need quite plainly. For that reason he would like to point out with all due emphasis that their work was something quite different from what Heller had called an attempt to put together a sort of heroic potted meat with the help of bay leaves and history. An action, an exemplary action, certainly had no unpleasant smell, it was always worth attention and recommendation, and, speaking from his own experience as a teacher, it was also palatable.

Is Janpeter Heller even listening? Is he satisfied? Has the ex-headmaster dispelled his aggressive doubts or at least induced him to make gentler comparisons? The young expert, whose eyes beneath their sparse lashes hardly ever leave the exotic weapons on the wall, who always has an arrow or a hunting knife in front of him, testing its sharpness on his own flesh to what seems the limit of endurance—Heller wakes up when he's addressed, visibly emerges from gentle contemplation, and waves a limp hand to show that he's taken it all in. He'd merely like to ask whether Pundt had said all he wanted. Yes?

Okay. Then he too has one or two things he'd like to point out. On behalf of unsuspecting generations of schoolchildren he would like to protest at the way in which the attempt was being made, as a matter of educational policy, to give young people an inferiority complex by forcing them to live under the oppressive gaze of ancient monuments. Why wouldn't people stop trying to intimidate others by means of authoritarianism? And why should people insist on devaluing the privilege of free will by making it slavishly dependent on models? The very thought of this rape on the part of smug schoolteachers made Heller want to puke. There were other ways of going about it. For example, they could accept the assumption that everybody was his own model or could become one if he only had the chance to actualize his finest potentialities. And any anthology must, in fact, explore this point and show how potentialities that were latent or were being repressed by circumstances could be actualized. Anything else was so much 1871 eyewash. And in case Pundt had any doubts about this, let him just relax and put himself honestly and objectively in the place of a schoolboy who sees the guard in "The Trap" set up as an example to follow. What can such a figure have to offer for his own petty day-to-day existence? What light can it throw on his problems? Heller himself would perhaps feel some excitement upon receiving such an out-of-the-way, almost exotic message, but he would certainly fail to understand it, and would immediately forget it.

Valentin Pundt's eyes are narrowing, his lips are dry and trembling, he gives a condescending nod of his head, he has something up his sleeve, he begins and then pauses—his normal pause before bringing out his final argument—but he either will not or cannot hold back any longer. "All right," he says, "if my proposal seems so out-of-the-way and exotic to you, then I assume that I have the right to explain to you that this is an actual report in the form in which we have it here. Those fortifications existed; there was an escaped internee and a guard who hid him."

"You?" asks Rita Süssfeldt.

"No," says Valentin Pundt. "I was the guard commander responsible for looking after the ammunition dump, and I felt that something illegal and forbidden was taking place without my knowledge, but I couldn't discover what it was, although I was on the track of it and had stepped up my patrols. But I learned what had really happened only when I was sent the report. 'The Trap' is not a manufactured legend or a model I invented but part of my personal experience, the truth."

And relieved of this heavy burden of confession and with his final, ominous appeal to truth, Pundt thinks that he has now in fact removed any doubts and objections and, leaning back in his chair, he feels almost tempted to apologize for having used this ultimate weapon.

Heller is neither surprised nor intimidated. "Let's not delude ourselves," he says calmly. "There are valid truths and there are invalid truths. There are truths that don't concern us and others which immediately shed more light on ourselves. In any case,

80

truth of experience is not in and of itself either exemplary or worth communicating." He didn't want to hurt Pundt's feelings and above all he was anxious not to become personal, but in the interests of their task he felt obliged to point out that the personal experience of many people is either irrelevant or just so much eyewash. Experience is of value only when others can recognize it as worthwhile for themselves. My experience is not worth anything unless it matches the experience of others. When someone offers me truth I should like to know more about myself. The abnormal experience of that guard looked to him like one of Rumpelstiltskin's presents: no one knew what it meant.

Without a word, Pundt rises to his feet. With expressionless face, he gathers his papers together, he straightens up, holding his chin exaggeratedly high in the air. This is not the attitude of someone prepared to be indulgent, open-minded, or conciliatory. Is there still something he would like to say? He takes a few steps toward the door, turns around, he's endeavoring to make a brief, stiff bow toward the table, but a sudden resistance forces him abruptly back to the perpendicular and in a deliberately frosty voice he informs the company that he is not accustomed to conducting differences of opinion in such a tone. And he says to Heller, "If I need any instruction, my dear Heller, I give it myself."

Thereupon Pundt leaves the conference room, gripping his papers tightly under his arm, blank-faced—or at least his face does not divulge what decision he has taken: whether to abandon the project temporarily or once and for all.

Listening provides no clue. Waiting is equally unprofitable.

"You'd better go after him," says Rita Süssfeldt. "Follow him and apologize. I've got the feeling that you went a little too far."

Janpeter Heller has a different opinion, he pushes an arrowhead into his eraser and holds the impaled rubber in front of his eyes. "The anthology may have three editors," he says, "but the responsibility for it can't be divided. And since I don't want to bear responsibility for something that I can't accept, there is no room for ambiguity. You can see all too plainly from other anthologies what happens when people are mutually considerate."

But Rita Süssfeldt is already on the move, holding her lighted cigarette in her outstretched hand as she sails downstairs, across the hall, and upstairs to the hotel rooms; needless to say, she has left the door open. Heller closes it with a sigh, inserts his finger into Dr. Süssfeldt's cigarette pack, discovers that it's empty, and thereupon, pleased with himself, walks over to the window, looks out for a while on Hamburg in November, all painted in gray, and then notices the odd pair of roof tilers who are working with a piece of sheet metal on a scaffolding above him at an angle.

A swarthy old tiler is teaching a very young tiler in a baggy pair of unfaded overalls how to cut sheet metal, presumably for a channel in the roof, and because the young tiler is obviously having difficulty concentrating, because his gaze keeps wandering to look at a low-flying airplane or to watch the flow of traffic or to pick out an old-age pensioner who is poking at pieces of paper blowing about in the wind with a pointed walking stick, because, in fact, the very young tiler, instead of watching and learning, is enjoying himself more by letting his attention wander, the old tiler cuts his thumb off with his metal shears, or at least he commands the metal cutters to go very close to the thumb and at the very moment when just one more snip will do the trick, the old tiler stops cutting and draws the apprentice's attention—he must be an apprentice—to the danger his thumb is in and, seizing the opportunity to point the moral, he holds up the forefinger of his own left hand, the first joint of which is missing. "That's what can happen and that's what will happen if you don't keep your mind on your job. And now go and get our lunch."

Heller watches the apprentice clambering down with numb fingers; he himself would like to be on the scaffolding in front of Pundt's window and, crouching down without being seen, hear what made the touchy Lüneburg headmaster become so annoyed as to leave the room. But he would also like to discover what Rita Süssfeldt has to say and what she thinks of his confessions. She is a woman who doesn't make it easy for him to behave toward her in a reasonable way: if he feels tempted to show her indulgence, he finds himself showing admiration, and when he sets out to pretend to be indifferent, she forces him reluctantly to agree with her, in his heart of hearts.

He gives the young tiler a nod; the apprentice gives a start, seizes a leather bag from the windowsill, grips its handle between his teeth, and, disconcerted, clambers up onto the scaffolding again, faster than necessary, as Heller observes, and just as if someone were after him. Heller goes to the door. He looks at his watch: this would be the time to telephone, but before he has a chance to go down into the vestibule, he can hear Dr. Süssfeldt's footsteps and as always she seems to be in too great a hurry, tormented and spurred on by all kinds of arrangements and fears, by real or imagined deadlines.

"Off you go," she says, "you've got to make an apology, he's ready to accept one. You can go up, I've prepared the ground."

"Later on," says Heller.

"A lot depends on your apologizing to him. How can we keep going if Herr Pundt quits? If he goes home? Who knows who the third man might be? After all, we've got to come to some agreement."

"Okay," says Heller. "I don't really know why I have to apologize, but as soon as I'm back from town, I'll extend the hand of friendship to our sulking denizen of the heath, so that we can continue to sing our three-part canon on the theme of exemplary lives. Meanwhile, there's something else I've got to do."

Rita Süssfeldt looks at him uncertainly, for she was expecting a different decision; now she'll have to have another word with Pundt, just a quick explanation, and then if Heller likes she could give him a lift into town, she's got to go in anyway. Heller agrees and goes off to the car, which is never locked, not even during the night—in Dr. Süssfeldt's view nobody is interested in unlocked cars and she can prove that up till now her psychology has been correct.

A gentle but pervasive drizzle. Poor visibility. Muggy November air which doesn't allow even the tiniest, weightless thing to float about. Everything is sticking to the ground. The windows are covered with grime and soot, you could write your name on them.

"The Stephansplatz?"

"That suits me."

The windshield mists up, Heller pulls a piece of cloth out of the glove compartment and starts wiping on his side with a few hasty excursions over to Rita Süssfeldt's side, as she has a cigarette dangling from her lips.

"That's one advantage," says Heller, "the windshield wiper that's working is on your side."

She shrugs her shoulders. "If it gives up," she says, "you'll have to wind the window down and direct me: we've seen it all."

Through the rain and the murk and the exhaust fumes, Heller glimpses the Hamburg Broadcasting Station and, next to the porter's lodge, the statue reclining on a patch of dirty grass and holding his hands above his head. "That's the bronze man," says Rita Süssfeldt, "he's wringing his hands at the quality of the programs." Heller has heard that joke before, he's known it ever since the time he was himself much in demand as a participant in debates on educational topics with political implications; as a debater he was barely tolerated but feared, there was an understanding between him and the program producer that he would act the part of a troublemaker and raise the temperature of the discussion. He had never known the Broadcasting Station as anything but a building site enclosed in scaffolding and occupied by bricklayers, concrete mixers, and painters, and they are still at it now, building covered connecting bridges, roof gardens, and a concrete wall for a pool in which goldfish over thirty inches long would feel at home.

They drive down the Rothenbaumchaussee where, further along, you can easily branch off, to the right, that is, after the Dammtor railway station. Where are those familiar ruins, thinks Heller, where is that cozy cellar bar? He can't find anything any more because at the critical moment the side of a tractor-trailer keeps cutting off his vision as Rita Süssfeldt endeavors to pass it first on the right and then on the left. The trailer is loaded with mattresses and on its sides it carries propaganda for Dr. Grotappel's mattresses: "By day or by night, you'll sleep all right." The language of advertising, thinks Heller to himself, and pointing his thumb toward the advertisement, he says, "One ought to examine the language of advertising."

"And its mentality," says Rita Süssfeldt.

"Instead of these hoary old exemplary lives," says Heller, "we ought to have a chapter in our book on the language and mentality of advertising."

"In that case, Herr Pundt will certainly be using his return ticket immediately. I've known him for more than ten years," says Dr. Süssfeldt, "he's a very competent teacher, you mustn't say anything against him."

"But politically," says Heller, "he seems to behave like a piece of blotting paper."

Suddenly he presses both hands against the glove compartment, the car is sliding and skidding gently sideways over the wet streetcar tracks, they're about to explore Dr. Grotappel's mattresses, but before the traffic light comes up, Rita Süssfeldt manages to get off the tracks and to apply the brakes. She hasn't noticed either Heller's movement or his fright and she says, in a tone of satisfaction, "When there's ice and rain, they ought to stop all traffic in the other direction." Heller eagerly agrees and reflects how much pleasanter it would be if there weren't any taxis or trucks and above all those two cement mixers with their gently rotating drums hurtling menacingly from the other direction as if they were trying to take on the little frog-green car.

But something must be happening ahead, policemen are standing in the street waving down the drivers, and then they can see a loose line of policemen facing the traffic as it slows down and directing it around the corner, all the vehicles follow the uniformed arms pointing at right angles and turn off into side streets —all except Rita Süssfeldt: with a short gasp she makes for the loose barrier of police, she's through it and on her way, and since she doesn't go in for rearview mirrors she doesn't realize that, in an automatic reflex, two policemen leap to one side and then pursue her for a couple of yards, waving threateningly, and finally have to be content with taking down her number. But she's on her way and is now driving all by herself down a street which has been cleared and on which there's no oncoming traffic; and when Heller looks back and remarks, "They'll have noticed that," she points out that the "Get to Know Your Police" week has only just begun. How effortlessly they sail past the Dammtor railway station and how easy it is to get into the proper lane when you have the street all to yourself, it's the only way to get to the Stephansplatz as quickly as that.

The Stephansplatz is not blocked but occupied, indeed swamped. They can see a wall of people approaching them, an irresistible quicksand surmounted by banners and placards like homemade regimental colors. On they come, joyful and angry, and their faces show that they can hardly believe how quickly they have achieved their objective: they've got control of the streets, they've paralyzed traffic, and there's no longer anything to stop them. Confidently, arm in arm and marching in step, the boys and girls advance through the rain, chanting the slogans that are written on their banners and placards. The increase in the price of school season tickets must be canceled. They demand justice and understanding. Instead of helping research and education, the authorities are making it more expensive to travel to educational institutions by increasing streetcar, subway, and train fares. A comic strip shows Hamburg in the process of becoming a wasteland.

The heaving procession is led by a hollow-cheeked young man with a megaphone and a Maori-Afro hairstyle. He is walking backward and, waving his arms to bring them all in together, he invites the crowd to voice their disapproval by chanting the slogan: "City fathers, don't be greedy, taking bus fares from the needy." Walking backward, the young man brushes past the little car in which Heller and Rita Süssfeldt are sitting and anyone with a bird's-eye view of the demonstration, say from the roof of the central post office, would be tempted to think of a stomach

86

drawing and squeezing something into its maw and digesting it, and in fact the car seems irresistibly caught up in the heaving mass, it's quivering like some foreign body that is being swallowed but finally rejected as too indigestible.

But although it's beginning to shudder and wobble and lurch, the car doesn't overturn, its glass windows remain unsplintered, no jet of flame breaks through the fury which is binding them all together and urging them on, and now, slowly, a door is being forced open against the pressure of the passing throng and a man dressed in an open raincoat, beneath which a burgundy pullover can be glimpsed, squeezes his way out. He's barely set foot on the ground and is still standing in a twisted posture beside the car when he's seized and carried off, arm in arm with those beside him, a new link in the chain—or perhaps one should say an old shackle which, still serviceable, has been joined on. It would be a more appropriate comparison, for none of those who are fitting Heller into their ranks and carrying him off come anywhere near his age, despite the liberal display of beards and luxuriant whiskers; they're all very much younger and logically they ought to be treating him as a member of the other side, but a sixth sense seems to tell them that despite the difference in age he's one of them, sharing their views, and that his indignation can switch on as and when required.

Heller changes places with a shy, chubby schoolgirl and moves out onto the edge of the procession, only a few yards away from the young policemen who are having difficulty avoiding infectious contact and are learning the hard way how not to listen to catcalls or become involved in conversation, how to show self-control when being taunted.

Janpeter Heller knows why he has joined the procession. Diagonally in front of him, pinned to a broomstick, a placard written in blue pencil informs him that the price of a single ticket on the city's public transportation system has been increased by fifteen pfennigs while that of a monthly school season ticket has gone up by three and a half marks. He's told by a schoolgirl who is busily providing his armpit with warmth from her own body that a member of the town council is going to be forced to discuss the matter with them and a suitable statement is going to be submitted. The statement has been prepared, the representatives for this discussion have been appointed. But hasn't anyone thought about the question of boundary limits?

The front of the procession has come to a halt on a line with the electric clock, their progress has been blocked and held up, people are overrunning one another, pushing and shoving, but there is heavy backward pressure from the front and all of a sudden everything comes to a stop. "What's up?" "Why can't we go on?" "How much longer do we have to wait?" "Go and find out for yourself."

Heller refuses to rely on the evidence of some of the taller students, he forms a spearhead with his hands in front of his chest and plows his way energetically through the ranks of the demonstrators, past damp wool, dripping hair, and shiny wet raincoats. No one knows who he is, yet they let him through without a murmur, simply because they feel confidence in him. In front there are two rows of police, staggered in depth, chatting and waiting while some of the officers in charge—immediately recognizable as such—are negotiating with the students at the head of the procession, good-naturedly, as their gestures show, but to the point, above all in their constant repetition of one single argument.

Heller is standing next to the youth with the megaphone and the Afro hairstyle, held in place by mother-of-pearl combs. Heller is told that they've reached the boundary limits. Heller is eager to talk; he inquires and is informed (he knew the answer already) what would be the result of overstepping those limits. Heller considers in what circumstances a deputation from the procession might be allowed to submit a prepared statement in the city hall. Heller leaves it to the demonstration's committee to decide whether they want to send the authorized delegation of three representatives to the city hall. Heller, still the only one talking, finds himself obliged to explain the demonstrators' rights to the superintendent in charge of the police contingent, since the officer seems to have different views. Heller utters the following sentence: "Once and for all, we must dispose of the error that people who have acquired extra power or information by underhand means are automatically entitled to give orders." And finally it is Heller who, when the delegation has gone off, instructs everyone to squat down and occupy the Stephansplatz until the return of their representatives.

The massed ranks squat down. All those who have raincoats pull them up over their heads, spreading them out with their arms like sails and offering shelter to those next to them. Half-clenched fists hold cigarettes between bent fingers. Transistors tuned to various stations begin to compete with one another. The police stand about in groups, listening to one of their number and unable to take their eyes off the crookbacked monster facing them, from which only vague sounds are emerging, ebbing and flowing like a tide.

And now a streetcar is approaching from the direction of the Lombard Bridge with its inevitable grinding and the metallic whine of its high-tension cable. Heller watches it coming with its protruding round metal front which seems specifically designed to push obstacles out of the way of the tracks, it's coming closer, slowing down, and then stops just in front of him—so close that, had he wanted, he could have reached out and touched the padded black bumper. The conductor gets down, looks in bewilderment at the squatting bodies, goes over to the group of officers in charge of the police, makes an inquiry and a protest and seems to get some results, for the officer superintending the operation accompanies him back to the streetcar and says to Heller, "You must all move off the tracks, the streetcar has got to get through."

Heller looks around him, everyone is winking and grinning his agreement, so he turns toward the superintendent and says, "As far as I'm concerned, the streetcar can get through."

The conductor tugs on his leather cord several times, giving the signal to start, but the streetcar doesn't budge.

"You've got to get off the tracks immediately," the superintendent says calmly.

"Notice was given of this demonstration," says Heller.

"I know that," says the superintendent, "but you agreed not to interfere with traffic."

"Is anyone interfering with traffic?" inquires Heller of the people behind him.

At a signal from the superintendent—a prearranged sign which is taken up and passed back along the ranks of the police —two dark-green trucks emerge from a side street and back up toward the streetcar. Bunched together, a first wave of police begins to advance, the officers shortening their stride and seeming to be automatically held back by some restriction or obstacle —presumably since they don't know exactly what's happening and they can't tell yet how they are to proceed. A few whistles and scattered catcalls greet their progress, a cracked boo from a breaking voice. This relentless advance, more or less in step: is it possible to go on sitting down? Here and there a few of the boys stand up with a jerk like plants in a speeded-up picture, ready to do something but uncertain when faced by the steadily encroaching police. The youth with the megaphone tells everyone to stay seated: "We're going to wait for our answer here."

The police wheel toward the streetcar, they're advancing so slowly now that they seem almost to be marking time. The superintendent believes in following the regulations and for the last time he tells Heller, primarily Heller, to move away from the tracks, otherwise he will have to use force, and so forth. Heller and the students grin. "Since I've given you several warnings, and you haven't complied," the superintendent says without raising his voice, "we're obliged to take the necessary steps." In the name of the community, Heller thinks to himself, in the name of the Deutsche Bank and all the forces of conservatism. The superintendent, who is wearing green leather gloves, gives another signal, obviously taken from the police manual and immediately understandable, whereupon the police break formation, calling out instructions to one another, and then, as required, and always in pairs, make for the squatters. One policeman vigorously grasps you under the shoulders, another takes a grip around your legs, and the refractory but sagging bodies are lifted up, dragged to the trucks, and skillfully slung inside onto the floor.

The police are working selectively, they are merely trying to open up a lane for the streetcar, but apparently they're not succeeding, nor will they ever succeed, for barely have they lifted one body from the tracks when another body takes its place. Heller has been inside the truck for some time now and he smiles as he watches the hopeless task of clearing a path; without any advice from him they are doing what he would have advised them to do and as they drive off he squeezes his way to the high tailgate, which is closed and tightly fastened, and gives the squatters a V-for-victory sign as a farewell greeting. Two policemen disapprove of the sign and cut short the performance by closing the awning.

Heller lets himself down onto the floor with the others. There's no smoking here. A dim light filters through the vinyl window. "Where are we going? Does anyone know where we're going?"

"The typical sort of question they set for competitive examinations," says Heller. "Surely you must know it. You're in a closed truck, from the estimated speed and duration of the journey and for all I care from the length of your hair, work out your eventual position."

The boy with the megaphone asks one of the escorting policemen, "I wonder if you'd be so kind as to tell us where you're taking us?"

The policeman doesn't reply, but his partner does: "Shut up," he says.

Heller feels his body being jolted, that must be cobblestones, so at least they're going past the Dammtor; perhaps past the university as well, if the students would only join in as they come out from their lectures and block the two trucks. Or are they going east, over the Kennedy Bridge? Suddenly the Beatles are heard in the truck, singing "Let It Be," but the policeman who wouldn't say where they're going doesn't give them a chance. "Turn that damn thing off," he says, "this isn't a picnic."

Are they going far? Is it worth trying to describe a Hamburg as invented from under the awning of a police truck? Perhaps it might be an opportunity to demonstrate the relativity of our perceptions. There's a horrible smell of fish meal, so I must be in Eidelstedt: something on those lines, perhaps? From under the awning you might perhaps dream up a Hamburg as valid as the real one or even better.

The trucks turn off, drive over a bump in the road, perhaps a gate entrance, in any case they've left the traffic behind them and seem to be crossing a blustery cement courtyard. The sharp tug of passing streetcars tautening the tarpaulin is replaced by gusts of wind which make it flap back and forth and blow the roof up into a kind of dome. They're stopping.

The tailgates are let down. "Out you come. Come on, let's get down! And get into line, you bums—assuming you know what a line is!" One of the girls, a long-haired ash-blond nymph, politely asks him to refrain from addressing them like that, whereupon the policeman, momentarily taken aback, gives her an ironical salute and merely says, "Your Grace is requested to show a leg. And now, ten–shun, right turn. Good God, what a bunch!" And now they're going into the administrative block. In single file, they shuffle off into the police barracks, go up a couple of worn stone steps, and line up in the well-scrubbed corridor smelling of thrift and disinfectant. "Have your identity cards ready," says a policeman, "we have to find out all about you; don't push, everybody gets his turn."

Heller is the fifth person shown into the office. A pale green light. In front of the window which overlooks the barracks square stands a scruffy little desk. Behind the out-of-date but serviceable Remington sits an equally aged policeman typing with two fingers, and a colleague is standing beside him, bending over the typewriter. No chairs. A condensed-milk firm's calendar is hanging on the whitewashed wall and a framed photograph of the former superintendent of buildings stares into the room with typical Westphalian stolidity. To the left of the desk they've squeezed a roll-front filing cabinet.

Heller comes in and waits beside the door.

The policeman who is standing says in an impersonal voice, "Please come over here. Your identity card."

"I don't carry an identity card, ever."

The old policeman: "Any other papers? A driver's license perhaps?"

With a lofty smile, Heller declares, "I'm sorry. Since I'm not a dog, I don't wear an identity disk, on principle."

The old policeman peers sharply over his glasses, which have slipped down his nose. "You do know that you're required to prove your identity?"

"It's incompatible with the dignity of the individual."

The policeman standing: "Perhaps, as an exception, you wouldn't mind giving us your name?"

Heller shrugs. "Janpeter Heller, Janpeter in one word, and as the next question is presumably my age, I was born on January 15, 1930, in Hamburg, in a taxi on the corner of Bundesstrasse and Rentzelstrasse, I can't recall the number of the taxi."

The policeman standing exchanges a glance with his colleague. "Born in 1930—that means you're going on forty."

Heller looks smug. "Does that remark suggest that I look younger?"

"Normally people have finished their schooling by the age of thirty-eight."

"You can see the result of that. . . . If I had my way, I'd send everybody back to school again at fifty."

The old policeman: "Profession?"

"Secondary-school teacher."

"Which school?"

"The state secondary school in Diepholz."

The policeman standing, in surprise: "Not in Hamburg? You don't teach in Hamburg?"

"There are secondary schools outside Hamburg."

The policeman standing, eagerly seizing on the discrepancy: "And what was it that led you to take part in this demonstration in Hamburg? Do you even know what it's all about?"

"Since you ask me—it was to protest against the profit motive."

93

The policeman standing, sticking to his guns: "It was about the price increase for school season tickets. And I'd like to know why you're demonstrating here when you yourself don't use public transportation in Hamburg. After all, you don't live here."

Heller, with a sigh: "I'd completely forgotten about that. If I take part in any future demonstration, I'll remember to take out a residential qualification."

The old policeman, personally interested: "Did you come to Hamburg just to take part in the demonstration?"

"No."

"For professional or private reasons?"

"I don't think I'm required to answer these questions. But if you really want to know, there's a conference."

"What kind of conference?"

Heller, not without a certain smugness: "An educational study group. Some colleagues and I are compiling a new reader. It's an official commission."

The old policeman, in amazement: "A reader?"

"Yes, something to read, if you know what I mean."

The old policeman, with a smile: "Well, I guess you'll have lots of useful things to tell the youngsters."

"It would be a great help if the police weren't so eager to compete with us. From an educational point of view."

The old policeman gives Heller a searching look. "Well, Herr Heller, perhaps nobody has ever said this to you, so I'd like to tell you something. In all my experience there's no one who seems to me more pathetic than a revolutionary who's getting too long in the tooth. Someone who hasn't got the guts to face up to his age and experience of life. A belief in the impossible is something that has its proper time and place, when you're young. Youngsters can afford to demand all or nothing. At your age, you ought to have realized that there are limits."

Heller, abruptly: "If the sermon's ended, I suppose I may go?"

"As far as I'm concerned, you may. You're free to go."

Heller goes out without a word.

In the corridor outside he's greeted with questions and cheer-

94

ful curiosity. What was it like? Did it hurt? What did the fuzz want to know? But Heller brushes them aside, he has no wish to linger with the youngsters. He leaps down the stone steps and hurries across the courtyard, he pays no attention to the guard at the gate. He knows what he wants to do. He immediately pushes his way to the streetcar stop, where a grumpy mother with a little plastic hood over her wispy hair, two shopping bags, and a bunch of flowers wrapped in sodden paper is abusing her superiority over a young boy whose chief desire is to rummage in the yellow public litter basket and if possible empty it. His mother keeps on tugging him away and giving him a smack on his flabby, obviously well-upholstered bottom, and when this doesn't work, she gives him a slap in his face. The little boy stamps his feet and bawls and stretches out his obese arms toward the litter basket. The mother gives the little boy a good shake, she's about to dislocate his arm, so Heller fishes a couple of old tickets out of the litter basket and pushes them under the little boy's nose, thereby earning a dirty look from the mother. With a laugh the boy immediately puts the tickets into his mouth.

The streetcar arrives. Heller gets in, is pushed toward the center, where he hangs on to a strap with his right hand. The streetcar seems to be reserved for people with bad colds, he's surrounded by dry hacking coughs and sniffles and wheezes. Even the driver seems to have caught it, for at every stop he noisily blows his nose and looks at his watery red eyes in his rearview mirror.

Heller presses his mouth against the sleeve of his raincoat. He shakes his head whenever anyone asks him about the stops. To avoid being touched he squeezes himself into the little niche beside the exit, rests his head against the window, and looks out: dark trees, walls, shopwindows. The lamps cast a sickly light. Heller came this way once before on a similar afternoon but without the same memories. That's the Isebek Canal, he must get out. Heller walks a little way back and then along the gravel path beside the canal, whose glassy surface is being cracked by rain-drops, the boat sheds on the other bank are deserted. He might just as well have approached the little rough-cast block of flats from the front, past the tobacconist, the hairdressing salon, and the savings bank, that would also have led him up to the bumpy entranceway and thence into a square courtyard, but Heller decides to go around the back way, probably because there's less risk of being recognized. He goes along the narrow footpath and through the back entrance, not wide enough for a car, not even for a normal-sized barrow, only for baby carriages and pedestrians. There are obscene drawings and graffiti freshly scratched on the plaster of the walls. In the inner courtyard, Heller stops. Over there are the hooks for beating rugs and stair carpets, and here, behind some scruffy shrubs, is the children's sandbox—once again a few forgotten sand molds will spend the winter outside, tin crabs, various ducks, and the inevitable shovel.

Heller looks around him and reflects: if he climbed up on the garbage cans beside the hooks he could see all of the kitchen and living room and perhaps even the nursery; so he climbs onto the cans and leans against the wall. Yes, there they are. They're both sitting in the dining recess, his wife and child, Charlotte and Stefanie. Charlotte is still wearing her hair in the same style, gathered at the nape of the neck and held with a clasp decorated —as Heller knows—with either a butterfly or a caterpillar. On the table are a teacup and a glass of milk. Stefanie puts her hand into her mouth, pulls something out, and hands it to her mother, who doesn't actually put it into her mouth but draws back her lips, holds it up against her teeth, and sits up straight to show what it's like: Well, is it as bad as all that? To convince herself, she picks up a white hand mirror and under the skeptical glance of the little girl she comes to the conclusion: No, it's really not bad at all.

It's a brace: so Stefanie's wearing a brace. The woman hands the brace back to the little girl, telling her to put it back in, then bends over the girl's face and, lifting the mirror and baring her teeth again, says: Look for yourself, Stefanie, there's not a big difference, is there? You can hardly see whether there's a brace or not. Charlotte takes Stefanie by the arm and gives her a quick kiss on the lips: You see, I don't notice it at all. And now they're holding hands, or rather Charlotte takes hold of Stefanie's hand, they seem to be coming to some arrangement, making a solemn promise, presumably she's offering the child another one of her bribes, just as she's always used bribes for everything, brushing teeth, tidying up, and now for wearing the brace. She'd like to change the whole world and keep everything going with a system of bribes.

Suddenly the woman lifts her head and sits up straight in order to listen: she must have heard a signal, she jumps up, looks at herself once more in the mirror before wagging a warning finger at the little girl, and goes out into the hall, smoothing her skirt and straightening her pullover. There's a visitor. As she goes off she turns her face toward the window, that set, doubting face that for a long time Heller thought would never change, simply because in everything Charlotte always believed that something else, namely something worse, was bound to happen, and was thus full of qualms, so that even when talking about herself her words were infected with doubt.

Left alone, Stefanie takes the brace out again, holds it at arm's length, makes a face at it, and then hastily puts it back as the woman returns. She's ushering a man into the kitchen, a curly-haired athlete in a raincoat who greets Stefanie in an avuncular fashion—no, not really, that's what Heller would perhaps like to think—but he greets her with a familiarity that shows he knows her. The man doesn't take his coat off. He sits down beside the child, puts his face close to hers, and speaks to her, possibly he's complimenting her on how well her brace fits. He even strokes her head with the palm of his hand, starting from the back of her neck and continuing upward as far as her forehead. Charlotte is excusing herself, she obviously wants to get ready to go out.

There's a noise and a rattle of bicycle saddlebags which obliges Heller to bring his observations to an end. He vaults down from the garbage cans, two men with bicycles are coming through the back entrance, so he saunters out through the front, turns sharply, and immediately stops in front of the savings-bank show

97

window, which is draped with gray velvet gathered up evenly in the middle, nothing is displayed there except a typed notice giving the current exchange rates. There's another notice hanging up on one side of the window: "If you own something, you are somebody." Heller stands in front of the empty window—after all, what have they got to display?—reads the rates of exchange, and then suddenly steps back and darts over to the telephone booth on the other side of the street. He knows the number by heart and always will. He imagines to himself how she listens, hesitates, and then comes out of the bathroom to pick up the receiver.

"Charlotte? Don't hang up, I know you're there and I know that you've got a visitor. You don't need to answer as far as I'm concerned, but do listen to me. . . . No, not later on, Stefanie's busy and you have plenty of time. . . . And even if he's twenty bosses, please listen to me or I'll have to come and see you at the office, I nearly did it today but in the Stephansplatz something happened to prevent me. You know I've got the right to see my daughter, you agreed to it yourself. Are you still listening? . . . Good, then I'm staying on for a few more days in Hamburg, I'm staying at Klöver's, the residential hotel on the Alster, you know where it is, you've already phoned me there. . . . Let me know when I can see her and whether we can have a talk together. . . . Where am I now? . . . Yes, that's right. Yes, there is a point to our meeting, I'll prove it to you. . . . Settlement? What do you mean by settlement? . . . Your quarterly payment? As far as I'm concerned, you can have it right away. So you will call? . . . Okay, I'll do it today, if you'd like. . . . Later on? . . . Tomorrow? Tomorrow then. Charlotte? Charlotte?"

Heller hangs up the receiver, comes out of the telephone booth, and hurries over to the bookshop on the corner. Will they recognize him? They've changed the staff. A gawky salesgirl offers to assist him, he waves her away, he knows his way around, he's an old customer who just happens to be passing by; he's already gone over to the revolving bookcases where the paperbacks are displayed, he bends his head down against his left shoulder, runs his eyes over the titles, and looks out past them into the street toward the entrance to the house, where they'll shortly make their appearance, in fact are already doing so, for Heller ducks down and takes cover behind the shelves. The man walks over to the car with Charlotte and opens the door for her.

Why does Charlotte hesitate? She looks sharply over to the telephone booth and then up and down the street. She can sense that he's not far away, and above all she can sense that she's being watched at this very moment; she stands there, searching, while the headlights flash on, and then she finally gets in.

The salesgirl has noticed the way Heller is using the bookshelf to conceal himself while he watches the car drive away, leaning over sideways at a dangerous angle as he does so. She's temporarily on her own in the shop, she feels she must ask him something: "Have you found anything?"

"Of course I have," says Heller, "this paperback on radio drama and the latest *Spiegel*, if you've got it."

6

How does one accept a formal apology? With his hands resting on the back of the desk chair, Valentin Pundt is trying to breathe gently, bending his head forward from the neck and staring intently at the bedside rug as if he wanted to burn a hole in it with his eyes; his legs, incidentally, are slightly straddled and bearing his weight evenly. He's listening with great concentration, he's turning the apology over in his mind, he's probably already assessing its form and content: "I really didn't mean it in that way, there was no idea, Herr Pundt, of describing your personal experience as irrelevant or so much eyewash—that was not my intention at all—and, to be honest, I'm amazed and upset that you could have misunderstood me so badly when it was you who made it plain from the start that nothing personal was involved in all our sessions and assessments; but if I actually did seem to say something that hurt your feelings, then it must be because I feel especially involved in this chapter of the anthology and ultimately each of us will have to bear the responsibility for the whole work; so that's why I feel I have to apologize to you."

Having said this, Heller makes a final gesture to indicate "that's that," but Pundt doesn't notice this, apparently still preoccupied with assessing the apology; but finally he gives a nod, a nod of acceptance, and the hand which he now holds out to Heller is ready not only to forgive but to offer his considered congratulations on having passed the test. They shake hands and Pundt's coat, hanging on a hook behind the door, is witness that the conference has not come to a premature end.

"Please sit down," says Pundt, "sit on the bed, if you don't object, and I'll pour us a drop of something." He opens his suitcase and with a smile lifts out a wrapped towel, which he tugs at and unfolds until a plain glass bottle emerges. "Made by me, I'll have you know. I christened it the Great Lüneburg Cock-a-doodle-do, it's a schnapps that I imbibe before breakfast and it's as cheering as a cock's crow." He half fills two glasses and puts the bottle safely back into the suitcase. He drinks to Heller: "I'm glad, my dear Heller, that you came to see me."

"Your good health, Herr Pundt."

They take two sips and look at each other.

"It's true," says Heller, "that stuff of yours—it really is like a great awakening!"

"Then I didn't overpraise it. It's a morning greeting, but you can feel it even at this time of day, even in the evening."

It's easy to be chatting away harmlessly, they could have gone on doing it, finding words to express their feelings and comparisons for their comfortable inner glow, but finally Heller feels bound to mention the brown envelope lying on Pundt's desk, especially as he knows what is inside it. He's got a similar envelope in his room, sent by the same person and containing the same thing. "After all this, Herr Pundt, that seems to be our last hope. Since our proposals have failed, if I may put it in those words. Dr. Süssfeldt's exemplary life seems to be the only one left. As it's a very controversial chapter, 'Exemplary Lives,' in any case trickier than we might have anticipated—if we go on like this, I mean, if the last proposal doesn't satisfy us either, then we shall doubtless have to adjourn our meetings, because goodwill alone won't be enough in this case."

But Valentin Pundt can't agree with this, what's more he would like to draw attention to the deadlines that have been fixed for the delivery of the text and for publication. "No, my dear Heller, when we go our own ways this time, we must have reached agreement; the chapter must be completed."

Then Heller asks, with appropriate caution, whether a suitable text has already been found, whether Herr Pundt thought that Dr. Süssfeldt's proposal might be one which he would be prepared to incorporate into the anthology without too many qualms.

"If we could perhaps add something to it," says Pundt, "a minor operation, working over some of it, then I think, with some improvement of that sort, we may have found what we want."

"We're only allowed to shorten, unfortunately," says Heller, "but is it really worth the trouble with that author?"

"Hartmut König is a well-known author and popular with anthologists."

"That's just the point," says Heller, "and he's been that for the last forty years; if we don't finally put him in cold storage he'll be persuading us for the next forty years that the Teutoburg Forest is inhabited by charcoal burners." He had read the story, "The Concession," only once, in fact, and he couldn't remember every single detail of it, but in his mind's eye he still had the picture of the mother, that indestructible anthology mother whose cheerfulness and care survive every disaster and every change.

The ex-headmaster held a different view, he had read "The Concession" a number of times and he had found the beginning alone more than convincing. Did Heller remember the beginning?

The dirty, bespattered basement window; the chamois polishing away; the sturdy, fleshy arm rubbing the chamois all over the pane of glass, first in a circular motion and then back and forth and up and down. And how gradually the mocking face of the good-looking boy looms up behind the window, clearer and clearer as if it were being wiped into existence, until it becomes plain to the mother that it's not just wishful thinking or an illusion but that the boy is actually squatting out there watching her—you remember, it's Kalle, whom she had no reason to expect. Oh yes, Heller remembers, and he recalls too that the joy of recognition lasted only for a moment and then vanished as the woman let the boy in—he *was* called Kalle, wasn't he?—and then followed him suspiciously with her eyes as he went to the bread-box and drank cold milk while he ate.

Up till then Heller had certainly considered it possible to approve the proposed story, and even if the thought of presenting mother love as a model to follow seemed over-obtrusive, too obvious, too commonplace, on the other hand he had recognized the opportunity of putting forward a woman as someone to look up to. But then this mother also turns out to be the typical mother beloved of all anthologists, an amiable worrywart, isn't she, full of love and resignation; she sees through her Kalle and immediately realizes that the reformatory hasn't let him out on parole for the weekend, as he pretends, but that he's run away; nevertheless, she doesn't reprimand him, but like the devoted mother she is, she cooks him his favorite dish, cinnamon rice pudding.

Pundt has to point out to Heller that he has forgotten something; the woman hadn't seen the boy for eighteen months—he'd already been that long in the reformatory—and her husband had been in prison for the same length of time, for a burglary they had committed together, incidentally. And if Heller were to delve a trifle more deeply into his memory, he would have to admit that the scene was not unimpressive: the jumpy boy on the run, hastily eating at the table, and his mother sitting quietly and patiently opposite him, aware of everything but happy neverthe-less. And if Heller had read the story again he would have known that Kalle's mother does indeed take him to task, at the point when, as soon as he's finished eating, he starts to talk about money. He needs money, his mother can't give him any, and when he decides to call on a friend so that the two of them might get some money for the weekend, his mother steps in and makes him abandon his plan.

"Don't the police appear at that point?" Heller asks, and Pundt, familiar as he is with the text, is able to confirm that that is the case and reminds his young collaborator that the mother hides Kalle in a hole in the floor beside the water clock until the coast is clear. "Unfortunately," says Heller, "that is the point where we embark on the tortuous path of all-embracing mother love, as inspired as vanilla sauce. Instead of doing the only sensible thing and taking the boy to the police station—after all, it's only four weeks before Kalle's due to be released—she hides him so he can have a weekend of fun. And then she goes off, after impressing on him that he must stay in hiding. And tries to get an advance from her employer at the snack bar. And when this maneuver fails, she tries to borrow money from a neighbor. And just as we're beginning to be horribly afraid and hope that she's not going to take something to the pawnshop just to make this brief weekend possible, out comes her engagement ring—you could hardly be more melodramatic—and she polishes it up wistfully, needless to say, and shuffles off to the pawnshop, where she's obviously a long-standing customer."

Pundt is amazed at this, he feels obliged to confess that not once did he have the slightest impression of vanilla sauce and he would like to ask Heller to explain why it should show lack of taste for a mother to want her son to have an enjoyable weekend, something he hasn't had for such a long time. And her visit to the pawnshop? Didn't he know how many people depended on pawnshops to pay their bills? Wasn't he aware that everyone needs some kind of model to imitate and eventually finds one? Those in distress as well as those who are above reproach?

"But the point in question," says Heller, "is what's the right thing for this young good-for-nothing. He's due to be released in four weeks' time, if he returns voluntarily he'll perhaps be given a slightly extended sentence, but at this point, instead of reason, it's the so-called maternal breast which starts to think and decides that the boy has earned some relaxation. It's true that everybody finds a model to imitate. But the pawnshop scene is too corny to be believable, and a proper model should be something unique and force us into a situation where all we can do is admit: that's how it is." However, he didn't mean to suggest that there was nothing in König's story that he didn't like; in fact, he admired the cutback technique which the author uses to describe the various stages of the action: The boy, now set up with pocket money, on the prowl in search of amusement during his weekend of freedom—typically enough, in the St. Pauli district—and on the other hand, his mother, all alone, shown patiently waiting. Heller had indeed found it extremely convincing, precisely because it was shown in action and was recognizable as life. A suggestive contrast between the boy on his pub crawl with old friends in a crowded, noisy atmosphere, looking for something which he'll never find because he doesn't know what it is, and his mother reading or listening to the radio, or just listening anxiously, trying just as hard in her own way to seek distraction in her loneliness. But that was as far as it went.

And how about the scene in the gambling arcade? asks Pundt. The games they play against each other, first on the pinball machines and then with dice? Didn't that have some value? Didn't Kalle's losing provide the right angle of incidence for a good story in which what was inevitable not only had to be justified but foreshadowed as well? The moment when the boy loses his mother's money—later on he borrows money from a friend and loses that too—prepares the way, as unobtrusively as possible, for what must inexorably follow. Wouldn't Heller admit that?

Heller's prepared to admit that, but he wonders—and he will never cease wondering—whether this mother provides the model that they need, an authentic one. For what happens? The boy loses the money that his mother has laboriously scraped together, goes on to lose some more, and so gets into a mess. What seems bound to happen in such a situation? One thing. As a result of all this, there's one scene that has to be put in and the boy has to be involved in it, as he's doubly in debt. Heller can't help it, it all seems terribly hackneyed to him, he can recognize all the stereotypes and he can see the novelette looming in the background. He would feel less annoyed if the friends got the money they need from a gas station, from the till of some all-night cinema, or, if it really was unavoidable, from some strip-tease joint, but who could defend the idea of having them break into the very pawnshop where Kalle's mother had pawned her engagement ring? Could you really spread it on thicker than that? And didn't Pundt feel a slight pain in the neck to see the author following such an obvious course?

At this point Pundt fishes out his bag of dried fruits and passes it to Heller, who takes an apple ring and sets it on his knee. "Later on; I'll eat it later."

"But, Herr Heller, have you ever taken the trouble to discover how many times coincidences have played a part in your life? You see, I can understand your difficulty in accepting that it has to be in that particular pawnshop that the youngsters manage to lay hands on some money, but you may find it less difficult if I tell you that pawnshops are one of the favorite targets for burglaries. In this case, the author is supported by real life—real life based on statistics."

"Hopeless," says Heller, "as soon as reality breaks in, then everything becomes hopeless."

Valentin Pundt can't see that at all, for him reality is the yardstick for everything; but if he might, he'd like to confess what makes him dissatisfied with the story and what he would like to see added to it: Kalle breaks into the pawnshop with his friends—Heller will remember—but there's only a few pennies in the till, quite insufficient to pay his debts, so he fills his pockets with as much jewelry and as many watches as they can hold. They're surprised by a night watchman, they have to take to their heels, and as a result they become separated. After searching for some considerable time, Kalle arrives home at daybreak. His mother has gone to sleep sitting at the table. Does Heller still recollect that episode? Yes? Then he will certainly remember that the lad goes straight to bed, and while his mother is tidying up his things, she discovers the loot. She empties his pockets and puts the watches, rings, and necklaces in a cardboard box. "And now, my dear Heller, I'd like to add something: among the stolen goods, his mother ought to find the engagement ring that she herself had pawned. Wouldn't that be more dramatic? Wouldn't that tie

106

the whole story together better? The boy unwittingly steals the ring which his mother had used to borrow money for his weekend's amusement?" What does he think?

"Tchaikovsky," says Heller; he could hear Tchaikovsky's music in the background, and if the UFA company still existed, they would surely turn it into a film. He wouldn't like to risk offending Pundt's feelings, but with the best will in the world there was nothing that could be done with that story, whatever changes one might make. But what about the ending? Yes, the ending did come down in favor of the mother, of course, for this time she did summon the police to pick up her son—presumably since she hoped to spare him part of his punishment, for there is an indication that she will send the cardboard box back to the pawnshop. Valentin Pundt finds it impossible to judge the conclusion so harshly and puritanically, he prefers to consider the difficulty of fathoming the mother's motives as an invitation to interpret her action: did the mother summon the police to pick up her boy in order to forestall further charges against him, or was she prompted by her sense of justice? There were indications to support both views, but what was surely indisputable was that in this story the example was not set on Olympian heights this time but belonged to ordinary life and moreover to the lower social milieu which Heller favored.

Janpeter Heller takes up the dried apple ring, looks at it closely, hesitates, gives it a short sharp puff as if to blow dust off it, inspects it again but still can't decide to take a bite—and then puts it down on the desk. He is unable, he says, to vote for Dr. Süssfeldt's proposal because, although it does offer a straightforward conflict suitable for an anthology—the struggle between affection and justice—as a whole the story seems to him inadequate. "Believe me, Herr Pundt, before I undertook this work I plowed through a dozen anthologies. If society is really as it is portrayed in those books, then it would appear that we're all living together like lambs in a meadow: fathers only need to roll up their sleeves for every problem to be solved and the mothers' only role seems to be to relieve any suffering that may arise with a big slab of cake. I was determined that the results of our collaboration shouldn't be like that."

At this Valentin Pundt springs suddenly to his feet, goes to the window, looks for longer than usual out into the darkness, and, half turning, says over his shoulder, "I'd just like to know how far we've got, whether we've reached the beginning or the end."

"We haven't reached the end of the road yet," says Heller.

"I cannot believe," says Pundt, "that in this day and age there is no example of model behavior which we can't agree on without difficulty. Exemplary acts are taking place everywhere, in secret or in public."

"But the fact that they take place," says Heller, "is not necessarily a recommendation to put them into an anthology of this kind. We've each put up a proposal and no doubt we're each of us surprised at the others' reservations. And that proves that we haven't found the right example."

"Shall we try and find one together?" Pundt asks. There was a knock at the door. "What did you say?"

"Someone knocked at the door," says Heller a second time.

Magda is standing outside the door, morose and irritated, everything she is asked to do seems to annoy her. There's a telephone call for Herr Pundt, she's transferred it upstairs to the telephone on the landing. Herr Pundt need only lift the receiver.

Pundt rushes to take the call; although he could have walked there differently, gently, he rushes out as if he were expecting news of exceptional importance. Heller drops the apple ring back into the bag of dried fruit. He bends over Pundt's desk and opens the bulky manuscript, which is as thick as a brick: *The Invention of the Alphabet*. He reads:

"Although quipu, hieroglyphics, and figure writing made some contribution, it can today be confidently asserted that the mother of all modern alphabets in current use is the Phoenician. There is no doubt that this alphabet represents an outstanding artistic invention. The syllable is formed by the consonants, which govern and express the meaning of the word; any vowels which the reader needs are supplied and inserted by himself. In this way the reader is required to provide his own shade of meaning by supplying these vowels of his own invention—what a challenge to his attentiveness and creative powers! Among the Semitic peoples, moreover . . ."

Heller quickly closes the manuscript, he senses that he's being watched. "Yes, Magda?" She's standing in the corridor at the entrance to the door. The girl has a request to make on behalf of Frau Klöver: Herr Heller has removed weapons from the conference room and taken them up to his rooms four times already and it's not permitted, so she has hung the arrow and knife back in their old places, she's telling him so that he will understand the situation. "So you see how afraid I am of you here," says Heller, and, pretending to be worried, he adds, "Can you find some way of making me feel less afraid, perhaps?" Magda doesn't understand, Magda looks at him with accusing eyes. Magda tosses her head and goes off toward the left.

Valentin Pundt arrives from the opposite direction, holding his hands behind his back, in meditation and doubt.

"Nothing unpleasant, I hope," says Heller.

Pundt replies contritely: "I would not have anticipated our joint decision, but I did in fact inform her of it. I explained to her that her proposal, 'The Concession,' had also failed to make the grade."

"And how did she take it?"

"She's invited us to her house for breakfast, an 'epic breakfast,' if you can imagine such a thing. In any event, it's reminded me that I still haven't had supper."

7

Over the canopied steps leading down to the August 4th cellar bar, there was a sign announcing: "Our Specialty: Goulash." Pundt opens the self-closing door and with a kind of crawl-stroke motion thrusts his way through the gap in the felt door curtain, to find himself standing on something soft and yielding, a large doormat. So this is it. He'd imagined the place differently: rough wooden tables, an oppressively low ceiling, clouds of smoke swirling around, barely disturbed by a clattering old electric fan, and the finishing touches: a concrete floor and candle smoke wafted about by a constant draft. Instead there is only the low ceiling which he'd expected, and even this is not covered with a layer of soot as he'd imagined but paneled with plywood and painted bright red. On the blue-and-white checkered table-cloths there are tiny plastic baskets of appetizers—pretzels, nuts, and potato chips. You're greeted by the modest nasturtium in its glass vase and the wall lamps peep out from cheerful rustic shades. So this is it.

Pundt wipes his feet on the doormat and observes how the people sitting at the tables, all of them very young, break off their conversations, discontinue eating, sit up, and look him up and down, not to reject him but nonetheless disapprovingly. Although they exchange glances to draw one another's attention, he doesn't hang back, he pushes his way through to the only free table; now you can sense the disapproval and rejection as, with a nod toward the balding young proprietor, he takes off his coat and sits down.

Why have they all come to a unanimous decision about him? Why are they examining him so indignantly? They obviously all know one another; is he the killjoy intruder preventing them from being alone together? A black-skirted waitress in a black sweater asks for his order—a goulash, please—and makes a sign to the proprietor, who thereupon knocks on the kitchen hatch and, when a half-visible face peers through the gap, holds his thumb in the air: one special. Is his presence a damper on conversation? Are spoons being lifted to mouths more slowly, with less enjoyment, because of him? I wonder where Harald used to eat, Pundt thinks—in front of that pale-green tiled stove, over there beneath the high skylight, or beside the glass case on the counter where people in a hurry could get cheese, ham, or roast-beef sandwiches? Was he on familiar terms with the owner like some of the youngsters here who are calling out from their seats to the bar: "Two more beers, Berti"? How had he and all these other people here hit upon the idea of making the August 4th cellar bar, of all places, their special haunt, a bar so tiresomely and, indeed, so compellingly domestic?

Pundt stands up and moves toward the counter, apparently with the intention of going to the toilets, which, with the customary humor of such places, are indicated by a girl in a very loose dirndl skirt—*Hers*—and a slim man wearing a top hat—*His*. However, Pundt stops at the counter and leans toward the proprietor, who, as he now discovers, is sitting on a revolving stool: Might he ask a question? "Go ahead," says the proprietor. Did he know someone called Harald Pundt, who used to be a customer here? "Are you from the police?" No, indeed, he has nothing to do with the police, far from it, he was asking for private reasons. "We don't give information about our customers on principle," says the proprietor. In that case, Pundt would merely like to know at least whether the landlord remembered this particular customer: medium height, gray eyes, very curly hair, Harald Pundt by name. "At a rough guess," says the proprietor, "that description covers about twenty percent of my customers." But how about the name? "I don't bother myself with names on principle," says the proprietor, still keeping his distance. Thank you very much.

Pundt goes back to his table, the waitress brings him his plate of goulash, hopes he'll like it, and under the proprietor's searching gaze he begins to eat, with his paper napkin tucked in at the neck, as is his custom. What do they think he's up to? Does the proprietor perhaps think that his spoon is fishing around for bits of glass or insects or rotten meat? There's a draft—where's it coming from?

Pundt looks toward the door, where a laughing young couple are trying to make their way through the felt curtain; they seem to have become entangled in it. They turn around and manage to free each other and then come in, waving hello to all and sundry; the young man and the girl are both wearing American army coats; the girl's black rat's tails are tied with yellow ribbon and her voice is twittering metallically, like a pair of fast-moving hairdresser's scissors. They prop themselves up against the bar and shake hands with the proprietor; now they're turning around and looking for a seat.

"Isn't that Rektor Pundt? It must be Rektor Pundt! Is it really you?" The young man drags the girl over to Pundt's table. "What on earth brings you here?"

"How do you do, Herr Eckelkamp," says Pundt as he stands up, crumpling his napkin in one hand.

"And so we meet again."

"I saw you quite recently, though from a distance," says Pundt, "at that musical entertainment." Pundt the headmaster, Eckelkamp his pupil.

"Come here, Mischa, and out with your tiny hand to shake with my old teacher Herr Pundt. May I introduce: Rektor Pundt, Mischa Kröger, my—well—my ermine. May we sit down at your table? . . . Berti, three beers!"

They sit there, surrounded by silence and noiseless communication in which even the proprietor becomes involved; at least his old pupil Eckelkamp tries to find something to say: "That's what I call a lucky coincidence!"

112

An unexpected meeting. So, at first, automatically, there are a limited number of things to say; the joyful outbursts are punctuated with too many exclamation marks and you're not afraid of repeating yourself as you search for a lead-in.

"No, I'm not in Hamburg on private business, we've got another conference, a conference for an anthology."

"Art history. I had two terms of art history, but now Mischa and I have switched to economics."

"What? You taking economics!"

"It's the only thing worth studying nowadays."

"And what does your father think about it?"

"He'll be told when I've finished the course. Well, really, Herr Pundt, what a surprise meeting you in the August 4th. Anyway you've managed to unearth the place where they serve the best goulash in town."

An unexpected meeting. Gradually the surprise begins to go a trifle flat, they plow on slowly through their common recollections, picking out what, ultimately, is all that's left—reminiscences. "And that handyman, Guntram, are you still in touch with him? He's studying history. And old pimples Klaus has gone in all seriousness into the Army. And Hebbi—you remember, the one who was always cutting things out of magazines under his desk—he's going in for dentistry."

The waitress brings the beer and they drink to their meeting. Now conversation is really beginning to flag, there are fewer and fewer things left that they both remember, it's time to dredge up personal memories, the sort of thing that will never be forgotten.

"Do you still remember, Herr Pundt, the argument the two of us once had? It was about being consistent. You assigned us an essay to write: 'Consistent and Inconsistent Behavior.' I'd love to know what you think about that now, after all these years." Pundt is sitting with a fixed expression on his face, meditating; he's obviously delving into his memory. "We disagreed because, to your annoyance, I not only defended inconsistency but said it was our only chance of self-affirmation, that really set you off; you claimed that anyone who said A must automatically say B.

I had to read my essay aloud to the whole class, and you not only tried to pick it full of holes, you even tried to make absolute mincemeat of it: inconsistency was a sign of fickleness and unscrupulous compromise. Do you remember that? Even at the risk of being wrong, you said, we must never turn back, we must go through with all our plans to the bitter end because our greatest allies are perseverance and endurance. You even used the expression 'the dignity of enduring.' I can remember that as though it were yesterday. I must say, Herr Pundt, that up till now events all seem to support my view. What's your experience been?"

First of all Pundt needs a schnapps, a large schnapps if that's possible, and then he says that he too can remember those differences of opinion, unfortunately rather vaguely, unfortunately not very fully, but he was pleased to see that a problem which he had assigned to his pupils, or perhaps inoculated them with, still continued to influence them now. Yes, he was still of the opinion that consistency was the most reliable way to behave and in the long run the most successful, simply because it stretched us to our limits, to our extreme limits.

At this point Mischa Kröger registers a complaint: "You never told me anything about all this," she says to ex-pupil Eckelkamp, to which Eckelkamp retorts, "When you're ready for it, Mischa, in time you'll learn all about that, too. The question is whether an ermine should go on as before and die in accordance with its principles as soon as its pretty fur gets a little spotty or whether it can resign itself to being inconsistent and go on living even if it has a few spots on it. I suppose you might be able to see the difference—or can't you?"

"Give me a pretzel instead," Mischa says, and makes a soothing gesture toward one of the nearby tables, as if to say, "Hold on, I'll be with you in a minute."

Pundt takes another sip of schnapps and a gulp of beer followed by another sip of schnapps—that's the right way to do it —and then suddenly asks, "Have you been coming to this bar long?"

"Eighteen months," says Eckelkamp, "almost every day, and in case you've been wondering about the name, everything important in Berti's life—Berti's the owner—took place on August 4th —born, married, failed his exams, and even the aunt who left him her money died on August 4th. That's the reason."

"Then you certainly must know a lot of the people who come here."

"Yes, a lot of them."

"Did you know Harald?"

"Yes, I knew Harald too. I often used to meet your son here, he used to like sitting over there under the fan and we've sat there many a time talking about you, Herr Pundt. Do you know how we used to refer to you?"

"Yes, you called me the signpost. Did you to see him much outside the bar?"

"He was studying education, we didn't have many points of contact," Eckelkamp says, and then, suddenly: "Why did he do it? Why?"

Silently Pundt stares into the distance across the tables, not so much wondering what to reply as hoping against hope that after his long and fruitless inquiries, he will be given the answer by Eckelkamp or someone else in the room. As he sits there with this expression on his face, filled with this unrelenting desire, once again he bears out Beckmann's portrait of him in which, all those years ago, he portrayed him with that brooding severity which can intimidate the person opposite him into laying his cards on the table.

Can he hear what Eckelkamp is telling him across the table? Is he even listening to him? Eckelkamp is telling him where he saw Harald for the last time, a few weeks before it happened and thus a few weeks before Harald's exams. It was in the St. Pauli fish market, very early one Sunday. "Have you ever been there? They not only sell seafood but absolutely everything that people think might be worth something. So Harald and Lilly were standing there early that morning in front of a barrow where a solemnly dressed man with an amusing patter was hawking eels. They walked on together through a bewildering array of goods—on that particular morning they had for sale an amazing number of secondhand water faucets—looking for a big old-fashioned bird-cage, for Lilly was anxious to acquire one. Lilly's like that, she has a desire for something and as soon as she's got it she forgets that she ever wanted it. We didn't buy a birdcage but a guinea pig, something else that Lilly had always wanted to have, and Harald carried it off in its cardboard box and later on fed it at the bar where we had breakfast. No, Harald didn't seem different at all. We sat outside the bar and discussed the antiquated system of examinations, and I can still remember how he put forward some good reasons why students who haven't yet taken their exams should get together to reform the examination system. Before we left he surreptitiously gave the guinea pig away to a little boy and his sister—she won't notice anything, he whispered to me, Lilly will never remember that she not only wanted a guinea pig but actually owned one. That meeting on that Sunday morning in the fish market was the last time we met and Harald was exactly the same as he always was: impatient at having to listen to others and always making plans."

Valentin Pundt stirs, his shoulders droop, he places his hands one on top of the other and turns his face toward his former pupil. It isn't like just shutting a door and going off, one knows that one has to put up with a certain amount; what can have gone wrong with him?

Had Pundt ever talked to Lilly Fligge? No, this was the first time he'd heard the name. But it was Lilly who knew Harald better than anyone and she would know the reason if anyone did. Lilly Fligge: a fiery ball of quicksilver. Then Pundt wanted to know, he really wanted to know, what the couple were doing together or, in his words: What was the relationship between them? But his pupil Eckelkamp can't understand that kind of question, he just ignores it, and instead of replying directly he volunteers a piece of unsolicited information: if you stand outside the August 4th, with your back to the entrance of course, and then look left, you'll see a delicatessen diagonally across the street with a tremendous show window and two immense windows

116

four stories up; and if there was a light showing at those windows, it meant that Lilly was at home and prepared to receive visitors, so Harald had told him.

The old schoolmaster acknowledges this information with a nod, he doesn't pursue the point nor does he disclose whether he has taken a decision and, if so, what. Anyway—Eckelkamp is doubling back and returning to his previous topic as though it were something quite natural—anyway, his present opinion would be that since all experience is recognized as being provisional, consistency in behavior is out of place. When we realize that our views have only temporary validity, surely we must alter our behavior—from time to time. Might not Pundt agree with that? Pundt won't say that he agrees but he does think that such a view has something to be said for it, they ought to discuss it further sometime, perhaps on some more suitable occasion; what he would like to do right now is to pay the bill. At that Eckelkamp protests, as a former pupil he insists on paying for his former teacher, and while he's making sweeping proprietorial gestures with his right forefinger on the tablecloth, he waves his left hand toward the owner of the bar: "This is my bill, Berti."

A lingering, somewhat overexpressive handshake as he takes his leave, closely watched by everyone in the room. "We'll be meeting again perhaps, possibly even in the August 4th, why not?"—and then Pundt leaves, buttoning his coat with its drooping hemline as he makes his way between the tables toward the exit, still being watched by Berti's young patrons and accompanied by the low murmur of their voices; and before thrusting his arm between the curtains at the door he looks back once more, aloof and unmoved, toward his pupil Eckelkamp.

Valentin Pundt clambers up the cement steps with the aid of the iron railing, peers across the road through the sleet, there's the delicatessen and two lighted windows four stories up. In the shopwindow Pundt discovers Herr Meister once again, against a Ceylonese landscape, he is portrayed cheerfully (but not unmindful of his heavy responsibility) tasting "the tea that's best for all of us." Above the row of shops you can see the dirty façades of old and very spacious apartment houses; the walls beside the unpretentious doorways are bespattered with white enamel nameplates which show that, whether by accident or by design, there are three professions that seem to be indispensable to the inhabitants of this city: lawyers, dentists, and tax consultants.

Why isn't the outer door locked? Pundt finds himself standing in the hall reading the list of regulations printed in old-fashioned type: it states that in winter the door must be locked at eight o'clock and in summer at nine o'clock. On the floor above he can hear a shuffling step dying away into silence. No sound of a key or of a door clicking shut. Pundt goes along the hall paved in two-tone floor tiles, hung with very tall mirrors, already stained around the edges, which have been keeping a watchful eye on each other for the last sixty years, past an elevator that no one ventures to use any more. He reads the nameplates on the doors in this Hamburg apartment house, each one painted a brownish yellow—considered here a "sensible" color—and although he finds it difficult to believe, it seems that behind each door roughly nine people are in residence, except for the consulates, the branch publishing offices, and the secretariat of some academy or other.

Here's Lilly Fligge's apartment. "Please ring four times," says a visiting card. Pundt operates the bell like someone familiar with Morse; relaxed yet accurately he gives four short rings, stands back from the door, and watches the peephole for the eye which must shortly fill it; but the peephole remains unobscured and, feeling that he hasn't been heard, Pundt rings again. There's someone coming, someone's on the way: a firm, rapid, purposeful step is heard approaching, to the accompaniment of a hummed tune, and then the door is flung open, rather than merely opened, revealing a red trouser suit in the doorway.

"Did you ring?"

"My name's Pundt, Valentin Pundt from Lüneburg." The name doesn't seem to produce any immediate impression, it's not going to give access to the spacious corridor, so Pundt adds, "I'm Harald's father."

The lively face under the short curly hair looks up at him with an expression of amazement and incredulity. "Harald's father?"

"Yes, may I talk to you for a moment?"

"Certainly, of course, although I'm afraid it's not a very suitable moment—I'd better tell you that now—please come in—it's not very convenient because I'm terribly busy going through my stuff and tidying up, let's go through—in fact, to be more precise I'm in the middle of packing because I'm off to Aberdeen tomorrow, I'm going to spend a whole term there—look out for the two steps—as an exchange student in Aberdeen, though of course there's no point in giving up my room, one of my college friends will be only too glad to take it over while I'm away because, of course, it's absolutely certain that I won't be staying in Aberdeen —now we go left—even so, one wonders whether even one term away isn't a good reason for making one's will, in fact one gets all sorts of weird feelings when one's packing all one's stuff, I suppose you've felt them too—here we are, please come in—in any case, this will be my longest stay abroad."

A machine gun, thinks Pundt to himself, she talks like a machine gun, and in the end there won't be anything worth repeating. "Please excuse the mess—do sit down—and if you don't object I'd like to go on packing—you can turn the record player off."

So the ex-headmaster finds himself sitting in an unbearably bright room in which all the furniture is so low that you wonder why she's bothered to have it at all: that table, for example, which seems to him to stand not much higher than a matchbox, this armchair which supports you a few inches above the floor—and bent double at that—or that chaise longue which certainly wouldn't allow any normal-sized man to stretch out when he sits on it. Everything is low, flat and squat, cut down, an extension of the floor, as if you were expecting a hurricane that must not be offered any resistance but must be allowed to blow itself out overhead. Valentin Pundt would be neither willing nor able, indeed, to decide how his present posture should be described, perhaps he's recumbent, but anyway he's occupying one of the armchairs and he feels as if he's on a raft drifting along on an ebbing tide surrounded by flotsam borne away past him: shoes and files and clothes hangers and boxes and fancy bottles, even a piggy bank, and of course books and suitcases and underwear and gaping traveling bags. In her red suit Lilly Fligge is wading through all this, salvaging it, sorting it out, piling it up, and stowing it away, including a few framed photographs, with Mike Mitchner's on top.

She seems to have forgotten who it is sitting in her room silently watching her pack, but perhaps she's also afraid of being interrogated and reminded and so she keeps on talking to prevent anyone from interrupting, thinks Pundt; but then suddenly she turns around where she's standing at the other side of the room by the window and says in a quieter voice, "I don't know why you've come, whether you want to tell me something or want me to tell you something, but I ought to say straight off that Harald and I had broken up a few weeks before it happened."

Pundt watches her expectantly, she's holding a sweater whose zipper has come out and she's trying to fix it under the standard lamp by the window, and now she's coming over toward him, accompanied by the flapping sound produced by the wide cuffs on her trousers. She holds the sweater against her body, throws the empty sleeves over her shoulders, and then, after a short, critical embrace in front of the mirror, holds the sweater at arm's length, folds it, and pushes it into a suitcase. What she needs is a course, thinks Pundt, a course on how to pack, perhaps an adult-education course.

"Yes, we'd parted by agreement, let's say as good friends, because we'd both seen that there was no point in going on like that."

"So that can't have been the reason," says Pundt.

"No, that wasn't the reason, there are always several reasons, two at least, Harald must have had several reasons, too." She opens a drawer, pulls out some gaudy kerchiefs, and ties them around her head one by one to see how they look, examining them doubtfully in the mirror; finally she rolls them all up into a ball and stuffs them into the trunk with a shrug of her shoul-

120

ders: it's likely to be windy in Aberdeen all the time, so you can't have too many kerchiefs.

"You knew him better than anyone else," says Pundt. "What do you think his reasons were?"

"I didn't know a lot about him, at least none of the important things," Lilly Fligge says, turning away and delving into the open built-in cupboard. "If you ask me—and if you'll let me speak frankly—at an early age, when he was young, he was taught to do something that became more and more sinister as he grew up until it turned into an obsession, a kind of mania. Yes, that's what it was, and perhaps you might be able to tell me the cause of it, why he was always searching for reasons, for proofs. Everything had to have a proof and an explanation, every thought, every wish, every absence, and if he was about to do something, then he had to find a justification for it before he did it. Only it's strange that, though he needed a reason for everything, he's left us in the dark about his reasons for taking the step that he took."

She pulls out a bundle of woolen socks, blue, yellow, and red knee socks, and holding them waist high, drops them one by one into the open suitcase.

"Perhaps you know," says Pundt, "what his main worry was?"

"Harald? I don't know. Often when he'd run out of cigarettes he'd walk over from the Alte Rabenstrasse and ring the bell at eleven o'clock and then he'd sit on the floor—he used to love sitting on the floor—and try to find reasons for some particular course of action, for certain things he was thinking of trying to do, and also reasons for supporting one policy or another. He never said what his worry was—perhaps with the exception of his exams, but I imagine that didn't count for him."

"And suppose he was keeping it hidden?"

"He must have been hiding something, obviously, because otherwise it wouldn't have happened; and since we don't know any reasons, we've got to fall back on conjectures and my own guess is that what Harald was hiding so successfully was the fact that he was afraid."

She slams down the lid of the trunk but the fasteners won't

snap closed because an enormous cooky tin, which can be seen pressing into the leather, refuses to be compressed, even when sat on, so the cooky tin will travel together with the books in their wooden crate, why not?

"Afraid?" Pundt inquires. "Harald was afraid?"

"He was sitting here and I had work to do, that's a long time ago now. He'd read something in the paper that kept running through his head: A boy had placed a folding chair in Times Square in New York and he sat there for a whole day with a gasoline can beside him. When evening came he wrote something on a piece of paper, poured gasoline over himself, and lighted a match. On the piece of paper he'd written: '. . . and it's not even worth it.' He was a student who was about to take his exams. I was busy working but I can still remember how Harald kept on going back over that uncompleted sentence to find out what it meant and looking for reasons, and then I remember he decided that it must have been fear and disgust, not only because of the exams but because of everything that he would have to face afterward—'. . . and it's not even worth it'—that's what was written on the piece of paper. I figure Harald was afraid in the same sort of way; if you ask me, he just didn't feel up to all the challenges he was facing, with this complex of his of needing to prove and justify everything. When something happens you have to find some explanation for it and that's mine."

She kneels down in front of a row of gaudy shoes, examines them helplessly, picks up a few plastic bags, and stuffs the shoes in, furiously knotting the end of each bag. Where can they go? Ah well, into the crate of books with the cooky tin.

"So you don't think," says Pundt, "that it was meant as a kind of protest?"

Lilly shakes her head. "It wasn't a direct protest; obviously you can't help feeling that he was rejecting something, it's quite clear that he was intending to say 'no'—and I still can't get over the fact that he didn't leave any reasons for the last thing he did, as he always used to, but left it unexplained."

With a sigh she casts her eye over her baggage and all the things that still need packing. "Really, Herr Pundt, for me packing is the most exquisite form of hard labor." She goes over to the sink in the makeshift kitchen, apologizing for not being able to offer him anything—everything ran out just at the right time. But Valentin Pundt waves her apology aside—"No, that's all right, please don't bother"—and casually watches her as she holds her wrists under the tap, jerkily breathing in and out. "I learned that from Harald."

"What?"

"This way of freshening oneself up."

Is Pundt falling over? Is he suffering from stomachache? Has he been suddenly bent double with pain? No, he's merely trying to get up out of the very low armchair, he slips, steadies himself, remains crouching for a moment, and then succeeds in achieving the perpendicular. "If you feel like it," says Lilly Fligge, "we could go over to the August 4th for a quick drink." But sensing the embarrassment behind her suggestion, Pundt declines with thanks and points to the urgent task awaiting her on the floor. There was little he wanted to add: he would like to thank her; he'd made some progress in his investigations; and he wished her a pleasant trip.

8

Janpeter Heller is against flowers or, rather, if not against them, at least against what he describes as the appalling traditional German custom of waving a bunch of flowers in the face of every host or hostess; this he considers to be certainly one of the most tiresome and stupid conventions in existence, since if someone invites you to breakfast, you don't after all expect the worst, and so the guest should be relieved of the duty of walking around flourishing a symbol of peace that is, in fact, not even worth very much.

Meanwhile Pundt insists on flowers: he's happy, he says, to bow to any convention that brings pleasure and his only doubt is: what kind of flowers would suit Rita Süssfeldt—perhaps long-stemmed carnations?

"Carnations," says Heller, "are acknowledged to be the favorite flower of construction workers, builders, and contractors; anybody inviting someone like that to his house must expect carnations."

"Well, what kind then?"

"It's no use asking me," says Heller, "in principle the only plant I'm in favor of is asparagus."

At that Pundt points a decisive finger at the yellow globes of a chrysanthemum: they seem to match Rita Süssfeldt; in any case, they look suitable to him, so may he have those chrysanthemums over there, but not too much decorative greenery with them. The salesman does not hesitate to congratulate Pundt on his choice.

They're standing on the Eppendorferbaum and the "epic breakfast" is due to start at nine o'clock. "Do we turn left or right?" Valentin Pundt, who is carrying the flowers and will be presenting them on behalf of both of them, knows the way; and they are striding along shoulder to shoulder, past the fronts of damp houses, against gusting winds chasing bits of paper or loose scarves. Past the post office, where a squadron of disconsolate mailmen are coming out pushing their loaded yellow bicycles, past the druggist's and the Deutsche Bank, eager to spring to your aid with a small advance in all weathers. With coats flapping, windswept, wet-faced, buffeted by the sleet, Heller and Pundt turn into the Rothenbaumchaussee and anyone passing in a car just then would gather that the old teacher is treating the weather with greater indifference, indeed with more contempt, than the younger man.

Bareheaded and, above all, erect, not so much huddled in his coat as Heller, he walks along talking into the wind, which carries his words away and cuts them off. He's asking something, he would like to know if Heller had ever been to Rita Süssfeldt's?

"No, never."

"Do you know her sister or her cousin then?"

"No, I don't."

"But you must have heard of Dr. Merkel or read about him; he's bound to be there."

"No, I've never heard of him or read about him."

"But there was so much about him on the radio and in the newspapers and any magazine you happened to open at the time. An archaeologist whose most important work is . . . *And the Ark Floated*, a history of boatbuilding before the Flood."

Heller is beginning to remember. "Wasn't there a film?"

"There was going to be one and Dr. Merkel had been commissioned as scientific adviser. The ark was built according to his instructions. . . . He said which animals . . . even down to the common field mouse. . . . He'd made all the preparations himself and just as they were about to start shooting, there came this offer."

"Offer?"

"The film company received an anonymous offer. Someone wanted to take over the care of the animals on board, you understand, he wanted to be paid to look after them. They wouldn't agree . . . not even after a second offer. And then it happened. . . ."

"What?"

"During his shift. They'd arranged shifts to guard them. They didn't make a third offer. A fire while he was on guard. He was badly injured. The ark was burned with all the animals and since then . . ."

"Since then?"

"You'll be meeting him shortly, Dr. Merkel."

"So he didn't make the film . . . ?"

"No."

"But I've an idea that somehow the name . . ."

"We must turn to the right here," says Pundt, wiping his watery eyes. "Frau Süssfeldt lives over there."

They cross the street diagonally and a squat man with a face like a bulldog stands waiting for them, shaking his head, and immediately asks, in a gruff voice, what's the point of having pedestrian crossings and who were they intended for; and without waiting for an answer demands a satisfactory reply to his next question: what did they think would have happened if a fast long-distance tractor-trailer hadn't been able to brake in time?

What's the man saying? Heller, annoyed at being scolded but amused by the question, draws the man's attention to the present acute shortage of policemen and advises him to go along to the nearest police station and join the force. And after passing through a knee-high gate and a front garden roughly the size of a postage stamp, Heller says to Pundt, "Auxiliary police; there's no country with so many volunteer auxiliary policemen as us." Pundt seems not to have heard, he's already got his eye on the bell and is tugging at the paper around the flowers with the tips of his fingers—what lovely asters, Rita Süssfeldt will say. However, he waits until Heller is standing beside him on the doorstep; and now he presses the button.

126

Here comes Rita Süssfeldt, holding out her hands, with recently washed hair which is not yet dry, and in her moss-green dress she opens the door with a smile and says, "Welcome, you murderers, so now you've killed my story too."

"It didn't struggle," says Heller.

"And we brought this to comfort you," says Pundt. "I hope they're flowers you like."

"What lovely asters," Dr. Süssfeldt says, and pointing to the clothes closet: "Hang your things in there."

They do so and now they make their way one after the other into the dining room, Rita Süssfeldt in the lead—the zipper in the back of her dress is only half closed, perhaps the hook fastening her brassière has brought it up short—and as if moved by clockwork, Mareth and Heino stand up from an immortal antique sofa and come forward to greet their guests, warmly extending their hands. They emerge so gently out of their background you might think that they had stepped down from one of the eighty-four frames out of which gaunt forefathers with narrow, harelike heads check every visitor's solvency or that they were escaping from the waist-high row of blank, staring, dignified portrait busts awaiting the next Ice Age.

"May I introduce . . . ?"

"I've heard such a lot . . ."

"How do you do?"

"How nice to meet you personally."

"How do you do?"

"Mustn't cross . . ."

"Entirely my . . ."

"And now shall we go and eat?"

Janpeter, whose reaction to any kind of greeting, including this one, is distinctly mixed, looks at the breakfast table and has a vision: these incredibly tiny bowls and plates filled with oatmeal, puffed wheat, cornflakes, and sweet corn are about to be swooped down on by hordes of local birds which have already gathered in the garden and are only awaiting a sign from Rita Süssfeldt. These miserable rye crackers, these pallid slices of toast, those barely recognizable cubes of ham, and the thimblefuls of jam must be meant as a breakfast for the sparrows and finches which are about to fly in any minute now and make for their food, squabbling and fluttering their wings. Surely this can only be, it must be, a birds' breakfast.

"Please do help yourselves to plenty of everything you want, you too, Herr Heller," says Mareth, Rita Süssfeldt's somberly dressed sister, and to set an example, she shovels roughly three grains of wheat and four of corn onto her plate, takes a deep breath, squints doubtfully at the quantity as though she had really taken too much, and then suddenly starts cheerfully munching. Rita Süssfeldt follows her example; Heino Merkel follows her example. What is Valentin Pundt going to do?

With a single movement, the old schoolmaster, in whose stomach an early-morning Lüneburg Cock-a-doodle-do has already bored a ball of fire, empties all the butter from the dish, scoops out all the jam from its container with his teaspoon, spreads and daubs both the butter and the jam onto two slices of rye crisp, sticks an unbuttered piece firmly on top of a buttered one, and, still not satisfied, makes the double-decker into a four-storied sandwich, and while the two sisters exchange a disconcerted glance, placidly sinks his teeth into the finished product. It's already becoming plain that Pundt, who has christened the meal "the breakfast of revelation," is determined not to deprive his body of the sustenance which it is accustomed to have every morning; so as a precautionary measure Heino Merkel is sent to get more bread and to bring some cheese and tomatoes as well.

"Now tea, who'd like some tea with crystal sugar?" Heller of course, and as he holds out his cup to Rita Süssfeldt he hears her inquiring whether, since her proposal has been rejected, the whole commission now falls to the ground; surely there now remain only two possible alternatives: either they would ask to be released from their contract or else they would press on in the hope that they still might unearth a model exemplary life that they could all accept. She realized that for a representative anthology for all Germany the "Exemplary Lives" chapter would have to be scrutinized with meticulous care; the three proposals so far put forward had not stood up to such a scrutiny; consequently, all that was left to them was either to part or to go on. She would like some clear statement and they needn't worry about the presence of her sister and her cousin, for they were aware of the situation and were used to arguing anyway. "Well, what's to be done?"

There they sit in the light of the cramped dining room, oppressed by the busts and the portraits and not even surprised by the directness of the question, which was bound to come anyway, but silent and uncertain all the same; the only sounds are the crunch of the rye crisps and a scratching and chewing and hissing noise through pursed lips. Then Pundt expresses his firm belief: if we hand back the commission, there'll be other people willing to accept it and presumably they'll have no difficulty in finding the right blend for the "Exemplary Lives" and in cooking it up into an anthology piece. Perhaps for that reason alone we ought to go on, in order to prevent something like that; and could he have a tomato, please?

Heller is looking down at the tip of his teaspoon, which is swirling tinkling sugar crystals round and round in his cup; and with a calm shrug of his shoulders he says that he'd anticipated all this, the moment of truth when the only thing left was the question: go home or continue under new auspices? It was the fault of the theme, of the impossibility of their task, of the authoritarian desire to thrust an educational colossus under young people's noses. As they'd all seen, every proposal had been tried and rejected and so it would continue, trying and rejecting, examples would be produced merely to be disposed of; yes, it was the fault of the whole theme of "Exemplary Lives" that they hadn't succeeded, of the appalling ambiguity of the whole idea, and if anyone else was surprised that they'd failed at their first attempt, he was not. And if it was up to him, they'd abandon their unsuccessful search and send back the commission, perhaps with the comment that all the examples they'd examined up till now had, on closer scrutiny, revealed themselves to be fat-assed pasteboard figures fit only for the educational Establishment—not in those words, of course—and they didn't need to pay back the advance, because they'd already done two chapters. Moreover, they could go home with the satisfaction of having saved countless school-children from being frightened. Janpeter looks up, but not across the table, he doesn't want to know whether or to what extent the others agree with him, he turns his face to look out on the dirty garden, where the wretched little hedge has long since given up its struggle against the wind.

Does Pundt want to say something? He would like to but decides against it because he's just then attacking a tomato with a saw-edged knife, vigorously cutting it into slices; and he is not going to eat the slices on their own; to the sisters' amazement he sprinkles them with kernels of corn, deposits them onto some modest rye crackers, and then tosses them down his throat with considerable panache, it must be confessed, his eyeballs protrud-ing with each swallow. Rita Süssfeldt, who is not only a quick but also an absentminded feeder, has long since spooned up her oat-meal and is now sitting with an unlit cigarette in her hand, all ready to smoke, squeezing it and tapping it on the table to make it firm. She would like to know from Heller whether their failure didn't spring from the fact that they hadn't properly agreed among themselves on the necessary criteria for a model life suit-able for the times. What could these criteria be? She was think-ing, for instance, of an example with a purely provisional and limited validity, which would leave it open to contradiction, according to the variations in the situation: whereas the present situation determines what kind of behavior can be considered exemplary, other situations might require other forms. Suppose they were to take this time factor as a starting point and accept the possibility of later contradictions; might it not then be possi-ble to find an example to satisfy all concerned? The advantage would be that the recommendations which they were making would be more modest.

Janpeter Heller doesn't deny this and if they have to find a model he would like to see them settle on one that was both modest and problematical at the same time—a coward could be a model person just as much as a looter or a social troublemaker —but the further he went into this question, the more he felt the need for pitiless self-criticism because any example that was put forward seemed, educationally speaking, to end by insulting the young: since you're too stupid to steer your own course, you need bright, towering beacons to guide you all the time, so keep your eye on Leonidas, Schweitzer, and Kennedy and take counsel from them. But wasn't the task of the educator to prepare for the inevitable shipwreck, for mistakes, disappointments, to inculcate a readiness to take risks? Was it advisable to try to protect a young man from certain necessary experiences, experiences which he would have in any case and which would provide him with his only yardstick for measuring reality? Instead of sticking an example in his way, blocking his view, ought we not to be more concerned with sharpening his critical faculties? Heller couldn't help pointing out that, basically, examples seemed to him to be a form of coercion for minors, imbeciles, and notorious scatter-brains.

Pundt is looking around for an egg but can find only radishes, which he stares at in some doubt for a while, as if they might have some use other than to be eaten, and then he suddenly starts cutting them up into tiny cubes, sprinkles them over the ham, and uses the sandwich spread which he's just invented on a slice of toast. "You ought to try this someday, my dear Heller, you've got a juicy, fresh flavor and the traditional smoky one blended in a hitherto unknown way; incidentally, I don't share your view at all." And as a reminder the ex-headmaster wishes to draw their careful attention to the fact that it's obvious that there's not as yet any consensus on what an example ought to be. It had been said that it should aim at replacing a person's own critical faculties—a handy breviary for every situation in life where you'd find answers to any question of importance.

But he saw things quite differently. In his eyes an example was, in fact, an invitation to develop one's critical faculties, it should help you to explore situations. "It shows what is possible in certain cases, it illustrates what unconditional acceptance can

131

lead to. The motto, we may call it the specifically educational, meaningful motto, must be: put yourself in someone else's place. We put ourselves strictly in someone else's place and in this way we can experience ourselves. By doing this we learn to recognize what binds us together but also what separates us, we consent and yet we set our own limits, we examine what we are capable of experiencing and acquire understanding. It's not a question of being able to repeat something but of weighing the differences and unless I'm mistaken that is very much a critical attitude; I wonder if I may ask for a little more tea?"

That's very much Rita Süssfeldt's idea too, she discovers a "striking resemblance" to her own views, and in the flush of sympathy inspired by the dizziness resulting from her first cigarette, she would like to point out that this represents a common approach which could lead somewhere. She had the suspicion that their doubts and even their dislikes could only have arisen because they'd been concerned with the wrong examples: the ship's doctor who turns his back on his duty, the reluctantly helpful guard, and, well, yes, the mother who acts against her own better feelings—examples that had been chosen strictly with the best intentions in the world—but that was not enough. They should have set about it differently. How? Well, first of all they should have drawn up a list of the suitable qualities of a model person and then looked for appropriate examples; but now *she* would like to suggest something. Although they were still not ready either to finish the job or to give it up, Rita Süssfeldt would like to suggest that each of them present his supplementary story, since she assumed that everyone had acquired a spare one in the course of his preliminary investigations, so she meant the second story, the emergency one that hadn't yet been mentioned because it hadn't been thought good enough to stand up to examination. What was the point of doing that? At least they could make comparisons, and Rita Süssfeldt had always been fond of comparing. "In my view we ought to tell these stories to each other as a parting gift. And so, briefly, here's my extra example."

132

A ship is stuck on a sandbar off the northern coast of Germany, abandoned by her crew and given up for lost by the salvage tugs, a prey to the winter storms. Photographs taken at intervals of several weeks show the gradual effect of the sea and the storms: the superstructure is smashed, the wreck is sinking deeper and deeper, it's heeling over more and more; the ship seems to be doomed. After eighteen months, the head of a small private salvage company buys the wreck, ignoring his friends' advice and warnings. He fits out a fleet of salvage vessels and in the spring he has a channel dredged in the sand. Calm seas, moderate winds, the weather is favorable, but during the first salvage attempt one of the tugs capsizes and they have to suspend operations for the time being. In late summer they come out again, dredge, get the wreck upright, and when they try to tow it off, it shifts, at least it comes free from the bottom. The salvage firm has made no profit at all by the time autumn comes and the work is halted again because during stormy weather the fleet can't stay out at sea for any length of time. They wait until spring, the head of the firm borrows money; first of all the channel has to be deepened, and this work is barely under way when a sudden storm washes some of the crew overboard and the salvage attempt has to be stopped yet again. Everybody advises the owner to give up, his wife pleads with him, yet he still risks two more attempts and before the onset of the autumn storms he succeeds in towing the wreck off the sands. It floats, the sea is calm, and with everyone holding his breath the wreck is towed toward the coast. At night, fog comes up, and in the fog the ship is rammed by a fast-moving ferryboat.

"That's roughly it," says Rita Süssfeldt, "just the main points, to give an idea of my additional example: an example of pursuing and never abandoning a dream." No one seems to want to comment, not to start with. Pundt spoons up the last few grains of corn from a china bowl; Heller can't help thinking of a medieval engraving representing a hunting scene, a boar hunt, in which two huntsmen on horseback are, strangely enough, spearing not the peaceful-looking boar but the hounds mad with the lust of the chase.

Hasn't Herr Pundt a supplementary suggestion in store? "Yes, I have, but after all this exchange of experiences, I'm not sure I'd like to tell it to you, or if I do, then only very briefly because the example which you can see in it . . ."

Very well, then, imagine the waiting room of a railway station, badly lit, with all its benches removed, it's evening. We've all experienced that. And this is an actual event, too. Lying on the wooden floor strewn with sand there are some prisoners of war, they are just about to turn in; the train that will carry them off to a prison camp is expected the following morning. Exhausted guards are squatting in front of the windows, the exit, and the door leading to the toilet. Later that evening, when the soldiers are already asleep, a troop train pulls in at the station, going in the opposite direction; it's taking home prisoners who've been released. Two trains, two directions, two different moods. Around midnight the released prisoners are brought into the waiting room as well; a rope is stretched across the room to divide the two groups and they are forbidden to mix. But in this small waiting room it's unavoidable that some of the soldiers from the two troop trains find themselves lying close together, as one can imagine.

And so we find two soldiers lying down there side by side, one old soldier who's just been released and a very young one who's going into captivity. Their bodies are touching and their faces are so close together that they can whisper to each other without the guard's hearing. The old soldier questions the young one in a whisper; first he learns how valueless are all the catch phrases and rumors and then he hears the news from home—they're both from the same town. But you needn't be afraid that at this point they discover that they're related, or that they spend the rest of the night going over common memories of streets, squares, and smells. In reply to a direct question, the young soldier says that he had wanted to become an ornithologist and then they talk about conditions at home and finally the old soldier advises the young one to go to sleep: "You've learned to sleep in all kinds of situations, you're not particular." When the young soldier is woken up, his train has already left, the one that is taking the soldiers to a prison camp. In the pocket of his coat, he finds a bird carved out of wood and a piece of paper, a release slip. The soldiers have to get up for the roll call, the count is correct, and they're allowed onto the train, which has been attached to a new engine.

"Well," says Pundt, "that was my spare story and you don't need to express your objections because I imagine I have more against this one than you have. Although everything in this story takes place in silence, you can't get around that very obvious roll call. And how often, in reality, does someone go off into captivity, how often does someone get the opportunity to take over a stranger's lot? An example without a moral or, at least, without any acceptable moral, and we can hardly offer that. May I have a little more fruit juice, please, and another cracker or two?" They all watch as Pundt, with deliberate strokes, daubs yogurt on the cracker, they're all expecting that at the first bite plywood will split, plaster will explode, mice will gnaw at the wainscoting, but all the surprising noises associated with crackers fail to materialize, because the cracker has obviously become moist.

Now it's the turn of the third member of the team, Heller, but nobody asks him for his emergency example because no one imagines that he has one; and so the amazement following on Heller's statement that he *does* have one is justified; not only has he brought an extra story along, but, he thinks, a perfectly respectable one, he has kept it under lock and key only because he was becoming less and less enamored of the whole project; he was really against any kind of educational manna from heaven. He was not asking them to approve of his second example, he would merely like to present it, not so much for them to judge it as for them to take cognizance of it.

So imagine a flooded land, for instance the North German lowlands after a tidal wave. In the dusk a raft made of gasoline cans is drifting past the tops of trees and stopping beside abandoned farmhouses. On the raft, surrounded by boxes and sacks, there sits an old man. With his makeshift paddle he lifts up the slack telephone wires hanging down in the water so that he can pass under them. He paddles gently, perseveringly on, there's no current. When the rescuers' motor launches appear he ties up to the tops of trees and waits until they're out of sight.

I'll skip his observations and precautions, the endless conversations he holds with himself in the actual story. He paddles toward a remote farmhouse and works around it, slowly circling the guttering at roof level, and he sees that the attic window is open. He ties up his raft. He climbs through the skylight into the house, which could be a fruit farmer's whose family has been there for generations. Through perseverance and thrift they've become well off. The old man opens cupboards and chests of drawers that have been floated up into the attic. He rummages in baskets. He examines all the things that are hanging from iron hooks fastened to the roof timbers. Here and there he finds some useful objects, which he either stuffs into a sack or carries to the attic window. As he's going through a cupboard for the second time he seems to have made his best discovery yet, some old-fashioned silver jewelry, which he immediately carries off to his raft and stows in a watertight bag. He casts off and is about to paddle away when he hears a whimpering noise. It needn't concern him. Without a sound he paddles off, quickly at first, and then, gradually, he slows down, and as he sits there, drifting, you can see that he is coming to a decision; he paddles back and discovers in the attic a woman with a baby at her breast, and although he must assume that she has seen what he's done, he lifts her onto his raft. They say not a word to each other. Grumbling to himself, he paddles toward the horizon, a railway embankment where lights can be seen. There's a rescue station there. They don't say goodbye to each other, there's no word of thanks, he watches the rescuers lift the woman off the raft, and she, who knows what he has in his bag, doesn't even look at him as, refusing offers of bread and hot coffee, he hurriedly pushes off and paddles away into the desolate floodwater.

"There you are," says Heller, "that's my example." He merely wished to put it before them, he didn't expect them to say whether it was suitable or not, but perhaps it would illustrate how he viewed their task: if it's to be exemplary, then it must have a living situation as its context; something like that. Pundt would clearly like to say something but decides against it when he notices that Rita Süssfeldt is not going to launch into a full-blown speech but under the warning eye of her sister sets to work with crumb brush and decorative crumb tray to remove a pile of ash which she has dropped beside her cup. Glutted but not satisfied with examples, and with their eyes wandering into the distance, they submit to the wave of silence which can have only one meaning: they'll give up the commission, they'll go their own ways and take the next train back to Lüneburg and Diepholz.

And then Heino Merkel stirs for the first time. This shy, emaciated man who can make himself so humble that you fail to notice his presence and who is assuredly anxious not to be noticed—he would like very much to confess something, as he's been listening for so long. Or add something. Or, if he might be allowed, to express a personal opinion. Hanging his head, plaiting and tangling and unplaiting the tassels of the crocheted tablecloth, he waits for Mareth to give him permission to speak and then carefully apologizes for what he's going to say. Well then, exemplary lives are like monsters which are frozen stiff in our memory, urging us on to hero worship. But in his view we no longer had time or sympathy for such things. All the same, there were undoubtedly desirable actions that might be called exemplary. What is it that makes these actions appropriate to the times? In Heino Merkel's opinion, the fact that they invite not only commitment but contradiction. Let's put it like this: a modern example can only seem so to us if it is a controversial one. A splendid confusion that points several morals at once. To quote an instance.

The archaeologist raises his head, hesitates for a moment, confronted by this ring of expectant faces around him, and then adds quickly, "Lucy Beerbaum," and then, lowering his voice: "Lucy Beerbaum, on our street. We knew her vaguely during her lifetime. She had every quality."

Is it worth noting the various reactions to this proposal? Mareth, for instance, her mouth dry with excitement, has stopped breathing; Rita Süssfeldt is shaking her head doubtfully like a Holstein brewer's dray horse; ex-headmaster Pundt is still vigorously munching away, contorting his always bloodless lips, and Heller shrugs his shoulders only once as he says that this name doesn't mean anything to him. Heino Merkel had guessed that his proposal would be met with amazement and had foreseen their surprise and their readiness to doubt; he sits waiting, withdrawing nothing.

"You know very well that she was an odd person," says Mareth, "and that she behaved oddly."

"Isn't there some oddity in every model person?" asks Heino Merkel.

"Yes, I suppose so," Mareth replies, "but her approach to things, for instance to her house—where else can you see on our street a house painted such a shocking pink? After all, this woman was only in her late fifties."

"I called on her twice," says Rita Süssfeldt. "In her house there was great importance attached to having a lot of superfluous space. I interviewed her after France had awarded her the Palmes Académiques, and she requested that I not ask her anything but factual questions, no personal ones."

"An actress?" asks Pundt. "Isn't Lucy Beerbaum an actress?"

"A biologist," Heino Merkel says. "She was a scientist with a worldwide reputation. She's been dead barely two years; she died on our street."

"Of her own free will," adds Mareth. "Lucy Beerbaum chose to die of her own free will: she had starved herself for so long that she no longer had any resistance against disease."

"A controversial woman," says Heino Merkel, "a controversial scientist, a model for our times."

138

Heller, who had never heard of Lucy Beerbaum, would now, very properly, like to know why this woman had starved herself to death, and Heino Merkel seems determined not to allow anybody to answer but himself: with his eyes fixed on the table he starts talking quickly, interweaving dates and opinions and happenings and revealing a hidden thread which he asks them to note and assess.

Twenty years ago—I must tell you that Lucy Beerbaum didn't come from these parts, although her parents lived here for a few years. She herself was born in Greece and came here twenty years ago. She lived with her housekeeper Johanna; she had her own department at the Institute. For a long time she had two nieces living with her who were remarkable examples of how different sisters could be. Every morning she walked absent-mindedly and amiably to the streetcar stop, belatedly returning people's greetings; she dressed exclusively to please herself; her profile, sharp and still youthful, wouldn't have been out of place on a coin. A discussion group met in her house every Wednesday evening; she had a circle of selected students with whom she talked about her social and political beliefs. She was extremely modest; her whole way of life seemed casual. When the Army seized power in her native country, she resigned from the Institute. And when she learned that the great friend of her youth and a number of his colleagues were among the political prisoners who were exiled to an island by the new regime, she expressed her sympathy in an original way. She allowed herself only the same living space that the prisoners had to move about in, and she lived under the same conditions that were imposed upon the prisoners. Although she was indispensable at the Institute, she refused to live any kind of life but that of a prisoner; often she declined to see her doctor, who was worried about her. She gave up reading, she rarely answered letters, and if she did, she used only the same number of words that the prisoners were permitted to use. She once asked the director of the Institute to keep to the visiting hours that the prisoners were allowed.

During this period of voluntary captivity, Johanna, who had been Lucy's housekeeper for so many years, handed in her notice twice because she didn't feel able to carry out her mistress's policy of deliberate neglect; but both times she returned after a few hours. A lot could be said about the changed conditions in that house brought on by these deprivations and about the relationship between Johanna and Lucy Beerbaum, who had given instructions that everything was to carry on as if nothing had happened. In any case, after she had lived on a starvation diet for twenty-eight days it became clear that she had been demanding too much from her body.

So much was definite; but a lot of what happened seems to be uncertain and impossible to prove, although a great deal has been written about Lucy Beerbaum's self-incarceration, including a play which actually reached the stage. But one thing is plain from all these accounts, which he has collected and preserved—there's even been a fictional biography—and that's that this modest, humble, middle-aged woman is a difficult person to define: as soon as she seems to have been recognizably portrayed, the outlines become blurred, and as soon as her extraordinary qualities have been carefully described, her earthy nature takes over and constricts our vision of her. But for that very reason something could be pieced together from this well-documented life, something of use for their project, an example which would need to be both confirmed and questioned. But it would have to be carefully worked out and explored and trimmed of all its extraneous material.

Heino Merkel would like to make a suggestion. He was willing to collaborate. He was willing to put at their disposal all the information he had collected. And he would, yes, he really would be delighted if Lucy Beerbaum's bold attempt to achieve solidarity, hopeless though it was, could be discussed by young people one day, somehow or other. It was true that for him, too, living without models meant living a more human existence, but in this case it might well be asked what a contemporary model should look like.

140

What is Heller going to say to this proposal? Especially as he is so obviously ready to give up and go home. He's about to speak, but Rita forestalls him as she points out that as it would be impossible to deal with the whole of Lucy Beerbaum's story, if they were going to do it at all they would need to restrict themselves to one section of it, one event that would illuminate the rest and serve as a guideline.

"So we must do some pruning," says Heller. "We must each of us arm ourselves with pruning shears, choose something appropriate, mark it out, and then we'll cut the most profitable pieces out of this sheet of biographical plywood which we can glue together later on. It's becoming almost creative."

And how about the ex-headmaster? He closes his eyes, clasps his hands on the table, and admits that he can see something here, that something seems to be emerging and making its presence felt, in a word the certainty that they're on the right track. "There's something in this story," he says, "something is taking shape, not in precise detail but certainly a definite promise of something. I don't suppose there's any tea left? Please don't bother. Don't make another pot just for me. But I will allow myself some crystal sugar to finish with."

Mareth pleads, as it were, extenuating circumstances for her judgment, but she finds it quite impossible to attach so much importance to Lucy Beerbaum or to see enough in her to provide material for an anthology: she'd lived close to her too long and observed her strange behavior too often; she couldn't for one moment see Lucy Beerbaum as a model person, not even in the spring migraine season.

An illuminated sign, Janpeter is thinking to himself, even this humble, silent protest can flare up like a suddenly illuminated sign if we can only give it the right emphasis and importance, but if need be, we should also point out how much of it still remains obscure. And he says, "There's a lot that's not yet known or else open to interpretation, but there's always the possibility of making a selection from this material. In any case, Lucy Beerbaum should be worth a try."

Rita Süssfeldt looks at Heller with eyes full of amazement and gratitude, she would like to give a nod or a smile to make him understand how sympathetic she is to his views, but Heller doesn't lift his head.

"I'll let you have all the information I possess," says Heino Merkel. "The material I've collected will make your investigations easier. Let me say in advance that you'll make discoveries and you'll certainly find things that you haven't found before. If you care to wait a moment, I've got the material in my room."

"Unless I'm completely mistaken," says Pundt, "that was a very profitable breakfast."

"I'll make you some fresh tea," says Rita Süssfeldt. "I feel like some myself now."

9

THE Landungsbrücken elevated railway station: how can we reconstruct it for you? First, you throw up a steep embankment, shift a tired railroad track—it forms part of the line that circles the harbor—put down a covered railway platform—very drafty despite the roof—put up advertisements for shoes and insurance companies on the walls, provide a receptacle with a slit in it for the traveler to dispose of his used tickets: you can almost see the station already. Vending machines for peppermints and cigarettes still have to be installed, trash baskets, and then clumsy, hard wooden benches for waiting travelers, who can, if they wish, ascertain that in the harbor which stretches out in all directions below them there are still plenty of signs of routine activity, even during this Anniversary Week when all the flags are out.

Seen from the platform, the movements on the water are confusing and haphazard: overtaking, passing, collision courses, evasive action, some craft being towed, pushed, or tugged—an onlooker always has something to make him apprehensive. What else? You need a swinging door to close off the station, a half-glazed door which is scratched and scarred at the bottom by the passengers' kicks and knocks; behind the door you place a few stone steps descending to a level space where a scale, as tall as a man, grumpily invites everyone to find out his weight. From this platform you throw a low footbridge extending over the street at a safe height and leading down to the groaning landing jetties floating on the water, hence "Landungsbrücken."

Janpeter Heller is standing against the handrail of the foot-bridge with a beret on his head, with his briefcase pressed against his hip, and wearing suede shoes, darkened where they are wet; he is watching the approaching elevated train whose coaches jerk upright after a gentle curve and brake to a standstill. Heller is standing at the prearranged meeting place. Now he walks away from the handrail onto the footbridge. His eyes dart along the doors, clicking and hissing as they fly open, and there they are, yes, that's them, Charlotte and the little girl, dressed alike in dark-blue lined capes and long checked scarves. What are these matching clothes supposed to emphasize or prove? Heller's arm shoots into the air and he waves toward the platform. Charlotte has spotted him some moments ago, but instead of waving back, she takes the child's head in her hands and slowly moves it like a telescope toward the place where Heller is standing—and now Stefanie has found him and is waving back, in her own way, with a pensive clutching motion. Why aren't they coming? Why is Charlotte resisting the child's tugging with her own stronger pressure and holding her back up there? Heller makes a sign to tell them to wait, I'll come and fetch you, and he runs up the steps, forces his way through the crowd at the swinging door, leaps onto the platform, and then hears the voice of the loud-speaker: "Stand back there!" and at the same moment sees Char-lotte take a quick step back into the train. The doors bang shut, the train moves off, and Heller waits for the approaching glass door behind which Charlotte must be standing, and now here comes the coach, and carries away inside it an unmoving face in which all her wary skepticism is concentrated.

"'Lo, Daddy, what have you brought for me?" The little girl has come up to him, puts her net bag on the ground, lets herself be lifted up, and brushes Heller's cheeks with a couple of vague kisses which also involve her brace.

"Let's have something hot to drink first and then we'll see what I've brought for you."

They take each other's hand, they cross the footbridge down to the port, past the untidy row of white flag masts from the top of which Hamburg bunting is standing stiffly out or lashing and flapping in the gusts of wind. Even the tugs are beflagged, the launches, the ferries, and, of course, the dull-gray warships; but the only ships which have really let themselves go with flags on every mast are the ships which till recently have been making the gay cruises to the bathing beaches and have returned in good time to celebrate the anniversary of their home port.

"I've brought something for you too, Daddy, in this bag; guess what it is."

"We'll go in here," says Heller.

Inside you can't feel the gentle yet determined exertions by which the Elbe raises the floating pontoons and then, within the limits of their moorings, lets them fall away again, the slow swell; here in this bare room where nothing is hidden, in which an old waitress is watching over the only customer, asleep with his head resting on the tabletop, you can't feel the heaving and gentle subsiding which outside forces you almost involuntarily to walk with your legs wide apart.

"By the window? Then let's go and sit by the window."

The little girl puts the shopping bag on the table, submits to being extracted from her coat, pushes herself back on the chair, which is far too deep, and struggles to open the bag, tugging and jerking at it, while Heller makes no attempt to help but watches her with relentless attention. "You do it." Heller opens the bag with a single tug and Stefanie shakes the contents out onto the table.

"What would you like?" asks the waitress, and in the way that a smile can appear quite involuntarily on a face she directs a slight smile toward the child, to enlist her sympathy.

"I don't suppose you have milk or cocoa? . . . No? Then we'll have one tea and one coffee and a kirsch with the coffee."

Stefanie is releasing small white sheets of pasteboard from their brown paper wrapping, she pushes them over to Heller, slips off her chair, and comes around to his side to give him, as on previous occasions, the necessary explanations: "See, I painted that for you! A boat and a duck on the Isebek Canal; here's the bridge, there's wasn't enough room for it, and you're standing on the bridge, there wasn't room for all of you either, and up here there's another little duck on fire."

So here they are again, these interminable attempts at painting, which Charlotte encourages her to work on, as a result of which, even in the old days, stacks of children's drawings would be produced, sheets and sheets which amazed her every time and which she collected almost reverently, sent them to other people and even took them along as presents when they were invited out. Heller looks through the painted pasteboards, holding them fanwise like overgrown playing cards: as before, the wild, voluble colors tell of flying boats and swarms of swirling rooks, cats and fish with pink bows, of Zwita, her doll friend, all dressed up in her Sunday best, and time and again a strange solemn man with a top hat beneath an unnatural sky. "And that's the Baltic, Daddy, we went there last summer. I buried my ball in the sand and there it is hidden in the sand."

"Oh, yes," says Heller slowly.

Now the little girl is all eager and inquisitive, with her eye on the briefcase. "And what about you? What have you got for me?"

"Oh, nothing very much, you have to open it yourself. Here it is."

Stefanie rips the rubber bands off the package as though possessed. "Is it a shop?"

"Look for yourself."

The child's narrow gray eyes, the brown hair gathered on the neck, the cheeks surrounded by soft, pale skin: Heller is watching every part, every detail, questioning everything in silence, as though trying to see what changes have taken place.

"A stove?"

"An electric kitchen for 'The Little Cook,' " Heller says, "with pots and pans, a kettle, and a roasting pan; now you can do some cooking for yourself at last, properly, and you can eat what you cook, too."

Stefanie unpacks the small bright-red stove, takes the tiny kitchen utensils out of their tissue paper, puts the utensils in the

146

correct positions, squealing with delight, shifts them around a bit, arranges them and puts them in order, and after a moment's thoughtful examination she decides: "I'll paint it, Daddy, I'll do it now. I always bring my paintbox with me."

"Not now," says Heller, "not here, you can paint it at home."

"Then you won't be able to see it."

Wearing a broad smile, the waitress brings the tea and coffee, and after setting the tray down, she runs her hand cautiously over the tiny stove and its equipment and asks Stefanie, "Are you going to invite me to dinner, too?"

"Your hands are all scratched," says Stefanie. "Did your cat do it?"

The waitress involuntarily turns and looks at the sleeping man, looks at her hands covered with scabs, and says quietly to Heller, "It's him and his scrap iron; whenever I help him sort it I always tear my hands to pieces." She looks with stern, reproachful eyes at the man, a hump of leather with a dull sheen, so relaxed and in such an abandoned posture that he seems to have dispensed with all the forces of gravity in going to sleep.

Heller pays immediately. "Drink your tea, Stefanie."

"I'd like to paint the little kitchen."

"You can do that later, at home."

"Will you be coming back with me?"

"We wanted to go and inspect a ship," says Heller. "Because it's the anniversary of the port, we're allowed to visit the ships today."

"But you can come back with me afterward. You're never at home now!"

"Please drink your tea first."

"I'd like to paint the little kitchen for you so you can take it with you."

"Yes, I see, but now drink up before your tea gets cold." With a grimace Heller tosses down his kirsch, gets some cigarettes from a vending machine, and while he is smoking watches the little girl as she puts the little kitchen and the paintbox back into the net bag, neither resentful nor disappointed but merely pensive—and as carefully as if she were due to receive a reward for it.

"You used to sleep at home, I can remember that."

Heller could reply to that, at least possibly utter a warning or reprimand her, but he says nothing and becomes aware of an increasing feeling of annoyance which is beginning to dissolve all the pleasure he's been feeling. He turns his head: outside, a group of schoolboys with their teacher are passing by on the floating jetty, they gather in front of the gangway of the dressed-up minelayer, and, at a sign from their teacher, storm on board to take over the proffered toy. Whose opinions is Stefanie expressing? Has Charlotte prepared the child for this meeting? Inoculated? Equipped her with questions? What should he regard as her share in all this? "Come on," he says, "let's get going, we'll go and look the ship over."

"I want to . . ."

"Hurry up then. The toilet's over there."

The little girl slides off her chair, steers uncertainly past the sleeping man; how dissimilar her legs look in the baggy wrinkled tights, how stiffly her dress stands out over her plump little bottom, and as for the upper part of her body—when he looks at her narrow torso encased in a pale-gray sweater, Heller can't help thinking of an electric light bulb. Stefanie stops in front of the door leading to the toilets, as if she needed a final encouragement, and looks questioningly at Heller. "Go on in." Why had he insisted so strongly on seeing the child? Hadn't memories of what had happened in the past given him sufficient warning? All those moments of impatience and annoyance, all the opportunities which it gave him to doubt his own adequacy as a father: had he forgotten all that?

As though of its own accord, a certain evening is conjured up in Janpeter Heller's mind, and his memory evokes a patchy darkness over the city; in the next room Charlotte has finally succeeded in talking her daughter to sleep, but in the room where he is—he calls it his study—whitewashed walls, a couch with broken-down springs, piles of books on the windowsill and on

148

the bare floorboards—he's sitting with his pupils from the school drinking light red wine and they have just agreed once again that a pupil must have a say in his curriculum. The air is thick. An odor of red wine and cigarette ash. The pleasure of playing at conspiracy. And conspiratorial whispering.

"We really can't leave it all to the grinds."

"Who's the curriculum intended for if not . . ."

"But the most ordinary advance in knowledge is not . . ."

"The final way in which the Establishment can . . ."

"What we lack above all, Herr Heller, is teachers like you . . ."

"That may be so but I'm going to chuck you out now because tomorrow morning we shall once again have to . . ."

And then Charlotte comes back into his room, opens a window, silently empties the ashtrays, collects the glasses, returns, and stands in the open doorway in an attitude of resigned protest. "No, Jan, it can't go on like this, I've told you many times and I'm telling you again: we can't go on living like this indefinitely, so publicly."

"You won't ever understand, Charlotte, that those young people need my help, at least my help in formulating what they want. They want to change something, but they're dependent on someone with experience to assist them. It's my task to help them."

"Oh, Jan, you behave as if you were one of them; you talk like them, dress like them, you play up to them as if their good opinion was the most important thing to you. Of course they're enthusiastic about you and you enjoy that. They confide in you, all those young boys and girls of nineteen, and you return the compliment by forgetting what divides you from them. It's a sad state of affairs, Jan, believe me."

"Charlotte, if you'd only take the trouble, if you'd listen to them—they need me. You would sense that. Why aren't you ever there? At the beginning all my problems were your problems too, you took an interest in everything, and now you've withdrawn."

"Oh no, Jan, I haven't withdrawn; but you've made me feel

that it doesn't really matter to you any more whether I take an interest or not. There aren't many things left for us to talk about; just the absolute minimum required for our day-to-day or week-to-week living. Just think for a moment, Jan—what do we have in common any more? Eating and the usual questions about how Stefanie is, and even that is conducted almost at shouting distance."

"I don't know what you think is missing, Charlotte."

"You don't know? Among other things, you used to give me the feeling that you needed me, that my advice or my interest meant something to you; in the first few years, when we shared our burdens, when everything was so difficult."

"How long ago is that?"

"Oh, Jan, I'm tired."

Heller raises his head and sees Stefanie come sailing out of the toilet with her arms spread out, a corner of her dress is still caught in her tights. She runs up to him and lets him lift her up. She asks, "Do you have to go back to school right away?"

"Let's put on our coats and go see a ship."

He bundles the little girl into her coat again, ties the scarf loosely around her neck, says goodbye to the waitress on the other side of the room, to which she makes no reply or at least no perceptible one. His fingers tap the child gently to propel her across the room and out onto the long pontoon jetty, where gray ships groan as they rub against the timbers. Guards are standing by the gangways, spick and span in their dress uniforms, friendly and good-humored, like town criers: "Come on up, come on up, everyone can come and take a look. It's the Hamburg anniversary."

The Elbe flows past, somber and gray; toward the middle, where the blustery winds blow unhindered, you can see an area of short, decorative waves, as regular as though sketched by a painter of seascapes. As always, objects are drifting downstream for everyone to puzzle out for themselves. The wakes of launches are tracing their usual network on the visible stretch of river. And that elephant over there, with his trunk tied fast, is a suction grain unloader. And that white spray, wheeling, with wings beating, always hungry: those are gulls.

Although for the moment it's neither raining nor snowing, faces are gleaming under the massage of the wet November wind and the general dampness, as are the flagpoles, the bollards, and the decks of the ships. "Which one shall we go on then? . . . This one? Good."

The young sailor on guard salutes them with a grin as hand in hand they go up the slippery gangplank and board the minelayer, where a boatswain welcomes them and protects them from a group of schoolchildren who are tumbling wildly down from the bridge and then, waving their arms about, rushing madly aft. They all stumble over the slide rails. They push and shove against the overgrown coils of rope. They press against the taff-rail and wave and scream triumphantly: the sea battle seems to have had a favorable outcome.

"Come with me," says the boatswain. "I'll guide you." His voice is a trifle too loud, accustomed to giving orders; it sounds as if it wanted to make itself heard to a large number of people and against the wind at that. Heller has not failed to notice the sharp, suspicious look which the boatswain—wiry, clean-shaven, and bandy-legged—has cast at his beard; he even thinks he detected a sudden dislike. Heller is familiar with that look and this mental reservation.

"This is a minelayer and thus a specialized vessel of the German Navy," the boatswain says, and stumps off with his bandy legs across the middle deck. "We must distinguish three different types of mines, E mines, magnetic mines, and acoustic mines; the last can operate either when moored or drifting. Our ship is called the *Admiral Tittgens*, after a minelayer commander in the First World War; we model ourselves on him."

"For what?" Heller asks in a quiet voice.

Without looking around, the boatswain continues: "All minelayers model themselves on Admiral Tittgens, you will see a picture of him in the wardroom. And now I suggest that first we go up onto the bridge, where we can get a view of the whole ship."

They climb up onto the bridge, the boatswain, Stefanie, and Heller, and there Heller holds the little girl up, supporting her on his bent knee, and shows her the forward part of the ship below. "That's how the *Admiral Tittgens* looks from above. Can you see the guns? And that's the anchor, can you see it? And those black balls; those must be the mines."

"I'd like to paint something here," says Stefanie.

"It's too cold and you're not allowed to sit down here."

"I'd like to paint the balls."

"Not today," Heller says, and to the boatswain: "Did your model admiral lay mines himself, too?"

"Admiral Tittgens, whom we regard as the father of all minelayers, had his finest moment off the Thames estuary in 1915; his minefields are still considered perfect examples."

"So he had actual on-the-job experience," says Heller.

The boatswain looks at him suspiciously. "How do you mean?"

"I mean you at least have a model with professional knowledge."

Heller first wants to take in the whole scene in silence: the upward-slanting guns with their muzzles protected by caps, the sturdy, well-rounded mines, the tall coils of rope looking like faded snails; the taut rhomboidal canvas tarpaulins battered by the wind; the slender bow, the dark openings of the scuppers and ventilators; the winch, stiff as a ramrod, the padded fenders: Heller does not have to search laboriously for a comparison; it presents itself of its own accord as he looks at these stiff, challenging forms, threatening and hard.

"Over there," says the boatswain, "you see the trolleys which are used to carry the mines to the stern of the ship."

"Am I allowed to paint them?" asks Stefanie.

"I'm afraid it's forbidden to take photographs on board ship," says the boatswain.

"When you come and see us, Daddy, I'll paint them from memory, the trolleys and the balls, and then you can take the picture with you."

152

"All right, keep quiet now."

He lets her slip off his knee and follows the boatswain, who obviously has to touch and stroke everything he mentions; the compass, the steering gear, the radio equipment are all being tapped and fondled. Tenderly he runs his hand over the knobs of a switchboard. Heller listens without interest to the complacent explanations; many of the phrases he can blame on the training manual: "What you see here contributes to the safety of the ship and its crew . . ." "An emergency occurs when . . ." "In mooring a mine there are three distinct phases . . ." Stupefied by this torrent of explanations, demonstrations, information, Heller puts on the expression of great astonishment appropriate to a layman, as well as a puzzled look, which, he hopes, will spare him any additional commentary. "This is the heart of the ship: everything starts and finishes here."

The child reaches up for his hand, he can feel her fingers bending and trying to twine into his and then slip into the palm of his hand, waiting for a sign which Heller either won't or can't give because he has to support Stefanie as they go down the iron companionway.

"I don't want to see any more. Mommy will be picking me up soon."

"Just a little longer, be a good girl."

They clamber down the steps and trudge through narrow companionways lit by electric lights—there's E room 2, there's the communications room, and further along, on the left, are the hoists for the mines—and at last find themselves in the wardroom, where three long-necked, fair-haired minelayers are playing cards, hardly making a sound. Soft music is coming from the ship's loudspeaker. "'Shun!" "At ease!" The boatswain waves aside the men's salutes, makes, as it were, an explanatory gesture toward the living quarters, please take a look; the coziness provided by the checkered tablecloths, the homeliness assured by a bench settee, firmly screwed to the floor, the comfortable chairs you can sit in without lowering your head. And here on the wall, as promised, Admiral Tittgens, the father of all minelayers.

Heller walks up to the photograph in its plain frame, less out of curiosity than out of politeness toward the boatswain who is acting as their guide, and looks longer than usual at this ascetic face with its impenetrable expression of irony.

"So that's what he looks like."

"Yes."

"Is that Uncle Gerhard?" asks Stefanie. "He's already given me two paintboxes."

"Nobody was talking to you," says Heller, wagging his finger at her in admonishment. With exaggerated attention, Heller examines a row of photos representing various classes of minelayers in action, in quiet seas and rough seas, moving half-speed ahead or gently drifting, quite harmless-looking boats on the whole as their black eggs go plop into the broken water.

"Here you can see minelayers in operation," the boatswain says. "A dangerous and exhausting operation."

"For whom?" asks Heller.

The boatswain, with his peculiar capacity for understanding questions, asks, "How do you mean?" He's turning away as he speaks, facing the bulkhead, because although it's not really his province, the boatswain would not under any circumstances like to deprive them of a visit to the vibrating, thunderous, oily, and smelly realm of the engine room: because if the bridge is both the heart and the head of a boat, then the engines are its belly; that's a fact.

Why has Heller stopped? Why isn't he following the boatswain into the belly of the ship? The young schoolmaster is suddenly starting to walk more and more slowly, seems to be remembering something, sways, shakes his head, takes hold of the child's hand, and turns to face the astonished boatswain: he'd seen enough, thank you very much, he'd got a good enough idea of everything; now all he needed was to ask the way out. Can the boatswain evince anything but suspicion in a situation like this? Hadn't Heller liked it, he would like to ask, was he unhappy about the way he'd been shown around or about the boat in any way? He wasn't? And he really wouldn't like the chance to look around the engine room? No? Then he wouldn't delay him from going ashore, we go along here, if you open that bulkhead there, you'll come out onto the quarterdeck. The boatswain wished them a cool, curt good day, not without a touch of contempt, squeezed past them, and went back to the wardroom.

"Let's get out of here quickly," says Heller, "come on."

"Don't you feel well, Daddy?"

"Don't ask questions, come on."

Panting slightly, Heller drags the little girl across the quarterdeck, down the slippery gangway, and along the floating jetty, the image of an impatient and, it must be admitted, inconsiderate man in a great hurry; Stefanie is almost stumbling as she's tugged along one step behind. A naval band is climbing out of a bus, carrying their instruments.

"Look, Daddy."

"Yes, yes, I can see."

The little girl is hanging back with her arm painfully stretched out to its full extent, holding her head turned as she stumbles along, unwilling to lose sight of the musicians as they carry their instruments in their cases down to a passenger boat covered with streamers.

Now they're over the footbridge and have reached the elevated railway station, where the imminent arrival of a train is signaled by the expectant gathering of passengers—picking up their luggage, breaking off their conversations, moving closer to the edge of the platform, and showing by the way they place their legs that they are all prepared.

"Is that our train, Daddy?"

"Yes."

The windows are covered with grime and sprinkled with scattered drops of rain which smudge the harbor down below, blurring its etched sharpness. Heller rests his face against the windowpane and lets the beflagged and bestreamered celebration glide by and disappear behind him: this flowing river, embroidered with shining streaks, the obliterated slipways and cranes, the fleet of moored launches—this port which was receiving its certification of more than seven hundred years' existence with an extended birthday lasting for a full week.

Heller hears the little girl ask, "Are you going away now?"

From the depths of his absorption he answers, "No, I'm staying on, I've got some work to do."

"What kind of work?"

"We're making a reading book."

"For me?"

"Yes, perhaps for you too, and now that's enough questions."

Stefanie slips between the curve of his arms, letting her net bag swing back and forth in front of her feet. She avoids the frosty gaze of an old married couple who are staring at her as if they wanted to interrogate her and blame her at the same time.

Did Heller know that game too?

"What game?"

"Someone has to go out, Daddy, and when he comes back in, he has to guess what the others have done."

"Is that a game?"

"We always play it with Uncle Gerhard. Do you know him?"

"No."

The child puts the bag in her lap, pulls herself up onto the seat, and tries to play at mountaineering by clambering up Heller— with the obvious intention of climbing onto his head. Heller pulls her down onto the seat. "Not here, Stefanie, you're too old for that sort of thing. Now be quiet till we get out."

By the time they reach the Eppendorferbaum, she has gone off to sleep with her head resting against his hip and her little paws on his thigh and he has to wake her, pick her up under her armpits, and carry her, stiff with sleep, to the exit and onto the platform. "Look, Stefanie, there's a market down there." Under the bridge of the elevated railway, between the iron pillars, they're selling boxloads and basketloads of autumn: weighing out autumnal pears and sandy potatoes and ribbed cabbages. Heller and the child push their way past open stalls and booths with patched canvas roofs in which jaundiced piles of whole cheeses are trying to attract attention and an array of cut sausage demands to be tasted. Pale yet powerful onions are already hinting at the tears that will be shed when they are cut up, bunches of celery are asserting their country smell.

"What shall we buy, Stefanie?"

"Ice cream, please, Daddy, that's what I'd like."

"Then we can go straight to the café."

On a market day like today they are not able, of course, to pick the seat they want because all the tables in the big front room are occupied by market people in their aprons or tunics, all sitting close-packed, rough-skinned, and warming themselves against the damp cold outside with coffee and brandy, with schnapps and aromatic grog. They have to go to the last table at the end of the narrow, winding hosepipe of a side room beneath the wretched blue-green daubs, two yards long by one and a half yards high, depicting a sea eagle about (and thus eternally unable) to pounce on a wild duck.

Isn't that Charlotte? Although they're half an hour early, Charlotte is already waiting for them, buttoning up her coat, already making her way over to them and pulling the little girl toward her with a violence suggesting that she has missed her dreadfully. She looks her over like a suspicious storekeeper inspecting an article being exchanged; all she needs to do now, thinks Heller, is to test for smell and viscosity.

"We're going to have ice cream, Mommy. I'm going to have cream with mine."

"Isn't it too cold for ice cream?" asks Charlotte. "Wouldn't it be nicer to go back home now, isn't it time to say goodbye?"

"But she's been promised an ice cream."

"All right, then."

Heller and Charlotte shake hands, unenthusiastically, standing as far away from each other as two people can when shaking hands; you could imagine that a chalkline had been drawn between them to keep them from coming too close. So they sit down at the table: Stefanie in an enthusiastic rush, Heller purposefully and from a deliberate rear-guard position as he slips off his coat, Charlotte, inhibited, awkwardly, and making it plain that her agreement is a short-term one in any case. "Shall we all have an ice cream?" asks Heller blankly, at which Stefanie claps her hands and Charlotte makes a curt gesture toward her cup of coffee, which she has not yet drunk. So just one ice cream with whipped cream and a double kirsch for Heller.

While the little girl is fishing the toy kitchen out of the net bag, unwrapping it and setting it up in front of her—"Look what Daddy brought me, Mommy"—Heller waits patiently until his and his wife's eyes cross, that is to say by persevering he forces her eyes onto the same path as his own, and with a pathetic smile says, "You've hardly changed at all, Charlotte." Her only reply is a slight shrug of her shoulders, which may signify either indifference or annoyance; and what should she say to it anyway, after all that time, all those years? You've hardly changed at all! Her face merely reflects what she feels and Heller can read no hardness in it but merely a cold, calm reproach which has set in since his departure.

"We ought to have a talk together, Charlotte."

"Now?"

"In a minute, if you like, or even later on. I'm staying on in Hamburg for a while." He offers her his open pack of cigarettes, she declines, she's given up smoking, and anyway she can't stay that long.

"But later on, Charlotte, I'll wait for you here."

"What for?"

"Even if it's only to reminisce together. Will you? I'll wait for you here, at this table."

Charlotte doesn't want to commit herself; she expresses her indecision by closing her eyes and turning her face the other way. "Perhaps, Jan; I'm not certain yet."

This seems to satisfy Heller; presumably he was not expecting anything more than that, he'll stay at the table and wait for her here because, of course—she would realize this, too—he's proposing something more than exchanging memories; after all, some decision would have to be made about the present situation.

His wife looks at him in astonishment. "Wasn't it decided long ago? Isn't it a decision that you're going your own way? And the different life which each of us is living, doesn't that have some bearing on our situation? Oh, Jan, why bother to try to find words for something that it's too late to change?"

She makes a sign to the child to hurry up, but Stefanie now has other things to do: she wants to divide her ice cream into its separate components and to put samples of them in the tiny kitchen utensils; this is for grated chocolate, that one for a lump of whipped cream, and this other one for squashy strawberries, each separately spooned into dainty pots and pans which are now apparently going to be warmed up. "What *are* you doing, Stefanie! Now eat that up and put your kitchen away." And now this scene needs describing: the way the two of them, Heller and Charlotte, watch the child with her ice cream as she eats it alternately from the glass, with moderate pleasure, and then with exaggerated pleasure from the kitchen utensils, tapping her spoon against her brace or offering a taste of it all around, which is declined with thanks. And the way the child then turns toward the table next to them, where people from the market are having a good laugh over someone's private misfortunes: there was a man living in the country who threw a lit cigarette butt into the toilet without realizing that someone had previously thrown in a gasoline-soaked rag. The jet of flame was said to have been considerable, but his bad luck wasn't over yet, for as he was lying on the stretcher telling the ambulance men how he'd acquired the burns in his nether regions, they laughed so hard that they dropped the stretcher and so he broke some ribs as well. Some people really get all the bad luck, the men from the market were saying.

And then the way Charlotte jumps up, packs up the toy kitchen, helps Stefanie into her coat, and immediately takes her around to Heller, so that she can say goodbye to him—not a lingering, protracted farewell but short and sweet—she achieves this by holding Stefanie tightly by her upper arm as the child says goodbye. "I'll wait here at this table," Heller says again. "Mm." A few of the people from the market say, "Hello, Charlotte," as she goes through the café holding Stefanie's hand, now they're both crossing the street, slipping between the booths and the delivery vans through the market; they can be glimpsed briefly here and there in the gaps and then they turn off and disappear.

Heller sits motionless facing the stiff curtain, impregnated with old tobacco smoke, in the vicinity of slightly tipsy men from the market laughing at other people's troubles, sits at this table with its spotty oilcloth top covered with crumbs at which he often sat with his pupils in earlier days and, for example, cast rather a jaundiced eye over Ché Guevara and Franz Moor. Should he telephone Mike? Or that gloomy Rübesam, who agreed with everyone and then relentlessly pulled them all to pieces? Or Ines, who insisted on wearing at least *one* red garment? The young schoolmaster lifts his briefcase onto the table and extracts from it some thin brochures and a book, orders a second kirsch from the attentive waiter, and props the briefcase against a chairleg. It's the book that he picks up first; its title, in white letters on a blue background, is easy to read: *The Price of Hope* by Johannes Stein, and in smaller, downward-sloping characters: *In Memory of Lucy Beerbaum.*

What's in the blurb? What promises does it hold out? Unique woman. Shrewdness and sympathy, outstanding scientific gifts, and an ardent compassion which led her to sacrifice her life. Ascetic way of life and social visionary. Naturally, inseparable unity of thought and deed. Naturally, decisions which concern us all. Heller heaves a sigh. Naturally, an example for many who are searching. In addition, the blurb recommends two other books by Johannes Stein which Heller hasn't heard of. He runs his thumb through the pages with a whirring sound, stopping at the few photographs scattered throughout the book, looking at them and reading the captions: a thin, large-eyed girl on the lap of a melancholy, stiff, mustachioed seated man: "Lucy Beerbaum as a child with her father"; a desiccated-looking man, frozen in the attitude of a lion tamer offering himself to the admiring glances of a group of girls, all without exception suffering from bad posture: "Lucy Beerbaum with schoolmates and her first teacher, M. Simferis"; a slender young woman with bobbed hair and a badly fitting dress is leaning with a smile against a muscular man dressed in the dusty clothes of his trade: "Lucy Beerbaum with the baker Th.P., whom she often helped out during school holidays in order to learn about the conditions of the working classes"; a pretty, self-conscious young woman standing by the rail of an antiquated pleasure steamer, swamped in a trouser suit far too large for her, and beside her a man, in a dark suit, rendered faceless by the shadow of a straw boater: "Lucy Beerbaum with her colleague, later Professor V. Gaitanides"; a deserted laboratory at the Institute for Genetics with a DNA molecule in four colors perilously perched on the only table: "Lucy Beerbaum's workroom"; a rectangular tombstone: "Lucy Beerbaum's grave in the Ohlsdorfer Cemetery in Hamburg."

Janpeter Heller closes the book and weighs it in his hand; so this is supposed to be the raw material for a worthwhile exemplary life, a model worth meditating on, credible because of its controversial nature, etc., etc.? Is it worth starting on it while waiting for Charlotte to come back? Reading it methodically? He opens the book.

. . . by the Innocentia Park on the way home not far from her house. Lucy had, as usual, departed early from a birthday party for one of her colleagues and was walking home alone. The long bell-shaped dress, the lightness of her step, and the way she held her body, twisted sideways in a right "on guard" position, gave the impression that she was sailing down Oberstrasse driven before the gentle breeze. Now and again, in her nearsightedness, she would say good evening to wet shiny trees which she took to be passers-by.

She gave a friendly greeting to the young man who came out of the shadow and stood in her way. She did not call for help or offer any resistance as with a quick twist he snatched her handbag with its snap lock, and, failing to see the barbed wire, ran off toward the hedgerow bordering the park. Lucy listened to the sound of his running, the flapping of his raincoat, until she heard his cry of pain and his swearing and then called after him in a subdued, urgent voice: he would be disappointed, the bag was worthless, he ought to come back. She did not realize that he had stopped under the streetlamp and was going through her bag, but she did hear him call back that he had put the bag at the foot of the lamp; and then she called out again, several times, asking him not to run away. She did so cautiously and perhaps it was her voice rather than any possibilities it opened up that made him suddenly come back to her from out of the shadow of the park, full of suspicion and ready to take to his heels. He was holding his hand pressed against one of his thighs. He angrily asked her what he wanted and made no reply when she asked whether he had hurt himself. She told him how little there was in her bag and he explained where he had put it. She picked up the bag herself. When she attempted to approach him and look at his face, he drew back and warned her, in a coarse, familiar voice: "You stay there, sister, and tell me what you want." And when she asked him in a sympathetic voice why he'd done it, he replied, "Mind your own damn business."

She told him she would give him some money if he cared to come back with her to her house—it's just around the corner—and then went off ahead of him without bothering to check whether he was following her, as if this went without saying. Only when she had reached the front garden and switched on the light above the door of the house did she turn around to look at him, standing in front of the knee-high front gate—so he'd already come up the three stone steps—and then, while she was looking for her key, she asked him several times to come nearer and go into the house with her. This repeated invitation, with its matter-of-fact, neutral tone that could arouse no suspicion, succeeded in unfreezing the young man from his immobility and drew him along the flagstone path up to the front door where he could see the woman at close quarters, under the light: an unexpectedly young face under a head of gray bobbed hair. Lucy went ahead into the hall, holding the self-closing door open for him, and said, "Come on, please come in"; she understood his hesitation and at any rate his terse inquiry as to who else was living in the house. He came in only after giving a further lengthy warning and he did not dare to follow Lucy into the living room with its antique wood paneling. A window full of flowers, a few pieces of brightly painted furniture. Pictures depicting nothing but landscapes without shadows. A small mountain of sifted periodicals. The young man listened to the sound of her steps dying away, first on bare boards and then on stone tiles, and when no further sound could be heard, he slipped through the gap in the door into the living room and called out "Hey!" and then once more, "Hey, you, don't try anything funny!"—but then she came back from the kitchen with her coat over her arm and invited him to sit down at the table. As she walked by she looked at him as he stood there in his glistening raincoat, his hair plastered down. Wouldn't he like to take his coat off? No. Lucy hung her coat up in the clothes closet, changed her shoes, and, speaking from the unlighted alcove in the closet, asked if he was hungry; should she get him something to eat? He didn't reply.

Still in the alcove, invisible to him, and no doubt thinking that it was easier for him to talk this way, she asked him, from the other side of the room, what had made him act like that. Did he need anything? What was the trouble? Because she couldn't imagine that anyone would do a thing like that merely because the opportunity presented itself.

The young man turned around, went over to her, and saw that she was leaning her hand against the cracked mirror while she changed her shoes. "I don't want any tea and I don't like being questioned either. Why did you want me to come with you, eh?"

"I want to help you," said Lucy, "because people don't do what you did unless they have to."

"And what," asked the young man, "do you expect to get for your help? I can sell you eighty-eight life stories, stories of my past. Which one will I dish up for you? Hm? Let's get this straight. I don't want to know anything about *you* and you'll be better off not to want to know anything about me. Then we can get along together."

Although standing in front of the mirror, Lucy had not once looked at herself in the glass, and now, raising her eyes, she saw the young man behind her making his way to the door.

"Wait a minute. Obviously that's not the only way you can talk."

"But what do you want me for?" the young man asked, pressing his hand on his injured thigh. "What is it?" And then, scornfully: "To help, eh? Your help has to be paid for in advance. With entertaining confessions, eh?"

"Don't go yet," said Lucy, but he was already out in the hall and was listening again for any sound upstairs before he went to the door. She ran after him, caught hold of his arm, and held him back while in the same subdued and urgent voice she had used earlier at the park, she asked him to wait. Her arm dug deep down into the folds of her dress, her body leaned sideways as she fished and rummaged about, and suddenly she stood still and smilingly produced a purse gripped by two fingertips. "I've got it." Lucy opened the purse and extracted a folded bank note; she lifted it up to her face and turned toward the light. Wasn't it enough? Too much?

She started to push the note back into the purse when the young man made a grab—not a very well-judged one. However, Lucy had perhaps expected or feared what he would do and so was holding the purse concealed in her hand; in any case, his hasty snatch only managed to catch hold of her wrist, which he grasped and twisted sideways. She did not call or cry out, but this time, unlike the previous occasion at the park, she offered silent resistance until he pushed her backward and the back of her head struck against the wooden post of the banister. Her fingers relaxed their hold as she collapsed beside the radiator, as quietly and gently as if she had actually chosen to fall, and even now she did not call out, although, through all her pain, she realized that he was tearing the purse from her hand and making off.

Several times Lucy tried to rise to her feet, to push herself up and support herself on the radiator, but she couldn't manage it: each time the pain forced her down. Why didn't she shout when a door was opened upstairs and Ilse said loudly to Irene, "The light's on downstairs, Aunt Lucy's back"? And why didn't she cry out when a female shape appeared at the front door, evidently a woman who had mistaken the number of her house? Why did

164

she stir only when the two girls came downstairs repeatedly calling her name?

Only when her two dissimilar nieces reached her—Ilse in the lead, as always in stocking feet—did she stretch out her arms toward them, immediately telling them that she had only fallen, they shouldn't be afraid; all she needed was to be helped to her feet, she'd soon feel better, she would just like to sit down, no, not upstairs, on one of those chairs over there. How light she was to lift, what little strength the girls needed to half help, half carry her slender body across the hall into the living room, where she was now able to sit upright.

"Did you fall, Aunt Lucy?"

"Of course, what else do you think? Don't you believe me?"

The girls were sitting facing her and watching as she clung to the back of the chair, flung her head back, and shut her eyes for a moment. "Shall we send for a doctor, Aunt Lucy?"

"No, don't do that, it'll soon pass."

The girls exchanged a glance and asked each other a silent question: shall we tell her? Ilse, thin and restless, wanted to; Irene, cautious and heavy, was not so certain; so they waited, made some tea as soon as the kettle was heard chattering away in the kitchen, asking themselves in whispers how anyone could manage to fall in the hall. And then Lucy did something that the nieces had often seen her do, and were now no doubt expecting, what they called "a typical Aunt Lucy": with a gentle moan, as if she had wasted enough time and attention on her pain, she bent forward, spread her fingers, passed them once again over her temples, and looked kindly at the two girls, first at Irene and then at Ilse, whom she gently rebuked for running about in her stockings. "And now let's have some tea, children, after this accident."

Once again the girls took a silent vote, and since Irene finally had nothing against it, Ilse said, "In the news, Aunt Lucy—did you listen to the news?"

"How could I? I was at a birthday party." So Ilse went on: "In Athens, the Army's seized power in Athens, on April 21. A lot of people have been arrested, including scientists."

165

"Yesterday?" asked Lucy.

Ilse said, "They're having a discussion of it on the radio now, we were coming to get you. Shall we help you upstairs?" Lucy was pressing her hands together, she sat motionless, looking out into the dark garden, at the lopped pear tree. "Did you hear, Aunt Lucy? Aunt Lucy!"

"Yes, yes, I heard. . . ."

"Are you Herr Heller? There's a phone call for you, at the counter, up front." Janpeter Heller places his forefinger in the book, closes it, and takes it with him into the front room, where a salesgirl, with a very smart hairstyle and wearing white overalls, points reluctantly behind the display counter at the telephone, and with that single gesture makes it plain that he could use the telephone there only in an emergency. He lifts the receiver, turns his back, looks at a round cream cake, a grinning, sickly sun whose light was dripping off it in thin threads of chocolate, and instead of saying "Hello," says, "Yes, Charlotte?" The salesgirl, pensive, with her arms folded across her chest, has no difficulty in following the conversation and in completing the sentences: they'd agreed to meet to discuss something essential, but now doubts have set in, something that had been essential has unexpectedly become much less so; nevertheless, they'll once again attempt to clarify something that has long since been clear.

10

Dᴇᴀʀ Maria [writes Valentin Pundt to his wife in Lüneburg]: First of all, I hope you are well, as I am. As arranged, we're staying in the Hotel-Pension Klöver, our colleague Süssfeldt discovered it for us and, all things considered, it's quite pleasant, even though the churlishness and lack of interest shown by the proprietress are hardly calculated to cheer her guests. Frau Klöver, roughly your age, spent a long time in former German Southwest Africa and now everything seems to be too much for her and her indifference toward her guests makes it plain to them that they're preventing her from indulging in the undisturbed contemplation of the memories which Africa has left her with. You ought to see our conference room—a private museum of exotic weapons.

My rheumatic pains are not as bad here as I had feared they would be; it was the same on all my recent trips; it looks as if any diseases that you take away with you have first to become adapted to the surroundings before they can get you under control again in their old way. All the same, I'm using the skin regularly. Have not worked so much on the *Alphabet* as I'd intended, unfortunately, the reason being the unexpected difficulties which our anthology has encountered. I imagine that you can realize who has been largely responsible for these difficulties. As I'm writing to you—looking out on the wintry Alster, it's snowing outside but the snow can't seem to settle—our young know-it-all colleague is sitting in his room listening to music. My colleague

Süssfeldt and I would long since have come to an agreement and indeed would already be on the next chapter if he hadn't sneered at everything and pulled it to pieces as he has.

Heller is, on principle, suspicious of anything that existed before he was born. He's too young to have experienced everything but too old not to have questioned many things and so he feels himself duty-bound to make it plain to us that exemplary people can only be shining examples of bogeymen, evil and authoritarian people who stand in the way of self-development. Can you imagine what it's like to come to an understanding with a man like that? It's no concern of mine how he dresses, but his behavior and manner of speech made a collision inevitable. He really believes that being young is an argument in itself. Still, I forced him to come and apologize to me. I dare not think how long it will take to compose the whole book since producing one single chapter is proving so troublesome. (I know what you're thinking but don't worry: if things continue like this I'll throw up the whole project.)

I've picked up all the rest of Harald's things and I have them here. I haven't yet been able to look through them, we ought to do that together when I come home. Have called on a few people who knew Harald or even were friends of his, a girl who was a fellow student and a singer, all queer fish without exception, hardly the sort of people one's likely to meet in Lüneburg. I learned a great deal through these meetings—but not enough to understand what happened. Gerd Brüggmann, whom I've just come from seeing, couldn't give me any further help either—he's an older former pupil of mine, you'll barely remember him. All the same, I have an idea that what he had to say will have a certain importance, even if it's a depressing one. So that you may know, I learned by chance through the Meisters that Harald and Gerd Brüggmann had had an argument that ended in our boy having to receive medical treatment—something which he hadn't mentioned to us at all. In the hope of obtaining more accurate information, I went to call on my old pupil, it wasn't easy to find him, he works as a scaffold erector with one of the big scaffolding firms.

They were in the process of erecting some scaffolding around a private hospital—all stocky men in overalls, wearing woolen hats, obviously well trained in working together, and when I tried to inquire from them, all they said was: "Out of the way there, look out," as if they were part of a conspiracy. Wherever I went, I found myself in their way; when they brought up their ladders and tubes from the side they made me run around in a semicircle, forcing me to duck out of the way, so that the only way for me to avoid being hurt was by continually crouching down. Gerd Brüggmann was putting planks between the ladders that they had erected and fastened. I recognized him and called up to him several times, but he didn't turn around, and so I simply climbed up to him and said, "Gerd, here's your old school-teacher." You should have seen his face, Maria, the first look he gave me, roughly at second-floor level. The hostility which made him go rigid. He stuck his pick—that's the name they give their tool—into a plank, reached for a rung, and hung on to it tightly, as if he wanted to stop himself from doing something rash. I'd forgotten that he had a speech impediment, nor did I know that since he'd left school he'd found it increasingly difficult to string words together in articulate sentences. His greatest problem was, each time he started speaking—but I'll tell you about that, and much else besides, when I see you.

On the platform neither Gerd Brüggmann nor I exchanged a single word of greeting, and when I asked him about Harald, he turned his back on me. I didn't ask about the argument they'd had, I merely inquired how his meeting with Harald had gone, and at that he told me—as far as it was possible for him to do so —to clear out. He didn't want my company and he wanted to be left in peace; in any case, he made it as plain as he could with his stammer that I had no business on his scaffolding. When I hesi-tated, he became more explicit. Speaking in an agitated voice, he congratulated me on the results of my educational efforts, the success of which I could judge by him. I couldn't understand what he meant and then he reminded me of a habit that I must in fact have had. When a pupil didn't know the answer, I am supposed to have let him just stand there, without continuing the lesson; and many lessons are supposed to have been spent like that. I wasn't aware of it and I'm still not, really and truly not, Maria, yet according to Gerd Brüggmann it must have been the case. You can imagine how I felt. He pulled his pick out of the plank and merely pointed down to the street and said, "There's no one up here whose will you can break now"; if I had any plans to do that, I'd better go and look somewhere else and if I wanted to know exactly what he thought of me I should inquire from Harald, because he'd told him everything. (So he didn't know and still doesn't know that Harald is dead.) And even if he'd never been able to stand him and still couldn't, in one respect at least Harald and he were in agreement, that none of the teachers in Lüneburg was better than I at breaking a boy's spirit without effort or without a sound! I simply can't believe, Maria, that I ever did that systematically. And if it did happen occasionally, then why didn't Harald protest against it? After all, he had every opportunity to speak to me and I remember that I encouraged him often enough to tell me about anything he disapproved of. You can imagine how I feel as I'm writing this now. But that's how things are today: it's not sufficient to have the strength required to do your duty; you need at least the same amount of strength to deal with the conflicts that you're exposed to and can't avoid.

Perhaps I ought to have come home, in fact, as soon as I realized the difficulties we would encounter when all the proposals which we'd brought were turned down. Not one was left, even the alternative proposals were talked out of court; that will show you how different our views are as to what constitutes an exemplary life in our times. What we're working on at the moment is going to be, at least as far as I'm concerned, our last attempt; we are in fact now occupied in producing our paragon from a considerable quantity of material already available. I must admit that this time we're on the right track: a female scientist, a biologist born and brought up in Greece but who worked and died in Hamburg, will, I hope, provide us with the example of exemplary conduct which we haven't been able to find up till now.

Her name, incidentally, is Lucy Beerbaum, and from my first acquaintance with her she reminds me of Frau Wischmann, Grete Wischmann, you know, the half sister of Harald's godmother: the same gray bobbed hair, the same delicate and, at the same time, strikingly chiseled features—and like Grete Wischmann, our model heroine also has a tendency now and then to dress with complete disregard for fashion.

The task we've set ourselves is to determine what period of her life would be especially suitable for inclusion in our reader. We've divided the material among ourselves and are now in the process of familiarizing ourselves with it and my first impressions confirm that we're pursuing a useful suggestion. (You won't be spared, at least, having to read the fictional biography of Lucy Beerbaum; suspense, admiration, scandals—I'm telling you now what to expect.)

You can hardly imagine, Maria, what discoveries I'm making in this strange life, the highlight of which, so it seems to me, is the chapter of her protest, or, as she described it herself, "a publicly expressed sympathy." When the Colonels took over in Greece, when scientists were arrested, as well as politicians and artists—including Lucy Beerbaum's oldest friend—she stopped working and of her own accord lived in her home under the same restrictions as those arrested in Greece were forced to live under. The same constraints, the same deprivations, almost the same isolation. Just imagine, this woman found out the amount of the prisoners' rations, how much living space they were allotted, how often they were allowed to receive mail, then she imposed the same equally harsh conditions on herself. That was the only thing that mattered to her and you must read sometime the reasons she gave her friends who tried to persuade her to go back to her work at the Institute.

But I must stop. A session is just about to start. My young collaborator has just turned his music off. If Uncle Schnittlein will be coming to Hamburg in the next few days, please give him two bottles to bring to me; you know, the unlabeled ones in the cellar. I hope the painters have now finished in the kitchen. (You should see what they earn here in the metropolis, we're still well off in Lüneburg.) I'll send a telegram as usual to let you know when I'm due to arrive in L.

Your affectionate husband,
Valentin

11

Rita Süssfeldt is asleep. Outside the circle of light from her bedside-table lamp, her sweater is embracing, with persuasive limpness, the back of an easy chair; her carelessly discarded stockings are hanging one over the other, trying to intertwine; a brown dress has collapsed and is nestling against the cracked leather upholstery; her brassière is dangling loosely beside a chair leg, and curled up on one arm of the chair a pair of white panties are slumbering, held by a piece of worn-out elastic. The shoes in front of the chair complete the double image of sleep: they are lying there, soles upward, their points turned inward toward each other, as though each wished to prevent the other from making any attempt to move. Nor must the book be forgotten, the book which has fallen off the quilt onto the floor, considerately one might say, in such a way that its title is showing: *The Price of Hope.*

It takes more than a knock from one thin knuckle to rouse Rita Süssfeldt from her slumbers; Heino Merkel ought to know that as he shyly tries to make his presence felt against this resounding silence with his repeated short-short-long tap on the heavy, white-painted, unfastened door. Obtaining no response, he eventually pulls open the door, laboriously carries a suitcase into the room, and then a traveling bag, cautiously now as if he ought not to waken the sleeping woman, sits down first on his suitcase, and then, after moving Rita's clothes—more tidily than she herself would ever have done—on the easy chair and contemplates the nape of her neck, which is not very informative. He waits. He is preparing for her awakening, anticipating everything that might occur, indeed shortly will occur—he parries a startled cry, and her anger, drunk with sleep, will have to be assuaged—and still he sits on where he is. He's wearing a lined raincoat, unbuttoned, and holding a lined cap in his hand. Anyone seeing him would assume that here is a man who wants to leave and is insisting on taking his leave at the most inconvenient moment.

Where his knuckle failed, his unflinching gaze directed at the cervical vertebrae looks to be succeeding, for under its silent challenge Rita Süssfeldt begins to stir, aimlessly at first—here her hand circles, there a leg is rhythmically stretching, and now finally the whole body starts to turn half over—and then, under the man's constant silent pressure, she blows some hair away from her face, passes her hand over her eyes, and sits up with a start. "You? What are you doing here? At this time of night. And you're wearing a coat." The man replies with ambiguous gestures which mean: Okay, I'm very sorry, but there was nothing else I could do, and now stop being angry and listen while I tell you why I've come.

The former archaeologist bends his head, she can see the piece of artificial skull, his calm sharpens her hearing, this unusual composure which hints at a crucial decision. "Well? Why did you come here? And you've got some luggage, too."

Couldn't she realize? he asks. The time, the state he's in, and finally the suitcase and the traveling bag, aren't they sufficient explanation? He couldn't stay on here any longer, in a house where he felt caught in a trap, a trap of gratitude for the rest of his life. He'd left a letter for Mareth, she'll find it as soon as she gets back from *The Flying Dutchman*, which incidentally is being televised, too. He didn't have a permanent address yet; in the beginning he'd probably live with a friend of his youth, a Bremen fruit importer.

Rita Süssfeldt looks at her watch, takes a cigarette from her bedside table, and lights it. She pushes her hair back over her shoulder. She inhales so violently that her body responds with a

174

burst of dry coughing. The ash—look out! All right. She doesn't look at him but leans forward, draws up her knees, rests her chin on them, and with her eyes on the mandolin hanging on the wall asks him why he came to say goodbye to her, he could have written a letter and left it for her, that would have been more reasonable, less painful in fact, if she could perhaps put it like that—so why? Amazement and increasing incredulity: surely she didn't need to ask that particular question, because one thing was certain and that was the link between them; they'd reached a sufficiently close understanding with each other, even if not explicitly, at least implicitly; hadn't they stood by each other because each recognized what the other had to put up with in this house?

"Why not just say you've come to take me away?"

"Yes, Rita," he replies, "yes, I'd like to suggest that you leave with me, because I know how difficult it is for you too to put up with everything, systematic humiliation, having to be dependent and say thank you all the time."

"You must have taken leave of your senses."

She flings back the blanket, a quick twist and she's standing in front of him in her shapeless but warm flannel pajamas, another gesture and the man stands up and goes over to the window. With her cigarette in her mouth she starts to get dressed, annoyed and bad-tempered, as though she feels she's being expected to do something that's not worth the effort; while the man feels impelled to produce evidence for the assertion he's just made. "Well, you remember, you can confirm that . . . You must admit that everything changed after my return; all of a sudden I'd become a sick man, dependent on help from other people. But before then, there was a time before then; have you forgotten it?"

And he describes what it was like in the old days, talks of the spacious attic where he lived all alone with his puppet collection: couldn't she remember how often she used to come and see him without telling her sister? And did she still know the special way of ringing the bell they'd thought up? And could she still remember their refrigerator—a watertight bag in which they put their

sausage, butter, and cheese and simply hung it out on the roof—
and what fun it was for her every time? He tells her she should
come upstairs again just as she used to and give the prearranged
signal with the doorbell; he would open up as he always did,
make her kiss his cheek as she goes by as he always did. There's
snow on the ground outside, he would make a hot rum punch and
then they would sit side by side and select illustrations for his
book, . . . *And the Ark Floated.*

Hadn't all that actually happened? "Certainly," says Rita, "but
what else?" He's surprised and reminds her of one night in
March, he can still remember the date—she had come back from
an examiner's meeting, tired but pleased because she'd succeeded
in getting her candidate approved; and with her feet all wet since
she had jumped out of the taxi into slush ankle deep and then,
after a hot footbath, just in case, she had curled up on the sofa
under the green Dutch rug and—it was all still so fresh and clear
in his mind—he had told her about Moslem puppets and puppet
plays for Moslem children; and she'd gone to sleep. "You didn't
even notice when I undressed you later on."

"Go on," says Rita Süssfeldt, as she continues dressing, "keep
telling me." And he wants her to admit that she often used to
come up to him and help him, sometimes with the proofreading
or to choose the illustrations, but especially in organizing and
writing notes on his puppets when he had been asked to lend his
collection for an exhibition. Did her memory go back that far?
And now could he tell her what happened at the fancy-dress ball
for which, without prearrangement, they had both come dressed
as Spaniards; all right, the majority of people there were dressed
as Spaniards but their two costumes were like the Spanish children's puppets which he had at that time; and after the ball Rita
had come home with him and spent the night as if it was the
natural thing to do. Would she like to deny that? "I'm listening
closely to everything you're saying," says Rita Süssfeldt.

"And then when the invitation arrived, you remember, they
asked me to be scientific adviser for the filming of my book, and
we were sitting in the Fisch-Keller and talking about the offer.

176

Mareth was there, too, and she advised me against it, because, she said, an outsider could neither improve anything in a film nor prevent anything from being put in, but you thought differently and advised me to accept, which I did because I hoped that you would follow me one day—after all, you'd had a share in the book; when I asked you, you wouldn't commit yourself. You didn't come. But you know what happened to me."

The effort of speaking, the effort of remembering are now becoming apparent. "Sit down," says the woman, "sit down on this chair, I'm ready now, and since you expect me to say something, I want to tell you everything there is to say on the subject; forget all those memories, because they're false: you've invented them because you needed them. I'm sorry, Heino, but I've got my memories, too, and they're not the same as yours."

Leaning stiffly back in the chair, the man points out that she has just admitted to a lot of them, and the woman doesn't deny that either, but makes it clear where hers are different from his. "Arranged to suit yourself, Heino, you've arranged them all to suit yourself. Mareth always knew when I was visiting you; not once did I spend the night in your room, and we never mentioned the question of my following you." She's speaking slowly to him; she clearly wants to spare his feelings and her kindness shows equally in her readiness to go carefully into all his questions and not try to explain everything too quickly. "If you're prepared to be accurate and collect your thoughts, we can go back over this together. Do you realize all the ideas you're going to have to give up?"

The man shakes his head, he can't give up either his reasons or his opinions, he won't allow her to destroy the things that help him to understand his plight and make his decision easier; so he produces a diversion and plays the card that she was expecting: his suspicions about Mareth. It was she who had planned to stand in the way from the very first and she'd achieved what she wanted, even if not in the way she had hoped.

"And what was that, do you think?"

"Don't you know?"

177

So he tells how, once he had proved himself to be a confident and single-minded producer, who had pursued a single idea throughout his life, *his* idea, which he had explored in every possible way, he directed every episode and laid down how each sequence was to be shot: the floating ark which had been built according to his specification; collecting all the animals beneath a guaranteed cloudless sky; the anonymous offer of protection, the night watches, and then the disaster in the night, the heavy blow which struck him down; and then the burning of the ark. He himself hadn't seen it burning because he was unconscious and remained unconscious for seven whole days, but later on he had been forced to fill in that gap in his waking dreams and the unwilling memories which always ended in the same way: his desperate desire to save the animals and the feeling of being unable to move. Unconscious for seven days; Mareth's rapid decision to come and see him, the difficulty of bringing him back to Hamburg, which was only overcome through her energy and her insistence on being proved right; the time spent in the hospital, with Mareth always here, there, and everywhere; her dogmatic and authoritative way of handling doctors and nurses; her attempt to keep him in the hospital longer than he wanted to stay; her detailed account through which he learned everything that had happened.

"And what was it she'd always wanted and had now got?" asks Rita Süssfeldt.

Did she insist that he tell her? She gives a nod, and Heino Merkel, seizing the arms of the chair and grasping and pressing them tightly, can suddenly feel resistance growing and this slows down his speech. "As long as I was independent . . . as long as I was alone, and in good health . . . I would never have come to live here. . . . Nobody could have persuaded me to live here. Only my illness and the dependence it inflicted on me made it possible. And that dependence was carefully pointed out to me and I was given proof of it every day: 'You've turned the room upside down . . . you've been lying on the floor . . . you've hurt us—or yourself —once again' . . . Whatever I do or don't do is always a sign of illness . . . it always serves as an explanation or motivation for what I do . . . its risks are continually trotted out for me: 'Consider what might have happened if you'd been without help.' . . . It's even reached the point where Mareth thinks for me . . . she talks for me and acts for me . . . she insists that she has to do it . . . and any attempt at independence is branded as ingratitude. I know that the worst thing I could do as far as she's concerned is to get my health back . . . because I would be reducing the value of the sacrifices she's made for me during my illness. So my condition is not allowed to improve because she's sacrificed so much for me. . . . Ask yourself whether anyone can go on living in such a situation."

The man stands up and looks challengingly at the woman. "Come away with me. If it is true that I sometimes need help, why shouldn't you give it me? After all, you might be able to gain something from it, too."

"And what might that be?"

"Independence, more independence."

"My poor throat," says Rita Süssfeldt, "I've been asleep, my throat's so dry, I must have a drink, there's some port downstairs." She quickly pulls the sheet straight, smooths the quilt, stuffs her pajamas under the pillow. "Shall we go downstairs? You can leave the luggage here."

Beneath the family portraits, beneath the gaze of ancestors who remind one of hares, they drink to each other's health in silence, from glasses out of which the skeptics on the wall presumably also used to drink the same sticky stuff, in dreary but, on the other hand, coolly calculated conviviality.

"But don't you see, you must also look at it this way"; and here come the second thoughts, the presentation of the opposite point of view will soon be under way, and if not exactly that, then at least the search for extenuating circumstances. "Just stop and think how unkind your explanation is and look more closely to see if you're really justified in passing such a harsh judgment after all. I know Mareth too. True, she's used to people paying attention to what she says. True, she's strict. True, she expects

179

more than her due. And this is true, too: she's never impressed by anything, she's incapable of being surprised. If you tell her that you intend to fly from Hamburg to Munich in a balloon tomorrow morning, she'll ask you what the difference in the fare is compared to the train. Margarethe is made of stone. At least, she's put on a kind of protective covering, ever since her episode with Nicolas."

The man slowly turns his head toward her. "Nicolas?"

"Yes, Nicolas Windschild from Rodenkirchen near Cologne. You've never heard of him? Hasn't Mareth ever told you about him? In that case, she's kept quiet about what's been the most important thing for her, or at least what's changed her most."

Can he be told? "You can't expect me to tell you, because in this matter I simply can't summon up the necessary objectivity, and if I tell the story unfairly, it won't really help you to understand it properly. Ask Mareth yourself, perhaps she'll tell you."

The man gives a resigned smile. "Our real illnesses," he says, "are our open-ended experiences, the ones that aren't concluded, and there seems to be only one therapy for them, to render them harmless by talking about them."

"You know, don't you," the woman says, "how much Mareth has hemmed herself in with principles."

"Yes, of course."

Then he would certainly have noticed how she takes advantage of every opportunity to go against them. All he has to do is wait for the right moment to question her and he'd be surprised at what he would learn.

The man is slowly twirling his glass, watching the viscous liquid lapping against its side, higher and higher, and then trickling down in oily festoons as soon as he stops; no, he doesn't want any more to drink; he'd just like to take off his coat but first he'll go to the telephone because it's been ringing for some time, couldn't she hear it?

Rita Süssfeldt doesn't hear it until she opens the door to the corridor; she pushes Heino back. "You be off, I'll take it"; but before removing the receiver she goes back into the living room and looks at the clock.

180

Who's that? A distorted but not unfamiliar voice apologizes, breaks off or rather is interrupted, begins anew, and again apologizes for disturbing her at such a late hour, but in exchange would like to offer something that will justify any disturbance.

"Who are you?"

"Dear Rita Süssfeldt, it's your collaborator, Janpeter Heller, yes, Heller, who's on the same painful search as yourself, for the great educational bogeyman." For the third time he apologizes, enunciating his words with some difficulty, and then it seems as though Heller is pushed away from the telephone, as if a friendly tussle is taking place at the other end of the phone: that is what it sounds like and Rita Süssfeldt has to ask several times, "Where are you? Where on earth are you ringing from?"—before Heller, apparently having successfully repelled the attack, replies, "At Mimmi's, Mimmi's Anchorage, Mimmi's bar by the fishing harbor. I'm waiting for you here."

He's speaking urgently, so something must be at stake, if not perhaps for their common cause, at least for him personally, but Rita is still hesitating, first she must recover from her surprise and she listens to the sounds that are coming over the wire with Heller's voice: the clink of metal balls, the whirring of spinning cylinders, a confused medley of cries.

She would be amazed, says Heller, he wouldn't like to say too much in advance at the moment, but what he was offering was the model for which they had been looking for such a long time, a model who could be seen and touched, who weighs in at an impressive one hundred and ninety pounds, at a guess. He could be examined and questioned. You could even have a drink with him. Wouldn't she like to make an inspection? They'd met by chance and they were sitting having a drink; Heller would be doubly delighted, and so forth. How about it?

Busy lighting a cigarette with one hand, Rita Süssfeldt finds herself repeating to Heller several times that in more convenient circumstances, at some other time, she would have been interested and come right away, but today of all days she couldn't because she had other plans for this evening and, incidentally, she'd already gone to bed. And as for the exemplary life, surely they'd agreed to stick to Lucy Beerbaum and work out something appropriate from her life? After all, what would happen if they started combing through bars, or perhaps even waiting rooms or public baths, on their own hook in search of an acceptable hero?

What is Heller saying? In fact, he's saying, "Rita"—and he repeats it, pronouncing the R slightly like an L—"I'm sitting next to Franz Pikosch, who can offer us everything we want, an exemplary life for our times, with the advantage of being complete in himself, in the round, so to speak; in any case, Franz doesn't need to be worked out." The clink of metal balls becomes louder, a wail of pain can be heard behind Heller, who places his hand over the mouthpiece and presumably addresses the hero in the living flesh.

Perhaps this is just an example of Heller's peculiar sense of humor, Rita wonders. Perhaps it's just a pretext to get me down to Mimmi's Anchorage at this time of night. And now Heller is about to speak again: in a persuasive whisper, he sums up in a few brief slogans the importance of his find, to give some idea of the unique suitability of Franz Pikosch, this delicious educational morsel whom he first describes as a bargee, and then, after correction from the background, as a shipowner.

"My dear colleague," says Rita Süssfeldt impatiently, "I can well imagine that it's a pleasure to be drinking with your paragon; you ought to stick to that. I can't spend any more time listening to you, nor can I come and examine him. Bring him along to the conference tomorrow perhaps. And now let me wish you a pleasant continuation of your amusing evening."

She hangs up, looks at the telephone, no, Heller's not ringing again, he seems to have got the message, her cautious rebuke has hit the mark. There's no light in the living room: is he sitting alone in the dark, as he so often does? Rita switches on the light and then immediately switches it off, she runs upstairs, the luggage is no longer in her room, he's carried it up to his own room and now he's going back and forth, silently putting away the things he had wanted to take with him.

"May I come in?" Rita Süssfeldt asks; she walks in without

waiting for an answer and stands beside the chair anchored to the floor. "It's better like this, Heino, better for both of you, and if you can manage to give up your theory, you'll realize why Mareth is doing all this for you. She doesn't want you to reward her by staying here on account of all her sacrifices, she just wants to go on helping you."

The man nods reluctantly; now that he has decided to stay and has removed all traces of his short-lived revolt, he has already abandoned his attitude of protest. He's unpacking and putting his things away: books, notebooks, woolen underwear, shirts, and, as Rita Süssfeldt observes to her amazement, a number of variegated glass animals, which he cautiously peels out of his woolen socks—her last birthday present to him. "So they wouldn't get broken," he says, and she, with exaggerated appreciation: "A very good idea. I must make a note of it." And now he's hurrying to put the things he had packed back in their places; he forces the suitcase under the wardrobe, shakes the contents of his traveling bag into two drawers—"I'll sort them out later on"— and to cover his haste, he asks, "Was that phone call about Lucy Beerbaum?"

"It was Heller, you know him of course, my collaborator, he's in search of a new persona himself. He's landed in a low bar and apparently he's found in the bottom of his glass the paragon who will relieve us of all our worries. He was insisting that I go over to make his acquaintance this very evening. I assume it was a pretext and tomorrow he'll be sorry he phoned."

The man is on his knees, pushing his traveling bag under the bed, and, without turning around, he asks how far they've got in exploring Lucy Beerbaum's life. Still on her early life? Anyway, if he had his way and had to provide the piece, he would devote particular attention to her early life because it was then that you could see her expressing, quietly but recognizably, the qualities which later on revealed her as a symbol and almost as a heroine.

Yes, she'd already noticed that; what had caused her some confusion on her first reading was the family relationships: there was a Georgios Beerbaum, Lucy's grandfather, who traded in

Greek folk arts and crafts—goldsmiths' work, earrings, lace, and hand weaving—now was it he who'd been married twice or Lucy's father?

"Both of them," says Merkel, "they both married twice; Lucy's father was born from her grandfather's first marriage, and she herself was the only child of her father's second marriage, his first marriage having been childless. If I understand their history correctly, Lucy's grandfather stayed on in Athens when he was on a visit from Hamburg to his brother who lived there, a ship's engineer; her father, Kostos Leonard Beerbaum, was born in Athens, tried living in Hamburg for a few years as an experiment, but then went back and continued his former profession as a sort of street-corner poor man's lawyer."

Heino Merkel listens, goes to the window, and looks down into the street, there still seems time to remove even the last traces of the unconsummated departure; and now that he shows no further signs of revolt, it can be seen that he is relieved and also tired. He asks the woman to let him have the anchored chair, sits down in it, lifts up the leather straps, and, with eyes closed, lets them slip lightly through his hands, then suddenly sits up and says, "I envy you that work. I can imagine all the possibilities and contradictions she offers: there are all sorts of strange things and you can't help asking yourself: How can any one of us manage to do that? And what makes him keep going? Yes, Rita, I really envy you."

"There are three of us as editors already," says the woman, "and we make things difficult enough for each other as it is."

"But just to follow what you're doing, perhaps you won't object if I can cast a critical eye over your work as it goes along."

They prick up their ears and look at each other, confirming each other's thought, both of them concentrating on listening to the inevitable stages of someone returning home: now she's putting the chain on, taking her coat off as she walks, hanging it up in the closet, now she's standing in front of the mirror, now she's opening the door of the living room and closing it again, now she's getting herself a glass of port, hesitating when she discovers the two empty glasses, finally she's coming upstairs. "Hello, you two—that *Flying Dutchman* had already capsized in the Elbe estuary; a typical one-horse show."

"Hello, Mareth."

"And what are you up to?" asks Mareth. "I thought you wanted to go to bed early." Disappointed but stimulated, she sits down on the stool at the desk, plainly wondering whether to open the window now or later on, obviously decides to do it later, and takes a sip of wine in a way that she surely must have learned from a bird.

"We're boring our way through the story of Lucy Beerbaum's life, so to speak," says Rita, "because tomorrow we want to put the lady under a magnifying glass."

"And what's happened? Have you struck oil?"

"Not yet, but Heino has opened up certain prospects; he even offered to help me today."

"Well, if you ask me," says Mareth, "I find her just as unremarkable now as I did when she was our neighbor."

12

THEY have just met in the dim vestibule of the Hotel-Pension Klöver and, with Heller bad-temperedly leading the way, have moved into the panoplied conference room; Pundt is renewing his campaign against drafts, while Heller is thinking up an apology for his late phone call to Dr. Süssfeldt, and at that moment, puffing and blowing to herald her arrival, in comes Ida Klöver, bidding them good morning with a limp wave of the hand; she doesn't want to disturb them, although she has already done so, but she wants to tell them that the maid, Magda, is not available today and so she will be attending to any orders herself. This is not said in a threatening tone, but you could detect a slight warning to refrain from ordering anything; she's too obviously bored and her lack of interest is too manifest. Since she intended to go and lie down again, it would be convenient if they could say now if they wanted anything. Yes? They don't require anything. That's good; then all she need do is wish them a good morning's work.

Now what? First, the conference must be prepared: cigarettes, dried fruit, and matches are set out in readiness, briefcases and bags unpacked, books with unusual book marks are stacked up—among other things, Pundt has used a torn shoelace—pads of paper and ball-point pens are laid out. "Can we begin?" They could, but first Heller would like to get something off his chest: his apology and the reasons for his late phone call; looking gloomy and unwell this morning, he would like to offer an expla-

186

nation, but Rita Süssfeldt waves it aside, as far as she's concerned the matter is closed, since Heller has given up the idea of bringing along the paragon he'd discovered last night. Moreover, the presence of his books and notes would seem to show that he'd fallen in with their joint decision, and that must mean that Lucy Beerbaum would, so to speak, be the raw material for their project.

At this point, Valentin Pundt, with his old smoking jacket pulled up around his ears, would like to "confess" something too: although he had not yet gone very deeply into her "Work and Personality," he would like to confess how ashamed he felt at being ignorant of Lucy Beerbaum until now. True, he was still only swimming on the surface, he hadn't yet immersed himself properly in the mass of biographical material; nevertheless, he thought it was already possible to believe—and he knew what he was talking about—that this personality was likely to provide the key for understanding our times. His nose for signs and portents confirmed it, his generally reliable instinct for ciphers, if he might express himself thus.

"We'll appoint Lucy Beerbaum chief gymnastic instructor," says Heller, screwing up his face, "for every type of gymnastics, too, including moral ones. A gymnastic instructor who can explain the world to us." Pundt asks, with more than a hint of suspicion in his voice, how that remark is meant to be taken, and Heller, with a shrug of his shoulder, says, "If you don't like the expression 'gymnastic instructor,' we can promote Lucy Beerbaum to the position of guide rail along which everything slides smoothly to its destination." And soothingly Heller admits that so far he's gained a favorable impression, he's even found a piece that could be used in certain circumstances, and incidentally he would like to hazard the guess that Lucy Beerbaum would provide the book with a special sort of piquancy. Was his colleague now reassured?

Pundt offers some prunes—no takers—and so helps himself to a double portion. "What line are we going to take then?" asks Rita Süssfeldt, and she is immediately dissatisfied with her question.

"I mean, how are we going to tackle the question? Exchange passages? Compare? Assess in writing and then vote?"

Left to themselves in this room full of African memories, the experts seek to find a method. "Well, how shall we do it? As we did before?" That much can be agreed upon without more ado.

So once again they'll be putting forward proposals to each other, offering each other what they have discovered about Lucy Beerbaum in their experimental probes, and expressing in the process their own temperament, character, and preferences; each of them draws attention to the extremely short time available for preparation, and that will have to be taken into account in their assessment.

Only the creaking of wicker chairs and the sound of fingers tapping on the rosewood table can now be heard in the room. Outside in the garden, where November is still busy mixing its slush, two young roof tilers are looking at them in amusement, puzzling over what could be the occupation of these people sitting beneath the antlers of a male antelope. What would they say if they knew? thinks Heller, and he stares so hard at the two youths in their blue outfits that they drop their eyes and hurry back to their ladder and their sheet metal.

Should Rita Süssfeldt begin? Or, since Heller is not eager, Valentin Pundt? We have the choice, but Dr. Süssfeldt has already decided, she's lighted another cigarette, settled herself comfortably in front of an open book, and merely issues the warning that since the example she'd like to put forward is taken out of context it would have to be reworked. "Moreover, I've deliberately picked an experience from adolescence so that the young reader will have the opportunity here of putting himself in her place and making an immediate comparison; we can find a title together. If you're ready, I'll begin. Here it is:"

Lucy seldom did her schoolwork at home. The old garden did not attract her, not even the ramshackle old garden house beneath the flat-topped trees which had a table and a chair. Almost every day, as soon as school was over she would stroll by herself down to the so-called Plaka, the old town of Athens, where people lived on frail wooden balconies, in unsightly courtyards, or simply on chairs set out in front of gloomy house entrances. She would make her way by the shortest route to this quarter where people openly displayed all their possessions, and go into a two-storied house and upstairs to her father's office, which consisted of two whitewashed rooms made available to him by the owner of the house, a male nurse, as a sign of special gratitude. And while her father, a lawyer and, in his own words, "counsel for the insulted," received his clients in the first room, Lucy would sit in the small back room with the door always ajar, doing her homework in the midst of slovenly tied and discarded documents and piles of abandoned books. Without being noticed, she could see the clients coming and going, could hear their voices, filled with care and guile and despair, and so could learn from her sheltered seat the alphabet of distress. How calmly her father could sit there when his visitors not only told of their distress but acted it out: gestures, motions, astounding ranges of pitch, helped to dramatize what had befallen them, but Lucy's father never straightened his bent back, the face with its melancholy beak seemed incapable of sympathy.

And how about Lucy? At first she couldn't see any way of changing her role and had to content herself with being an eavesdropper on various kinds of misfortune—at least until Andrea appeared. Suddenly she found herself dissatisfied with merely knowing about someone's case; she realized that she must actively intervene in her own way, not so much because she had by now learned enough about legal matters as because Andrea bore such a striking resemblance to herself.

Lucy was startled the first time she saw the strange girl from her hiding place, thin like herself, big-eyed like herself, and with the same color of hair and eyes. Andrea was barefoot. There was a watchful and precociously wary expression on her face; a sign of premature awareness. On her lap she was holding one of her younger sisters, whose vocabulary seemed to consist of a single squawk. She had come with her mother and was listening attentively, as though she wanted to impress the essentials on her mind just in case she ever had to come to the lawyer on a similar mission, and she was watching for the effect which her mother's words were having, or ought to be having, on the man, while she jerked and shook the little girl to keep her in order. Her mother was a stocky muscular woman, with a black kerchief around her head, a black knitted sweater, a black skirt, faded and aged by the sun, and with a face which would light up suddenly and equally unexpectedly would become overcast again; speaking rapidly, she was trying to tell the man her tale of woe.

Well, her husband was in prison, that was predictable, her Elias, an unusual man, full of bright ideas, ah, nobody could touch him! And his bright ideas were the best protection against unemployment; his whole family was able to live satisfactorily on his bright ideas, including the grandparents, but now he was in prison and his magnificent bright ideas were knocking against prison bars. And what for? Pah, all he'd done was to dye the feathers of common sparrows—and weren't they common enough?—then he put them in cages and sold them as singing birds to tourists down by the harbor just before their ship left. Well, nobody lost very much, did they? And it gave a family enough to eat. Until one day a stranger came along, bought up all the birds, and had them sent on board the ship. He paid with a large bill, and when Elias tried to change it in the bank, he was arrested. It was a trick. A counterfeit. They thought Elias was a member of the gang and took him into custody and so they clipped the wings of all the bright ideas he had for keeping us alive.

While Andrea's mother was going on about her misfortune at great length, Lucy had eyes only for the barefoot girl, who was still expectantly watching the lawyer, but less intently now, her attention had wandered and her eyes were darting around the room, seeing which objects were loose and which were nailed down, and suddenly her brown arm shot out. She snatched two oranges from the glazed fruit dish and hid them under the little girl's clothes.

Lucy had seen it happen but she did not come out, she remained in her hiding place and waited until Andrea had gone off with her mother; then she went after them. Quietly she followed behind them. She made a note of the house with high windows into which the three of them disappeared, peeped at the well-trodden, shady inner courtyard, and on the way home she decided to go back.

She returned with a small shopping bag full of oranges; she waited in the courtyard for a while but no one came out, so she called Andrea's name and soon the girl appeared. She approached suspiciously as Lucy stood there with an embarrassed smile, holding out her hand. "What do you want?" asked Andrea in a hostile voice. Lucy held out the bag toward her, said, "For you," and saw an intense look of doubt and scorn spread over the girl's face, which was so similar to her own. Lucy was trembling, perhaps because she felt that she'd been found out, but perhaps, too, because she hadn't expected such a haughty refusal; and all of a sudden Andrea tugged the bag away and flung it at Lucy's chest with such force that Lucy felt as if someone had struck her. The oranges rolled to the ground.

Andrea went back into the house without a word, but Lucy picked up the oranges, took them to her father's office, and put them on the glazed fruit dish. She felt offended, but although her disappointment lingered in her mind, she did not give up the idea of another attempt and kept thinking what she could bring the girl instead of oranges.

Since she refused to abandon the idea of winning the friendship of the girl who looked so much like herself, she decided to visit her without bringing a present. Before she could carry out her plan, however, Andrea again came to the office with her mother. Lucy was already settled in her hiding place; she shut the door, put a chair in front of it, and was now sitting and watching the strange girl through the keyhole. And then it happened again: as Andrea's mother bent over the desk, took hold of the pen and was shown where and how often she had to sign, the brown arm moved toward the fruit dish, not once but several times, and once more the oranges disappeared under her little sister's clothes. Lucy was pleased, she admired Andrea.

She had to see her the very next day and on the way home from school she went past Andrea's house, peered into the courtyard, then sat down on the step of the house opposite and waited. Andrea was not long in coming; angry and bewildered, she discovered Lucy first.

"What do you want? Why've you come here again?"

"I've been waiting for you," said Lucy.

"Why?"

"People would think we were sisters," said Lucy, "we look alike. Have you noticed how alike we are?"

Andrea laughed scornfully and ran an appraising eye over Lucy's appearance: black buckled shoes, knee socks, pleated skirt, dazzling white shirt blouse. "Us?" she asked. "We look alike?"

Lucy handed her a pocket mirror. "There, take a look and you'll see."

"Get lost," said Andrea.

"Take a look and then I'll give you the mirror."

They were standing facing each other, tense and uncertain, both looking at the mirror lying in Lucy's outstretched hand, almost covering the palm; then Andrea hit Lucy's hand with a sharp upward slap, so quickly that the movement was hardly perceptible. "I don't want anything from you," she said. "Get out of here and take your present with you. Go away and don't ever come back."

Lucy picked up the mirror, which was undamaged, waited until the girl had gone into the house, and then went off to her father's office.

Her father was surprised at the interest that Lucy was suddenly taking in the case of the man who dyed birds and equally surprised at her pleasure when he told her that Andrea's mother would probably be coming to his office a few more times. She almost felt like asking him if he could speed up his handling of the case.

And on the day of the next visit, he was once again surprised when, instead of asking for permission to stay in his consulting room, possibly even beside him, at the desk, Lucy said she wanted to go into the back room and be alone; she didn't want to be "betrayed."

This time, unknown to her father, Lucy had put two coins on the edge of the dish, hidden under some oranges, and she was once more sitting on the chair watching Andrea, seeing as before how intently she stared at Lucy's father; and she was so captivated by Andrea's face that she forgot to pay attention to her fingers. Had she? Hadn't she? Lucy waited hopefully, but no brown arm let go of the struggling child, no clutching fingers reached out toward the fruit dish, however much she may have wanted them to; yet later on Lucy discovered that the coins had vanished as well as some fruit. Then she decided that, for the time being, she would not bring gifts to Andrea at her house, but would simply put everything she wanted to give her on the dish, covered by fruit, and on her next visits she left her candy, the mirror which the girl had knocked out of her hand, and once more a few coins from her own pocket money.

Andrea came with her mother for the last time on the so-called "day of the eagles," when everybody goes out to the hills near the town to fly painted kites. Even Lucy had her kite; she'd painted the parchment herself and stretched it on the frame: green eyes and yellow tongue, breathing fire underneath; and on the day that Andrea was due to come, she brought the kite with her; she did not take it into the office but left it hanging in the hall, tied to the banister by its tail. The fruit dish was empty. Although Andrea came with her mother, she seemed restless and fidgety and left the office early, without saying goodbye and without her little sister, whom she handed over to her mother as she left.

Lucy wanted to go downstairs straightway but forced herself to wait in the back room until the woman had also taken her leave; not till then did she come out and immediately dash down to the hall, where she found that what she had hoped for had happened: the paper kite was no longer there. She ran into the street. There behind the house the kite was climbing barefooted to the hills, its tail trailing in the dust, and a gust of wind pressed the gaily colored paper against the ribs of its frame. Lucy followed the girl as she went up to the hills, where kites were already dangling in the air, supported and flung to and fro by a gusty sea breeze; like strange old birds hovering patiently over their chosen prey, the kites were looking down on the rock-strewn hills through their flashing, wheeling, and, at any rate, many-colored eyes.

As she went up the slope Andrea could already feel the kite trying to escape, tugging and pressing and kicking and fluttering over her head, but she held it tight and carried it to the top of the hill and cast it off into the wind, which immediately bore it away at the end of its waxed string. From a distance Lucy could see the kite rising up, no bigger but wilder and bolder than the others hovering in the air; it even seemed to be soaring higher than all the rest.

She slowly climbed to the top, unnoticed by Andrea, who was having trouble letting out the string and was bracing her feet against a pile of stones in an attempt to keep the bucking kite under control as it strove to free itself completely. The string which she had wound twice around her hand was cutting deeply into her flesh, causing a burning pain each time she let out more slack, but she didn't mind as long as the kite went on climbing until it topped all the others.

Then came a sudden gust, the kite dived downward, went into a spin, and suddenly shot up so irresistibly that Andrea was no longer able to hold it on her own, and without looking to see who was standing behind her, she shouted, "Help me, help me!" In a flash Lucy ran up, sprang toward the taut quivering string, seized hold of it, and after a struggle, leaning their bodies back, the pair of them managed to control the kite. Delighted, they exchanged a look of excited understanding: together they had subdued the kite. No dislike, no suspicion, not even surprise was shown on Andrea's face when she saw Lucy standing beside her, determined and pleased, intent only on hanging on.

They were both holding on to the kite but a second gust flung it spiraling wildly downward, it stalled, spun around, and finally, as if struck by an arrow, it plunged to the ground, striking a pile of stones. They let go of the string and ran up to the fallen kite. The cross-members were shattered; the paper torn. Lucy knelt down, pulled out of the painted piece of paper a broken slat which had pierced it like a broken rib, and as she raised her eyes and was about to show it to Andrea, she found herself looking into a face full of hostility.

"You've followed me again," said Andrea, "it's your fault that my kite crashed."

"I'll repair it," said Lucy, "you can watch."

While she was still on her knees, bewildered by this accusation, Andrea picked up the kite, raised it in both hands, and brought it down so hard over Lucy's head that the paper split and the wooden frame came down around her body. "Don't ever let me see you again," said Andrea. "Never, you hear?" Then she ran off.

Rita Süssfeldt leans back, protrudes her lower lip, and puffs smoke about her face; and now at last there occurs what Heller had long been anticipating: her cigarette, which has gone out, deposits its ash over her thigh; she makes a purely automatic gesture to wipe it off. Well, that was her proposal, an episode from Lucy Beerbaum's childhood, lending itself quite well to interpretation and, in any case, very revealing of the central persona and completely characteristic, because what became plain, didn't it, was the unconscious realization that in certain circumstances a theft is justified. This strange girl Andrea, who, out of a sense of pride, wouldn't accept something as a gift, would be prepared, given the opportunity, to acquire it with her own methods, and Lucy, recognizing the girl's dilemma, if only in-stinctively, endeavors to provide such opportunities. "But I would like to stress that this is an example which I found very quickly on a first reading"; she's certain that, if need be, she can put forward other suggestions.

So shall they start going into details and assess this childhood episode, dot the *i*'s and cross the *t*'s so to speak?

Valentin Pundt grunts and makes a gesture of disagreement; although that example did have possibilities, he would, nevertheless, suggest that they should first consider other episodes because direct comparisons would automatically expose the weaknesses in certain proposals; in saying this he didn't mean, goodness knows, that he considered Lucy Beerbaum's childhood experience weak; he wouldn't like anyone to misunderstand him —only they would surely make quicker progress if each of them made his proposal first and if they then confined themselves to considering what had met with most general approval. Was his colleague Heller not also of that opinion?

His colleague Heller is dehydrated and, as he puts it, he couldn't care less how they get their exemplary life, but he would merely like to say once again: if an anthology was going to bear his name as an editor, then any possible saving of time was completely irrelevant for him. Incidentally, he was in favor, as it was morning, of having the light off now, because it was hurting his eyes and bothering him, not to mention his headache, he adds. So the light is switched off; then Valentin Pundt confesses that he has already read that childhood episode and that it immediately struck him as worth discussing, but later he opted for another episode because in it—however, he doesn't want to anticipate and, above all, to influence anybody, the text must be allowed to speak for itself. Were they ready to listen? Good. The beginning would no doubt have to be rewritten; and then it goes on like this:

. . . at the window, while her mother was noisily changing her clothes, as if the noise would magnify the scolding which she felt compelled to give Lucy. The girl was standing by the window; slim, self-assured, watching the policeman smoking by the garden gate—he was disturbing and scaring away the lizards sleeping in the crevices of the walled gateway—and listening to the content and sequence of her mother's reproaches, not contritely

196

or downcast, but almost entirely in order to note the variations. The ponderous woman went moaning on and on, drawing her attention to advice that had obviously gone unheeded: "How often have I told you? How many times have I warned you . . . ? You knew what the consequences would be when you deliberately tried to mix with other social classes, when you went outside your own milieu. You knew that you could be infected with their ideas. So why didn't you, haven't you, weren't you . . . ? And it's not taken long to get us into a mess: the police. It's the first time a policeman has ever knocked on our door. And your grandfather was commander of the Evzones for a short while. He was a General. He was! But you have to go and help out in a little back room, you spend your holidays with bakers; and now you've learned what happens when you associate with such people."

Lucy turned her face away and smiled: she couldn't detect any variation in her mother's reproaches; they were all her usual accusations and remonstrations which Lucy could have picked up and finished herself; she had had to summon up all her patience to listen to them so often; and she nodded her head as her mother went on talking, not really hearing what she was saying but rather listening to her rehearsing her views, as with sighs and moans she prepared for the second performance, which she had already announced. "Today you'll not be going there on your own, I'm coming with you to that miserable hole, that baker's room where they do more than bake bread, it seems. You won't go with the policeman by yourself. Oh, why did your father have to go away, today of all days?" She was hectoring her reflection in the mirror, suddenly became dissatisfied with her tweed suit and decided on white; white hat, white gloves—where's her white bag?

And now Lucy remarked calmly from where she was standing by the window, "Grandpa wasn't commander of the Royal Guard, Mother, he was going to be, he'd been as good as promised it."

"Well then," said Lucy's mother, embarrassed as well as annoyed, "what difference does it make? Isn't it enough that he was promised it? It's enough for me, heavens above."

Her excited, fleshy face was glistening with sweat; you could see from the careless way she was strapping up her heavy body, doing violence to all her bulges, how strongly she disapproved of all this: Lucy's determination as well as the trend of the times. She whose life for the last few years had consisted of phonograph records and candy, who had grown fat through indulgence and inactivity, Lucy's mother, who had finally retreated into the tottering shell of her past, needed only one word to express her disagreement: "nowadays . . ."

"Shall we go, Mother?" Lucy asked. "Let's go."

The policeman saluted when he saw the woman in white ponderously descending the stone steps, and when he saw Lucy he raised his shoulders to express his regret: I've got my job to do, I can't help it. They walked down the steep street in single file, Lucy's mother in the lead, a wrathful white frigate leaving harbor on a punitive expedition; then the young policeman, with Lucy bringing up the rear and endeavoring all the while to learn more about what had happened or was still happening in the bakery, but the policeman knew only what he had been told to do, and would say no more than "I've been told to take you to Psathas' bakery."

Theodoris Psathas' bakery was easier to reach through the courtyard than through the front entrance of the house, where any new arrival found himself facing a confusing labyrinth of corridors; so Lucy peeled off and went ahead across the shady courtyard. On the walls were fastened racks to place the bread pans on and springy, flour-covered shelves used for cooling the bread. A worm-eaten wheelbarrow with its handles sticking up at an angle, earthenware jugs in which water was evaporating, a worn-out oven door, a pile of fired bricks: this was the inventory of the courtyard which they were now crossing side by side.

"Down the steps," said the policeman.

"Yes," Lucy replied, "I know, I know my way around here."

The steps were messy, covered with a grayish-white layer like

198

all steps leading into bakeries; similarly, the cement floor had a dirty, doughlike covering which would defy any broom and which could only be removed with a scraper. The bakers were standing in front of the oven, in dusty white undershirts and sticky aprons tied in the front: the master baker, Psathas, scared and stooping; Semni, his assistant, with greasy hair and, as usual, chewing grains of wheat; and Stratis, the flabby-lipped apprentice, whose admiring gaze never left the assistant. Opposite them, sitting on a sawhorse, the police superintendent, wearing an open topcoat; beside him, with his notebook and pencil stub at the ready, stood the superintendent's assistant.

From the stillness, the prevailing silence, and the obvious air of patience, it would seem that they had finished with each other or at least had gone through the standard performance and were now waiting for the person who could provide the denouement.

Lucy came in first, but before she even had time to greet the bakers, who, each in his own way, were showing how pleased they were to see her, her mother had pushed past her and was standing between the two camps demanding information and looking challengingly into their faces: "Which one of you is in charge here?" And on the assumption that only age would entitle you to be in charge, she addressed the master baker: "I've only come to tell you once and for all that I disapprove of Lucy's coming here; I can't forbid her to do so, but I disapprove of it. Don't say a word! I warned Lucy, I told her a long time ago what the consequences would be. I hope you can understand where the responsibility lies."

At first Psathas could find nothing to say and then was about to say something, but not without permission from the superintendent—who ignored the baker, slid off the sawhorse, introduced himself to Lucy's mother, and not only made it plain that he was in charge but also explained what had brought him and his companion here. The authorities had for some considerable time been wondering how prisoners in the city jail had come into possession of information and small tools which could have only one purpose; the superintendent had followed the trail, with his officials, and it had led here, to this bakery. Since, rightly or wrongly, the master baker had enjoyed the confidence of the authorities, he had been allowed to supply the prison with bread; news and tools had been baked in the bread: he could prove it.

The fleshy woman looked at Lucy in alarm, gloomily triumphant: now you can see why I advised you not to come and how right I was to warn you. Her painful triumph overcame her suspicion and her indignation, and now that she had been proven right she turned to go up the slippery steps and out to the courtyard. But Lucy went quickly over to the bakers, and after a whispered greeting, stood among them as if she unquestionably belonged with them and was prepared to accept equal responsibility for everything that might involve them. "Come along, Lucy," said the woman; and then to the police superintendent: "You surely don't imagine that my daughter can help you in your inquiries even if by some strange aberration she's been coming here now and again." The superintendent calmed her down: in a second, in a second, just a general question or two, a mere formality.

"You're a student?" he asked Lucy.

"Yes."

"Of biology?"

"I'm studying biology and chemistry."

"And you've occasionally helped here during your vacation?"

"Yes."

"With *your* constitution?"

"Yes."

"May I ask what your work consisted of?"

"Mainly assisting."

"You weren't being paid?"

"No."

"How long have you known Psathas?"

"Since I was twelve."

"And the others?"

"Since I've been helping here."

"And why did you come and help out here?"

"I wanted to know something."

"What about?"

"About the work; the hopes and desires it fulfills and the ones it fails to fulfill."

"And are you satisfied with what you've seen here?"

"No."

"And your studies leave you time to pursue this sort of experience?"

"These experiences provide a justification for my studies," said Lucy.

The superintendent nodded, not because he was in agreement with her answer, but because he seemed to be expecting it; it obviously completed the picture that he had formed of Lucy. "Working at such close quarters," he said, "you're bound to observe things. Did you know that this bakery supplied bread to the prison?"

"Yes."

"And did you also know that other things were being supplied with the bread—information and tools, for instance?"

"Yes," said Lucy, "I knew that."

The superintendent nodded again, as though he had also expected to hear that; he was about to continue his interrogation when Lucy's mother, standing by the exit, burst into a furiously indignant protest: "What are you saying, Lucy? That's not true, Lucy. You'll withdraw that at once." And to the superintendent: "Please, you're not to believe that."

The superintendent made a soothing gesture with his hand and asked Lucy casually, "And you were there when information and tools were being baked in the bread?"

"Yes."

"Perhaps you helped?"

"I did help."

"Why was that?" Lucy made no reply, and the superintendent continued calmly: "Did you have personal reasons? General reasons? Or were you given instructions to do it?"

"General reasons," said Lucy in a low voice, while her mother made tiny gasping noises with her lips as she stood frozen and incredulous.

"Are you prepared to specify your reasons?" asked the superintendent.

"They come from my convictions."

"Well?"

Psathas turned toward Lucy with fear and admiration in his eyes.

"Well?" the superintendent repeated.

"Certain crimes," said Lucy hesitantly, "go beyond the intention of the person who commits them. They become a general misfortune for mankind. With certain crimes we must all feel a sense of identification because they are a reflection of the world and of economic conditions."

This confession did not seem to surprise the superintendent; he said quietly, "Yes, under certain circumstances a crime can become necessary. What sort of circumstances did you have in mind?"

"When someone is deprived of basic essentials, then a crime can lead to a new chance in life."

"According to that," said the superintendent, "you believe that certain crimes are justified?"

"Yes."

"And that certain culprits, who could be rehabilitated, are unjustly detained?"

"Yes, I think that."

"And so, because of these beliefs, you helped to supply information and tools to the prison?"

"Those were my reasons," said Lucy.

The superintendent walked thoughtfully over to the door and then spun around suddenly and looked closely at Lucy: the fragile, almost sickly girl, splendid in her certainty; the narrow shoulders; the light, slender body that seemed unfit for any exertion; then he went slowly up to her and, in the same tone as before, asked, "And you're convinced that there are many people in our prisons who need your help?"

202

"Yes, many of them."

"Although they've committed a crime?"

"Although they did something that in some peculiar way we've agreed to describe as a crime," said Lucy, "and perhaps our help ought to begin by redefining what a crime is."

"In your opinion that hasn't been done?"

"No," said Lucy. "A crime at a desk or in a conference room is shrugged off, but we're not willing to show sympathy for a crime caused by poverty or passion."

The superintendent nodded, apparently satisfied, as though to put an end to the interrogation—had he been expecting these replies? In the course of, at a rough estimate, some thirty years' service, had he often heard them? Now that he knew or had had his view confirmed, the only thing that now interested him was the tool. He asked Lucy, "The tool that you were smuggling into the prison—would you describe it to us?"

Lucy, taken aback, exchanged a glance with Psathas and his assistant, Semni; she stood very still and screwed up her eyes.

"What did the tool look like?" asked the superintendent.

"It was to help prisoners to escape," said Lucy. Her mother gave a loud wail, covered her face in her hands, and shook her head incredulously.

"Well, what tools were they?" asked the superintendent patiently, and as Lucy remained silent for longer than usual and then merely repeated her previous answer, he touched Lucy's mother on the shoulder and said, in an official sympathetic voice, "You may go now, both of you, thank you"; and to Lucy: "You've helped me comply with the formalities."

Nonplussed, Lucy walked toward him; less because she was relieved than because she was unhappy about the situation: whereas this was the end for her and, to all appearances, she was to suffer no consequences, for the bakers, or at least for one of them, it was by no means over, since the superintendent now went back to the sawhorse on which he had been sitting when they came in. And as if he had detected Lucy's disappointment and understood what she wanted, he added with a smile as he

203

dismissed her, "I might be needing your help again; if so, I'll call on you."

Still bewildered, Lucy took her leave of the bakers, gave the superintendent a curt nod, and followed her mother, who, still in the throes of spasmodic chewing motions, was stumbling along as if she were balancing a heavy load, all the while directing a high-pitched moan toward the crumbling walls. Deaf to any appeal, solely concerned with what had just happened, she was completely unaware whether Lucy was walking beside or behind her; swaying, she dragged herself up the street in the meager shade and allowed Lucy to lead her through the garden and into the house. She must lie down. She must have her anisette and then lie down. Lucy slipped off her mother's shoes, turned the maternal mass onto its side, and unbuttoned the dress, releasing hooks and eyes, coldly and unemotionally loosening laces and straps and zippers until all the bumps and bulges were relaxed and had collapsed once more into bearable flaccidity. Lucy sat on the edge of the couch, picked up the warm plump hands, and massaged the hollows and joints, answering her mother's still bemused look with an expression of superiority and certainty, as if to say: Don't worry, there's nothing for you to be afraid of.

The woman gathered her strength and launched into a hug— albeit rather a panic-stricken one, which didn't quite come off, which, indeed, rather resembled an attempt to put Lucy into a half nelson, and during this rough caress she moaned, "Why, Lucy? Why? Why do you always have to take such risks in everything?" She let herself fall back and stared at the ceiling. "Sooner or later," she said in a low voice, "people like that have the police down on them."

"Listen, Mother," said Lucy, "you must believe me: no information got into the prison through anything I did, no information and no tools either."

"No? But you admitted it! And you explained your reasons."

"You were there," said Lucy, "they weren't impressed by my reasons."

"But why on earth did you do it then?"

"They can't afford to be out of work, none of them. The baker himself can't, because he has to look after his wife; the apprentice can't, because he's supporting half his family; and Semni, the assistant—he's had to take on a responsibility that will keep him tied down for a long time, an obligation from which he can't release himself."

"You seem to know a lot about it," said her mother with a worried air.

"It's because I do that I had to say what I did; I volunteered because I can afford to do it more easily than any of them, and because Daddy would have helped me. Do you know why Semni is working in the bakery instead of being in prison, as he really should be? Because his family's council decided that one of Semni's brothers, who was unemployable, should take responsibility for what had happened and go to prison so that Semni himself could work."

"Don't you realize what you're asking us to do?" moaned the woman, and her head drooped sideways.

"We're asking more from other people," said Lucy.

"Oh, you're ungrateful," said the woman, "you're so ungrateful."

Toward the end Valentin Pundt, who has been reading faster and faster, and stumbling increasingly over the words, jumps suddenly to his feet: has he been stung or bitten or perhaps pinched? He jumps up so abruptly and noisily that Rita Süssfeldt looks at him in alarm and Heller is roused from his undisguised lethargy; yes, something serious must have befallen him, for he gives no explanation, sticks both hands simultaneously into the pockets of his old smoking jacket, fumbles about in search of something, and finally produces a paper handkerchief, from which he tears off a corner no larger than a snowflake—obviously to stick onto a tiny wound. The irritated schoolmaster, whom nobody dares interrupt, finds the small scrap of paper too thick and with well-directed puffs manages to blow its layers apart, until the single pieces are even as light as a snowflake, and then carries them on the palm of his hand toward the radiator: a twirl and then here, into the conference room itself, November has come, it's snowing in here, too, if only artificially and for the purposes of experiment. Pundt is observing the scraps of paper drifting around the radiator, crouching lower and lower to keep level with them as they float down, and suddenly he thrusts out a vigilant forefinger: "Here it is, that's where it's coming from."

"A draft?" inquires Rita Süssfeldt with relief.

"A gale," says Pundt, "it's practically unbearable, we're jeopardizing our health."

"It's high time that education had some martyrs, too," says Heller, "perhaps we'll all manage to catch something together. In that case, I'd like to propose the following inscription for our tombstone: 'They gave their lives in the cause of an eternal essay topic. In search of an exemplary life. Honor their memory while continuing their search.'"

Rita Süssfeldt laughs and pushes the pack of cigarettes over to Heller while Pundt kneels down in front of the radiator and shreds off pieces of the paper handkerchief to plug up the crevices beside the pipes. "And the old builders have such a wonderful reputation," says Pundt bitterly, "but I assure you that in those days construction was even worse, both in terms of the materials and in terms of the care they took." Would he like to go on reading now? asks Heller. No, he'd finished, he'd just come to the end of his sample, the last part was rather rushed and he would like to apologize for that. Mistrustfully Pundt waves his open hand in front of the place where the pipe disappeared into the wall: "That's better now, that'll do, and now I'm ready."

To the amazement of his colleagues, Heller now states that he would like to make a statement of principle; Heller, who'd been listening without interest and with a pained expression on his face, is not afraid, at this juncture, to open his heart: well, he thinks the two samples that had just been read were more acceptable than any previous ones, they were more topical and authentic and, yes, more questionable in the best sense of the word. Lucy Beerbaum's career seemed to be a real treasure trove for educators—and he didn't mean that in any derogatory way; all you had to do was put in your hand and pull out a plum, ripe for anthologizing. That was not Lucy's fault, in fact, but Johannes Stein's, whose book *The Price of Hope* had provided both examples —samples which led him to wonder whether they hadn't been over-elaborated, too well "dressed up," he was worried because a real life had ended up as a story, as a memorable tale, and as a result it was open to the suspicion of having been manipulated. However useful the text might seem, he would like to issue a warning that such a risk existed, and to obviate this risk, to avoid any suspicion of anything of that sort arising, he had opted for something else, for a real find that he had made in a periodical.

Pundt smiles; after a whole life of teaching (now almost finished) he finds such scruples exaggerated. "Every life ends up as a story, my dear colleague," he says, "and I'm not scared of stories, since they are that part of us that survives; in addition, everyone who wants to make people aware of anyone else's life is bound to add something of his own to it. What you call 'dressing up' is only helping to serve the truth."

Is Rita Süssfeldt going to agree? No, she wants merely to pin down what now needs to be examined, to sum it up under headings. "Well, there's Lucy's childhood experience—which can be summarized as legitimate theft—and then there's Herr Pundt's proposal, which by general agreement we can sum up as the opportunity for personal sacrifice; shouldn't our colleague Heller make his suggestion now, so that . . ." He should and will. Let's arrange it like this, then: Heller is to produce his example for comparison with the previous ones, and afterward they'll see. Everyone agreed? Everyone's agreed.

Heller is already thumbing through the magazine but wants first to make a point: If they were to agree on his proposal, it would be necessary to write a short introduction, since what he was going to read presupposed some knowledge of Lucy Beerbaum's life. He would skip certain time factors, dates and events, chronology, normal sequence; that wasn't what really concerned him; that was also why when he was slicing his way through Lucy Beerbaum's life he hadn't started from scratch; he'd branched off in various directions, crossways, so to speak. The provisional title: "Simultaneously." "May I draw your attention to the fact," says Heller, "that in this case one thing throws light on others, a personal decision mirrors general conditions, and so on. After a short introduction, then, this is how it would read:"

While, in her home in Hamburg, the biologist Lucy Beerbaum was creating an artificial state of captivity to which she then consistently and voluntarily submitted herself, a West German Chancellor, despite serious qualms, opened a letter from the East German Minister-President and managed to read it to the end. While, in order to manifest her solidarity with her Greek colleagues who had been placed in preventive detention by a military government, Professor Lucy Beerbaum was accepting all the external conditions of voluntary captivity, the National Bank of Germany lowered its discount rate to three percent, whereupon all the banks rushed to put their liquid assets into fixed-interest securities. While Lucy Beerbaum, without knowing how this captivity would end, was deciding to undertake her practical demonstration of sympathy, in West Germany consideration was being given to finding emergency accommodation for prisoners to relieve the current shortage of prison space. While Lucy Beerbaum was granting a three-minute interview to a deputation from her Institute—they were quietly trying to persuade her to give up her voluntary captivity on the grounds that she was indispensable to the Institute—abstract paintings and cuckoo clocks were being shown to the American President, who happened to be in West Germany at that time: he decided to take some cuckoo clocks back to the States with him. While Lucy Beerbaum was listening to her housekeeper Johanna giving notice for the second time—Johanna was hoping through this maneuver to bring her mistress's voluntary ordeal to an end—on the square in front of the Rathaus you could listen to the band of a naval squadron anchored in the port, consisting of submarines, a tender, and the inevitable minesweepers. While, after a week of voluntary captivity, Lucy Beerbaum suffered a fainting spell, the police authorities issued an optimistic statement regarding the vehicular accident rate: only six hundred eighty-four accidents had been reported. When the professor of biology Lucy Beerbaum, holder of the French Palmes Académiques, member of the Soviet, British, and French Academies of Science, learned from a reporter that her protest had received scant attention in Greece, she seemed neither surprised nor discouraged. On that same day, she insisted that a previously scheduled birthday party for her niece Ilse should not be canceled, although she herself did not attend. While Lucy Beerbaum caught Johanna secretly trying to improve her strictly measured food ration, in Hamburg a liter of milk cost seventy-six pfennigs, a roll of bread ten or twelve pfennigs, while an oyster cost from one mark sixty to two marks eighty, depending on size. While Lucy Beerbaum, since no one could persuade her to give up, went on with her demonstration, the Egyptian President announced a Holy War and the final struggle against Israel, after dismissing the United Nations peace-keeping forces; no one thought that it would come to war. While Lucy Beerbaum was inventing a new way of expressing sympathy, an interested public read about the death certificate of a German Chancellor (ret.) which had not stated his profession properly: Member of the West German Parliament—the title of German Chancellor (ret.) not being an adequate description of a profession. While the biologist Lucy Beerbaum was considering it necessary to react to a *coup d'état* in her native country— privately but consistently, persistently but amateurishly—a marriage advertisement appeared in a Hamburg newspaper asking for a wife with the following qualities: "As fresh by day as by night, straight out of a bath of Fenjal *crème,* as elegant as a Bach fugue, as tender and burning as a steak *flambé au whisky,* as darkly sweet as Turkish coffee from Dalmatia; private means would not be unwelcome." While the scientist Lucy Beerbaum was deciding to draw attention to the misfortune that had befallen her Greek friends and colleagues, the heir to a worldwide chain of hotels declared that his executives had already worked out plans to build a hotel on the moon; there would be wall-size television screens and a cocktail lounge; as for the rest, everything would be the same as on earth. While Lucy Beerbaum was accepting her voluntary captivity, the new government of her native land was enumerating its reasons for seizing power: these included "the deplorable and unscrupulous haggling between the parties; the impudence of a large part of the press; the systematic attacks on the foundations of the state."

Heller has just reached this point and seems almost to have finished—Rita Süssfeldt deduces this from the fact that his fore-finger is resting on the manuscript some five lines from the end of the passage, reminding him to go thus far only—when, to-gether with his colleagues, he turns toward the door, which has been opened cautiously, indeed, but nevertheless noisily: and there stands Mike Mitchner. He's standing embarrassed, in his tight suede trousers and in his frilly pink shirt which peeps out from beneath his fur-trimmed jacket; he's holding the tip of his finger between his teeth as if he had scalded himself; by this gesture, as well as by assuming an expression of mock fear, he is trying to apologize for disturbing them.

"Neidhart," says Heller in surprise as he greets his ex-pupil, who is trying to justify his unannounced arrival: he'd waited outside, rung the bell, called out without succeeding in attracting any attention; and so he'd taken it on himself to start looking. "May I introduce my old pupil, Neidhart Zoch, better known perhaps as Mike Mitchner—the idol, I may say, of some hundred thousand maladjusted people—this is Frau Dr. Süssfeldt."

"How do you do."

"And Herr Pundt you do know, I believe?"

"Yes, we know each other from the show the other day."

"As you can see, Neidhart, we're hard at work concocting a splendid anthology; I didn't expect you to call so early."

"Doesn't matter," says Neidhart, "I'll wait outside and read the German hotel trade journal. It's something I've always wanted to do."

"We may be quite a long time," says Heller.

"Doesn't matter," says the singer, "there's a whole pile of journals in the vestibule." Suddenly he walks over to Pundt and puts an envelope down in front of him. "We were talking about Harald, do you remember?"

"Yes, of course," Pundt replies, taken aback.

"Here are a few letters Harald wrote at various times. I suppose the last one will interest you most, it must have been written shortly before that happened to him; it may even be his last letter."

Pundt stands up, is about to say something, raises his hand as though expecting a few words to spring from it, a few words that even if they didn't mean much would at least match his gesture, but before he can make any utterance Neidhart is being led, arm in arm with his former teacher, to the door, and upon reaching it he asks Pundt to let him have the letters back sometime and he leaves the conference room with a soft-shoe shuffle.

"Mike Mitchner," says Heller with emphasis, and with a wink at Rita Süssfeldt: "If we don't strike oil with Lucy Beerbaum, we can always come back to him, the most gifted pop singer we've got and lord and master of a rapturous community."

"Won't you read on," asks Rita Süssfeldt, "just the last few sentences?" Heller shakes his head, he doesn't want to pursue the matter, because as he was reading aloud he noticed that this series of sentences didn't really produce the tension which he'd felt on his first reading and in addition, as he is now ready to admit, they seem to him too deliberately cut off from the ramifications of the actual happening: congealed moments which might possibly throw light on an event but which are not sufficient to show how the event came to take place. And that was exactly the point: to define the elements, the motives, and the influences that were responsible for an event. He would like to withdraw his first suggestion. Herewith. He would provide other examples. Moreover, he asks them to consider whether they were doing Lucy Beerbaum justice by prematurely agreeing on one period without viewing the whole rich range of her biography, to start with, anyway. "Isn't that the least we must do?" he asks Pundt and himself. "Don't we owe it to her?" Heller need not explain his doubts further because the old schoolmaster has already nodded his acquiescence to the first question.

13

Never before has Janpeter Heller heard a car horn like this one: first, as though clearing its throat, it gives a croak and expectorates; it then produces a challenging, melodious, flutelike note not unworthy of a song thrush, finally modulating to the contented lowing of a cow. In the spacious parking area between the tower apartments, Mike Mitchner twice activates his horn and, as always, is filled with pleasure at the sight of bewildered and frightened pedestrians who could have sworn they heard a cow mooing and now look around to see where she is. He waves toward the twelfth floor, where, unlike Heller, he has glimpsed a face at a window: the message is received, his arrival has been noted. "Let's go, Herr Heller." They cross a deserted children's playground, walk past some trees firmly anchored with taut guy ropes, past some bronze figures—"Child Rolling a Hoop," "A Young Gooseherd"—which are being washed down by the chilly sleet. They make their way to the main entrance, battling against the gusts of wind, past the row of brightly lit drugstores, shoestores, and delicatessens. "We're nearly there—watch out, that's a glass door. . . . Who's monopolizing the elevator?" Mike Mitchner presses the button and keeps it pressed but is unsuccessful in bringing the elevator down; it descends to the second floor, only to shoot straight up to the thirteenth, up and down, as if it were a shuttle service or—this seems more probable—an office on the move. They walk up to the second floor—where Mike Mitchner manages to catch the elevator, in which two worried-looking little girls are squatting on the floor in front of a white cardboard box. "What on earth are you up to?"

"Good morning, Herr Mitchner, we saw you on television," the little girls say. At the bottom of the box, half covered with lettuce leaves, there is a tortoise. "His name is Albert," the girls say, "and he isn't feeling well, because he hasn't been eating, and so we're taking him up and down in the elevator. You can hold him if you want." Both of them, Mike Mitchner and his former teacher, give the tortoise a good-humored prod, express the hope that he will soon recover his appetite, and then get out at the twelfth floor.

There's a door without a nameplate, that must be his, thinks Heller, but although not unexpected, nonetheless this unremarkable, standard-sized matte door seems hardly appropriate for Mike Mitchner's apartment—surely a door made of brightly colored panes of glass or a curtain of rustling strips of tin foil would have been more suitable? "Please go in—and once again, glad you could come." "Thank you," says Heller, "thank you," and he allows himself to be propelled wonderingly across the hall into a large bright room: no posters on the walls, no pictures, no flowers, nothing to give warmth or life or to gather dust, nothing to persuade you to stay, nothing, even, to invite you to make comparisons; instead, nothing but glass surfaces on metal frames, metal fittings and supports, plastic furniture, white and indifferent, a transparent glass clock, a glass bookshelf on top of which, to Heller's astonishment, there lies an old pair of binoculars. Between these white hospital walls you would expect a white coat to be the appropriate dress, and had someone come and forced him into a white coat and tied a sterile white gauze face mask over his mouth, Heller would have accepted it without a murmur as a concession to the room.

Over there a life-size celluloid doll, with long hair and long eyelashes, is sitting looking vacantly at the brass-colored innards of the clock—no, it's moving, it's standing up of its own accord and producing, specially for Mike's benefit, a parsimonious but unmistakable smile. Even Jürgen Klepatsch, who is resting his bent leg on the windowsill, interrupts his search for a kingdom in four letters, drops his crossword puzzle, and greets the new arrivals with a smile. "Well, you both know my old school-teacher, I've invited him in for a bite to eat, I hope you've got something to offer us. This is Herr Heller and this is Jürgen Klepatsch and Tamara."

"Sardines," says Klepatsch, "we've got cans and cans of sardines."

"But we used to have some soups," says Mike, "crab and oxtail and eel and onion soups—what's happened to all the soups?"

"Tamara," says Klepatsch, making a gesture more of explanation than reproach, "Tamara lives exclusively on soup."

"Then we'll get something from the delicatessen, and lots of potato chips. But first let's have something to drink, apple juice of course." They drink apple juice laced with spirits and Mike Mitchner shows his former teacher around the apartment, expatiating on the advantages of coolness and bareness; the stimulation provided by a lack of decoration was in his opinion the only thing suitable for contemporary society and even the only true expression of it; he admires its concrete utopias as much as its harsh trivialities.

"Do you remember once saying, Herr Heller, that trivialities are more honest than any metaphysics?"

"Doesn't sound too bad," says Heller, "and what's more, I still think the same as I did then. But I wonder if I can ask you what those field glasses over there are for and why you've given them such a place of honor." As he speaks he picks them up from the bookshelf, puts them to his eyes, and immediately takes them away, surprised, for in the glasses the house opposite appeared in a field of dark-red light. "Night glasses?"

"Yes," says Mike, "night glasses, a friend gave them to me as a present—Harald Pundt, incidentally, the son of your collaborator. Binoculars with a story attached to them."

"You know he's dead?"

"Yes."

"And you know that it was suicide, after he'd taken his examinations?"

214

"Yes, I know. We lived together for a while, a long time ago, when I was a protest singer. Poor guy, he used to spend a lot of his time in a kind of ecstasy; he would dream of trying out new ways of protesting; even suicide seemed to him justified in order to draw attention to social evils."

"Does his father know that?" Heller asks.

"I've never really talked to him," Mike says, "at least not about that."

Janpeter Heller puts the glasses to his eyes again and looks at the many windows in the wall of the neighboring house. "Russian," Mike Mitchner says, "they're Russian binoculars. Harald's father brought them back after the war, as a souvenir of an unfortunate incident. One day at dawn, out in no-man's-land, presumably in a fog, old Pundt fell into a water hole which someone else had already fallen into earlier, a Russian soldier, in fact, who welcomed him with a grin, up to his knees in water. They had to spend the whole day in each other's company, both of them armed—what a day that must have been for them; they couldn't talk to each other, they didn't dare sleep, they couldn't risk looking the other way, and it wasn't until night fell that they helped each other out. When they parted, they exchanged field glasses. Harald gave them to me more or less as a symbolic gift."

Mike takes the binoculars out of Heller's hand, carefully winds the thin leather strap around his knuckles, and listens to Jürgen Klepatsch talking in a flat voice on the phone in the next room —the phone is on the floor—trying, with remarkable economy of words, to disclaim any knowledge of Mike Mitchner, while at the other end he is not being believed. He protests, he gives his word, he repeats himself so irritably and with such practiced ease that suspicion is bound to be aroused.

"Who is it?" asks Mike in an undertone.

Klepatsch, covering up the mouthpiece, tells him, "Some stupid department store, Hillmeyer and something, you're supposed to be signing autographs, there are hundreds of people waiting."

"Tell them I'm on my way."

So quickly can Mike Mitchner make a decision. He's going to

drive over, perform his duty, then come back straightway, with the ingredients for a really chic menu, as he calls it. He asks Heller to bear with him, to be understanding. Meanwhile Heller can make himself cozily at home here—and Mike really means cozy; Tamara will help him there, he can listen to some music, relax, perhaps have a bath; there were all kinds of things he could do. All those people waiting there, perhaps some of them might have come a long way, they'd given up their time for him; so Mike Mitchner couldn't let them down, he couldn't let them wait there all alone, he would have to go.

"How lonely are they?" asks Heller with gentle irony.

"Very lonely," says Mike, "and so they have a claim on me; in any case, the arrangement was made a long time ago."

"And you have the impression that they need you?"

"Yes, I really think they do."

Now Klepatsch appears from the next room waving a piece of paper. "Well, here it is: the thing's at Hillmeyer and Knokke's, whose palatial premises are on Mönckebergstrasse. We go to the furniture department and while Mike is scribbling away they're going to inflate pieces of furniture."

"Furniture?" Heller asks with interest. "Inflatable furniture? I'd like to see that."

"Then let's all go; Tamara can come too," Mike says, "provided we can all get into the car."

They board the hard-sprung little car, not exactly tying themselves into knots but squeezing together to save space, with a leg stretched around here and an arm sticking out horizontally there; and not by way of complaint but merely to discover whether the cool, long-limbed, odorless Tamara can speak, Heller remarks on the faulty structure of the human body and inquires whether she hadn't on occasion had thoughts about possible improvements. Tamara doesn't quite grasp what he's saying; she gasps, "I don't understand what you mean." Well, at least she can speak, thinks Heller, and he points out how useful it would be if in particular circumstances people could screw off certain limbs or unhook them and take them off; now, for example. "Or in bed," says

Mike. "Or on the Millerntor football field." Tamara opens her pouting mouth, which is never quite closed, and states, with another gasp, that she really can't understand, because your legs and arms grow onto you, whereupon Mike not only agrees but also approves of the way she always looks for the logic behind the facts, the hard and fast facts. Heller would like to take that up and under the stimulus of his irritation pursue it further, but one glance at Tamara's profile, at this drooping face, makes him afraid that, not having understood him thus far, she will understand him even less well now; but he does feel he has to do something, at least get something off his chest.

"So it's an autograph session?" he inquires.

Passing a streetcar, Mike replies, "Department stores are doing that sort of thing now, to kill two birds with one stone."

"And what do they do with your autograph?" Heller asks. "I mean, do they carry it around with them or frame it or use it as a bookmark or do they eat it with sugar and cinnamon, like a eucharist from the body of their Lord?"

"They exchange them with one another," says Mike, rather at a loss, "they exchange them and sell them as well."

"So it's the profit motive," says Heller, "even these looted relics are only used as a means of increasing their profits. You see what a pernicious instinct your community is motivated by: not even the objects of their adoration are exempt from barter and you're encouraging inflation by flooding the market with your autograph."

"At our old school," Mike says, "the going price is three bars of chocolate for one of my autographs."

"Doesn't that sort of barter make you wonder?" asks Heller. "Cocoa, milk, and sugar, that's what you're worth, perhaps with a few bits of chopped nuts thrown in. That's your contribution to social enlightenment and greater critical awareness."

As he's speaking, Janpeter Heller feels a sense of relief, a grim satisfaction as he yields to the cold pleasure of getting his revenge for something which he himself couldn't even define at that moment: the phony invitation for a bite to eat, the bodies pressing against his own, or his former pupil's views, which annoy him all the more because they're being delivered with such self-assurance. "You were saying, Neidhart, that they need you because they're lonely. But what do they need you for? To lead them through the Red Sea? Out of Hamelin town in Brunswick to fall into the welcoming river Weser? What do they see in you? What role are they giving you in this private drama they've composed for you of their own free will? Let's assume they're taking you as their idol. They would like to resemble you, emulate you, imitate you. But do they know what kind of a person you really are? How much information do they actually have about you? You've been taught to ask questions—don't you sometimes ask yourself the reason for this mock alliance? What they really want is to abdicate, to escape, to hand over their responsibilities as they go in. They need a flame to warm their dreams which have gone stiff with cold, their dream of rejection and withdrawal and union in a mysterious landscape. And you fan that flame, you burst open the door hung with flowers and behind it they find something which they haven't in the least deserved—in a word, oblivion. You're the high priest with a guitar preaching the cheap religion of oblivion; isn't that rather inadequate? Do you realize what you're protecting them from? You're driving them into a Garden of Eden and preventing them from seeing the things that need altering." Heller stops talking and reflects on what he has just said: wasn't his conclusion too harsh?

Tamara is trying to keep her distance, to avoid any further contact with him. She keeps tugging at the hem of her shiny white plastic jacket to pull it down over her thighs, while staring straight ahead at Mike's unwashed neck. She wants Heller to realize how much she feels involved in his comments. What about Mike? Mike emits a good-humored snort as a request for attention and then says, "I get it, Mr. Schoolmaster, we can do whatever we like but it's no good unless we have a proper awareness of what we're doing. Is that it? As far as I'm concerned, all I really want to do is make music, if you know what I mean. But if you insist that some sort of awareness is absolutely essential, perhaps you can recommend one to me? My favorite color's yellow—even at the risk of disappointing you."

This is how they talk. This is how they show themselves off to each other. This is how they often clashed in class, by devious paths, for modest historical reasons, pursuing the echo of a name, of an idea or a deed—Heller had seen to it that opinions were divided so that the class would be split into opposing camps and he thought it was a promising sign when famous characters were toppled, when opinions were formed under pressure and indecisiveness finally prevailed. At this moment, Heller and his former pupil seem to recall those days; they both laugh.

And now they've reached Hillmeyer and Knokke's, a dreary temple dedicated to the consumer society; you're allowed to get into and out of your car: but what about parking it? Tamara volunteers to drive it to the multi-level parking garage nearby, she'll join them later, now all of you get out. Through a wall of hot air at the entrance, squeezing into a stream of wet coats, pushing, waiting hesitantly, threatened by umbrellas, molested at knee level by shopping bags, submerged in a flood of music, they find their way unrecognized into the store; nobody bows to them or waves to them; that doesn't often happen to Mike.

They can't break away, so they let themselves be carried along to "Belts, Buttons, and Zippers," where the flood disperses, and you can peel off and identify yourself, to this haughty, incredibly bored salesgirl, for example.

"Here we are," Mike says, and waits for the customary outburst of enthusiasm.

The salesgirl eyes Mike reprovingly. "May I help you?" she asks.

Mike is unprepared for this kind of a welcome, so he doesn't object when Jürgen Klepatsch answers for him: "May you help us? We want the manager, girlie, right away and make it snappy. Tell him that Mike Mitchner has just entered his store."

As the expression on her face suggests, the salesgirl is plainly used to being addressed only in respectful terms, and is unable to conceal her distaste at being spoken to in this fashion; she hesitates and then stalks solemnly over to a colleague, whispers to her, indicates the little group with a glance—they're over there —and now Mike's normal expectations are fulfilled: there's the convulsive smile, the embarrassed, what one may describe as the sidling, approach: "Good morning, Herr Mitchner, you're already . . . May I show you . . . We'll take this elevator, it's not for customers. After you, please, gentlemen, we go up to the fifth floor, to the furniture department."

And here is the furniture department, they've rearranged it specially for him. In front of a low rope which cordons off an area of the department, a man whose face is familiar to many from the television screen is holding a microphone at an angle in front of his mouth, as if he wanted to drink out of it, and walking up and down asking the tightly packed, damp and perspiring crowd witty questions about their relationship to furniture: How old is their couch? How many positions are possible in their favorite chair? "He's trying to make people furniture-conscious," Mike Mitchner whispers to his former teacher as he works his way toward the rope barrier. The objects lying on the cordoned-off square of parquet flooring could have been mistaken for the cleaned, prepared, and then dyed organs and offal of large animals or at least for the limp integuments of such organs: brown kidneys, yellow pericardia, skins shaped like spleens and livers, large intestines, appendixes, flabby rust-red stomach linings—all with a dull sheen and carefully displayed, like a bag of game after a hunt.

This impression of high-class butchery which has achieved the peak of its artistic ambitions is strengthened by the six blond girls dressed in short white tunics and forage caps who are standing along the wall—salesgirls or hostesses or whatever you want to call them, they are all set to leap forward as soon as the demonstration begins. But first Mike Mitchner must be publicly welcomed: "Mike—despite all the many calls on his time—Mike has agreed to make an appearance, and all of you, ladies and gentlemen, whether on the radio or television or on records," etc., etc. . . . And the man with the microphone vigorously shakes Mike's hand. "Hello, Mike, nice to see you." By comparison, the official welcome for the singer seems rather flat and amateurish. It's made by a bald old man with sagging cheeks whose name is either Hillmeyer or Knokke, Mike doesn't notice which; whoever he is, he looks as though he might well have liquidated his partner.

"What shall we play today then, Gunnar?" Mike asks hypocritically, and the man with the microphone makes a broad, expansive, lingering gesture, almost a gesture of benediction, toward the many-shaped and many-colored sheaths and skins and says, " 'Premiere.' Here is the furniture of the future. It's having its premiere today." An encouraging wave of the hand to the blond assistants, and the six girls, who fulfill almost all the requirements of shopwindow dummies, walk over to the bags and covers with standardized smiles, seize some air pumps that have been placed there in readiness, the type you can work with your foot, attach the short tubes to the valves, and begin to pump; not at random but straightening up in unison, they put their feet in unison on the pumps, and listen with concentrated attention for the order to start. And now, as Mike's first hit booms out from a loudspeaker—"The bench is empty, the chairs are empty too" —in unison they begin to tread with their feet, that is to say, to pump, cheerfully of course, playfully of course, because even the act of inflating must seem to be a rewarding and indeed pleasurable process.

Heller pushes his way to the front. The girls are pumping in rhythm, sticking out their little bottoms, giving their bodies a forward tilt which they counteract by bracing their right foot. Heller has now reached the cordon. The air is being forced, hissing, into the skins, bags, and covers, expanding them and blowing them up. With sharp gasps, something is coming alive, stirring, awakening from its state of flabby limpness, and bulging upward.

A woman with a bag of potatoes and herself possessing a cheerful potato-dumpling face can't restrain her laughter any longer; a high-pitched breathless laugh which sets others laughing, too. Heller pats the woman on the back, but she doesn't seem to notice and, obviously under the powerful compulsion of memories impossible to express in words, points to the swelling skins, now becoming tauter and bigger as they vibrate under the relentless pressure of the air and gradually assume their predetermined shapes.

Heller has long since abandoned his first impression that these swelling, rearing objects might be extraordinary kinds of organs; at present these monsters, still uncertain what shape they will adopt as they are steadily pumped up by the indefatigable efforts of the six girls, seem to him like particularly clumsy sex symbols, as tyrannical as they are menacing. More and more of the spectators are starting to laugh. People are nudging each other and pointing to those of the swellings and stretchings and bulges which are particularly suggestive. The girls keep on pumping and smiling: See how effortless it is! Well, they're certainly sexual organs, thinks Heller, but what sort of creatures can they belong to and what part of the body can they be attached to so as to be more or less meaningful, that is to say, capable of use?

"You're witnessing, ladies and gentlemen . . . ," says the man with the microphone, "here, in front of your eyes, you can see the birth of the furniture on which we shall all shortly be sitting and lying. The furniture of the future. Inflatable furniture. Note how little effort is involved. And observe how form is created out of formlessness. All with the aid of air. And, of course, conceived and planned by an artist. Now, my dear Mike, perhaps you would also like to say a few words, because you've got many admirers here, I can see a few autograph albums already."

Mike Mitchner takes hold of the microphone, throws a quick glance toward Heller, who is following him with rapt attention, and then: Although no expert, he says, he doubts that very many members of the public are really furniture-conscious in their lives. In other words, too many people put up with old furniture; they don't object if their legs go to sleep in chairs that have been glued together without thought or consideration; they don't complain if they get pressure spots from lying on cheap, shoddy beds, or if their vertebrae protest whenever they're sitting in certain

222

chairs which may well cut off the blood supply to the brain. Furniture-conscious: by that he means turning pieces of furniture into friends and companions who can help us in many ways. "And doesn't everything of importance in our lives take place *on furniture?* Yes, indeed. For that reason, people like yourselves must examine closely what you're lying on, sitting on, drinking coffee on, writing letters on, and adding up your bills on. Well, so much for my general remarks. As far as this particular exhibition is concerned, Gunnar, it seems to me that lots of surprising things are happening. I keep asking myself what these stout little fellows here remind me of; anyway, they don't seem exactly unfamiliar to us, do they?"

The girls are now pumping more slowly to the tune of "The Last Waltz"—this doesn't mean, however, that any sign of fatigue has become apparent, it's intended rather to give the spectators a chance to see how the different pieces of furniture are filling out and assuming their intended shapes—shapes that can, of course, be reproduced indefinitely. The nature of some of them can already be accurately determined: a settee, a chair, a mushroom-shaped table; though one well-padded fellow, who looks like an egg provided with an arm, is for the moment refusing to reveal his identity. What now?

In unison the girls stop pumping, unscrew the tubes from the valves—surely they've earned some applause?—yes, they're now receiving some rather faint applause and they take their bow standing beside the results of their labors. Now the man with the microphone pushes "dear Mike" toward the inflated friends and companions of our lives and asks him to try them out by lying and sitting on them on behalf of all of us; tell us how it feels. Mike sits down, sprawls, bends, stretches, bounces up and down a little: how does it feel? Well, the first impression is that you've sat down in a bowl of pudding; then you snuggle down and finally you have the feeling—how can he express it exactly—that your body is being caressed by the chair.

"May we try it, too?" asks a tieless young man from the crowd; he is immediately applauded. Everyone may and everyone shall,

223

promises the man with the microphone, but first he would—
"Can you all see well enough?"—he would like to demonstrate
the advantages of this inflatable furniture with a living model.
Although no one is really bothering to listen any more, he keeps
trotting out his phrases, talks about a new experience of lying,
a completely new concept of sitting, invents farfetched comparisons, mainly at the expense of marriage, and he illustrates his
meaning with Mike Mitchner, who, at his request, finds himself
forced to fall, to turn on his left side, to pretend to read, to
pretend to sleep. This last advertising gimmick can surely be
ignored, and even Janpeter Heller pays it not the slightest attention; he has eyes only for Mike Mitchner, and when the cordon
is finally unhooked and removed, he presses forward with the
rest of the crowd, not so much in order to try out the pieces of
furniture—which are, of course, immediately taken by storm,
mounted, and tormented by children—as to be near the table
where his former pupil is giving his autograph. With deliberation and concentration. Often putting his face so close to that of
the autograph hunter that he gives the impression of having a
confidential chat with him or her. He's confronted with school
notebooks, photos, writing paper, even a paper bag with something in it—Mike seems to be used to everything. But not quite:
as the woman with the cheerful dumpling face comes up to his
table and holds out a pair of white canvas shoes to sign, he is
taken by surprise and has to inquire cautiously where he is supposed to sign. On the toe cap? On both toe caps? So his first name
on the right shoe and his surname on the left one? He's managed
that one; the woman laughs, shaking her head as though she can
hardly recognize herself, and then goes off to look more closely
at the furniture.

"Excuse me," asks Heller, "is it true that you've just asked for
an autograph?"

"A what?"

"A signature," says Heller.

"Yes, on the shoes, they're for my daughter. Surely there isn't
any charge?"

"No, they're free, gratis, and for nothing," says Heller. "I'm

224

just interested in finding out one thing about it: Have you known Mike Mitchner for long?"

"No, not at all."

"But you do know his profession?"

"Is he an actor possibly? He looks a bit like one."

"Then before today you didn't even know his name?"

"My daughter must certainly know it, her walls are covered with names and photos and that sort of thing."

Heller thanks her rather too effusively, even in his own opinion, perhaps it's the atmosphere of the whole performance, he thinks, all this forced official joviality is contagious; and he goes and stands behind Mike again, watching the progress of the line of autograph hunters, whose high spirits also seem rather exaggerated. How differently they behave once they've got their autograph: some of them push it hastily into their wallets as though afraid of being asked to give it back; others brandish it in the air; while others carefully inspect the signature, as if afraid of being stuck with a counterfeit.

But that girl, with her severe-looking face, straight black hair parted in the middle, is approaching the table in an untypical manner; unlike the others, she's moving along with a listless air, she seems to regret having joined the line; while she doesn't actually give the impression that she is about to be inoculated, she looks even less as though she were waiting to collect an autograph. Has she, in fact, got a piece of paper in her hand? Now she's bending down to Mike Mitchner and pushing a piece of paper toward him—something's written on it, as Heller discovers—and gently tapping the piece of paper, she whispers something to him which makes him first smile and then agree; a quick handshake and she goes away without an autograph while Mike pushes the note into his breast pocket.

"Excuse me," says Heller, "may I take it that you're an admirer of Herr Mitchner?" The girl stops and eyes him aggressively. "We're Herr Mitchner's friends," says Heller. "Your answer will help us with the survey we're conducting on contemporary hero worship."

"I'm too busy," says the girl in a quiet voice, almost as if

225

speaking to herself, "and in any case I refuse to let you pry into my affairs."

"But perhaps you wouldn't mind telling us what impresses you about Herr Mitchner."

"What impresses me? The size of his shoes. And now please excuse me."

"Don't be offended," says Jürgen Klepatsch's voice suddenly, "the girl was only bringing Mike an invitation and there's someone waiting for her over there behind the pillar, can you see?"

Had Klepatsch witnessed what had happened? Had he heard what had been said? Heller gives up. Heller believes that the line patiently moving toward the table will not reveal any more secrets. He'll go up to the store's restaurant and wait there until the performance is over. "Will you come and get me when it is?"

"Of course," says Klepatsch, "one of us will drop by and get you."

So Heller asks his way to the elevator and has himself taken up to the restaurant, where people relax after a successful shopping expedition or gather strength before launching upon one. He clambers over parcels and cardboard boxes piled up in the aisle, he finds a free chair at a corner table, next to a taciturn old married couple who have ordered coffee but forgotten to drink it. Was this chair free? The amiable wave of the hand comes too late, Heller is already sitting down, he's lifted his briefcase onto his lap and is now pulling something out of it. What would he like? "Tea with rum and, in any case, a curried sausage." As he wipes the table, the waiter eyes the two old people and shakes his head; he's about to invite Heller to share and thus justify his amazement, but Heller is looking at his books and papers and thinking of the title, *The Price of Hope.* In a couple of hours' time he'll have to be back at the hotel, equipped with new knowledge, fresh judgments, and perhaps even some more examples.

Our young expert Heller is reflecting on a question of method; here we have a clear picture of a whole life, so we may assume that it contains high points and extraordinary situations, but surely these can only exist against a backdrop of everyday events, a gray stream that doesn't carry anything with it as it flows along; and that means that even the long periods when nothing happens are part of the whole and have their own importance. What would Lucy Beerbaum say if she knew why her life is being scrutinized and X-rayed? That a committee is trying to select, out of a whole body of living experience, the tastiest morsels for teaching purposes? How valuable are such deliberately chosen examples of model behavior? Why shouldn't what happened *before* an exemplary action—or afterward—be of significance? Might not the unpretentious, colorless things, the even tenor of the days slipping along, provide us with food for thought? Why not look for the center at the perimeter, in some overlooked event, some remote occurrence? Shouldn't we extend our search to unimportant things, things which at first sight seem to lie outside our province? For instance? Well, for instance, that night with the shepherd in the dark hut with dry-stone walls up by the cliffs of Meteora. Isn't that typical of Lucy Beerbaum? But typical in what sense?

First of all the landscape; that can very quickly be reconstructed: in the middle, he inserts the cliffs of Meteora with their steep slopes and in front of them he unfolds a stretch of Thessalian plain, fits in the fretted pattern of a river and christens it Pinios; and that fringe of light on the skyline can only be the Aegean Sea. The two moving points must be Lucy Beerbaum and her fellow student Victor Gaitanides—weren't they making their way diagonally from the base of the cliffs to the road and the bus below? This is what he had read:

They had driven out to the cliffs at Meteora during their short vacation—both had just passed their intermediate examinations —had walked over the rising plain, picnicked out of their hamper —Victor Gaitanides so smart and formal, as always, as though anxious to shelter behind the strict observance of all the rules of deportment, or at least to disguise his youth. And while they were eating at the foot of the cliffs, the storm was gathering, revealing itself first with a tremor, a stirring of light which bathed the cliffs and made the river glitter more harshly. Victor carefully folded the handkerchief on which he had been sitting and looked up at the sky as they were packing up to go: the quickly forming and dissolving shapes of the clouds, gleaming fish and the glowing red tops of phantom trees growing upside down. "We must hurry—that's the father and mother of a storm brewing over there."

He seemed more concerned than Lucy, who didn't want to be rushed and insisted on eating all her melon at least, even if she couldn't finish her bread, and she made fun of his eagerness to get down to the road and the bus. "Are you so worried about getting wet, Victor?"

"I must confess"—he was one of those people who look upon a simple answer as a confession—"I must confess that I know pleasanter sensations than having a wet suit clinging to my skin."

"Because of you, this will be the second time I've not had a decent meal," said Lucy, "and our doctor's always telling me to eat all I can manage."

"You must have eaten your quota long ago." He stood there impatiently, his boater on his head and the picnic hamper in his hand, a man whose desire for propriety concealed and disguised everything, not only his readiness to participate in things but even his amiability, which always gave the impression of being mechanical. "We'd better be going, Lucy, I don't like what's going on up there at all."

All of a sudden, the edges of the clouds seemed to catch fire: they overflowed with red and lilac, and among the clouds there was a black whirling eye beneath which the whole plain wilted, all the way down to the coast.

"That at least is unique," said Victor. "I mean these Thessalian thunderstorms of ours."

"I don't think so," said Lucy, "as far as I know, lightning is discussed in every school geography book in the world; in any case, they are really only electrical discharges, partial discharges, to be accurate, which take place throughout the lightning from particle to particle."

228

"It was the light that I was thinking of in particular," Victor said. "We celebrate our thunderstorms in color."

"Yes," said Lucy, "our storms and our poverty are very picturesque in Greece."

She took hold of the handle of the basket, not so much to help Victor carry it as to let him drag her along, over the overgrown slope, diagonally down to the road, where, as could now be seen, there was no shelter except for isolated trees. "Come on," said Victor, "it's starting already, I can feel the first drops." The first few drops were large and refreshing, they hit you hard, one by one, so that Lucy felt she could still distinguish them as they splashed on her shoulder and neck or in her face. The wind was coming in short gusts; the storm's own wind.

"Not so fast," cried Lucy, "I can't run that fast." The sharp stones concealed in the undergrowth, the hidden cracks in the ground, and the rocky outcrops, washed smooth, made her lurch and stumble; the rain was now pouring down heavily and steadily, drumming on the thirsty ground, so that, as it splashed up, the spray formed dirty gray streaks in front of them. Lucy's knee socks had slipped down, the grass was whipping against her thin calves and wetting the hem of her skirt. Visibility was becoming worse and worse. "Over there," said Victor, "there's a hut, we'll take shelter." He grasped her wrist and dragged her over to the low hut, a shepherd's hut with dry-stone walls, blackish in color, and boulders on the roof to hold it down. Two openings in the walls, like narrow loopholes. Roughhewn entrance posts covered with scars. A pile of brushwood and the glistening roots of trees. Between the doorposts was stretched a curtain made of cured skins stitched together; the man lifted it up, let Lucy go in first, and then slipped into the hut himself, quickly removing his hat as he did so.

Behind a hollow in the floor where a fire was smoldering, the shepherd was standing beside one of the peepholes—so he must have seen them approaching. On his head was a greasy military cap, possibly dark-red in color; a grayish-white stubble on his chin; over a collarless shirt, a faded vest and an equally faded three-quarter-length jacket; from a cord slung diagonally over his shoulder, a hand-sewn linen bread bag was hanging on his hip; an old man but of uncertain age; he was looking toward them with half-closed eyes, waiting for them to greet him; and he then bade them welcome. He vacated his post by the peephole and suggested that they look at the landscape under the "blessed rain." His eyes twinkled at them and he poured out some bitter herb tea, handing the only enamel mug to Lucy and making a sign for her to share it with her man.

Peering over the rim of the mug as she sipped, Lucy looked around the inside of the hut: the sagging bed, the homemade blanket, a closed wooden box, wire strung along the walls and pieces of cord, a carving board with a knife stuck in it, and bread, onions, and olives all around, and then the bed again, spread out and rolled flat, a sack filled with grass and herbs.

"Where are your sheep?" asked Victor.

Pointing to the second of the peepholes, the shepherd said, "Look through there, they're standing all huddled up just like they do in a pen."

Their hands and faces were dripping wet. "If you don't mind, Lucy, I'll take my jacket off and dry it by the fire."

"And if you don't object, I'll do the same with my blouse and scarf."

By propping a stick between two wooden pitchforks, they were able to hang their things up to dry beside the fire.

"There goes the bus," said the shepherd.

"There's another one later on in the evening," said Victor.

All the time they kept looking through the peepholes; alternately and sometimes both together, they stood watching the storm, the flashes of sheet lightning which lit up the beating rain from underneath the low-hanging clouds over the plain. The storm seemed to be moving out to sea and then turned and was blown back as the wind veered.

"Victor, are you sure we're not missing the last bus?"

"Yes, I'm sure."

Lucy opened the picnic hamper, crouched down, pulled out

what had been left over from their meal, and offered it to the shepherd, who apparently took the offer as an invitation to offer something in return, for he flung a coat over his head, went out, and came back with a leather haversack. With ritual deliberation he unpacked some strips of mutton, which he exhibited to them for their approval, seasoned and salted them as they stood watching, and then cooked them on a handmade grill, fanning the fire into a flame. Then he looked at them expectantly, with a smile on his face, as though encouraging them to do something that was long overdue. Victor realized why he was waiting and, before eating, told him their names, where they were from, and what had brought them there, whereupon the shepherd gave his own name and asked Victor for permission to make a comment about Lucy. "With pleasure, we'd like to hear it."

Sitting on the bed, Lucy was hunching her shoulders, and putting her thin, bare arms together, she squeezed her hands between her thighs and waited. From the hem of his jacket the shepherd fished out a ball of paper, opened it up, and revealed a coin, which he silently held out to Victor on the palm of his hand. Victor took the irregularly shaped disk and looked at it closely by the fire.

"What is it?" asked Lucy.

"A very old coin, at least two thousand years old," said Victor, "and there's a head on it, a girl's head, presumably the famous nymph Arethusa. Would you like to take a look?" He handed the coin to Lucy and as Lucy turned her head sideways, showing him her profile against the light of the fire—the smooth, high forehead, the barely noticeable base of her nose, her mouth always on the point of smiling, the energetic, prominent chin—he realized what the shepherd was trying to tell them.

"You really do look like her, Lucy," said Victor, "we'll appoint you the local nymph."

"Then I'd have to lug a water jug around for all eternity—do you really want to do that to me?"

"Nymphs are mortal," said Victor. "It's true that they're allowed to bring up gods and help mankind, but they are mortal."

"That's some consolation," said Lucy, "and as for my resemblance to that lady, I personally can't see it."

"That's because Arethusa looks so robust and well fed, almost aggressively healthy."

"In other words, in contrast to me this well-built nymph didn't have her meals interrupted or wasn't prevented from eating them."

She gave the shepherd back his coin with a word of thanks, the old man gave a gratified nod; and then they ate, the men squatting on the floor of the hut, Lucy on the bed, while outside the rain pounded on the tin roof and darkness set in early over the plain.

"Will we be able to see the bus coming soon enough?" asked Victor.

The shepherd reassured him. "You can see the headlights in the hills, the bus comes down to the plain slowly; when you can see the headlights in the hills, there's still plenty of time to get down to the road."

He put the dishes out into the rain. He lit a much-mended pipe and talked about his brother: he had been a shepherd here, had lived in the hut for many years, and then one day he was found dead, no trace of injury, no previous illness, he was sitting in front of the hut, leaning against the wall; he had found him like that and not only found him but buried him and then simply taken over from him, that was a long time ago, at any rate too long ago for him to expect anyone to notice either his brother's disappearance or the fact that he'd taken over his crook and his job.

The coin was the only thing his brother had left behind, probably he'd found it down by the Pinios, by the river, and later on sewn it into a case. If someone's young—can he die without being injured or having any previous illness? His visitors felt unable to settle the matter, whereupon he hastily went on to tell them about his father, who had also been a shepherd, just like his grandfather, not here but nearer to the sea; he was good at rounding up his sheep, and one day he was found dead, too, having fallen from a height, they said at the time, but to this day he

232

couldn't believe it, because his father knew every pass and every ravine, he thought rather that it was an "intentional accident," because it happened just before his father was due to receive two years' pay. When something like that happened, wasn't it natural to draw one's own conclusions?

He went on talking and telling his story, anxious to come to terms with himself and find peace of mind, and all the while Victor stood at the window slit and looked across to the hills— the swinging headlights which were supposed to herald the approaching bus still failed to put in an appearance. The shepherd poured out some of his bitter herb tea and went to the peephole, rather as though he would be more likely to succeed where Victor Gaitanides had failed; but even he couldn't see the bus coming.

"Perhaps it's because of the storm, it may have broken down."

"But what's going to happen now?"

They continued to look up toward the hills, and later on, when the last departure time had long since past, they scoured the plain for the twisting headlights; but there was no light to be seen, all they could hear was the rain.

"If you don't mind," said the shepherd, "you can spend the night here."

"No, we can't do that," said Lucy.

"You can stay in the hut by yourselves, I'll keep my flock together, there's another shelter out there and I've got my heavy coat," said the shepherd.

"It's not necessary," Lucy said quickly, "really it isn't—what do you think, Victor?"

"Or stay in the hut," said Victor, "there's room for everybody."

"But you're my guests, this hut is yours and I must go and see to the animals." The old man flung on his coat, waved goodbye with his crook and went out.

"We'll wait for him," Lucy said, and stretched out on the bed; her slight body fitted into the hollow, she spread the blanket over her legs, rested her head on her bent elbow, and stared into the fire and beyond the fire at Victor, who had settled down beside the wall of the hut—a wall that had not even been plastered inside and smelled of age and smoke—as though expecting a lengthy wait. The fire was casting lively patterns of reflection, throwing tongues of light over their skin and sending out random slivers of shadow. They were silent while the piled-up logs caved in as the fire died down, leaving nothing but gently crackling embers which flushed their cheeks. When their eyes met, they immediately glanced away, turning their heads. Their faces: alertness personified. Then, as the glow died down under the ashes, leaving only a pale gleam insufficient to illuminate either themselves or the ceiling of the hut, at a moment when their sharpened sense of wakefulness lent meaning even to the slightest sound, Lucy sat up violently, moaning with pain, grasped her left wrist, and held it up, whimpering.

The man sprang over to the bed and squatted down. He poked the embers with a stick until they flared up again, and now, as Lucy turned her open hand toward him, he could see the head of the pin sticking into the ball of her thumb; it was the brooch, depicting a rearing silver snake, which Lucy was wearing in her scarf. The whole pin had gone right into the ball of the thumb, pushed or stuck deep into the flesh. The wound was hardly bleeding at all. "Good God, how did that happen, Lucy? Lie still and look at the wall." Victor held her firmly by the forearm and jerked the pin out. "Suck it," he said, "go on, suck the wound. How could that have happened, Lucy?"

He folded his handkerchief and put it on the wound as an emergency bandage, as it was now bleeding quite freely and steadily. He helped her to stretch out on the bed and drew the blanket over her. "How did that happen, Lucy?"

"I don't know."

"Any pain?"

"Not too bad."

"In any case," said Victor, "I'll look after the pin until tomorrow morning."

"I'd like you to keep it," said Lucy. "I'm making you a present of it."

Once again, Janpeter Heller can feel a gentle touch on his shoulder, two fingers are tapping him there to attract his attention. What is it? The old married couple who had let their own coffee get cold are thinking that it's a pity for him to let his curried sausage do the same. "It should be eaten hot," the wife says in a friendly voice, convinced that her advice is sound enough to justify disturbing him.

"Thank you very much, I hadn't even noticed that it was there." They're watching him approvingly as he eats, the wife is even nodding and is apparently on the point of uttering a word of praise: that's right, that's how sausage ought to be eaten. The two old people put their heads together, their lips are moving, not a word is said, but there is a slight sign, a gentle smacking sound, which Heller believes may have been produced by himself. "Waiter, the bill," he calls out, and, still chewing, wishes the old couple good day.

He must go downstairs, he must take the elevator to the furniture department, where the demonstration is now probably coming to an end. Down there, amid the bulging chairs, the assistants are answering questions and handing out brochures. But what about Mike? And where's Klepatsch? Where's the bald man who goes by the name of Hillmeyer or Knokke? And Tamara: where's she? Heller pushes his way through the department looking for them, slaloming between the beleaguered furniture: where are they? At lunch, an assistant tells him, there's a special lunch being held upstairs—she points with her thumb—up in the holy of holies. "Oh, I see."

Heller goes to the elevator and waits, faces are floating up and down in front of him; he can hear people talking beside him and behind him, and, strangely enough, there seems to be only one topic of conversation: the bargains which people have found; against all expectation, everyone seems to have been lucky, at the expense of Hillmeyer or Knokke. "The elevator's always full here," a voice says, "let's walk down"; and not only Heller but all the other people waiting for the elevator stream toward the staircase and go down through the various departments as though through outer circles of paradise; carefully dressed men exuding dignity are standing by to receive potential buyers, to help them discover exactly what they want and then lead them into the thicket of what the store has to offer. Bed department. Men's wear. Sports department. Toy department.

Heller has already gone past and then he goes back a few steps and with his face at floor level looks through the triangles made by people's legs toward the two identically dressed harbor pilots, both wearing red sou'westers, both in yellow raincoats, wife and child, Charlotte and Stefanie.

"Please don't block the stairs." All right. They're standing just beside the rack where the most pretentious toys are displayed, toys for the imaginative child: "The Little Needlewoman" or "The Little Doctor." What's it going to be this time? Heller has already turned Stefanie into "The Little Cook."

Hidden behind a pillar, where he stands thumbing through some children's books, Heller is trying to discover what they are buying over there in the distance merely by watching their movements, and he would bet anything that Stefanie has set her mind on something that Charlotte will object to for at least two reasons: first, because it's too complicated, and second, because it's too expensive. But Stefanie wants it, she wants that or nothing, so it must be the "Little Doctor" set, which Heller had once looked at himself: a darling clinical thermometer, sweet little syringes that really syringe, all the operating instruments a child would need to restore the health of aging dolls, a tiny silver hammer for testing reflexes.

"If I can't have that, Mommy, then I don't want anything."

"What shall we get instead?" Charlotte asks the salesgirl to hand down various boxes from the shelves. "Look at this, Stefanie, this doll's carriage with red curtains; Mützi and Empfi could both sleep in there."

"No, I don't want it." Whines and sulks and snivels and general disgruntlement. "Then I don't want anything."

Heller immediately recognizes the man again, the curly-haired athlete who walks rapidly into his field of vision—a fashionable flat briefcase in his hand still bearing an airline luggage ticket—and makes his way toward the two pilots, slips a vast hand under Charlotte's bent arm, and gives Stefanie an affectionate cuff. Here I am and I'm not even late. A quick impromptu diagnosis, he's already in the picture, he realizes the reason for the annoyance on one hand and the pouting face on the other, well, if it's like that—because bad temper can't be allowed—then let's get Stefanie what she wants, after all we should always try to encourage fair competition—what's the price of "The Little Doctor"? No, that's all right, Charlotte doesn't have to go through the motions of protesting, it won't happen every day but just for today, all right? Yes, wrap it up, please.

Heller slips off toward the side, quickly calculating how to take advantage of the pillars, ducks into the stairwell, and walks jerkily down, turning his face to look once again at the relaxed group of shoppers, now reunited over their purchase. He works his way purposefully toward the exit, through families and groups and laden customers finding it difficult either to move or to see where they're going, and finally through the wall of hot air. He's reached the street and he leans against a shopwindow where a grinning skier amidst a cloud of artificial snowflakes about as large as saucers is swooping toward him. He lights a cigarette, looks up at the sky, where a hailstorm is at this moment preparing to rattle down—where's the streetcar stop? Heller allows himself the luxury of a taxi.

Refusing on principle to respect the speed limit, the driver gives a running commentary on the driving methods of other road users: "Signal earlier, you idiot. . . . Get into line, you jerk; a woman driver, of course. . . . When you spend twelve hours at the wheel every day," he says to Heller, "you get to know what people are like."

"Only at the wheel?" asks Heller.

The driver stops, the flap of the glove compartment falls down. "That's the way to the Isebek Canal, I can't turn there. Do you want a receipt?"

Heller pays, takes his receipt, and goes off without wishing the driver goodbye; he hurries toward the gate and enters the house through the inner courtyard. He doesn't need to press the three-minute time switch but waits beside the cellar door until a painful, halting step, presumably that of a cripple, has died away on the second floor and then he creeps cautiously to the street entrance and with his back to the wall slides toward the ground-floor flats, to the brown-painted door, and reads the nameplate on the door: Ch. Heller. So it's no longer J. Heller or even Heller by itself, but Ch. Heller—leaving the sex indeterminate, however. He keeps the door key, a flat one, in one of the compartments of his briefcase. He opens the door. J. Heller is paying a visit to Ch. Heller; the spring lock clicks shut. Shall he take his coat off?

The same hand-crafted hanging cupboard is still there for coats and next to it, that's new, another one for the child's clothes. Coats of the same color. Caps and scarves ditto—all this is presumably intended to represent solidarity—or perhaps conspiracy. Directed against whom? Against him? If at all, it must be against him.

Here's the kitchen with the dining recess: blue-and-white checked rustic curtains, the table, as always, set for the next meal —"You feel that you're expected if that's been done"—the rows of glasses, pots, and gravy boats all standing at the ready, all arranged in order of size; the china face of the kitchen clock whose mechanism is even noisier than it used to be; two shelves with dish towels—Stefanie obviously earns her reward, offered even for drying up, for the bright-colored towels are no bigger than handkerchiefs; piles of cups and saucers; in the breadbox, as always, only the doughy white bread which they both prefer. And the bathroom? Is the pink toweling cover still on the toilet? And is there still a dripping faucet in the bathtub? And is the wastebasket, which is far too small, still overflowing with used wads of cotton covered with blackish smears? And the collection of butterflies and beetles, the brooches which she uses to keep her hair up?

Why, thinks Heller, do we suppose that any absence must lead to change? The walls of the nursery, of course, are plastered with the latest artwork, Stefanie's brightly colored paintings, and on the floor, under the window, a big council meeting of toy animals is in progress; wooden monkeys are hanging happily, with outstretched arms, from a rope ladder and over there, on the bedside table, fastened to a stick, two offended old clockwork birds are drinking in turn out of a glass of water.

How can you explain her preference for heavy pretentious furniture which bears no relation to the size of the room? Is it a pathological desire for property? A longing for durability? Or an ingrown tendency to endow her home with the impregnability of a fortress? Heller slides sideways over the carved arm of a massive chair, sprawls out in it, and looks at the bloated white foot of a lamp, at the leather blotter, at the calendar to be turned over once a month; shaking his head, he looks at all the accouterments, hateful acquaintances whom he'd once had to live with.

How far back was it, Heller wonders, that evening when he returned from a school trip with his pupils, a trip he had himself suggested, to North Rhine-Westphalia, to the "black country," to see "how the workers live"? And now he looks back on that summer evening and sees himself coming in and Charlotte greeting him mysteriously—how obvious it is that she's got something up her sleeve, a big new surprise which is so much on her mind that she doesn't even ask about the trip; but before she will tell him anything, he must first have something to eat, here are some sandwiches and some tea to wash them down—hospital tea, Heller himself calls it. Her impatience. Her excitement. Her preoccupied look. . . ."Are you listening to what I'm saying?"

"Of course I am. You were saying something about running off the Bessemer converter at night."

He tells her about all he has seen and done during the trip (you meet people who simply haven't the slightest idea that they're being exploited), describes scenes of the way the workers live (you have the impression that they are growing smaller and smaller as they stand at the conveyor belt, that they're on the point of melting into bolts and threads and will end up by rattling off to be assembled), describes his pupils' reactions to what they saw (the place cries out for a labor contract), but he can't fail to notice that the longer he talks, the more impatient she becomes.

"Well now, what is it, Charlotte? Let the cat out of the bag now."

"Come with me, I'll show you something, then you can go on telling me what you did."

He has to shut his eyes and let himself be led along, in we go and now you may open your eyes. So that's supposed to be the surprise: this carved monster, occupying half the room, big enough for the asses of a whole board of directors, and this ponderous desk behind which someone might well count oil shares but never grade school papers.

"Oh God," says Heller, "that's a pretty kettle of fish."

And Charlotte asks, anxiously and expectantly, "Do you like it, Jan?"

Heller moves in a semicircle around the outfit and ends up in a corner, staring at the "surprise," completely at a loss. "Who's going to use it, for heaven's sake? I mean, who's it intended for?"

"For you, Jan; I thought you'd earned it. Are you pleased?" She wonders why—for she can see that Heller is embarrassed and practically horrified—the surprise she has arranged for him seems to be causing him more perplexity and bewilderment than glad acceptance; and as if feeling that she must show off the advantages of the chair to him, she settles into its inviting embrace.

"One thing at least is certain," says Heller, "anyone who sits down in that chair has got to wear a tie and write with a silver pencil."

"But look at the quality: that'll always be worth something."

"That's just it," says Heller. "The more valuable a possession is, the greater the terror it spreads."

"Ah, Jan, now you're talking the way you've started talking recently; you despise everybody's acquisitions and anyone who wants to possess anything. Hasn't everyone the right to want to do that?"

240

"But you were there when I used to mark my exercise books on the kitchen table or even on the large windowsill; why shouldn't I go on doing it? Why do we have to burden ourselves with such pretentious and expensive furniture that forces me to change not only the way I sit but my whole persona? You're right, Charlotte, I'm suspicious of possessions because they either tie us down or else turn us into opportunists."

And now her long, questioning gaze and the uncertainty in her voice as she asks him to tell her whether he isn't pleased, at least a little bit pleased; after all, perhaps he'll get used to this furniture and one day he'll find he can't do without it.

"I don't know, Charlotte. I've known what it is to feel the sort of imprisonment that comes when we own things."

"Don't talk like that, Jan. Once upon a time you used to talk very differently and you know you did, in the days when we only had my salary to live on. Or have you forgotten what you used to say when we were looking into shopwindows? Have you forgotten all the things you wanted to have, all your plotting and planning for the future? And now isn't one even allowed to be pleased over a new desk; do you have to be so suspicious if someone just goes out and buys a new chair? But I know the cause of all this, all the theories that you've taken up with. I've heard you and your little group of pupils talking often enough."

"I hope you'll give me credit for some ability to think, too," Heller says. "You must understand, Charlotte, it's not just a question of the desk, it's something fundamental—as long as we possibly can, we want to keep our independence, and the surest way of doing that is not to make any concessions to the new creed, I mean the religion of material possessions."

"Oh, Jan, how odd that sounds! Just big words, big ideas, and not one atom of experience. I'm afraid of people who don't understand the meaning of compromise; you want to change everything from top to bottom, a hundred percent. Why not let your pupils get around a bit? Don't just show them the way the workers live; let them talk to all sorts of people. You'll all be surprised how many people want to be able to take something home, to acquire something. People have always wanted to do that and they still do; they say it makes them happy; at bottom, it's perhaps simply a normal human desire."

"It's strange, Charlotte, how you always have to bring everything down to a personal level."

"That shows you that I'm getting older, Jan; at the beginning, you react to everything theoretically; later on, when you've realized how little can be changed, you view everything personally."

Heller doesn't look at her, he knows that she's going into the bathroom, and he knows, too, without hearing anything, that she's sitting on the edge of the tub and, in her usual way, is crying quietly to herself, dry-eyed.

No, thinks Heller, its quality is indestructible, they'll outlast everything. He taps the furniture, scrapes his fingernail sharply over a corner of the desk, and gives the chair a kick with his toe: how goes it, you lanky old bastard?

The sound of a key being vigorously inserted in the lock of the flat door takes Heller completely by surprise. He looks hastily around to see if there's anywhere to hide, but steps can already be heard in the corridor, Charlotte's steps, she rushes into the kitchen, drawers are flung open one after the other and slammed shut again, she swears quietly to herself, and then there's a sudden silence; relief, relief, she obviously seems to have found what she was looking for, the clasp of her handbag clicks shut. Is she leaving again? She goes to the door of the flat, then, surprisingly, comes back, disappears into the bathroom, comes out again, and walks into the living room with a wet blouse to hang it on the windowsill in front of the radiator.

Three times, to make her meaning plain, she says, "Good God, how you scared me"; and then, slowly lowering the iron she had picked up, still at a loss: "You don't expect me to say welcome home, I imagine?"

Heller takes a step toward her and apologizes in some embarrassment: "I don't know how it happened, Charlotte, I can't even explain it by force of habit—I just suddenly found myself here in our old flat."

"Jan, you've got no right to force your way in like that, after all this time, now that we've finally managed to get back to some sort of normal life at last. Please leave at once."

"At any rate, I'm not here by mistake," Heller says, "even if I can't actually find a reason; perhaps the past isn't completely dead yet."

Charlotte hangs the blouse on the windowsill in front of the radiator and, turning off the switch of the iron, she says, looking toward the window, "I can't talk to you now, there's someone waiting for me."

"Is Stefanie with him in the car?"

"Oh, Jan, what's the point of answering you?"

"So they're both waiting for you?"

"Yes, they're waiting for me and I assume you're not trying to tell me that you object. Please leave now, but let me go out first."

"Would you find that unpleasant?" asks Heller, and when she doesn't reply: "He seems to have bought Stefanie's goodwill already; and how about you?" He nods his head toward the photograph on the heavy lamp-stand table which shows the curly-haired athlete in a high-necked doctor's tunic, standing in front of a well-kept lawn, obviously on the grounds of a hospital; at the edge a man can be seen driving a mower. Have the two of them reached an understanding?

"I must go now, Jan, please appreciate my position. You'll only hurt yourself with your questions."

"So I'm right?"

"Yes."

Heller walks slowly past her out into the corridor and waits there for her with his eye on the door. "As far as I know, Charlotte, we're not divorced yet, are we?"

"Call me this evening, Jan," she says.

"You won't pick up the receiver."

"Yes, I will."

"Since I know the way, why can't I come straight here?"

She looks at him in astonishment and holds out her hand toward him—no, she's *about* to hold out her hand, but when she sees that he's not expecting it, she changes it to a gesture urging him to be quick. "When the child's asleep," she says, "not before."

"Off you go," Heller says with a smile. "I'll wait on the stairs." He stands beside her watching her lock the door of the flat and then walks back into the shadows, places his hand on the handlebar of a bicycle, and waits to hear the hissing sound made by the automatic door as it swings shut.

14

WELL, they don't seem to have recognized him in the August 4th cellar bar—neither the young people who have placed several tables side by side and are now putting their heads together like conspirators over their empty plates of goulash nor the young bald-headed proprietor, who is brooding over a stained notebook, perhaps his order book. But as on his first visit, they raise their heads and eye him suspiciously and with surprise as he walks over to the pale-green tiled stove—as if they were counting his steps or, more probably perhaps, as if they wanted to block his way with their unfriendly stares.

Valentin Pundt is not put off by their gaze. With a grumpy greeting, he shakes off his waterproof cape and sits down beside the stove. Although he knows what he's going to order, he first waves his finger with a flourish over the menu before saying to the proprietor, "A plate of your goulash, please." Then he reaches into the inner pocket of his jacket, pulls out some papers, places them on the table in front of him, and looks at them with his face resting on his hands.

"Dear Mike." That's Harald's writing, perhaps he used to sit here, perhaps he even wrote that letter here, next to this stove, amid the clatter of spoons, in this "healthy," warm atmosphere.

What's that hawk-faced young man saying at the next table? Take over the professor's rostrum? Pundt is sitting there as though exhausted, but he still can't help listening: yes, they're going to take over his rostrum during his first lecture unless he allows them to discuss with him not only the intellectual content of his lectures but his career as well. He had accepted the chair without heeding their warnings—Pundt gathers—and as a result he will have to face their questioning, in particular on the articles he's published on Slavonic architecture, of which there are forty-three in all. At the very first meeting of the term, they're going to ask a certain Riemek, who apparently will be lecturing on the history of architecture, about the characteristic features of the "tumbledown" architecture which he had himself discovered in the course of a trip through the cities of eastern Poland and on which he had written at great length in the *National Architectural Review* at the time. "If we're putting the content of the courses to the vote," says one of them approvingly, "then we must do the same with the people who are giving them."

That can only be Alfons Riemek, thinks Pundt; Professor Alfons Riemek whom they're discussing at the next table, and he can visualize him with a look of pleasure written all over his commonplace face, with its respectable pince-nez, walking tirelessly up and down in front of the freezing soldiers in the cold gymnasium—Major Alfons Riemek, the latest and last commanding officer inspecting the final batch of soldiers at the end of the war, his convalescents whom he is adjuring, in a bullying voice, to follow him loyally and whom he himself is nevertheless going to abandon to their fate at the first opportunity and without warning.

Pundt admires the sober arguments with which they are justifying taking over the professor's rostrum and recalls that he himself had intended to call on Riemek or at least write to him —long after the war, when Riemek was delivering himself of opinions on the government—simply in order to tell him what he thought of him.

"Here's your goulash," says the waitress, "I hope it's nice." The old schoolmaster wipes his spoon and fork on the paper napkin and mechanically, without thinking, he starts to ladle up the liquid as he reads, over and over again, the beginning of the letter: "Dear Mike." The savory fumes rise up into his nostrils

246

and excite his taste buds. And now he's unfolding the letter and placing it beside his plate.

Dear Mike,

I didn't go to the performance of your new program last Saturday, even though I wasn't doing anything. According to the papers, it went very well and soon you'll be going on tour and so we'll be witnessing in sixty other towns the same scenes that we've been seeing here. You'll be gratifying their dreams and afterward you'll have to slip away through a side exit to escape their frantic hero worship. I understand that it was your own compositions, "All My Weaknesses" and "Only a Stranger in the Waiting Room," which they liked best. I'm not surprised, you've got your ear to the ground and at least you haven't yet cut the umbilical cord that joins you to them. Or, more accurately, you've succeeded in joining it again. You're able to express all their unspoken needs—and not only that, you liberate them from all their shortcomings. So you're bound to be a success; be careful what you do with it.

But it's not because of your success that I'm writing to you. I'm writing because the papers have found a new name for you which you yourself don't seem to object to, perhaps you even chose it yourself: the singer in love with life. According to the reports, you've stated that you've "lost interest in simply despising the world and showing how pointless it is"; you don't want to criticize it any more as you used to, you want to "point out all its advantages plainly enough for even doubting Thomases to accept it." Understanding, that's what you're aiming at now. I assume that you realize, Mike, how far you've moved away from your earlier attitude and what this means for your old friends who offered you their friendship under very different circumstances. With this new discovery of yours, you've definitely stopped being one of us. Whatever it is that may have induced you to give up protesting and look on the bright side of things, we can't follow you. Since there's no point in telling you what you've now become as far as I'm concerned, you should at least know what you used to represent for me.

This may surprise you a lot, Mike, but the very first time I heard you—it was at a faculty party—I had the feeling that my doubts were suddenly all resolved. You were announced as a protest singer, and people were skeptical until you began singing —"Ballad of the Bank of Germany" and your "German Ra-Ra-Ramblers' Song" and finally "You Want It Like That," and it was that last song that seemed to be telling me to start doing something; all of a sudden, I knew what my choice ought to be. I wrote to you that same night, you invited me to call on you, and I can still see the worried look on your face as I told you how much I owed to you—as you told me later, it was my enthusiasm which made you worried. And I admit it, I was enthusiastic because at last I'd found what I'd been looking for for a very long time, you might call it a mission. Yes, Mike, and you remember how we joined forces and what we agreed on—not only during all the evenings we spent together in the August 4th; it was an active partnership, which perhaps didn't have any great future but at least we refused to remain silent, because silence might seem to imply approval. So we took action. We protested if any injustice that had come to light threatened to be forgotten too soon. We put our finger on the sore spots so that they wouldn't heal up too quickly and become insensitive as a result of indifference. We took up and put into practice what you were trying to do as a protest singer with your songs and ballads and skits. And you set the pace in all this. Yes, Mike, it was you who got everything moving: the protests, the action groups, and even our inspiration, at least you showed us what to look out for.

It was you and you alone who were clear-sighted enough to draw our attention to all the issues and social conditions which posed a challenge for each one of us. You were the first person to point out the things which should arouse our sympathy or protest: from delays in the legal process to the table-cigarette-lighter culture, from the white-slave traffic to Bonn's Christmas crib. I often felt that it was no effort for you to expose an unsavory state of affairs and find the right name to describe what was

248

happening; anything that caught your eye immediately became significant and looked ugly. I don't need to tell you what that led to, do I? Or at least what it led *me* to? We weren't prepared to accept the world as a *fait accompli*, with all its fathers and judges and consumers and bosses, and it was you who supplied the voice to express our refusal to accept. And because you were able to do that, you automatically became our spokesman, we didn't even need to elect you.

Can you imagine how happy I often was, even when you sometimes said, "Ease up a bit on the enthusiasm, old friend, you've got too much pressure in your tires"—and especially when you sang the words that we had written together? Even now I'm amazed how dependent I was on you. When I needed a catchword or a slogan, you gave me one. And you showed me what I could make of myself and what I was capable of.

Don't get alarmed, Mike, but it's the truth: you were something of an idol for me and being with you all the time and familiarity with your way of life couldn't change that. And if you want an explanation: before I knew you I usually did things haphazardly, but during my time with you I acted out of conviction. It was from you that I learned that we shouldn't do merely what we liked but should systematically do what we owed it to ourselves to do.

We went over the state of the world together. We said no. We accused the times we lived in. We made it plain to everybody that we were not going to conform and we taught lots of people that it was wrong and corrupting to look the other way. It may be that people smiled at our protests and that they lost their impact as people began to get used to them, but at least we'd tried to do what we thought was necessary.

And now ask yourself, Mike, was that the only basis of our common cause? Were we united only in saying no to the present state of the world? Was it really just a question of protesting? You don't have to answer and I know you well enough to realize that you won't answer me—and after all no one can require you to justify yourself. The time when we were all working together no longer exists. You're the man who sings about how lovely the world is and that means you're reconciled to it. We don't come off so well: we've outlived our enthusiasm, we've outgrown our plans, we've lost our sense of direction. And it's your leaving us which has shown me what it all adds up to (and that's shabby enough): we can no longer refuse to grow up and for me that means, among other things, learning how to say goodbye. So now that you find that you need success, I hope you get it and I don't begrudge it to you.

Harald

Pundt turns the letter over and looks at the address again, looks in vain for a date, and stares down at the letter as he steadily spoons up his goulash, which by now is lukewarm. Does he hope that one sentence will stand out on its own and provide the evidence he's looking for? Or is he trying to assess and interpret and pass judgment? What kind of marks do you give disappointment? Involuntarily he brings the letter closer to his plate as these wet-haired giants come into the bar, dressed in blue-and-white-striped sweat suits and wearing handkerchiefs around their necks instead of scarves. They move soundlessly on their thick-soled sneakers, with Adidas tote bags in their hands. They push their way through the felt curtain at the door, wave genially toward the bar, and, probably from sheer habit, make a beeline for Pundt's table, although there are two other tables free. Let's see what they order, thinks Pundt; this short-necked Praetorian Guard with identical aggressively angular chins, let's see what the proprietor is going to produce on his brown tray in response to their call: "Same as usual."

Pundt feels cribbed, cabined, and confined, and since, as if by common agreement, they all ignore him, he also feels unpleasantly belittled. He quickly puts the letter away and moves his plate in closer so as to leave the top of the table free for them as they casually strew it with nuts and salted crackers which they are extracting from cellophane bags.

So it's Florida Boy, they're actually drinking something called

Florida Boy. Their way of ignoring you and talking across you, thinks Pundt, makes you feel superfluous, as if you're an intruder; you really must escape somehow, if only because they're casually informing you of the reason for their disappointment and, specifically, what they are soon going to have to tell a certain Sammy Flotow, who has completely failed to come up to their expectations. They admit that he did all that they expected of him in the breaststroke and butterfly but in the backstroke he lost ground hopelessly, not because he's not good at the backstroke but because at the age of twenty-nine he doesn't really belong on the team any more, he should swim with the old-timers: the great Sammy, who used to be so reliable, who always used to win.

So they're student athletes, swimmers, a swimming team, and the absent Sammy is serving as a scapegoat to explain away a defeat. Valentin Pundt would like to pay and above all he would like to stop listening, but as the proprietor and the waitress fail to notice his signal, he is forced to hear how difficult it is to get rid of a man whose very name used to spell victory and who's obviously still on the team only through sheer force of habit, even though his performances no longer justify it.

So who's going to speak to him? You? Or you? Or how about the coach, Karl Heinz? Naturally no one wants to do it himself, so they'll inform him jointly, in chorus, that he must step down, but they will try to spare Sammy's feelings and make him realize that even the greatest athletes live on borrowed time.

"My bill," Pundt hears himself calling out in an unusually loud voice, and as though he had shocked even himself, he adds in a whisper, "Can you let me have my bill, please."

15

The sight brings even Rita Süssfeldt to a halt: an empty bow window where only yesterday carefully cultivated potted plants were vying with each other. Now it's empty, the curtains have been taken down, and the only thing that can be seen through the windowpane is the gymnastics of a nimble old woman on a stepladder. She is relieving the climbing plants of their green beards and dropping them on the floor. The stepladder wobbles and the old woman grabs on to the curtain rod, quite calmly, however; and now she looks down and recognizes her neighbor standing outside, and recognizes as well the alarm still written on her neighbor's face; she smiles, taps on the window, and from the top of the ladder issues an invitation: "Please come in, I've got something for you."

Rita Süssfeldt hesitates but nevertheless rings the bell of Lucy Beerbaum's house, which now belongs to Johanna, for many years her housekeeper, Johanna with the scald mark on her cheek, who now opens the door and instead of holding out her hand offers the back of it to shake. "I'm repotting my plants." Rita walks past the hall stand without taking off her coat, across the big room and past the sliding door, and now music can be heard, a request program for young and old coming from a transistor radio. The oval room looks like a devastated gardening shop: heaps of glistening compost, crumbling peat spread out on old newspapers, bare shriveled bulbs, plants with mossy soil still clinging to their roots, and, in between, pots and enameled bowls and stands, the tail ends of climbing plants, and a container filled with crushed eggshells.

"I've always been wanting to give you a plant," says Johanna, "and now you must choose one for yourself." Embarrassed but pleased, Rita looks at the plants on offer; she makes a point of picking her flowers purely by their color and never by species or name, but she would like to know whether Lucy Beerbaum perhaps had a favorite flower. And what it was. And whether it would be possible to have a cutting from it. "The professor's favorite flower? If you'd like a fuchsia, she was fond of those. No, she didn't have one special favorite flower, except perhaps that model in her study, the DNA molecule, composed of nothing but brightly colored needles, the 'flower of life' she used to call it, but you can't have cuttings of that."

Rita Süssfeldt sits down on an empty flower stand and looks at the woman who is squatting down and cleaning out a small flower pot for her. "You were with her a long time?"

"Yes, many years but not long enough."

"You knew her better than anyone else?"

"I often used to think so, but then something would happen and I was as puzzled as when I first knew her. Just look at these photos here; each time it's her and yet each time she's different." Johanna fills the pot with damp soil, presses it down firmly with her fingertips, and rubs in some leaf mold.

"If you could live with her again," says Dr. Süssfeldt, "for as long as before, would you want to do it again?"

"Yes," says the woman, "but not on the same conditions."

"Is it true that you gave notice twice?"

The old woman, breaking off her work, surprised and at the same time suspicious, inquires, "How do you know that? Why are you asking about it?"

Before replying, Rita Süssfeldt asks whether she's allowed to smoke in here and after inhaling a few deep puffs she tells Johanna about her present work, her colleagues, and their task. Johanna listens. On the radio, congratulations are being offered, a centenarian admiral (ret.) who has no fewer than thirty-eight grandchildren and great-grandchildren is being wished all the very best for today: keep your chin up, they tell him, steer full speed ahead toward the next hundred years, they tell him. And to help him do this, they will now play for him, as well as for a lockkeeper and a man taking a cure who has just spent his fortieth vacation on the island of Sylt, apparently unscathed: "Where the North Sea's Waves . . ."

"When I gave notice the first time," says Johanna, "when I think about it now, so long afterward, I always had the same reasons for giving notice. It was a warning, you understand, it was intended as a warning, a reminder, for her lack of consideration."

"Lack of consideration?"

"Yes, toward herself. When I gave notice the first time," Johanna says, now holding the pot in her lap and thinking; and then she tells how Lucy Beerbaum first managed to disappoint her: it's a story set in a period of wretchedness and shortage, a time of need which forces everyone to rely on his wits, shortly after the war. "Can you even imagine it?" asks Johanna.

Hard times are here again and the two very different women have to live together in cold rooms, with virtually everything made of ersatz material. Lucy Beerbaum comes back exhausted from her lectures—"You should have seen her as she was then, her lovely hands all numb, her feet paralyzed with cold, and then she had shooting pains in her shoulders"—and the two women sit in the twilight or early dusk, with a hot drink in front of them, groping for it with stiff fingers every time they want a sip. They're talking about the housekeeping. It's not until after the second, not the first, sip that Lucy Beerbaum tries to work out exactly what this drink is that's burning her throat like fire: "It's wine, goodness me, Johanna, where did you manage to get wine? As things are now—you surely can't have . . . ? You must tell me where you got it, as well as those eggs a few days ago and the unrationed butter." But Johanna doesn't want to answer and asks to be allowed to keep a few small secrets to herself, not least because too many questions might spoil the taste. Since they have to conserve electricity, she listens in the dark to the effect of the warm drink and is pleased to hear her mistress becoming more and more talkative; she suggests bringing her another glass, but Lucy Beerbaum still has work to do. "Can you imagine, in those days her salary as a professor was just enough to buy three pounds of butter." As always, Johanna decides what is useful and good for her, what will help to put the exhausted woman "on her feet."

What impatience and what pleasure every time Johanna is able to put something special on the table, some unexpected windfall, cheese or eggs or wine, and how blunt and good-humored her domineering voice becomes: "We won't have any questions now, Professor, we'll just take a bit more, to keep our strength up."

Lucy is struck by the fact that Johanna's rare and unannounced extra provisions almost always appear just after she has had her day off; when she goes off in the morning she takes her basket with her and on her return she manages to avoid being seen. When they have visitors—and there often are visitors, mainly students but also colleagues and their wives—Johanna insists that they all bring something to eat with them; and if there's anything left over, she puts it away in the kitchen and gives it to Lucy Beerbaum for supper before she goes to sleep.

"Someone had to look after her, you know, because she was so easily satisfied herself that she had no idea what you needed to live on and because she would have shared or given away all the things that I'd found it quite hard to collect." Johanna finds herself obliged to lecture Lucy and get her to agree that Johanna should look after the housekeeping herself, simply so that they wouldn't run short. And the more independent Lucy Beerbaum allows her to be and the greater her control over the running of the house, the better the housekeeping becomes, despite its relative frugality. But that won't satisfy Lucy Beerbaum; she finds it impossible to stop asking questions and worrying every time Johanna puts something on the table that can't be obtained with a ration card.

"I can see now that she had a guilty conscience, because she

255

was continually asking whether it was right for us to enjoy having these things in secret at a time when things were generally so scarce." So it was inevitable, perhaps, that one morning, with snow flurries starting up, Lucy Beerbaum leaves the house right after Johanna, and although she is hopeless at shadowing because of her nearsightedness, she sets off in the same direction, to the streetcar stop over there, and, looking across at the miserable display outside a news vendor's shop, waits for the streetcar, catching it at the very last moment and crouching down on one of the end seats all muffled up to disguise herself. She has to sit near to the rear exit in order to be able to follow Johanna as soon as she gets off the streetcar at the front; it would all be much easier if her glasses didn't keep misting up. Dammtor station: it's not too difficult to remain undetected here, there's a constant stream of passers-by. Through the broken panes of glass, snow is drifting past the swaying lamp down onto the rails.

"I can only think that it was because she was so worried and anxious that she decided to follow me on my day off, keeping out of my sight. I really didn't see her, I suppose that you just don't think about being followed."

They both get into the same suburban train, though not into the same coach, and at each station Lucy Beerbaum gets out onto the platform to check and doesn't get in again until she hears the conductor's whistle. And then suddenly, through the window of her compartment, she sees Johanna striding resolutely past and she follows her, looking for the name of the station: so it's Barmbek.

As they walk along, nobody would have thought that the two women were pursuer and pursued, even though the distance between them doesn't vary and one of them doggedly follows the other through the driving snow, through almost deserted streets; in fact, the pair of them look as if they just happened by chance to be making their way to the hospital at the same time.

At the porter's lodge, Johanna is required to identify herself; she produces a piece of paper from her basket and passes it through the window; they hand it back, apparently with some jocular remark, for she laughs aloud before going through and walking down the street behind a barrowload of food containers.

"She couldn't have found out yet what she wanted to know, because until then she might well have assumed that I spent the first part of my day off visiting someone in the hospital."

Cautiously, Lucy Beerbaum walks up to the porter's lodge, following Johanna with her eyes as she disappears into a building which is still dressed in its greenish war camouflage, and she looks after her so absentmindedly that the young porter has to repeat his request: "Your donor's card, please. May I see it?"

The woman looks at him, puzzled, and shakes her head. "Donor's card?"

"I thought you'd come to give blood," says the porter.

"No, I haven't."

Johanna, now, looks over at Rita Süssfeldt. "And even then, all she could know was that I hadn't come to visit someone in the hospital, but that I'd come to give blood, which everyone is free to do, after all."

Lucy Beerbaum decides not to pursue Johanna any further and returns home by herself; that evening she hears Johanna come back and go furtively upstairs, taking care to make as little noise as possible. As expected, once again there appears on the table something not available on the rations, white bread and butter, for instance, and although Lucy can't refuse to eat some of it, she does insist that Johanna eat the same amount. And Johanna doesn't fail to note that the woman on whose behalf she's gone to so much trouble and employed such guile, whom she's taken under her wing—Johanna can sense how sad and sorry Lucy is as they sit at the table together, and that she is looking at her as if she's done something underhanded by providing all these good things.

Winter. Evenings when the electricity is cut off. Lucy Beerbaum often works by the light of the candles which Johanna has managed to pick up at a reasonable price, although she doesn't say how she did it.

"You ought to have seen her during all those difficult times; she wouldn't accept any excuse for not giving her lectures, whether because she was hungry or had frostbitten heels, and once when she'd slipped on some ice, she still insisted on being taken to the Institute."

And then she does cancel a few lectures, not because of herself but because of Johanna; although apparently so delicate and vulnerable, she looks after her housekeeper when she has to take to her bed with influenza. One evening, when Johanna is getting better, Lucy Beerbaum sits down by her bed and tells her to have a drink, something "very good for you," which she has prepared herself. Johanna guesses that it's eggs beaten up with sugar and red wine, and when her suspicion is confirmed, she sits up, quite at a loss—not only because she feels that Lucy has seen through her trick; she's also afraid she might be losing some of the power she wields in the house—and begins to interrogate her mistress. Lucy Beerbaum has foreseen this reaction and prepared for it, so she evades her questions by demanding the same right that Johanna had previously claimed, the right to keep a little secret to herself on occasion.

"I already had my suspicions, so I asked the professor straight out where all those things had come from, but she had a way of looking at you when you said certain things that made you feel sorry you'd ever opened your mouth."

There's nothing Johanna can do but get well as quickly as possible and then, while Lucy is at work, she makes an inspection of the house. She lifts lids, rummages in wastepaper baskets, reads labels on empty bottles and sniffs in them when she is in doubt. And now it's time for Lucy to come home. Johanna is standing stiffly behind the table, she mumbles "Good evening" in a voice full of resentment. The atmosphere is like the Last Judgment and after a brief moment of surprise Lucy Beerbaum inquires, "It looks like we're in for a discussion, then?" But no discussion is necessary; Johanna knows everything and this gives her the right to say that she feels let down; she has completed her investigations and she's got the proof in her hand: "You've been giving blood, too. You've been collecting special rations. Then

you've shared them with me, and you in your condition, too."
And to give Lucy Beerbaum no chance of refuting the accusation,
Johanna places a little strip of adhesive tape and a bloodstained
wad of cotton on the table.

"You must realize that in her condition she couldn't afford to
do what I'd been doing and yet she still did it—well, how can I
put it? I felt that it was directed against me, it was as though she
was devaluing all the care I was taking of her; after all, I had
proved to her which of the two of us needed special rations
more."

Lucy Beerbaum looks at the proof which Johanna must have
fished out of the trash can, trying to find not only an answer but
some way of defending herself, on principle, because she feels
that Johanna's reproaches are too harsh. So Lucy asks Johanna if
she herself doesn't think she's gone too far in her accusations and
Johanna refuses to agree. It's plain enough what Lucy Beerbaum
is trying to accomplish with her questioning: Johanna herself
must acknowledge the difference that exists between them and
once that difference has been established she must decide herself
how solicitous she needs to be and what form her solicitude
should take. Without a word, Johanna picks up her knife and
fork, takes them into the kitchen, then goes up to her room and
starts to pack, quickly and grimly at first and then more slowly,
presumably in the hope that Lucy will come up to her room and
at least ask her what she's doing; but Lucy remains sitting at the
table.

"Yes, that's how I came to give notice the first time."

And then Johanna comes down with her meager luggage, sets
it in the hall, and waits, something should be said before she
leaves, a contract has to be ended, if only orally, so she knocks at
the door and walks in—no doubt still secretly expecting her
mistress to meet her halfway and make it possible for her to
retract her decision—and is surprised at the way Lucy Beerbaum
is still sitting in the same posture and this time doesn't even turn
her head. In the face of such detachment, Johanna doesn't say,
"I'm giving notice," but instead: "I'm off," and when she sees that

it does no good to linger at the door, she reluctantly goes out of the room and leaves the house, still expecting to hear a voice calling her back. And perhaps it's this that disillusions her most and which continues to rankle inside her for some time afterward, the fact that her mistress makes no attempt to detain her and, as she half-consciously wants, to calm her down with soothing words, to try to make her change her mind. Does she know that Johanna will come back? And does she perhaps also know that Johanna will never mention her departure but will move back into her room the very next day and after unpacking and arranging her things will start work again on the jobs that seem most urgent?

"As I've already told you, whenever I gave notice or left, it was for one reason only, because she needed a warning or a reminder. . . . Are you going to take the fuchsia?"

"And how about her," asks Rita Süssfeldt, "how about Professor Beerbaum herself, did she ever mention your giving notice?"

"Never a word, she acted as though I'd never been away and she left it entirely to me to go on doing the work where I'd left off. . . . I hope you'll like this fuchsia."

"I'm certain that I will."

Rita Süfsfeldt accepts the flower pot, turns it around, and examines it from all angles. She would like to express both her admiration and her gratitude in one and the same breath. "You must come and visit it yourself," she says, "so you can be sure that it's settled down with us." The two women walk to the door, they don't shake hands but nod vigorously to each other several times, and then, carefully holding her pot in front of her, Rita goes down the stone steps, lifts it up once again like a newly won trophy—at which Johanna gives a short wave of her hand—and then goes back to her house past those very narrow gardens.

Where should the flower be placed? Not here, not over there; there's nothing else to be done, so she takes the pot up to her room, but before she slams the door, Heino Merkel catches sight of her; he's sitting on the floor with scissors in his hand surrounded by piles of newspapers and periodicals, which he is attacking with gusto.

"Look what I've got, Heino."

"A fuchsia, if I'm not mistaken."

"Lucy Beerbaum's favorite flower—her own cultivation or planting or whatever you call it.

"You've been over there?" the man inquires.

"Johanna called out to me to come in, she's repotting her plants and she made me a present of this one."

Without looking up, the man waves his scissors in a semicircular motion over the clippings, files, index-card boxes, and periodicals and says, so softly that she has difficulty understanding him, "And I'm on the hunt, as you can see, I'm extracting all the appropriate items from this heap of papers." He flourishes his scissors like a barber, inserts them into a large Sunday supplement, a few sharp snips and he holds up an illustration, with a caption underneath: "Wheels of a Persian chariot." "I'm going to write it, Rita, I'm going to write the history of the wheel. Do you think I can do it?"

"You can do it, Heino."

The woman sits down on a pile of newspapers, lights a cigarette, and watches the man, who, after her laconic remark, is pressing on even faster with his work: an expeditious judge who runs his eye rapidly over the individual cases, sums up the situation in a single glance, and immediately decides what deserves to be preserved for posterity in the battered cardboard boxes of his archives. "It's not every flower that can stand ash," he says suddenly, "cigarette ash, I mean," and he points with his scissors toward the flower pot, into which Rita has flicked two gray lengths of ash. The blades are waving about in his hand and with a clatter they snip into a gray periodical as he casually asks, "Made any progress? Any further insights? Johanna must have lifted part of the veil . . . or did she?"

"Corroboration," says Rita, "all you get is merely corroboration that her life was made for anthologizing. Even from Johanna that's what you get—one example after another suitable for quoting. You slowly begin to wonder whether anyone could possibly have lived like that, so unselfishly and without any contradictions."

"Just wait," the man says, "you'll find out what was missing all right. Lucy wasn't exactly all of a piece like that."

"It's a pity," says Rita, "but up till now one can only agree with everything; with her there's nothing to be explained or interpreted in different ways, there's nothing at all obscure. And agreeing with everything is not enough, you understand, at least for our purposes it's not."

"Perhaps you must remove a few more layers," the man says, and silently holds out a clipping from an article for her to see: "Classical Forms of Death—5. Breaking on the Wheel."

"Do I have to read it now?"

"No, I just wanted to show you how rich my subject is."

The woman won't let him evade the issue. "You knew Lucy well, didn't you? In any case, better than you're prepared to admit."

Heino Merkel shrugs noncommittally, leans his head back, seems to be reviewing the extent of his knowledge, and then gives a half-contented nod. "Not as well as you seem to be assuming, but I did know her, certainly."

"Where did you first meet each other?"

"Where? We had the same publisher."

"At Butenfels'?"

"Yes, at one of his so-called bread-and-butter parties, so it was on a Friday. Like everybody else who was there for the first time, she was having trouble; among all those sweaty pink sides of salmon, the lobsters and piles of smoked eel and jars of caviar, she couldn't find a slice of bread and butter; after all, everybody had come because they'd been promised bread and butter."

"And you made her acquaintance at one of those evening parties?"

"And how!"

"What do you mean by 'and how'?"

As he rummages in his collection of periodicals, the man replies, "Thoroughly. I got to know her thoroughly, right from the start; it would happen, wouldn't it, that we rubbed each other the wrong way that evening, in the house of our publisher."

"But I don't suppose you actually had a real battle, did you?"

"For me it ended in a resounding defeat," says the man with a sour smile, as though the confession brought back the pain or the humiliation that he must have felt at the time.

"Was it you who opened hostilities?"

"On the contrary, I was like all the others, we were all eager to listen as soon as Lucy opened her mouth. You know, Butenfels wanted to inaugurate his 'Hamburg Conversations' with these bread-and-butter parties of his."

"Was Lucy—I'll call her just Lucy too from now on—was it Lucy's first appearance at these parties?"

"The same as myself—the very first appearance, and while the rest of us moved around and conversed, she stood in a corner and held court—as was her due. Not nice."

"What wasn't nice?" asked Rita.

"The colors she was wearing; three different shades of red which clashed, and when she was holding a smoked-salmon sandwich in one hand as well . . . But of course that wasn't the reason why we fell out."

"Well?"

"Possibly, in a bold sort of way, what she was wearing was in good taste; at any rate, people were pushing their way toward her corner and Butenfels himself was making sure her plate was never empty."

"But tell me now, Heino, what happened between the two of you."

"That was later."

"What was?"

"Our clash. We were already sitting in a circle around the hand-carved coffee table, each of us with a glass beside our chair, people from the university, editors, and of course that pompous blockhead Hanker-Schmühling, who always has to add a dab of theological mustard to everything that's said or thought in this town."

"And what were you talking about?"

"Naturally enough, Lucy was the center of attention and

her presence automatically settled the topic of conversation."

"So it was biochemistry?"

"Yes, biochemistry, and all the hopes and fears connected with it."

"Do you know anything about that, Heino?"

"That was just it. As she was sitting there like that, talking—dressed rather outrageously, it's true, but looking gentle and girlish, with a kind of modest satisfaction—when she talked, let's say, about a cell in the intestinal tract of the frog containing the whole genetic program of that frog—then I could understand her without any trouble at all. I don't know how it happened, but when she defined a man as a particular molecular series of various atoms five feet eight inches tall or when she explained the genetic code to us, it seemed to me that I already knew it all, in various vague connections."

"And how could you have a quarrel over that?"

"It was Hanker-Schmühling. It was his fault, the way he talked nonsense. He kept agreeing with Lucy, emphatically approving her statements or, in his words, meeting her halfway from the theological point of view. Once he detected God's presence in amino acid, another time he turned Him into a technologist, controlling sixty billion human cells, and finally he even made Him climb the famous DNA rope ladder. He actually set God up in a white tunic—and Lucy didn't correct him. She didn't stop him, she didn't ask him any questions, she just listened attentively, and yet she could have burst all his hot-air bubbles with a single sentence."

"And that irritated you?"

"Perhaps. I'm not sure. There was a heated discussion going on between two opposing camps: one side believed that research could produce godlike creatures and the other side was afraid that, once it got out of control, research might populate the world with specialized slaves, with programmed robots."

"And that's when you intervened?"

"I didn't have any particular purpose in mind and I didn't want either to gloss over or to exacerbate the differences of opin-

264

ion. I merely mentioned—to prevent that bumbling old driveler from sticking his oar in—something I'd recently read about a young biochemist who had drawn the public's attention, with some embarrassment, to the possibly disastrous consequences of his work, in which man was confusing himself with God. The scientist had left the research team and taken another job. And that was all I said."

"If I guess right," says Rita, "that was grist for Hanker-Schmühling's mill!"

"He didn't say a word, he waited for Lucy's response, he needed someone else's opinion first, so that he could put his dab of mustard on it."

"And that was your first contribution to that 'Hamburg Conversation'?"

"Yes, up till then I'd just been listening. Oh, Rita."

"What?"

"You should have seen the look of amazement on Lucy's face as she turned toward me, very slowly closed her eyes, and just as slowly and incredulously opened them again—her look was full of such deep, pained astonishment that it filled me with foreboding. You should have seen how the others suddenly stopped talking and eyed me with distaste, doubt, and pity; I didn't realize what I'd done."

"And now you do?"

"I discovered that very evening the gaffe I'd made—but how was I to know that the young scientist who'd left his team was Lucy's assistant?"

"All the same," says Rita, "Lucy couldn't help taking your remark as a reproach; you'd suggested that her work was extremely arrogant."

"She took her revenge for it, too."

"How?"

"In her own way. She merely asked me questions, twenty or a hundred questions, shyly, even deferentially, and each question brought me closer to my execution, as the others recognized, taking satisfied little sips from their glasses. The very way she framed her questions: 'I don't know if you share my view that . . .' or 'If you happen to be of the same opinion, then . . .' She was concentrating so hard on putting me down that she failed to notice the smoked-eel sandwiches with scrambled egg that Butenfels was trying to press on her."

"But how about the actual deathblow?" asks Rita Süssfeldt. "Presumably she did, in fact, give you your *coup de grâce.*"

"She made me give it to myself with her questions. First she repeated my remark in her own words and then she let fly: Would I not agree with her that man, having had to suffer a ready-made fate for so long, should try to become master of his own fate; hadn't he the right to make himself the subject of an experiment; should we refrain from deciphering nature's code merely because we don't know the consequences? And didn't I, like her, reject the simplistic assumption that new knowledge whose consequences were unpredictable should be put on ice or proscribed until such time as all risk had been removed? It went on like that, Rita, and I didn't know how to defend myself, all I could do was express agreement and understanding in this free-ranging self-defense of hers which I hadn't intended to provoke in the least. You can imagine how the others enjoyed it, and when I was finally floored and as Butenfels put his hand on my shoulder and offered me a full glass of wine to console me, she said, 'We can desert under pressure from all kinds of things, even under the pressure of irresistible knowledge.'"

"And that was the end of it for Lucy?"

"Yes. I'd had my punishment and she'd vindicated herself."

"Well, one can see that there are all sorts of ways of getting to know people."

"That was only the beginning. We went home together."

"You two? After what had happened?"

"She asked me whether I wasn't the subscriber to the Greek periodical which she had seen in the bag of the mailman who delivers on our street. I was so surprised that I admitted it and afterward we went home together."

"You never told me about that, Heino."

266

"She invited me in."

"I said, you never told us about that."

"There was no occasion to. Anyway, Rita, I went in with her, we sat in front of the open window and drank sherry. Outside there was a procession of children who were going 'lamplighting,' they were on their way to the park swinging their moons and their painted Chinese lanterns."

"I suppose she offered some sort of apology then or what?"

"Not a word, we didn't talk about the party at all, we reminisced about our school days. We wondered whether people had always wanted school to be what most people today expect it to be—namely, a springboard to qualify you for the more important jobs."

"That was what you talked about?"

"Lucy showed me her house, too, and I couldn't help meeting Johanna, who was preparing apple juice using a very primitive press, and I was not only allowed but required to try some."

Rita Süssfeldt flips a cigarette out of a new pack, looking at her watch at the same time, and springs to her feet with a shrill cry.

"What is it now?" asks Heino.

Tightening her headband and frantically brushing ash off her dress, Rita says, "Our session, good heavens, it went completely out of my head, I suppose they'll have started without me. You must tell me more some other time!"

She makes for the door. The man points his scissors at the flower. "Shall I look after it?"

"Admire it," Dr. Süssfeldt cries, "and then take it to my room."

"Shall we wait dinner for you?"

"Not today," she calls, already on her way downstairs, "but tell Mareth that the chimney sweep's coming tomorrow and someone must be at home."

16

Bᴜᴛ from time to time they have to get down to work and be shown at this rather special labor of theirs: talking, interpreting, appraising. So once more we open the door of the conference room of the Hotel-Pension Klöver—proprietress, Ida Klöver— it's afternoon and we sit Pundt and Heller down at the rosewood table and let them cover its brightly polished top with papers, books, and notebooks; we provide sufficient light to reveal two gleaming schnapps glasses, which have obviously already been used and will no doubt shortly be used again. Heller must put on his burgundy sweater and Valentin Pundt, under whose chair we shall place a bottle of his homemade Lüneburg Cock-a-doodle-do, will be wearing his old smoking jacket, in which he nevertheless looks stiff and formal enough.

At the moment the conversation is still desultory and deliber- ately skirting their topic; they are waiting and these two school- masters, so very different, give the impression of athletes warm- ing up. Outside, let us for a moment draw aside the heavy cloud cover over the Alster, and we can imagine a shaft of light, a somewhat austere, perhaps indeed pathetic gleam beneath which the shimmering waters stir uneasily. In the Anglo-German Club, a reception might be taking place, perhaps celebrating the tenth birthday of the Lux advertising agencies, and the guests—all dressed in those dark-blue suits which are de rigueur in business —are greeted by flash bulbs, which, as they flare up in the dis- tance, penetrate even into the conference room itself.

268

And finally, it's not Heller (who might be expected to show the greater impatience) but Valentin Pundt who suggests starting without Rita Süssfeldt, whose late arrival once more seems most remarkable and in any case justifies the presumption that she has either forgotten or else mislaid her waiting colleagues. Heller is agreeable, if Pundt will first pour another glass.

"You weren't exaggerating, this homemade schnapps of yours really does taste as if it had a message."

"Yes, it does, doesn't it?"

Heller gets his second glass, he leans back, ready to listen, he waves his hand for Pundt to begin, to chew over, as it were, for his benefit the instructive slice which Pundt has cut from Lucy's substantial cake of life. This time Pundt wants to dispense with any introduction, he thinks he's found what they need for their third chapter, and with a look full of promise and inviting the strictest attention, he merely says, "Just listen to this."

Toward midnight they surrounded Lucy—not all of them, but certainly the majority of those present—and sang and clapped their hands in rhythm as though the hopes they had placed in their newly elected student representative had already been fulfilled. They shook their heads in rhythm whenever Lucy tried to escape their homage, and whenever she tried to duck under their outstretched arms and slip out of the circle, she was pitilessly pushed back into the middle, into the center of their enthusiasm; they spun around where they stood and forced her to join in the rhythm of their stamping feet. Pleased yet embarrassed, Lucy kept making signs to them: Please stop, that's enough, and then, exhausted, once again: Now, please, please stop; but they continued their applause as though determined to prove to her the full extent of their enthusiasm.

Victor was not in the circle, he was standing outside on the balcony in the warm night, not perhaps disapproving of the fact that the newly elected student representative was being acclaimed for the second time, but nonetheless expressing his reservations by deliberately keeping apart.

It was his party. He had invited his fellow students because he felt he owed them something—after all, the best oral exam since the days of the great Marangas could hardly expect to go unpunished—but it was Lucy who had found a name for the party: "Out of the Test Tube."

And now she was surrounded by stiff-legged homunculi, slim, long-tailed, whiplike creatures, sunburned robots in T-shirts with genetic instructions on their chests; there were cheerful tadpoles on stork's legs and three-eyed beasts and masks showing the complete human brain, in full color, under glass. They were stamping their feet and going through the motions of sawing and chopping and reaping. They were in no mood to be put off by gestures or dissuaded by words. Dogged and undaunted, with single-minded and convincing boneheadedness, they were carrying out their allotted tasks, prepared only to execute the orders given by numbers, by their inventor. They insisted on paying tribute to Lucy, a bag-shaped amoeba, for as long as the program required, while she was trying to catch Victor's eye, waving to him, throwing him happy and resigned little signals: Get me out of here, please get me out. Victor was the only one who had not, or at least not yet, congratulated her on her election as student representative; Victor Gaitanides, who had not needed to add very much to his own stiff formality in order to lend credibility to the medieval homunculus that he was representing tonight. Stiffly and solemnly he handed out retsina and chose music suitable for arousing mechanical reactions; he admonished fellow students who forgot their roles, but it did not escape Lucy's notice that he carefully avoided being left alone with her in this large house which his parents lent him every time they went to the Pagasaean Gulf in the summer.

He didn't return Lucy's wave, he merely acknowledged it with the slightest of bows from the balcony, in the dark: You're enjoying it, really, so I'll bear with it for your sake. And Lucy had to put up with a second round of their homage, defenseless inside the circle, held prisoner by their enthusiasm, which was trying to produce the appropriate noises: bubbles were bursting, there were hissings and rat-a-tats and pit-a-pats; there were rattlings and gurglings and imitations of prehistoric animal sounds; many howls and wails were heard. And now a general moan of relief, a long-drawn-out collective gasp, and the ring opened up to let Lucy out, and while the exhausted artificial creatures collapsed, reaching for their glasses to cool them off, she went to the open balcony door. Victor was already coming to meet her, and on the pretext of getting her something to drink, he squeezed past her and disappeared into the greenish darkness of a back room.

"Come on, Lucy, let's dance." She was dancing with Kitsos, who had put his claws firmly on her shoulders and was working his arms like wrenches, so that she had the feeling he wanted to unscrew her trunk from the rest of her body. Vagilis was dancing next to her and every so often he released yellow fumes from a concealed bag, tiny poisonous-looking clouds such as hang over boiling lava and which in this case produced either tears or sneezes; at any rate, with his moaning and groaning, Vagilis would have you believe that he was being dissolved in acid. And that gnome over there, eyeless but with a gigantic head to make up for it, towing an electric plug attached to a wire behind him, was Stratis, whom they called the sponge. Not only this room but the whole house was lighted by only a few lamps, with greenish-colored shades, suggesting a dim primeval or underwater light, or even, in fact, the light at the bottom of a test tube.

People were leaving and once outside they were allowed to return to human shape and speech: "All the best, Lucy." "See you soon." "You can rely on us." Victor put Lucy's glass down and insisted on accompanying his friends to the door and out into the tranquil street, where protracted farewells were in progress. The echo of footsteps. Whistling. Laughter dying away. A thin, gray, sulphurous thread had fallen onto the skyline over the sea. "Can you see that? He's joining our celebration." Through the open window Lucy could see the foreshortened forms of her friends, saw them turning to wave to Victor from the hill, by the stone seat. One after the other she straightened Kitsos' fingers and lifted them off her shoulder. "Excuse me just a second, Kitsos."

Jerkily, with her arms moving like pistons, she went out of the room, stumbling over a strange couple lying in the hall—two bottle-shaped bodies locked in a clumsy embrace—and went downstairs. The light was on in the kitchen. Victor was standing at the sink holding his left forefinger under the water, pressing it and sucking it; he pulled a handkerchief out of his pocket and tried to tie a bandage over it with one hand.

"What are you doing, Victor?"

"Nothing, one really shouldn't use a sharp knife to peel an orange."

"Tonight," said Lucy, "I mean, to judge by the theme of this party, it shouldn't be possible for any real blood to flow."

"Yes, I know, the most one would expect would be a solution of common salt."

"Don't you have any adhesive tape?"

"Over there in the wall cupboard," said Victor.

Lucy examined the cut, dabbed it, and got a roll of adhesive tape, scissors, and cotton out of the cupboard. Without looking at him, she said, "You're the only one who hasn't congratulated me on my election, all the others have."

"I know."

Lucy, cutting a strip of tape, asked, "Why's that? What's the matter with you? Aren't you glad for me?"

Victor gave another suck at the blood still oozing out of his finger, and then, looking down at the back of her neck as she bent forward, he said, "Are you sure that anyone ought to be congratulated on that kind of election?"

"Why not? Wasn't everything done according to the rules?"

Victor lifted her head so that she could see his face and, with a look that was both piercing and perplexed, said, "Don't you know? Do you really not know, Lucy?"

"What?"

"Surely, it must have been done with your consent."

"What?"

"I was on the election committee," said Victor, "and we were all of the opinion that according to the votes cast Kitsos had won the election and not you."

"Kitsos?"

"But surely you must know, Lucy. In their enthusiasm, your friends allowed an error to creep in and that decided it."

"Give me your finger," said Lucy. She put cotton on the wound and wrapped the strip of adhesive tape around the finger, pulling hard on the ends so that they overlapped. "Listen, Victor. The election's over with. I don't know anything about an error, but if you know something, then you're free to dispute it."

"I can't do that, Lucy, everybody knows about our relationship."

"So what?"

"I don't want to lay ourselves open to their speculations."

"So what are you hoping for then?"

"For you to do something, Lucy. It's you who ought to question the result of the election now that you know everything."

Lucy turned away, put the dressing back into the cupboard, and closed the kitchen door in order to shut out the noise that was now coming from upstairs—the rhythmic stamping and puffing of a human locomotive. "So that's the reason," she said, "that's why you've avoided being alone with me all evening. Just because you know more than I do—and you didn't want to embarrass me by telling me about it. Perhaps you even suspected me?"

"Lucy, you must question the result of the election yourself."

"Why?"

"As a matter of principle. You'll be acting in accordance with the rules and then new elections can be held to decide who the representative is to be."

"And what if I don't do it, Victor? Suppose I decide not to do it, precisely because we know what Kitsos is like, how amiable and unsuspecting he is, how weak in character he is, all of which, of course, makes him popular but it won't help us change things. Or do you think that Kitsos will bring strength to our cause?"

"No, I don't, Lucy, yet I still think we should stick to principle."

"Even though, if we do, nothing will get changed?"

"Yes."

"Even if the election, then, would actually have achieved nothing?"

"Even then."

"And so to stand by our principles we should give up all hope of putting through the changes that I've already initiated and which I am certain of getting through?"

"Yes, Lucy, because we can't sacrifice our rules on the altar of opportunism."

"Is that written down anywhere? If principle is so dictatorial, don't you think, Victor, that now and then we ought to ignore it, so that we're not blindly controlled by it?"

"You're forgetting, Lucy. This principle represents a consensus which we accept so that everyone can exercise his rights."

"Very well, then," said Lucy, "you do that, Victor, make sure that the consensus is respected and once again we'll get the weakest man as our representative."

"You won't do it?"

"No. I won't do it because in this case I can't act against my convictions."

"Not even now that you know how you came to be elected? Now that you're an accessory after the fact?"

"No," said Lucy decidedly, "it's only if we are prepared sometimes to violate a principle that we shall be able to change things. All I know is this, Victor: I've been elected as representative and I'll try to achieve everything they expect from me. Even the majority can be wrong and often we can do something for them only by going over their heads. You wouldn't have thought me capable of acting like that, would you?"

"No, Lucy, I wouldn't have thought that of you."

Victor looked at his finger, bent it as though he were pulling a trigger, and took a half-peeled orange from the kitchen table. "Don't bother," said Lucy, "I'll peel it for you."

The house was trembling and rattling, heavy bodies were stumbling downstairs on insensitive feet. Just like pieces of furniture, thought Lucy, tables and cupboards and chairs would leave the house like that if they were giving notice to quit their jobs. But they were only coming downstairs and then the door flew

274

open and the gnome towing a piece of electric wire behind him picked up the plug and looked around for a socket. "A recharge," he said, "we must recharge ourselves, our batteries have run down." And now the others came in too, gnashing their teeth like nutcrackers and jerking their arms about, going through the motions of eating, complaining, pretending to be exhausted.

"Fuel," said Lucy, "I think they need refueling."

"This way," said Victor, and the hungry fantastic creatures were led to a table and given bread, cheese, salami, and olives. Victor saw to it that they ate in accordance with their roles—that is, without enthusiasm or enjoyment, with the proper reluctance. A recharge, they must recharge their batteries. Lucy poured them some wine, as businesslike and cool as if she were looking after engines, and as they chewed and drank cheerlessly, the group of weird creatures seemed to revive. Once more a number of them decided to leave, and this time Lucy, too, accompanied them into the street, submitted to long embraces, and heard once again how pleasant it could be in a test tube; and then the shadows tottered away.

Without a word Victor turned to go back into the house, as if he hadn't noticed Lucy's presence and, above all, as if he had forgotten what they had arranged to do that evening. And how disagreeable his formality was as he turned toward her when she addressed him, how painfully he was straining to conceal his emotions.

"Well, what about it?" asked Lucy. "The guests will soon be leaving."

He shrugged his shoulders and made a gesture indicating that any decision was entirely her affair: You know the situation, do what you think best.

"Isn't it peculiar?" said Lucy. "That shudder that comes over you, as though glass were being shattered. Do you have that feeling, too?"

"I don't know what you're talking about."

"When the others leave," said Lucy, "Kitsos will be going my way. I'll ask him to take me along with him."

"He'll certainly take you home safely."

275

"So you'd prefer that I leave?"

"We shouldn't keep the others waiting so long," said Victor, and then . . .

A pause, an unbearably long pause carefully staged by Valentin Pundt now that he has finished reading; so deeply moved is he that he doesn't even stir or look up, perhaps to demonstrate to Heller the effect that a passage like this can infallibly produce, but Heller, reaching out for the bottle of Lüneburg Cock-a-doodle-do and without a by-your-leave proceeding to fill both glasses —Janpeter Heller interrupts this meditative pause since he thinks it's more important to release Rita Süssfeldt from her posture of frozen immobility.

So as not to interrupt the reading, she had frozen as soon as she came through the door and has been listening to the last third of it motionless, staring at the floor, an unlit cigarette between her lips, successfully stifling an urge to cough. Genially Heller signals to her to come and join them, raising his glass toward her. "Even though such things ought not to be remarked on between colleagues," he says, "I must say that that look suits you, I mean that embarrassed expression which goes with a guilty conscience."

Rita Süssfeldt flings out her arms, she's ready to confess all if only she can be excused and forgiven this time. "And incidentally, I know that passage and I'm prepared to agree anytime you like," she says, sweeping to her seat. Papers are spread out on the table, the green headband is adjusted, now all that she needs is a cigarette. "Go ahead with your drink, gentlemen, cheers, I'll catch up with you later." The men upend their glasses, Heller in great good humor, Pundt noticeably pensive and theatrical, as though still unable to abandon or emerge from Lucy's world, and since his collaborators don't seem to be over-eager to express their views concerning his suggestion, as a start he would like to confess something himself.

Well, if anyone would like to know, if anyone were to ask him to state the justification for an exemplary life, he could now answer with renewed confidence: it was because it brought to light certain deficiencies and offered a watchword, a slogan that would make it possible to remedy those deficiencies, and, if need be, rules considered sacrosanct would have to be broken! From such an example, continues Pundt, you could learn that we shouldn't do merely what we please but should systematically do what we felt we owe it to ourselves to do. He hesitates, but since no one contradicts him—or at least not yet—he gives the reasons for his view, in a monotonous, very deliberate voice. He'd been reading letters, letters written in a state of distress; they'd been written by his son and addressed to someone of roughly the same age whom his son had hero-worshipped. And these letters confirmed his belief that a hero, an exemplary person, draws attention to the fact that we need something. That something has to be done. That the world is not a *fait accompli* but can be changed. And it was in this belief that Valentin Pundt had put forward this chapter about Lucy, who, having been elected student representative in a dubious way, rebels against old-established and thus unproven prejudices by questioning the power of principle; she instinctively takes the part of a majority which perhaps hasn't even elected her, and that surely provides the educational point to the story —it's always worth doing something even if your first effort seems to lead nowhere.

Do they follow him so far? Do they agree with him? Gloomily he passes around a triangular paper bag of dried fruit and is not offended when neither of them takes any.

Heller stands up. Heller snatches a panga from the wall, makes a few passes in the air with it as if amputating superfluous limbs. He concentrates. He shows concern. He wants them to realize how difficult he's making everything for himself. And then: "My dear colleague"—such a beginning bodes ill. But first he would like to admit that he hadn't disliked the passage which has just been presented; it was as serviceable and as suitable as many other passages which they'd had the opportunity of listening to; honest, to the point, agreeable to interpret, and in addition the inevitable message was handed to you on a platter, staring you in the face.

Doubtless none of their readers would find it strange if they decided to put this example into an anthology. It was sufficiently unequivocal: on the one hand, blind principle, and on the other, a dangerous infringement of a principle—it was easy enough to handle, and totally familiar; basically, it was the well-tried recipe of either/or. Lucy was a ready-made model straight out of a perpetual calendar. "But this is where we should start to feel misgivings," says Heller. "If we're looking for a message, if we're cooking up a moral, if a passage is being twisted and turned merely in order to pick up encoded signals, then we ought to refuse to play along. For there's nothing more arrogant than passing on concealed messages to defenseless schoolchildren, messages for universal salvation which you make them dig out of their sumptuous wrapping. Let's put it like this: the modern view is that every ego should discover its own authentic content." Heller can't help it, but, when he thinks how eloquently Lucy rejects the burden of tradition, behind the scenes he can see looming up a gigantic admonishing forefinger, made of teak.

Valentin Pundt had not expected such a reaction in the least and he eyes Heller in astonishment as though he had met an unexpected opponent. Is it worthwhile, at this point, to attempt some form of self-defense? After such a judgment, should one try to solicit support for one's proposal?

"No," says Rita Süssfeldt abruptly, "no, my dear Herr Heller, you're on the wrong track, your judgment's at fault. What Herr Pundt has put forward here is certainly worth consideration. All the same, it may well be asked whether in this case it's not perhaps Victor who offers an example worth copying. You said 'a message.' I understand why you're so suspicious of anything that smacks of a message, of didacticism—it's manipulation, isn't it? You scent manipulation in everything, even in our autumn weather. But what does the word 'message' mean? I know you look on it as simply a dishonest proclamation, a magic formula to be swallowed whole, uncritically; for you a message is a broad hint from the authorities indicating the new direction which is to be followed. But what if you change the name and instead of 'message' you call it 'experience' or 'conviction'? An experience is put forward for comparison or as a challenge: isn't that precisely the task we have set ourselves in our reader? And isn't that our only chance of success? A passage which doesn't pose any questions or obligations, which offers no problems with regard to its meaning—any passage of that kind leaves me quite indifferent. It must have some purpose in order to interest me. And if it reveals something of that sort, I mean if it makes me aware of an experience or an attitude, that's not a disadvantage. On the contrary, that's just when I start to become interested. I can't understand the reason for this universal fear of being taken in. Certainly, Lucy's revolt against formal principles is too obvious, but who's going to be harmed by this obviousness? Doesn't the subject still remain controversial enough? I'm in favor—even if you do keep looking at me so skeptically—I'm in favor of putting this passage on our short list. Under another title, of course."

Heller takes the panga back to the wall and hangs it up. Are they going to vote on it immediately, perhaps a disputed vote? No? In that case, he would like to enlarge on his statement, simply because he's afraid he may have been misunderstood: perhaps he'd been too aggressive. That might well be the case, but unfortunately there were reasons for that. He was, in fact, fed up with playing this dishonest game of selling suitable exemplary lives. And the situation was always presented in these terms: you're faced by chaos, aren't you, and black despair, you're suffering from uncertainty, there's no end to it all, in the long run you have to come to terms with it, for better or worse, and then, in a moment of crisis, a heroic act springs to your attention and spawns a meaningful message. What happens? Everything in the garden is lovely and hope returns once more. "Well, I don't have much sympathy for this accountant's type of mentality," Heller says, and as Pundt looks at him disapprovingly he adds: "That's not directed against you personally, Herr Pundt, we've agreed on that."

279

"That passage convinced me at least," says Dr. Süssfeldt, "and I agree with the view put forward by Herr Pundt: an exemplary life must be seen as an active, stimulating force that sparks something off. And now you may give me a drink, Herr Pundt; but before I drink, I'd like to say something else to you, Herr Heller. Of course there are reasons for packing up and putting an end to our search. Of course we can declare, like any old obscurantist who's been following the wrong track, that there's no greater blasphemy than searching for a meaning and foisting a meaning onto certain attitudes or actions. If nothing has a meaning, then of course an exemplary act is meaningless, too, and in a particularly blatant way. But every day I feel convinced that it is meaningful to do something—if only to prevent reason from being driven into a corner. Or, as Lucy Beerbaum said, to prevent suffering from becoming a matter of indifference."

Heller raises his empty glass toward her, Heller acknowledges her statement with an approving nod. "You're in good form today, one hardly dares put forward any suggestion of one's own."

"So you do have one," says Rita Süssfeldt.

"With Lucy Beerbaum," Heller says, "one's bound to find something." And so, with no particular purpose in mind, he would like to state that he has never yet X-rayed a life—he actually says "X-rayed"—which contains such tension, such elementary and self-evident tension between a person and her society. And in his view, that was precisely what you could learn from this woman: the obligation to disturb and to participate. It was from this point of view that they should judge the example that he would like to put forward for discussion, an extract from *The Price of Hope*, they'd have to settle on the title later. "Are you ready? Here goes:"

They brought Nikos back and flung him on the plank bed and immediately left without taking the next person on the list. They didn't even glance at Lucy or Alexis; it was as though they had learned all that they wanted, or perhaps they were saving them for some special treatment. They left them alone in the cold,

280

unbarred room; but only one of them walked away down the corridor.

Nikos was shaking, his lips were swollen, the top buttons of his shirt had been torn off. He turned his face to the window, writhing with pain, and seemed to be listening to his own gasping breath. Alexis walked gently up to him, put his hand on his shoulder, and forced him to turn over toward him. "Quick, Nikos, before they come back for the next one." The man on the plank bed sank back and seemed about to tip over toward the wall, not only indifferent to the questions but temporarily unconscious; but Alexis kept hold of him and persisted: patting his cheeks, he pulled Nikos to the edge of the bed and whispered, "As we agreed? Tell me, everything as we arranged?" Nikos was still looking at him as if from a distance, as though he had forgotten what had been arranged between them, but then he made a sign without speaking, with an expression of pained amazement which could only mean: What else? Did you think I could possibly do anything else?

Alexis gently laid him down and lifted his legs onto the bed. "Well done, Nikos," he said, "they'll be told the same by me, I promise you."

Alexis bent over his comrade, who with his eyes closed was now moving his lips, trying to confirm in words what he had just expressed in signs: "The two of us . . . I told them . . . that both of us . . . wrote the article . . . that was all they wanted to know . . . who wrote 'The Whip' . . . exactly as we agreed."

Alexis stroked his forehead to show that he had understood, gestured to Lucy standing beside the door to come over to the bed, and whispered, "He's accepted the responsibility and I'll do the same. You mustn't admit anything, Lucy."

"But I must," said Lucy. "I wrote the article and I'll admit it."

"It'll be easier for us if we know that our journal is still appearing occasionally," said Alexis.

"It will appear," said Lucy.

"But they need your articles. You must go on writing them and that's why you're not to admit anything, Lucy."

"It's easier for you," said Lucy, "but not for me. When I'm

outside, I'll be thinking every moment about what you've done for me; I won't be able to bear the burden. I'll be thinking of you whenever I'm doing anything."

"You're needed more than we are," the man said. "That's why we're taking the responsibility; none of our friends would understand it if we came out without you."

"Other people depend on you," said Lucy. "I'm on my own."

They sprang apart and looked toward the door as it was flung open from outside. Two men with gun belts came in, gaunt, joyless men who pointed briefly at Alexis: Your turn, and they led him away between them. Lucy rushed to the door and pressed her ear against the smooth, cool wood and listened until their steps died away.

"Sit down," said Nikos from the bed. "You won't learn anything by doing that. Come and sit down here, it'll be your turn soon enough."

Lucy went over and sat down on the end of the bed. "Did they beat you?"

"It was my memory," said Nikos, "they weren't satisfied with my memory and so they tried to help it along."

"Why are you doing this for me?"

"It's not for you, or at least not for you personally. We must make sure that more articles like 'The Whip' are published; you must see that they are. You should have heard the way they talked about it, you wondered whether they were more furious or more frightened. Anyway, they showed that we were right."

He was trembling and his feet were gently twitching and then he lifted his clenched fist to his swollen lips and bit the back of his hand. "They won't do it to me," said Lucy, "they won't dare. If I'd confessed right away, you'd have been spared all this."

Nikos gave her a worried look over his bent elbow. The youngest of the editors, he had been caught with the stencils in his hand when the police burst into the warehouse where they used to discuss their factory journal after work. Nikos sat up, seized with the sudden suspicion that everything that they had discussed and for which they had agreed to accept responsibility might turn out

282

to be pointless. "You must confirm that *we* wrote the articles. They haven't accepted it yet and so you've got to confirm it." He seized Lucy's wrist and immediately dropped it, frightened by the twisted smile that had appeared on her lips and perhaps sensing once again the controlled and cold indifference which Lucy was able to summon up whenever she had to pass judgment on and dispose of something unexpected; an indifference which still amazed him every time he saw it.

"You're in a better position than I am," said Lucy, "you're *giving* all the time, but all I can do is accept it and try to endure it."

"You must ignore it," said Nikos, "and then it's okay, you must think of the others." And he inquired, anxiously and suspiciously, "You will do it, won't you?" And calmly, as though he had to deprive her of a forbidden hope: "And don't count on Alexis, he won't give in, he'll accuse himself." And probing still more deeply into her silence, which he was finding increasingly disquieting: "You owe it to us, Lucy. Now that Alexis is also accepting responsibility for it, you just can't confess now."

Lucy stood up, walked to the door, to the window, and then back to the door. For a long while she stood in front of the wall trying to decipher initials and marks and signs scratched in the mortar, marks which had become shallow and sometimes difficult to make out under the layers of dried whitewash. The young man on the bed moaned. She opened the door and listened down the corridor; far away, near the iron water drum, light was coming from a room and she could hear the clatter of a typewriter. She heard a call, the young man on the bed was calling to her and making signs to her to close the door. "No, don't do that," he said. "Don't try to escape; you won't get very far." Lucy didn't sit down on the bed as Nikos wanted her to but hoisted herself onto the table and sat facing him, dangling her legs and resting her hands on the edge of the tabletop. Instead of sinking back on the bed, the young man struggled to hold himself propped up, looking her in the eye as though he had to watch her closely, and they waited in this position until Alexis was brought back.

You knew they were coming because of the noise of something being dragged along the floor and the sound of surly voices. The men wearing the gun belts were holding him tightly under the armpits, and as he hung stiffly between them, face downward, they dragged him into the room and straight to the plank bed, while Nikos moved to one side and drew himself up to the top end.

Behind the men in uniform appeared a sad-looking and extremely tired civilian and a young man, no older than Nikos and just as pale; and the civilian, with a grubby white collar and unshaven double chin, bowed to Lucy as he came in, not in the least ironically but rather mechanically. Lucy slipped off the table and moved instinctively toward the bed, where the uniformed men were lifting Alexis into a sitting position and supporting him as they ordered him in a low voice to pay attention to the civilian. She raised her hands, getting ready to do something, though she didn't know herself what she could do at that moment. The civilian made a reassuring gesture, it won't be long, he'll soon recover; he asked her to go back to the table and came and stood beside her.

The two men were on the plank bed in front of her. Lucy was obliged to look at them while the civilian was speaking, and in a businesslike tone of voice he inquired whether Lucy's father knew where she was now, and as she raised her shoulders uncertainly, he said in a matter-of-fact voice that Mr. Beerbaum had been informed a few minutes ago. He didn't go into personal details, but merely asked her for confirmation that she was a student of biology and chemistry, and then made her answer various short questions, without ever once showing any surprise at her answers: Yes, she knew it was an illegal factory journal; yes, she had written several articles for it; yes, she did realize that it might cause unrest in the factory but for her it was more important to improve the working conditions there; yes, she did participate in various editorial conferences; yes, friends did recruit her for the journal.

Admission, confirmation: as she faced the two men on the bed, Lucy made no attempt to hide behind vague replies or to

284

seek any advantage by answering ambiguously; she seemed rather to be anxious to get the interrogation over with by corroborating everything. It was hard for her to understand the seemingly pointless questions the civilian directed at her in a droning, monotone voice. She did not take her eyes off the two men who were listening to her with concentrated attention—even when Alexis lifted his head and watched her, bemused, with bloodshot eyes. And then, as if spontaneously, a relationship seemed to establish itself between her and the two men, for as a result of the "special treatment" they had received, their lips were constantly quivering and this created the impression that they were in fact commenting to themselves on Lucy's answers. "Yes, I did distribute the factory journal, too, in the rain while the workers were waiting outside the gate to be let in." Lucy could not fail to see how much effort the men had to put out to follow her answers or how anxiously they awaited each new question.

"Yes, something in particular did precipitate my decision to collaborate on the factory journal." Lucy was thinking of the girl whose hair had got caught in a machine one morning and who came to work again the same afternoon after she'd learned that the management of the factory regarded her accident as "rank carelessness" and was not going to give her any sick pay.

Now the civilian was simplifying his questions by prefacing them with the same phrases: "Is it your view that . . ." or "Do you also believe that . . ." or "May I conclude from that . . ."

Lucy pretended not to notice that he was closing in on her with his questions and trying to pin her down. "Is it your view," he asked, "that the decisive conflict is between those who control machines and those who are controlled by machines?"

Lucy, with her eyes on the two men, nodded and said quietly, "Yes."

"And do you also believe that the most urgent task is to set up a workers' organization which can do without bureaucracy?"

"Yes," said Lucy, "because it's always the officials who reject every project."

"And is it also your view that the attitude of most people

toward their work is one of alienation and that among workers the predominant attitude is dislike and even hatred?"

Lucy could see that the men on the plank bed were waiting expectantly. Returning their look, in which she thought she could detect a silent request for extreme caution, she said, "Yes. If work is to lead to a free and close relationship with life, it must be given greater dignity."

Without raising his voice, the civilian pointed out, with no sign either of satisfaction or disappointemnt, that every one of his questions was, word for word, a sentence taken from a certain article called "The Whip," printed in the last issue of the factory journal. As he spoke, he handed her a copy of the journal, asking, "Are you familiar with that article?"

Lucy nodded, but that was not enough for him and he repeated his question. "Yes," replied Lucy, "I am familiar with the article."

The men on the plank bed stirred, as though they were preparing to object. "Do you know who wrote the article?" the civilian asked.

Alexis bent forward to free himself from the grip which one of the uniformed men had on his shoulder; his eyes narrowed.

"The articles are all unsigned," said Lucy.

"So you don't know?" asked the civilian.

Lucy pressed her fingers against the edge of the table. "No, I don't know."

"So it's pointless to ask you whether you perhaps wrote this article yourself." He nodded, neither pleased nor disappointed. He said something but she didn't catch it—she was trying to engage the eyes of the men on the bed, for now she was relying on some sign from them; but they sat there in silence, although less tense than they had been at first.

The civilian repeated what he had said: "You may go, I don't need you any more," and since Lucy still seemed not to have heard him: "We don't need your cooperation any more."

Lucy walked uncertainly toward the bed, thinking: I can't leave without saying something. She stood there a moment as though waiting for the men to shake hands with her, but now that she had done what they wanted they seemed to be leaving the rest to her, even the way she would say goodbye to them.

She walked out without saying a word. No one paid any attention to her. Tight-lipped, she went to the door, swaying slightly as she looked down the corridor and then quickly putting her hand against the wall for support. She walked hesitatingly, more and more slowly and still hesitating, soon she would come to a halt and reflect, perhaps change her mind. And then she stood still, leaned back against the wall, and lifted her face toward the ceiling. But she didn't go back.

Without looking, Janpeter Heller reaches for his glass, gulps down the small amount that remains, moistens his lips with his tongue, and reads, no, he's not going to read on although the passage is obviously not yet finished, but he wants to end his selection here, with this sentence, and he concludes with a vigorous jab of his finger. That seems to him quite sufficient, he can lean back and confidently await his colleagues' reactions. However, his colleagues are in no hurry to voice an opinion. The silence drags on; the air is filled with reluctance. Embarrassment is concealed by a pretense of being otherwise preoccupied. Rita Süssfeldt shakes her hair as though removing snowflakes; Pundt applies himself to scratching off the label on his bottle, which is arrogantly flying the false colors of an ordinary schnapps instead of the Lüneburg Cock-a-doodle-do. "There's one thing, at least, that nobody can deny," says Rita Süssfeldt. "We're not making things easy for ourselves. I'd like to meet the publisher who would take as much trouble as we have. Over an anthology! Over one single chapter of an anthology! Nobody's likely to be following our example in that respect in the near future."

Valentin Pundt has nothing to say to that, but this ironical self-praise visibly relaxes him, he passes his hand once over his unparted hair and announces that, in all sincerity and without wanting to take sides in any way, he would like to ask, without beating about the bush, how his colleague Heller means his example to be taken. What was exemplary in Lucy's decision to keep the authorship of the article secret? And what would the school-boy, the young man for whom this reader was intended, gain by trying to interpret this particular example? He'd like to ask this quite bluntly, simply because he feels completely in the dark.

Age obviously has its own explanations, Heller is tempted to say, but doesn't, because he knows how sensitive Pundt is. Instead he sits up, complacently contemplates his open hand, and, tugging at his fingers, tries to explain his proposal to the old schoolmaster. "In general, an exemplary person surely acts for other people, doesn't he? But in this case, in order to be able to represent others, he must first act against his own views. An exemplary person has to earn his role, doesn't he? In order to appear credible, he must first pay a price—in order to be effective for the many, he must have an understanding of the sufferings of the few. On his way to a greater purpose, the exemplary person must have an understanding of the tribulations of the few, which are offered to him as—I'm almost tempted to say: as an unwelcome sacrifice. How much easier it would have been for Lucy to confess and suffer the consequences of writing the arti-cle! The common purpose requires her to accept the sufferings of others. In the interest of the common cause, because she is expected to make a contribution that is beyond the powers of the others—she has to disregard everything, not even the sight of suffering can be allowed to weaken her resolution. And that represents for me," says Heller, "an extreme variant of the exem-plary person." Does his colleague not view it in the same way?

The old headmaster's posture of gloomy meditation evolves into an increasingly violent shaking of his head: no, he couldn't quite go along with that; although he had some vague idea, a nebulous inkling, the whole passage seemed to him not conclu-sive enough, not convincing enough. "Don't you think, Herr Heller, that there's something a trifle farfetched in the example you've chosen?" Above all, Pundt would like to know what a schoolboy would make of this insight that was being recom-mended to him. Even assuming that he saw what the passage was all about, what else was there for him to do except shrug his shoulders?

They turn abruptly toward the window, beyond which a black shower is falling, flat black objects and splinters which float and spin past the scaffolding and hit the ground with a series of sharp cracks, like whiplashes.

"Tiles," says Heller, "they're replacing the worn-out tiles on the roof." Among the shower of splinters, whole tiles are whizzing down, like heavy swooping birds; some of them perform a somersault, spin sideways, strike the scaffolding, and are smashed to pieces. Suddenly a bucket drops, bounces with a resounding clang, and rolls off.

Rita Süssfeldt springs to her feet and rushes to the window, but the men on the roof or at the top of the scaffolding are not to be seen. And now a hammer drops past and right on its tail a few more tiles rumbling like a load of snow sliding off a roof; and then still more tiles.

"It'll be an interesting sight when the first tiler comes down," says Heller, and Pundt, speaking as if from experience: "They're known for being quarrelsome, presumably it comes from the great heights they work at." Rita lifts a black wooden blowpipe from the wall, puts it to her eye like a telescope, and, making a face, aims it upward through the window.

"Finding a meaning," she says in a strained voice, "nowadays you have to find a meaning for everything. Since we're so good at it, perhaps we ought to interpret what's happening up there as meant for our amusement." She puts the blowpipe to her lips and points the tiny aperture at Heller. "Don't you agree, my dear colleague? We can see from your example what it all adds up to: it's no longer enough to see, and hear, we have to explain what we've seen and heard to each other. An action without its interpretation is worthless. An event without its explanation is incomplete. An idea without a commentary is meaningless. In the old days people lived, didn't they; nowadays life is merely an occasion for interpretation. And in the process, gentlemen, a great deal is lost. Interpreting, analyzing, explaining: we do it as a profession, many of us even make our living from it, and at the end of the day, what's the outcome of it all? At best, just assumptions. We lift the cloak, we draw aside the curtain. We remove layer after layer to get to the heart of the onion. Interpreting: so you break open the shell and it's empty—and one's left with the mother of pearl and that reveals nothing, you put it to your ear, you hear a murmur, and you can say: that's the sea."

Dr. Süssfeldt swings the blowpipe back from the window to the table, searching for a target, and then, holding it to her lips like a flute, she informs her surprised colleagues of her doubts, doubts that are by no means recent ones, for now she confesses that the interpretation of actions and characters and ideas has always seemed to her a highly dubious matter: usually you end up with: on the one hand . . . on the other hand. If interpreting meant assimilating something in a new way, if it meant the same as finding out for yourself, Rita Süssfeldt would perhaps not be so much against it. But what does it all end up as, almost always? Secrets are forcibly exposed, deep-rooted obscurities are made to appear acceptable. Everything is put under the spotlight, everything categorized. And what's the end result? Our interpretations turn our life into enlightened boredom.

Valentin Pundt is restless, he's tapping the tip of his ball-point pen sharply on his notebook and, as an older man, ventures to point out that something has just been done which he, at any rate, regards as questionable. "You were trying, my dear Dr. Süssfeldt, to interpret the act of interpretation. In so doing, one may, indeed, receive the impression that our work is superfluous or, to say the least, odd. So please permit me to say that, for me, interpretation and discrimination are surely two of the most important aspects of teaching."

"That's my view, too," says Heller, "and so that we can have something to discriminate about, shouldn't we listen to the last proposal now, before we've discussed everything to death; it may provide the solution to all our troubles. Or haven't you got a proposal?"

"Me? Even if I did arrive late," says Rita Süssfeldt, "I have at least come prepared; of course, I haven't any passage ready to read and I don't even know if this example is written down."

"Did you invent it then?" Heller asks, and at the thought of this possibility he immediately adds, enthusiastically: "Perhaps that would be our real salvation: we'll invent an exemplary action for ourselves."

"This is a story I heard," says Rita Süssfeldt. "It could be called 'Desertion,' all it needs is to be written up."

" 'All it needs'?" says Heller. "That's rich."

Pursuing the matter no further, Rita says, "We see Lucy Beerbaum at the peak of her career in her Hamburg period; her Institute, of which Lucy is deputy director, enjoys the highest professional reputation, and a scientific publication of hers, *Purpose and Chance*, even becomes a best seller—but, of course, that's not the beginning of the story; according to my own rough idea, it ought to start something like this:"

Lucy Beerbaum and her assistant Rainer Brachvogel are sitting in a narrow-gauge railway compartment and are hurtling along at a good ten miles an hour to attend a conference, a weekend conference. An evangelical teaching establishment has asked the eminent scientist to attend, and also to bring along a collaborator, preferably a "dissenting collaborator," so Lucy Beerbaum has chosen from among her assistants the one who has expressed the gravest doubts about the work of the Institute. The theme of the conference is "Science and Faith" for the umpteenth time. There will be television coverage this time, and the radio station and interested newspapers will have representatives on hand as usual.

As the narrow-gauge railway toils through orchards and pastures, the two passengers are conversing, their heads involuntarily bobbing up and down all the while. What are they discussing? Let's say they're discussing all these learned institutions, not one of which is easy of access, whose purpose is to remove the scales from people's eyes. Anyone who spends a weekend at one of these establishments becomes a seer almost overnight and acquires a disturbingly new angle on contemporary problems. Are you with me up till now? Good.

Professor Beerbaum and her assistant have to travel to the end of the line, where the station consists of a "Ladies and Gents" nestling among vine leaves, and here they're met by a youngish, prematurely bowed giant of a man called Dr. Turrini, who inquires with a melancholy smile how they have fared on the journey—without showing the slightest interest in their answer. They would not have been surprised if they had been offered bicycles to finish the last part of the journey; it turns out, however, that Dr. Turrini has a car, though such a tiny one that Lucy Beerbaum is amazed and asks whether it was intended for export to territories populated by pygmies.

They drive in silence to the Institute, through country lanes and then up an avenue of poplars and into the paved courtyard of a former Electoral palace. In front of the stairs at the main entrance, the director, Dr. Hoelzgen, is eagerly pacing up and down. Seen from the level of the car, he looks so overwhelming that you wonder whether he's going to tuck the vehicle under his arm, carry it into the building, and dump its contents into various rooms.

Introductions. Delighted, etc., etc. Expressions of gratitude, of course. Eager expectation and general excitement. He insists on accompanying the new arrivals personally to their rooms; somewhere in the house a girls' choir is practicing: "Jesu joy of man's desiring"; an odor of wax candles and Lysol hangs about the corridors. The doors of the rooms have no keys. On every table there's a small basket of fruit, with blunt fruit knives and table napkins made of unbelievably tough paper. Dr. Hoelzgen suggests taking a rest until dinner or a walk through the gardens or a tour of the building; they can spend the time as they like but are expected for the big dinner, at which everyone will be present and which will be announced by a gong.

Does Lucy change her dress? Doubtless she will continue to wear her chlorophyll-green suit and the same comfortable black shoes; nor will she abandon her bulging handbag, because she knows that it contains everything she needs in case of emergencies: small change, packs of paper handkerchiefs, pills against every known ill. She doesn't have to ask her way to the dining hall, for at the stroke of the gong Dr. Hoelzgen comes to get her; a man of restless geniality who hardly ever finishes a sentence.

A great performance over the introductions at the head table, where Lucy's opponents are already assembled, including, not surprisingly, Hanker-Schmühling, the theologian and publicist who never misses any gathering where contemporary phenomena are being debated; Hanker-Schmühling, the great traveling salesman of theological sauce, which he pours over every discussion. Professor Kannebichl, dapper and dogmatic, with a little goatee, is also present, and then there's a benevolent-looking moon-faced man with crafty eyes, the newspaper editor Ewald Kregel, and finally Hilda Dupka-Moersch, the worthy president of a women's welfare organization, knock-kneed and flashing a set of massive horse teeth. Is that everybody? I think we're all here; they seize hands, Dr. Hoelzgen says a cheerful grace, and, pumping their arms up and down, up and down, the whole row wishes each other in rhythm: *Gu–ten Ap–pe–tit*. Unbelievably pale girls lug the largest teapots ever invented to the tables and, using both hands, pour out the thinnest tea ever brewed.

"I know it," says Heller, interrupting. "I've had it at home."
"But I hope," says Rita Süssfeldt, "that you didn't have to drink it out of institutional teacups like Lucy, because they're heavy, hold a terrifying quantity, and are so thick that many of the guests walked around with anguished, wide-open mouths long after they'd finished dinner. It's caused by the cups, you know. Although it could, of course, have come from the sandwiches, wads of such massive dimensions as to test the flexibility of any jaw to the utmost—and incidentally, they used razor blades to slice the sausage."

What kind of conversation would there be at the table? Since Hanker-Schmühling is present and takes the leading part in it almost as a matter of course, they'll no doubt talk about their appearances on television: technical problems, human errors—and fees. After another cheerful grace the participants stream out into the conference hall. The back rows are occupied by the nuns' pupils, long-suffering and attentive girls, and it is already plain that nothing is going to induce them to leave their seats; in the middle, those indispensable participants in any conference, "enlightened housewives"; the two front rows are reserved for the press and guests of honor, while the young people are lolling about against the radiators or sitting on windowsills.

Now the intellectual gladiators make their entrance and are assigned their seats—science here, faith there; next, Dr. Hoelzgen: presentations and welcomes or vice versa; and then, in accordance with the tradition of the house, a cautious introduction to the evening.

We can imagine how Hoelzgen "develops" the question of the different approaches: faith is an affirmation, a socially constructive, purposeful force; science a blind force, seeking knowledge and having no imperative but itself; on the one hand, irrational experience which makes moral demands on its believers; on the other, concrete experience which leads to fundamental theoretical principles; on the one hand, certainty, on the other, knowledge; faith as increasing security in the world and so on; science as disinterested enlightenment, whose results are controversial. At that point, you can link on, take up, put into focus, the television camera swivels around; the fight is on.

There are too many people smoking. From the platform, you have the impression that the nuns' pupils are dissolving into small craft drifting away under pale sails. One man, in addition to his silver mane, has brought along an explosive cough and in the view of many people had far better stayed at home. The television technicians, faceless beneath their bushy beards and shaggy tousled hair, might at least make some attempt to pretend that they're listening. Only the housewives are taking notes, classifying the points of the discussion under separate headings; the young people are listening and waiting in moods varying from indolent to sullen.

Meanwhile, on the platform faces are hardening because Frau Dupka-Moersch and the dapper dogmatist are insisting on believing in a divine act of creation to which we owe the multifarious universe of phenomena. This is disputed, on technical grounds, by Lucy's assistant, speaking in a quiet voice. As of now, he says, we are in the position of being able to copy nature, to produce every imaginable biological system artificially. Why? Because life will necessarily be created whenever certain chemical and physical conditions are present. And then he brings out his big guns, leaving Hanker-Schmühling speechless: all you need do, he declares, is to send a flash of artificial lightning through a mixture of hydrogen, ammonia, and steam—that is, through the sinister primeval slime—and inevitably the basic elements of life will be produced, namely the amino acids glycine and alanine. The idea of a single act of creation, Brachvogel states, is a fable, because nothing can be created out of nothing. This idea has lost its credibility. Though it may have wound itself around our hearts, we must reject it because it's being disproved every day in our labs.

And now Hanker-Schmühling trots out his pet idea—the reconciliation of faith and science—and after he has endeavored to conceal all the contradictions under a gooey sauce, he pulls Kant and Newton out of his bag: why did Newton describe space as *sensorium Dei*, he would like to know, and why had Kant regarded certain laws of nature as providing a proof of God's existence, he would like to know. Unless he's been misled, in those days science and faith did not stand so far apart.

"I would think," says Rita Süssfeldt, pausing a moment, "that this particular discussion should be rendered dramatically and informatively—at least we should say something about the dramatis personae."

Hanker-Schmühling is famous as a guest who never knows when to leave, and his splendid platitudes are greeted with no more than the usual silence; no one else is inclined to pursue them further. Rainer Brachvogel meanwhile has awakened as much disquiet as acquiescence, and though he has not won the sympathy of everybody, at least he has attracted considerable attention. No one has registered this more carefully than Professor Kannebichl, the dapper dogmatist. He is alarmed and feels called upon to intervene; with an amiability that bodes little good, he turns toward Lucy's assistant, first of all to express his agreement: It's correct, he says, that today any biological system can be produced artificially; he is also aware that man has gained control of his experiments with living matter; he had even heard of an attempt which, reportedly, led to the discovery of a mathematical formula for the self-organization of matter—in fact, the formula for a universal law. Yes, it's true, he says, things which it took nature some millions of years to produce, science can now accomplish with breathtaking speed. And having stated all this, he clears his throat, changes his tone, and asks, almost sharply: What has been gained as a result? What help could this new knowledge provide for a mankind perplexed and not yet liberated from suffering? And what is the contribution of modern science to a stabilized view of the world, to an understanding of man's place in the world as a whole? He would like to hear an answer to that question.

Applause from the housewives, of course, but also from the nuns' pupils, and this encourages Kannebichl to fire a rapid supplementary question: he would also like to know in whose hands lies the responsibility for the humane application of these results of modern research.

There's a whispering and a stirring of chairs and a straightening of backs as the questioner on the platform leans back and tries to light a small pipe, curved and obviously hopelessly clogged up. What will Rainer Brachvogel say in reply? Brachvogel, who a moment ago was expatiating on the immense possibilities of modern science. He hesitates. He admits that in this instance he can only speak on behalf of his own science of biochemistry. And then he confesses that even if the possibilities are immense, the results to be expected make him dubious, and not only that, he sometimes shudders to think of the consequences of unbridled advances in the life sciences. The most frightening victories of alchemy, he says, are still to come—that is, if man takes himself as the subject of his great experiment and becomes both the creator and the created.

At this point, and for the first time, Lucy smilingly starts taking notes and she nods her head in acknowledgment of the reasons her assistant gives for his feeling of horror. Many things are no longer inconceivable and we shall be able to accomplish them; among them, he would mention: detached brains; the culture of fertilized egg cells in a laboratory; the postponement of life and death; specialized human beings produced to fulfill certain functions only, both higher and lower ones; biological wars in which whole peoples will be turned into idiots. And in conclusion he says: If man wants to play at being the creator, then eventually that game might turn out to the disadvantage of mankind.

Professor Kannebichl manifests vigorous agreement, although his questions have been answered only indirectly, and even Frau Dupka-Moersch and editor Kregel are in agreement, while Lucy, who up to this point has been making only brief and indeed barely intelligible comments, now collects herself as though she had received the signal to join the fray. She ignores what has previously been said and turns to talk to her assistant in a quiet, intimate tone of voice that takes people by surprise; it's as though she were merely continuing an interrupted conversation. Tense silence falls.

You know quite well, Rainer—she says, more or less—that what forces us to believe is an irrational experience; what leads us to accept a scientific discipline is the desire to determine our position in the cosmic process of evolution. We have the privilege of knowing more than earlier generations; true, we must be prepared to face the fact that knowledge can also be a tragic privilege. It may be that knowledge can lead to self-destruction; but it doesn't follow that stupidity is likely to lead to salvation.

The audience is already betraying signs of disquiet, anxious glances are being exchanged, gasps are clearly audible.

Lucy Beerbaum reminds everyone what biochemistry has already given us, from sleeping pills to insulin and hormones. And still addressing Rainer Brachvogel, she describes all that can be achieved by deliberate intervention in man's genetic programming: curing hereditary diseases; artificially producing organs and limbs; predetermining the sex of future generations; successfully combating cancer; and, yes, even brains joined by computer. Fate, which used to be a matter of belief, has become for us, Lucy Beerbaum says, a question of the chemical construction of a cell in the body, and she asks: Doesn't that represent a gain? Isn't that something of a contribution to the understanding of man's place in the world as a whole?

Further signs of disquiet, a murmur of protest. Rainer Brachvogel inquires where this quest by man's intelligence will end, and Lucy replies: We don't know and it's a risk we have to take. To and fro the exchange goes between Lucy and her assistant, each skeptical query is met by a prompt affirmation, sometimes despairing and sometimes dubious, as when Lucy talks about honor—there can be honor in the pursuit of knowledge purely for the sake of knowledge—and at that the audience finds itself listening to a dialogue which leads to dismal conclusions: "casual arrogance" is the term Brachvogel uses to describe this godlike application of our knowledge. And Lucy retorts that surely this impression of hubris could arise only because we haven't yet become familiar with our knowledge. Many of our colleagues are beginning to play at being God, says Brachvogel—to applause—and Lucy, once more defending a hopeless position: Anyone who can't cope, who can't face up to modern knowledge, is free to back out. Desertion in the face of irresistible or unbearable knowledge has always existed and it exists today.

You can imagine how they now descend upon Lucy, the dapper dogmatist above all, but also the housewives, who interrupt with spontaneous shouts; only her assistant remains silent, perplexed, I would say, and bitter. The discussion spills over beyond the time allotted, of course, and later they are still talking together in a small circle, more or less willing to be reconciled as they sit drinking their weak red wine; only Brachvogel is missing.

"He's presumably flung himself into a trout stream," says Heller. Rita Süssfeldt, with an admonishing look, continues:

Rainer Brachvogel catches Lucy at the door of her room long after midnight. He refuses her invitation to come in, he merely asks her point-blank in the corridor whether in her view there could ever be good reasons for deserting. But of course there can be, says Lucy, that goes without saying. And could she imagine someone deserting purely out of a desire not to be a collaborator? Professor Beerbaum can imagine that as well. And then Rainer Brachvogel: Well, from now on you may look upon me as a deserter. Perhaps he adds a word of thanks, perhaps it's just a bow and a formal leavetaking; in any case, the story ends with a break, a separation for reasons of conscience.

"There," says Rita Süssfeldt, relieved, "that's my proposal. I've written down a lot of notes, everything's checked, but the story still has to be written, and in the course of that, our topic—I'm saying 'our topic,' you notice—should be brought out more plainly."

Pundt is nodding his head. Valentin Pundt puffs out his cheeks and makes a brief, imperious gesture over the table: there's our example, we've found it, our search hasn't been in vain.

"But who's going to write up the story?" asks Heller. "Who's going to undertake that 'trifling task'? I admit that the action is attractive, not least because I can see in it a perfect example of ambiguity, a big Yes and a small No, only it seems to me too soon to make a final decision. For us to be able to judge how good something is, it must surely be put into writing first."

"Well, not by me," says Rita Süssfeldt. "I hope that nobody expects me to do it."

"Our colleague Herr Pundt will, I'm sure, agree to undertake the 'trifling task,' he's had the most experience and he writes the best German. So we perhaps can celebrate the completion of our third chapter tomorrow; it's taken us long enough."

Pundt immediately objects: no, he can't do it, it's impossible, quite impossible, not for an official reader, he doesn't feel that he's at all adequate.

"But we really must come to a decision," says Heller, "I propose that we reach agreement tomorrow. We've got enough examples; if need be, there's always the well-tried principle of the vote."

There's a visitor: Rita Süssfeldt draws her colleagues' attention to the door, where Magda, the gloomy maid, is standing in silence while somehow giving the impression that she would like to be noticed. What is it? A parcel has just arrived with a gentleman who didn't want to leave it. He insists on handing it over personally, his name is Herr Schnittlein, by the way.

"It's for me," says Pundt. "Uncle Schnittlein from Lüneburg has brought fresh supplies, we'll be able to wet our whistles any moment now." Pundt follows the maid into the hall, whence voices expressing mock surprise and lavish thanks then become audible, interspersed with the sound of the palm of a hand slapping a raincoat.

"Do you really want to reach agreement tomorrow?" Rita Süssfeldt asks Heller.

"Do you think we're going to make any new discoveries at this stage?" he replies.

17

O~N~ THE table, near a pair of eyeglasses and a pencil, there are more catalogues, green ones, so they're about gardening. Pundt reads: "Everything for the Garden," and bending over into the circle of light he looks at the illustrations of spades and dibbles and shears, sees smiling, long-legged girls striding proudly along behind power mowers and wheelbarrows; the prices are boldly underlined. He involuntarily thinks of his first visit, when Frau Meister was copying the names of bulbs, mainly tulips, out of catalogues and he remembers how surprised she was at their names. Over there, behind the curtain, Herr Meister is whispering to his wife, presumably soothing her, explaining that it's "only" Pundt, the headmaster from Lüneburg, whom he had invited over to pick up the rest of the stuff—you know, the books which his son had lent to someone and which had been returned last Sunday.

Somewhere in the flat a phonograph is playing, Pundt can't locate it exactly. He's holding his briefcase on his lap and running his eyes swiftly over the dimly lit flat, as though objects might start moving around if you paid too much attention to them. But he still feels he has to sum it up. That giant brass-colored shoehorn topped by a horse's head, for example; or the Tyrolean couple in national costume, he the saltcellar and she the pepperpot; or the bottle opener ending in the body of a water nymph.

Herr Meister returns. Herr Meister pushes the curtain to one side and pauses, holding it back with his arm bent and thereby breaking the fall of the material. He says, "My wife asks me to give you her regards."

"Thank you," says Pundt, and then, for further confirmation: "Thank you very much." As Herr Meister walks past him, almost noiselessly, toward some books lying on a radiator, Pundt feels he ought to say something more to this quiet man and, pointing to the catalogues, he suddenly produces the thought that next summer will certainly come. "When we can get out into the garden again," he says, "then certain illnesses will go out by the back door. Colds. Influenza."

"We don't have a garden," says Herr Meister, "unfortunately." He picks the books up from the fluted radiator; they're warm. He slips them one by one into Pundt's open briefcase.

"You don't have a garden?" asks Pundt in surprise.

"Not one big enough to walk in, at any rate; my wife designs and plans and cultivates her gardens in her imagination. And she lets me say what I think of her ideas."

They go out into the corridor; at the end there's the door with the frosted pane of glass: that's where Harald died. "May I?" asks Pundt, and Herr Meister nods and moves out of the way and waves him past with too mechanical a gesture. Light is visible behind the glass and the music is becoming louder. Pundt hesitates, turns around uncertainly, but, anticipating his hesitation, Herr Meister has already gone ahead and knocked and without waiting for an answer opened the door. Tom, tall and slight, is sitting at the desk in his parka; he has a bundle of loose, lined sheets in front of him, some of them written on. On his upper arm he's wearing the Iron Cross. The record player is within reach: "Songs of Hate and Memory."

"Excuse us for butting in on you like this," Herr Meister says, and turns sideways so that the boy can understand why he's been disturbed. Tom looks up, recognizes Pundt, and stares at him fixedly and at length with increasing distaste, offering not a single word of greeting or even of surprise. And now it's Herr

302

Meister's turn to find the silence unbearable and feel that he has to ask a question: "Are you working?"

"Not so, oh my papa," says the snow hare, making disclaiming gestures with his ball-point pen. "I'm just giving myself a little pleasure by tearing you to pieces."

"Tom, how often have I told you to watch what you say."

"Okay, if you want to know, we have an essay for homework and for once it's on a sensible subject—the language of advertising—and since there's no one closer to me than you, Daddy mine, I'm gossiping a bit about my experiences with you: my father's dear smile. Surely you don't object to that?"

"Tom," says Herr Meister reprovingly, "I've got Herr Pundt with me, Harald's father. Perhaps you can pull yourself together and wish him good evening."

"But of course," says Tom and, crossing his arms over his chest, he bows in mock-respectful deference to Valentin Pundt.

At that Herr Meister pretends to be indignant and outraged, perhaps he actually is indignant and outraged, for he laboriously puts together a reprimand; following it up with another one—incomplete—and, vigorously rapping his knuckle on the table, he requires, expects, and demands, he insists, once and for all. The boy obviously sympathizes with the knuckle and counts under his breath each time his father raps the tabletop. And what is Pundt doing? He's looking stealthily around, he's searching for something even though he knows there's nothing to find, and at the same time the expression on his face indicates regret at the dispute between father and son while also suggesting that he even feels guilty himself.

"I'm just moving in," says Tom.

"Yes," says Pundt.

"It'll look a bit more cheerful than when Harald was here, more casual and cheerful."

"I can believe that," says Pundt, his face turned the other way.

"And above all, I won't keep any book of accounts where you have to vomit up everything you've done every day. Do you know what Harald called it when he wrote up his statement of

303

accounts in the evening? Throwing up. He used to say: now I have to throw up what I've done today."

"That's enough, Tom," says Herr Meister, putting a soothing and restraining hand on Valentin Pundt's elbow.

But Tom isn't finished yet. "You end up by not living properly at all, you just live for what goes into your statement of accounts. A load of bullshit, that's what it is, and I suppose it's meant to be a signpost to guide you through life."

"I don't think we ought to disturb you any longer while you're working, Tom," says Herr Meister, and he gives Pundt a little nudge to indicate that it's time to leave. They don't shake hands, they don't say a word, just a vague gesture as Pundt goes out of the room with the suspicion that father and son are exchanging rapid signs behind his back, furious or perhaps smiling and conspiratorial, but he doesn't stop, he walks down the corridor to the door of the flat, where coolly but still gratefully he takes his leave.

That's that and since the all too familiar Hamburg November weather is awaiting him outside, Pundt buttons up his raincoat and turns up his collar in the hall before going out into the cold dirty slush. He walks down to the Alster, which is being whipped up by squalls. A dog attaches itself to him and trots along beside him for a few steps, discovers its mistake, and stops under a streetlamp. The passers-by are protecting their faces. The car headlights look like balls of light dimmed and obstructed by the driving sleet. Over there, under the dirty red bell, a suburban train is crossing the Lombard Bridge, its lighted windows coalescing into a single luminous strip. As he walks along Pundt has the sensation that the distance from his feet to his head is steadily increasing and that his feet are definitely going through an area of darkness which doesn't exist at eye level. Although he is certain to run into puddles on the soggy paths of the public gardens, he goes down into them, by now already accustomed to the biting wind and untroubled by the sleet beating against his face and making it glow.

Accounts: their hostility as soon as you ask them to account for themselves. But it's not a question of revealing or admitting or confessing in the hope of forgiveness; keeping an account of your actions ought instead to help you to discriminate and then to evaluate. And he called it throwing up!

He hears a very clear, whistling sound of wings beating in the air. Ducks? Do ducks alight even after darkness falls? The silhouette of the squat boathouse resting on its piles; the long slippery jetty on which the boats are laid up on chocks for the winter beneath their tarpaulins. Voices, thinks Pundt, those are human voices, coming from a whole group of people; one of them is obviously in distress and is protesting to someone else, who is doing most of the talking, and on the long jetty between the laid-up boats he can now make out the group, a loose circle of very active figures, and in the middle—and the threatening nature of the scene is immediately evident—a man and a woman are standing back to back as if trying to defend themselves from all sides.

The slippery greenish wood of the long projecting jetty; the decorative waves lapping at the piles; the bottoms of the boats looking like friendly sleeping animals; and the delicately mottled background, which gives the active figures not only the necessary sharpness but even an allegorical quality: wouldn't you say that this automatically creates the effect of a stage set?

An open-air ballet, in fact, which the sheepskin coats and leather jackets and matching sweat suits are putting on out there, without an audience; and the title is: "The Surprise Attack." No calls for help, but distorted words of warning and indistinct protests—and seeing all this, the former headmaster cannot possibly walk on, he must stop and see what's happening, and when he has understood the situation, he must get closer to the scene, on the assumption that there might be something here for him to do. Some calming down to be done. Bringing order. Restoring peace. And thereby providing a remedy. He walks determinedly onto the jetty and then gradually slows down.

The slippery jetty demands concentration from the dancers; it prescribes which leaps can be made and cautions you to control your movements. So: *Préparation!* And more lightly in your *Petits battements dégagés!* And then, after a beat from a distance, a *Grand battement.* There's no rail here.

The wind is testing the tightly lashed tarpaulins and elsewhere a loose piece of canvas is flapping and drumming against the wooden hull of a boat. Two reddish specks flare up brightly and are then extinguished in the semicircle over there; they're sucking at their cigarettes.

Is his briefcase becoming heavier? Pundt feels as if the weight of his briefcase is increasing as he continues to walk out along the slippery jetty, as he draws near the group, who have not yet noticed him. He hears the sound of blows and hollow thumps on the greenish wood. The woman inside the circle is whimpering, the man is holding his elbow in front of his face to protect himself. In all this activity, one person remains inactive. Pundt takes a closer look at him: the angular face with the furrowed forehead, the glittering amulet on his bare chest, the short sheepskin jacket, the tight-fitting zippered sweat-suit trousers. The youth is standing apart and giving his orders from the sidelines; imperious and menacing, he seems accustomed to being obeyed.

How do you intervene, what words do you use to break into a situation which you think is unjust? And especially when you have to deal with an overwhelming majority?

His coat fluttering, Valentin Pundt thrusts his way into the ring with outstretched arm and shouts: "Stop it!" followed by: "What's going on here?" and once again: "Stop it!"—and then gives a peremptory gesture with which you might perhaps send an impertinent pupil back to his seat but which here, on this slippery jetty, is incapable of making any impression on these vigorous young men, so superior in numbers. He walks toward the leader. He threatens him. He says, "If you don't stop this immediately, I'll summon the police." Pundt turns abruptly away and in a few steps is standing beside the frightened couple, who are holding hands; he is just about to lead them out of the danger zone in the appropriate manner when one of the youths says, "A nut, Hubert, look at this nut"; and an Afghan coat adds, "A little too old for this stuff, wouldn't you say, Hubert?"

The old headmaster is about to reply, he obviously has a word on the tip of his tongue which will express his frank opinion of the youths, but the situation seems merely to warrant a dismissive wave of the hand, an ordinary gesture of contempt: you're not worth wasting my breath on.

So back to terra firma and the overhanging streetlamps. As he turns he throws his arms in the air, not because he's lost his footing on the slippery wood, but because his feet have been knocked from under him, in such a narrow space that his fall seems inevitable, in a kind of slow motion, so that he may even manage to put out his arm and break his fall. And he does succeed in doing so. Hardly has he measured his length on the wooden floor when he lifts his head, looks for and discovers his briefcase, on which a high-heeled shoe has been planted as though on an animal to keep it from escaping. He tries to crawl toward it. His eye can see no higher than the knee of a pair of legs in tight leather shorts. The first kick gets him in the armpit and then he feels several kicks in the ribs, and just as he's thinking how hard their toe caps are, a resounding kick behind the ear jerks him upward; pain shoots through him and he lies motionless, his head stretched forward as if expecting another blow. His arms, on which he is supporting himself, are forced outward and his trunk sags and falls flat on the planks, he draws up a knee, is struck by a kick, rolls over onto his side, and is caught by another one. His muscles still have some strength, some power of convulsive movement, he attempts to do something with his shoulder—and then they get him on the chin and temple and now his fingers unclench, his body becomes loose and slack and is finally subdued.

They could take to their heels, a few of them no doubt expect a signal to make themselves scarce, but the youth they call Hubert bends over Pundt, flicks a corner of his coat away from his face with a flexible steel rod, peers closely at him, and seems to be meditating something, almost solemnly. Then he hits his steel rod against the side of a boat and says, "Get moving"; and since they still haven't understood or are perhaps scared of understanding him, he makes signs to them that he wants the boat put into the water, the man placed into it, and the boat pushed out into the somewhat dark, turbulent waters of the Alster.

They stand there for as long as they dare. He won't repeat his request. So they sever the ropes holding down the tarpaulin, pull it off, turn the light boat over, and manhandle it into the water. How the boat plunges in, how skittishly it's bucking and prancing. One of them has to lie flat on his stomach to hold it. Behind them, the couple are taking to their heels, they've already reached the lights, hand in hand. "Let 'em go, hurry up now." Feet first they hoist the man into the boat, dump him in the stern, for a second the center thwart supports him and then he topples over to one side. The painter, where's the painter? Holding on to the short painter, they pull the boat to the end of the jetty, faster and faster it moves, it's becoming easier to judge which way it's going, and now a small swirling, foaming wash can be seen at the stern as with a final spurt and a vigorous tug they throw the rope into the air and watch as its loose coils splash onto the water. They don't wait to see how far out the boat will glide as it begins to drift under the choppy cross waves. Their feet thud on the wooden boards, no longer stepping like dancers but striding out like runners. Who's got the briefcase?

The foxy-faced one, the one with the long, innocent eyelashes like hinged lids, has to go back and get the briefcase, sulkily moaning: Why pick on me, why does it always have to be me? But no sooner has he put the briefcase under his arm than he starts to run and concentrates solely on finding his way out of the gardens, up the asphalted private path to the cozy houses, nestling close together, which will shortly be torn down to make way for "a new residential development." Over there bulldozers and tractors are standing beside the builder's hut on hard rubber tracks; past those, too, and then over the crumbling debris of a wall to the cellar entrance of an empty house.

Tiles, discarded churns, and damaged, forgotten cans: this was once a dairy. The youth shuts the door behind him and gropes his way forward. His hand slides over the water oozing from the smooth, greasy wall: it's dripping from old waterpipes. Here's the recess; it must be behind this door.

They're already there. They're sitting in a circle on boxes and churns, the candlelight glides over wet clothes and flickers on beer bottles. Damp and stuffy. They're sitting with their legs sprawled out, pleased with themselves, as though enjoying a hard-earned rest from honest toil. Only one of them is standing, slender and domineering, in front of a poster on which horses have discovered a very photogenic motorcycle which they have surrounded and are sniffing at. Hubert is holding his flexible steel rod like a British officer carrying his swagger stick. He's walking up and down, taking short, aimless steps. You could imagine that he's meditating on something important. Now and again he looks vacantly at a table, a rickety garden table covered, as though for some ritual, with a sheet that is hanging almost to the floor. How quickly they can make themselves understood: he lifts his eyes, and the foxy-faced one, unhealthy-looking and with shadows under his eyes, walks up to the table, heaves the briefcase onto it, and in response to a tight-lipped command empties it out: books, files containing manuscripts, a package of tea, paper handkerchiefs. Is that everything? A box of paper clips and that's all. The steel rod taps the books and manuscripts, springs back of its own accord, and swishes down again. Foxy-face sidles off and would like to go and have a drink of beer, but Hubert, having now put on an American officer's peaked cap, gives him a sign to sit down at the table.

"Read something!"

"What should I read?"

"Take a book, open it, and read!"

"Me?"

"Read something! Now. We want to hear your voice," says Hubert, and he is not just pretending but is waiting, solemnly and expectantly.

"Anything?"

"Anything out of a book."

Grins run round the crates and churns. Beer bottles are silently lifted to mouths. Once again Hubert seems to have hit on a good idea.

"Where should I begin? And how?"

"If there's nothing else you can do, then start at the beginning, for practice."

Foxy-face drops his eyes and to the accompaniment of even broader grins he suddenly manages it: "Dates . . . of . . . Ger–man . . . po–et–ry." There, you see! Applause. Cheers!

The tip of the steel rod inserts itself between the pages of the book. "Here, read us some more from that, it doesn't matter what it is."

"Some more?" One by one, in a toneless voice, as if quite unconnected with each other, the words appear: " 'The ode or hymn cast off its intellectual ballast and in Goethe and Schiller soared beyond logical categories. In Schubart's political odes, genuine anger and a personal feeling of vengeance replaced theoretical considerations and a vicarious hatred of tyranny.' " Foxy-face looks up at Hubert with a beseeching air. "What the hell does that mean? I can't understand this crap, choose something else but not that."

Hubert seems to rouse himself, he runs his eye quickly over the title and subtitle of the manuscript and makes a decision. "Let's try that one, perhaps it's more exciting."

"Why me, only me?" Foxy-face asks with a worried look, whereupon one of the gang, squatting on a tub, shouts, "Professor—from now on you're our professor. We want you to read us something."

"It says here: 'The Invention of the Alphabet.' "

"Okay, go on."

"Well: 'We know from the history of the letters that they are more than a written sign, more than the vehicle of a permanent content. When letters are brought to life in the form of a picture alphabet, they make clear the meaning of many symbols . . .' " He breaks off again and peers at Hubert with a puzzled look.

Hubert, all set for a ceremonial appreciation of the passage, angrily turns his head toward him and asks, "What's the matter? What's holding you up?"

"It's these words," the youth says, "I just can't get through all these words."

"They're just everyday words," says Hubert. "Keep reading."

18

"Just tea"; all that Rita Süssfeldt wants this evening is some tea and peace and quiet. The tea can be put on the floor beside the chair, because the free space on the overcrowded desk is taken up by the monstrous glazed earthenware ashtray. "We've got to reach a decision tomorrow, so please understand why I'm not to be disturbed; and shut the door. Thanks, Mareth, and excuse me for today."

She hoists her legs onto the table and smooths her dress down over her knobby knees, as though disapproving of her bulges and hollows. She opens the book, bristling with book marks, and reads:

Four hours after she had given notice for the second time, Johanna stood up from the bench, picked up her suitcase and bag, and followed the shady path around the edge of Innocentia Park toward the exit, waited there for a while—not so much because she had changed her mind again as to recover from the exertion of carrying her luggage—and then discovered that she hadn't handed in the house key when she left. Now that she had ascertained this, the last part of the journey went more quickly and she didn't have to put down her bags again. She unlocked the self-closing door and held it open with her back while she pushed her suitcase and bag into the hall, waiting for a moment before taking off her hat and coat. She would take her bags up to her room later on, but first she must go into the kitchen and brew some tea, it was getting late, and then she would walk up to the bedroom with the unsweetened tea and make known her return as though it were a matter of course. She bustled about the kitchen in her best clothes, put some water on, carefully warmed the teapot, making sure she didn't make any noise, and while she waited she looked out into the tiny terraced back garden where spring was trying out its colors. A white day with a misty blue sky.

She poured out the tea, knocked on the door after she'd already opened it, as was her wont, and carried her tray across the half-shaded room, through its artificial twilight, to the couch where Lucy Beerbaum was lying; she looked very frail. A large part of the room was closed off by a sliding door and the window was blacked out up to the very top except for a piece cut out for the skylight, so that you could imagine a narrow confined space, forcibly enclosed, especially since the sleeping area seemed to be hemmed in by stools and chairs.

"Here's your tea and it's not sweetened, not even on the sly," said Johanna, and she placed the tray on the stool with the same reproachful air of sympathy which she had shown in the past. No surprise or amazement or pleasure at the fact that it was Johanna who was bringing her her tea, although she had given notice only four hours before on the grounds, she said, that all her warnings and pleas were no longer of any use. But apparently she was expected, for Lucy immediately sat up, smiled, held out her hand before taking the cup, and since she said nothing, was evidently not going to comment on Johanna's decision. Johanna looked around the room suspiciously to see whether any changes had been made during her absence: there were the two hard, squat stools; the breadbox, in which she had to put the day's ration every morning; the enameled crockery, which the professor herself now washed every day; under the hard bed there was a pile of still unread letters and telegrams and periodicals, and on a shelf, as though inaccessible, the still unused notepaper; and the photograph still hung on the wall, the portrait of a very correctly dressed man whose face, despite the bright sun, could not be seen clearly since the shadow cast by a straw boater made him almost featureless. And Johanna said, "Someone has to look after you, because you do all you can to do yourself harm."

Lucy was sipping her tea but she didn't eat anything, she wasn't feeling hungry on this, her ninth day of voluntary captivity. "You're wrong, Johanna, all these things I'm imposing on myself I'm doing on my own behalf, too—it helps me to bear my memories better and feel closer to my friends."

"Your friends don't know anything about it," said the woman bitterly. "I don't suppose they've even heard about all these things you've taken on yourself, so far away. If you only had something to fall back on, physically, I mean." She shook her head back and forth uncertainly, wringing her hands; how could she reconcile this complete refusal to be looked after with all the things she was forcing herself to accept? Persuasion had led nowhere and all atempts to improve her diet had been detected. Reminding her of her professional commitments had proved of no avail; even giving her notice, which was intended to bring her to her senses, had had no effect.

Outside in the corridor the doorbell was being rung repeatedly. Johanna ignored it until her anger was sufficiently aroused and then she stood up and went to answer it, her neck as red as a turkey cock, she'd already worked out how she was going to tell him off. Beyond the glass door of the house, against the light, she could see a giant paper bag—"Eat More Fruit"—and a lively bunch of lilacs, waving to and fro and above the paper bag, as if emerging from it, and a robust, cheerful face underneath a mushroom of blond hair, like a pineapple underneath an explosion of fruit leaves: it must be Professor Pietsch. Not only was he clutching the paper bag, the flowers, and two small parcels pressed against his body with his arms; in addition he was holding two books and a bottle of brandy in his short hairy fingers; he was maltreating the doorbell alternately with his elbow and upper arm. When she saw him and recalled his amiably booming presence, Johanna toned down the rebuke she was going to administer and greeted Lucy Beerbaum's chief with the words: "Anyone would think there was a fire from the way you're ringing, Professor Pietsch," whereupon she first unburdened his freckled fingers of the gifts he'd brought and then took the flowers out of his embracing arms. To his question: "Well, how are we?" he seemed, on principle, to expect a reassuring answer. But after Johanna had relieved him of his load in the hall and he was about to launch a booming welcome outside the door, she asked him, contrary to all the rules, to wait, stating that she was not certain whether Professor Beerbaum would be able to receive her visitor, welcome though he usually was. He expressed his own view by lighting a very dark *colorado claro*, a cigar whose very dimensions indicated his willingness to accept a protracted wait, and while Lucy, still lying in bed, began to work out when she had received her last visit and when the next one was permitted—during all that time everything was arranged precisely in accordance with the regulations governing her interned friends—he walked the length of the hall, contemplated the figures on the illustrations of painted Attic vases with a twinkle in his eye, even Theseus who had just come to grips with the Minotaur, and was neither particularly grateful nor particularly delighted when Johanna came back and showed him into the living room.

From the kitchen she could hear his relaxed, booming greeting, his cheerfulness hiding his concern; but they had never adopted any other tone in their relations with each other, so why should he change it now, in circumstances which he had never even inquired about, let alone been aware of? Holding his cigar out sideways as though to help balance his powerful, albeit malproportioned body, he walked toward Lucy, who looked at him, shaking her head and presumably already anxiously calculating how she could get out of his way if his brakes failed; but as with everything else he did, this too was quite deliberate, tried and proven: checking his stride, Professor Pietsch came to a halt almost elegantly just before reaching the couch. His two hands clasped Lucy's like waffle irons and the phrases with which he greeted her were as generous as his gifts: having just returned from a business trip, he's been told the general details of what has happened and he brings her the sympathy and good wishes of all their colleagues. At last, however, he came to the obligatory question: "Well, Lucy, and how are you?" And as a sign that he had come ready and willing to listen, he lowered himself onto one of the stools, not indeed before ascertaining that there was no more comfortable seat available. "Well, what's it all about? I take it that there's some background to your decision?"

"Would you like tea or coffee, Richard? Johanna can get you either," said Lucy. Professor Pietsch wouldn't like either, but he wouldn't object to a brandy and an ashtray if that was within the bounds of possibility. While greeting her he had noted Lucy's appearance and condition and had gathered information that would be difficult for her to contradict in words. He would venture first of all to drink to Lucy's health and he carefully knocked the ash off his *colorado claro* into the ashtray which Johanna had placed on the second stool. He knew that what he was saying was absolutely true when he once again assured Lucy how worried about her they were at the Institute.

Johanna was becoming restless, she would have liked to reply because she felt that she had found the right address for her complaints; but she did not dare and left it to Lucy to explain in person a decision which she had already justified in a letter. "I imagine you've read my letter, Richard? Yes? Well, in that case you know all there is to know." For Lucy Beerbaum nothing had changed, and even after having nine days to think about it, her decision still seemed to her to be something absolutely normal and, in this case indeed, necessary.

When the nine generals and colonels seized power in Greece on April 21 she was not yet certain about the form her protest would take. Richard would surely remember how surprising it had all been; even their avowed opponents reluctantly acknowledged "the brilliance of the military operation." This all changed when the new regime took men and women into custody because it felt threatened by their independent views. Through a telephone conversation which she had had one evening—the connection had been unexpectedly cut off and couldn't be re-established —she knew that Victor Gaitanides was among those who, after being arrested, had been deported to an island; on hearing this, not only did she realize that she must certainly do something but she also already had some idea of how she might express her sympathy and solidarity.

"So you can see, Richard, what I've decided to do: to share their lot. To remind myself of—and to draw attention to—the conditions in which they are being forced to live as a result of this deliberate violence, I've imposed the same conditions on myself. That's all. I've asked for indefinite leave from the Institute."

Lucy Beerbaum seemed to have nothing further to say, but at this point Johanna intervened with the comment that, in anything you undertake, you surely ought to ask yourself whether you're in a position to do it and, above all, physically capable of it. Professor Pietsch took this as an appropriate moment to ask for another glass of brandy and with his glass and his cigar in his hand he stood up, walked toward the curtained window, and stared at the gray, unpatterned material as though it did not prevent him from seeing into the garden. Then he relaxed, emptied his glass, and began to walk back and forth in front of the couch. They hardly looked at each other throughout their dialogue:

PIETSCH: You can't stick to your decision, Lucy . . . For your own sake . . . for ours . . . You must . . .

LUCY (*prepared for this approach*): Withdraw it?

PIETSCH: Think it over. I think you owe it to us to think your decision over.

LUCY (*sadly*): I know, Richard. But I do owe something to myself as well.

PIETSCH (*persuasively*): At the Institute, Lucy . . . There's no one at the Institute who doesn't recognize that. In one department, they even considered following your example . . . following it, Lucy. . . . They all have the greatest respect for what you're doing . . .

LUCY: But?

PIETSCH: . . . but they doubt whether your example . . . well,

316

whether your example is the best or the most effective form of protest.

LUCY *(who has considered this point carefully):* It's not so much that I'm assuming the right to protest, Richard, what I'm trying to do, primarily, is to assert my right to express my sympathy publicly.

PIETSCH *(trying another approach):* Lucy, you've spent more than twenty years with us. For the last ten we've been collaborators. . . . You belong here. . . . You're part of us.

LUCY: I'm grateful to you for that, Richard. . . . But everyone comes from somewhere. . . . And the older you grow, the more you begin to think about it. . . . Going home. . . . It's a kind of involuntary homecoming.

PIETSCH: That kind of homecoming always ends abroad. Your home is here, Lucy. . . . You're not responsible for what's happening down there . . . in the country where you happen to have been born.

LUCY *(placing her fingertips on her temples):* And I don't feel responsible, either. . . . But I do feel concerned, Richard. . . . Yes, I feel concerned in every way.

PIETSCH *(anxiously):* You must tell me, Lucy, if it's becoming too much for you. . . . If I'm pressing you . . .

LUCY: No, it's all right, I've recovered now.

PIETSCH *(as though speaking from experience):* You know very well that anyone seizing power can't risk being unsuccessful . . . he has to go through with it. . . . They're precautionary measures, Lucy. . . . What the military are doing in Greece is just taking normal precautions . . . *(thinks over what he has said and, placatingly:)* the usual, traditional measures which apply only at the beginning and which in any case don't seem strange to us any more.

LUCY *(echoing his words):* . . . strange to us.

PIETSCH: I mean which no longer surprise us. . . . They always arrest—as a preventive measure—the people who can't be relied on, in every country . . . *(with grim irony:)* And the people who can't be relied on are all those who are inclined to speak for themselves. That includes us too, Lucy, and those like us.

LUCY: We don't have anything to fear.

PIETSCH: No, we have nothing to fear, not immediately. . . . But neither have our colleagues.

LUCY: Their Institute was closed down. They were detained without any reason being given.

PIETSCH: They'll be released. . . . Those people—I mean the new regime—can't afford to lock up the country's scientists . . . for an indefinite period.

LUCY *(bitterly):* Can't afford?

PIETSCH *(righteously):* World opinion—they have world opinion against them.

LUCY *(almost sardonically):* There are many people, Richard, who feel themselves positively confirmed in their views when they have world opinion against them.

PIETSCH *(confidently):* That merely proves their initial fear, it's a sign of crisis, that's all. . . . Those measures were adopted hastily, and our colleagues will be released just as quickly. . . . In case you weren't aware of it, Lucy, attempts are being made already . . . at several levels.

LUCY: They only know one level. That's why they always have the advantage.

PIETSCH *(after a pause, imploringly and vigorously):* Lucy, you must think your decision over.

LUCY: I have thought it over and I'm thinking it over all the time. . . . I know that I have to justify it. . . . *(quietly:)* I'm going to keep on, Richard. As long as our friends aren't free, I shall remain here. It's something that concerns only me.

PIETSCH *(pulls a newspaper out of his pocket and puts it on the stool):* No, Lucy, it's not just your concern. . . . When a scientist of your eminence, your ability . . .

LUCY *(defensively):* Please, Richard!

PIETSCH: . . . decides to act as you have done, then it ceases to be a private matter. Read what the press is saying about this protest of yours, our press and the foreign press. Even if you won't admit it, it's still important who does certain things.

LUCY: I'm not so much concerned with protesting, Richard. . . .
Please do try to understand me . . . it's sympathy. I want
above all to demonstrate my sympathy. Because I feel a special bond with those people, I'd like . . . to share their lot.

PIETSCH *(stopping in front of her):* Imprisoning yourself out of a
feeling of solidarity?

LUCY: I come from there. They're my friends. What other people
are demanding them to do, I want to demand from myself.

PIETSCH *(officially solicitous):* But what will you achieve? What
can you achieve? You're starving yourself. You're shutting
yourself away. You're subjecting yourself to the same conditions as our colleagues are being subjected to. You're voluntarily accepting for yourself the wrong that's being done
to them. . . . But what do you hope to achieve by all this,
Lucy?

LUCY *(equally prepared for this question):* I don't know yet. . . . Does
one have to ask, in everything that one does, how much one's
going to achieve? How useful it is? Isn't it sufficient to do
something to justify oneself?

PIETSCH *(after a pause; he knows that he's about to play his trump card):*
Lucy, I need you at the Institute. We all need you.

LUCY: That's the thing that makes it hardest for me.

PIETSCH *(swiftly):* We know how much your work means to us,
now . . .

LUCY: Richard, if only I could . . .

PIETSCH: . . . and that we depend on your work.

LUCY: I've considered everything.

PIETSCH: *(in a cautiously plaintive tone):* Really, Lucy? Even the fact
that there's another kind of solidarity—toward us? Or don't
we have the right to expect that?

LUCY: Oh yes, you've got the right. . . . I know what I owe you,
Richard. You personally and our colleagues at the Institute.

PIETSCH: I was thinking only of the work. Of all that you've
succeeded in doing. . . . The Americans, too, are now trying
to find enzymes capable of repairing damage to cell walls.
You know what that means. . . . What couldn't we accomplish with your help, if . . .

LUCY (*sadly*): Ah, Richard, you're reminding me of my duty to biological research.

PIETSCH: Is that so unimportant? Just think what we might achieve if we continue our work.

LUCY (*quietly, unperturbed*): That's not everything. The people at home are defenseless. They've no voice to speak. Shouldn't there be someone willing to speak on their behalf? Or merely to draw attention to what's happening to them? I've asked myself, Richard, which is easier . . .

PIETSCH: You've given your answer.

LUCY: . . . and I'd like to say that we're not in this world to achieve success . . . success in our job. If we want to make life worth believing in, then we must always react to injustice, yes . . .

PIETSCH (*shifting his glance from her to the oval framed portrait*): And Victor? Have you any news of Victor Gaitanides?

LUCY: Under arrest . . . he's under arrest along with his colleagues.

PIETSCH (*has an idea*): Perhaps that's one of your reasons, too, Lucy? In your decision, I mean. Gaitanides is a colleague . . . well, to some extent he's working on the same problems as we are. As far as I know, he's also reached the same stage as we have—as far as the tertiary structure of proteins is concerned. . . . He's not only the friend of your youth . . .

LUCY (*quietly and decidedly*): No, Richard. My decision isn't connected with the fact that Victor is working on the same problems. I can see what you're thinking now. . . . You think that I would like to avoid gaining any advantage—an unsought advantage—that might now arise. It's not that.

PIETSCH (*looks at her for a long while, not without hidden reproach*): I'm worried, Lucy.

LUCY: And you're disappointed.

PIETSCH: Yes, I'm disappointed, and if you'd like to know why I'm disappointed, it's because sooner or later you'll come to see yourself as a martyr. . . . You'll realize that your decision hasn't achieved anything. And to make it up to yourself,

320

you'll talk yourself into being a martyr. I'm even afraid, Lucy, that you'll come to enjoy being a martyr. . . . No, I can't understand your decision. You could help large numbers of people through your work. But what you're doing is of no use to anyone. It's a waste, it's a pointless sacrifice.

LUCY: You're not the first person to tell me that, Richard. . . . Believe me, I know all the arguments against what I'm doing.

PIETSCH *(aggressively):* Then I'm surprised you don't listen to them . . . their objections are, in fact, sound ones . . .

LUCY *(politely):* Excuse me, Richard, long visits . . .

PIETSCH *(ironically):* I see, the consultation is at an end. . . . But you must let me say one more thing, Lucy, after all these years . . . it's you we're more concerned about. . . . There's no chance that we can make you change your decision, but because of the friendship we feel for you, we must tell you how much we regret it.

The longer the conversation lasted, the plainer it became that he was talking himself into a state of excitement; and excitement made Professor Pietsch seem a very different sort of visitor, his face seemed to change, at least it seemed to Johanna to take on a hard, angular look, and even the extravagant gestures petered out as he was spurred on by disappointment to comment on Lucy's decision; he was irritated and unsympathetic and acted as if he had had personal experience of similar situations.

After these exchanges and accusations, the scene could hardly end as it had begun; it may be also that he had been expecting too much from his visit; at any rate, he suddenly walked up to the couch, and in a tone of voice that may be described as official, he inquired how long Lucy had set herself to accomplish her "undertaking." And by his attitude he made it plain that this time he was merely interested in obtaining accurate information. At this, Lucy looked at him nonplussed, as though she had expected any question but this one and, shrugging her shoulders, said, "How do I know how long? Does it depend on me?"

Whether he came to a decision then and there is doubtful, but this information seemed to give him food for thought, as though it would be of importance for future decisions. His final mumbled query as to how and when they might meet again came out so sarcastically that he immediately proceeded to take his leave, and after a rapid handshake, in which he was unable to suppress an expression of mock respect, he went to the door. And Lucy? She lifted her legs laboriously onto the couch and remained lying doubled up for a moment and then gave a deep sigh of relief as she stretched out her thin wiry body and shut her eyes as though comforted. She paid no attention to the parting words exchanged in the hall and she was lying in the same position when Johanna returned. "I imagine you both came to the same conclusion, eh, Johanna? At least you were able to confirm your opinions."

"Your visitor's gone," said Johanna, "and I ask myself why I don't go, too. There's nothing for me to do here, or practically nothing. Did you even know that I had left?"

"You brought me my tea on time," said Lucy.

"I'm used to doing more for you than that," Johanna said coldly.

"I know," said Lucy, "but you must get used to the new situation: the more careful you are not to look after me, the more you're helping me."

I can't read with that racket going on upstairs, thinks Rita Süssfeldt, all that bumping and jerking and rumbling in Heino Merkel's bedroom as he storms around: it's like being in a switchyard with all those bangs and rattles, even the steam pipes are taking part as their loud clanking resounds through the whole house. She directs warning glances toward the ceiling and acknowledges a particularly violent bang with an absentminded call to order; and then her suspicions make her leap to her feet.

She flings her book down on the table, rushes into the hall and upstairs without waiting to listen—automatically registering how dangerous the red carpet runner is, it's always shifting and sliding—and without knocking she flings open the door of Heino

Merkel's room. Where's Mareth? When she sees the man on his knees, crawling toward the chair anchored to the wall, she calls out her sister's name, and then in a couple of strides she's beside him, and is swiftly bending over to help him when she realizes that he has noticed her. Then she holds herself back and slowly retreats, not too far, just enough to be out of his reach. She has seen this face before, this face swollen with effort, the head swinging back and forth, the purple, discolored lips, and the convulsive jerking of his body as though electrical shocks were passing through it, painful but at the same time stimulating. Once more she calls out for her sister, but less loudly, just in case she might need her, for as she draws back she recognizes in the man's wide-open eyes another kind of look, a gleam of energy and revolt which explains to her why he is dragging himself trembling in this direction, toward her and the chair which is standing behind her.

Although in the grip of his affliction, he has managed to summon up reserves of resistance, and not only that—even though forced to his knees he still seems aware of the goal that he has set for himself and no doubt measured in moments of sanity. She watches as he advances with a calculated effort of will. She can see the layered hair around the edge of the artificial plate in his skull.

"You're going to make it," she says suddenly. And although the words frighten her, she repeats them: "You'll certainly make it, Heino." And slowly retreating, encouraging him, leading him forward, she urges him up to the chair, where his head sinks into the cold leather seat as he supports himself until he has gathered sufficient strength; then bracing himself, he pushes his trunk over the seat of the chair up to the backrest—all the time to the accompaniment of whispered encouragement and praise—and now he seizes the back and pulls himself up; a twist and he's sitting upright on the chair. He gropes for the leather straps, pulls them crosswise over his lap, feels blindly for the self-fastening clasps, pulls them together, and their click tells him that they have joined and locked. As he is immediately jerked upward, so

323

that the straps are at once tested to the full, Rita says, "You see!" and, still frightened, adds approvingly: "You made it, you see!" and for a second she seems to glimpse on his wasted, contorted face a look of satisfaction, but it is immediately obliterated by a painful expression of protest.

The pills; she gets the tiny yellow pills, dissolves them in water, pours the liquid into his mouth as he bends his head back, and then lets him thrash about for a while, straining against his bonds, before she cautiously begins to massage the back of his neck. As soon as he's less rigid and his tension has relaxed, I'll be seeing that look of surprise on his face, with the inevitable feeling of guilt, thinks Rita Süssfeldt, and she casts her eye over the moderately devastated room. The things he had brought down with him as he fell, the damage or changes he'd caused in his clumsy, inhibited efforts to control himself: all traces of that she will remove herself, because what you managed to do today, Heino, was wonderful, we must tell Mareth about it, too, especially her.

"Really, we wouldn't have imagined you were capable of it." Standing behind the back of the chair, she surveys the stools, books, writing materials, and scattered files with the press clippings, and there, underneath the shelf, are the scissors stuck into the wooden floor, in the middle of a sheet of newspaper pinned to the planks. She pulls the scissors out of the wood, picks up the paper, goes back behind the chair, and reads while she continues her massage with one hand: " 'Lightning strikes at Sottje Böhnitz's: During a freak November thunderstorm which has fascinated meteorologists, the Kullenried stables at Tremsbüttel were struck by lightning; the owner of the stud farm, Horst Böhnitz, better known as "Sottje," is not only one of the most successful but also one of the most popular of German show jumpers. Eight horses perished in the fire, although the watchman and Sottje Böhnitz himself had succeeded at first in getting the horses out into the open and herding them into a paddock. As a witness explained, a clap of thunder panicked the animals and they tried to seek refuge in the stables. In their efforts to

324

restrain the animals, the stableboy was seriously injured, Sottje Böhnitz himself receiving slight injuries. The loss was all the greater because at least three promising young foals . . . in addition Nona, whose reputation in puissance competitions . . . the total damage is assessed at . . .' "

Rita Süssfeldt crumples the sheet into a ball, looks in vain for a pocket, and shoves the paper into her bodice. She talks soothingly to the man. Although she knows what he has to live with and what he has to be prepared for at all times, she speaks of the prospect of being able to make his suffering bearable by trying to forget. "You've proved that it can be done," she says. She'll presumably be saying such words to him often.

As far as his bonds will allow, he's using the edges of his hands to massage his stiff thighs, pounding them to loosen up his cramp and bring some feeling back to them. He would have felt surer of being able to guarantee his actions were it not that at the critical moment he was almost crippled from the hips downward. "Yes, Heino, I know." How actively his hands and fingers are moving, how concerned he is to distract attention from his situation. The fact that she now begins to tidy up makes him somewhat embarrassed, not only because it's all his fault, after all, but because he would like to be able to find things after the tidying has been done; but the woman is gathering things up and packing them away so willingly and cheerfully that he has the impression she is doing it in appreciation of his recent "performance." He watches her as she works and doesn't dare to correct her when her idea of order doesn't necessarily coincide with his.

Where can Mareth be? She had said she was going to complain about the noise which the young men in the post-office hostel were always making. His silence is becoming too prolonged for her comfort, especially at a time like this. "Did I tell you that we're going to decide tomorrow? Yes, tomorrow we're going to define for perhaps a whole generation of unsuspecting schoolchildren whom they should model their life on, just think of that, Heino. As a matter of fact, we've got too much material and our choice is becoming more and more difficult because of all the options." The man nods as though these are difficulties he had anticipated; the more deeply you go into her life, the more surprised you are at how equivocal the things you admire seem to become. He'd foreseen that when he made his suggestion. "If we didn't have quite so much material," Rita concedes, "it might well have been easier to reach a decision, but there were still lots of gaps and missing connections and correlations of events and periods which remained in the dark."

What for example?

"Well, something I haven't been able to discover yet is when and for what reason Lucy Beerbaum decided to remain in Hamburg; true, her grandfather came from here, but she herself was born and grew up in Athens, all her friends lived there."

The man in the chair releases the catches and loosens the long leather straps, exhausted and still uncertain. He remains seated and asks for a handkerchief. Why did Lucy Beerbaum come to Hamburg and stay here? He could tell her that and something more. "The grandfather's brother—perhaps you remember, he was the ship's engineer—had died in Hamburg and had left everything to Lucy. Since her mother would never attend a funeral, on principle, because she was too deeply affected by them, and since for reasons of health her father didn't feel up to the journey, the family decided to send Lucy and she could then use the opportunity to look over her inheritance."

"Was she able to make that long journey in the few days left before the funeral?"

"That was the point, it really is worth mentioning. The man who'd invited her to the funeral was Henry Beerbaum, the ship's engineer himself; he had a presentiment of what was coming, he'd heard the bell toll for himself, so to speak, and of course, when he tendered the premature invitation, he'd taken the long journey into account. He did. He must have. During the whole journey—on the Orient Express, there's a film about it that everyone knows—Lucy hoped that she might still see him alive; she didn't succeed in doing that but she was in time for the funeral. Just imagine the situation: a young woman comes from a far

326

country to attend the funeral of a man she has never seen, although she has written him extravagant letters of thanks for the postcards he has sent her from all over the world. The coffin has already been firmly screwed down, it's one of those stifling hot August days with not a breath of air, all the seats at the Ohlsdorfer Cemetery are occupied by exhausted visitors. Lucy said that she was far too warmly dressed. At the grave, a group of mourners turned up that you can recognize at a glance, old buddies from the engine room, but in particular three veiled women, each of them laying claim to be the one who mourned him most. They grieve volubly and now and again they manage a sob for three voices. Out of embarrassment, or even suspicion, Lucy said, they'd at first barely acknowledged each other's presence, but later their grief brought them much closer together, so that they supported each other, since nobody else seemed inclined to do so. As the deceased had requested, the song 'La Paloma' was sung over his grave, first by just one friend and then with everybody joining in; the three women knew absolutely every verse. You can imagine Lucy's feelings after an experience like that. At any rate, that same evening, after the funeral, she began to look more closely at her inheritance. She was living in the house that had been bequeathed her and she'd arranged to stay only a week. How can I put it? When she looked through his things—she told me this herself—she discovered an album containing photos of the ugliest women and girls you can imagine, and from his letters and his uninhibited diaries she learned that this was obviously a specialty of Henry Beerbaum's: you might describe him as the enlightened friend of plain women. Every harelip, every double chin immediately attracted him, he collected bulging eyes and cross-eyes and he wasn't even put off by incredible gap teeth or goiters. Even the three veiled women, whom Lucy recognized again on a side table, must have been, according to what they said, the victims of a grumpy or envious portrait photographer. Yet he himself was a tall, clean-shaven Hamburger who could have been the model for any recruiting poster advertising an engineering career in the merchant navy. Why did he do it? Out of pity; perhaps out of an erotic sense of justice. The female visitors who called on Lucy during the next few days to express their condolences received, as mementos of Henry, cigarette holders, shoehorns, and can openers. The longer Lucy stayed in the house and the more closely she went through his papers, the more she regretted having known the man solely through his postcards. She had a gravestone put up: *Here lies Henry Beerbaum. His motto was Compensation.* "

"But surely it wasn't because of him that she finally decided to stay here?" asks Rita Süssfeldt.

"Definitely not; it's quite probable that she had several reasons for not using her return ticket; but there was presumably one reason that tipped the balance."

"And that was?"

"If you really think you need to know that too, Rita, well, she had definitely decided to leave when during her last few days here she received a letter from home telling her that Victor Gaitanides had published his banns and that he was going to marry, moreover, the secretary who had worked for them both at the Institute, the one they'd had to share. I didn't learn this from Lucy herself, though she did mention it once, dropping it casually into the conversation in passing, you know the sort of thing, but even if this must remain pure surmise, this time she was certainly right: she stayed on because something had come to an end in her life. She furnished the house according to her taste, gave away the things she considered superfluous—and there were a lot—and applied for a post at the Hamburg Institute, not right away but after a few weeks. Don't ask me whether her decision was motivated mainly by disappointment or by misconstrued expectations, I imagine that question can never be decided, and since the friendship between them lasted right up to the end, it can't be proved—or even imagined—whether it was caused by a sense of grievance or hurt feelings that she wouldn't admit. It's surprised me how long their friendship lasted; at any rate, he never seemed to me good enough to be a partner for Lucy Beerbaum."

Rita straightens up in amazement and turns around to look at him, now sitting relaxed in his chair. "Did you know him? You knew Victor Gaitanides personally?"

Heino gives a calm nod; he'd been down to Greece a number of times and on the next-to-last trip Lucy had given him something for her colleague and companion; it was a letter, which Heino had been asked to transmit, as a neighbor.

Rita Süssfeldt can't contain her curiosity any longer, she lights up a cigarette, reaches for a chair, and insists on looking him in the eyes. "And now tell me about it; so you met him?"

Her high hopes are bound to be disappointed, because he doesn't attach as much importance to the man and his meeting with him as she assumes; so he goes on with his story, telling her how he arrives in Athens, telephones the Institute for Biology, and asks to speak to Professor Gaitanides, who with some hesitation invites this visitor from Hamburg, Professor Lucy Beerbaum's neighbor, to his home. "That was all there was to it, Rita."

A silent, timid woman opened the door, took his coat, asked him to come in, and offered him a choice of refreshments, since the professor was still in his study—she said "the professor," referring to her husband. Never had he witnessed so much devotion, so much unobtrusive solicitude at such close quarters before, says Heino Merkel; the visitor couldn't forget the way she smoothed the cushion on the chair before he sat down, the way she brought him his comfortable jacket, the quiet care with which she polished the glass he was going to drink out of. And the professor? He rewarded all this bustling humility with impeccable politeness and attention. He took the envelope to his study and put it into a drawer; his questions were courteous and concerned mainly with the external circumstances of Lucy's life, Heino couldn't recall the details. Although Heino was the guest, he must have received only a fraction of the attention that was shown to the professor, Victor Gaitanides. "I presented him with a copy of . . . *And the Ark Floated;* just imagine, he seemed to recognize the title!"

"And what about Lucy," asks Rita Süssfeldt, "didn't he have anything interesting to say about Lucy?"

"I don't think he saw any reason to bring out any of his recollections of her; it may be that he also wanted to be considerate; as I said, he merely inquired about Lucy's welfare. At any rate, I can't remember having gathered any other information; and after all, we can learn all about his reputation as a scientist here."

Unable to find an ashtray, Rita Süssfeldt stubs out her cigarette on the box of matches and, lost in thought, walks over to the window; she looks disappointed. A youth dressed in shining leather and wearing a painted crash helmet swings his leg over a heavy motorcycle, kicks on the starter, and with an enormous gauntlet throws a kiss up to a lighted window. She senses that Heino Merkel has just thanked her for the second time, and with her face turned toward the misted-up window: "Not at all," she says.

19

It must be true! The papers say so and the covers of the magazines carry additional evidence, it's being announced in black and white and blue on advertisement pillars and kiosks and dingy billboards: today he's going to make positively his last appearance, he's finally going to hang up his boots to devote himself to private life and family: Charly Gurk, the irreplaceable king of the midfield, the leader, etc. etc., is today giving his farewell performance, under floodlights; he's going to captain this last match, which is being given in his honor.

Janpeter Heller would like to avoid seeing it, but he finds it impossible to escape it: that squat face with the drooping eyelids, the astonishing ears which sprout like savoy cabbages from his sparsely covered skull, the amazingly small and literally heart-shaped lips—wherever he goes he sees Charly Gurk quietly appraising him with his eyes, and even here, in the Zur Funkuhr café, he catches sight of him immediately in the newspapers that are lying around and on a notice hung in the window.

At the moment, there's hardly a soul in the café, only a few aging radio producers, seemingly part of the furniture, who are crouching around a nearby table and over numerous whiskeys are hatching out a smash hit; if Heller understands them correctly it's a kind of hare-and-hounds game with celebrities as the hares—involving audience participation, obviously.

Heller hadn't expected to find such a desirable place to sit; between the wide-spaced letters forming the name of the café he can see the gas pumps of a garage and on the other side of the street, exactly in his angle of vision, the enamel plate, set diagonally on the patch of grass and thus easy to read, announcing the office hours of Dr. Gerhard Thormählen, internist. Behind the frosted glass on the ground floor everything is still in darkness; only the offices of the insurance company above are lit up and in the fluorescent light he can see a man collecting notebooks and files and reference books from deserted desks.

Now this flat-assed waitress who propels herself from the glass showcase and with studied distaste makes a beeline for him, stiff-necked as her ash-blond superstructure demands—a pair of storks could easily have nested in it—and then through her hairy lip breathes: "What's it to be, darling?"—this kind of waitress tempts Heller to say: Before I recognize your existence, I'm afraid you'll have to pass an intelligence test.

He doesn't say it. He doesn't even correct her mode of address. "Schnapps," he says, "a rye if you have it"; but in this establishment they'll have no truck with such vulgar tastes and he has to order a raspberry cordial in order to earn the privilege of sitting there. And what a sight as she hobbles away on her cork soles that are far too high for her! What a cozy mechanical grin she puts on as she goes past the radio producers! I'd like to see how she walks when she's in a hurry to take a pee, thinks Heller. What does the paper say? Charly, the mentor and driving force, is retiring. Heller reads an interview and learns that the interviewer, a sports writer, is more or less a friend of Charly Gurk's and presumably that's why he's allowed to sit at the coffee table too and stick his fingers through the crocheted tablecloth. Along with the interview the paper publishes a telegram from Hanker-Schmühling, the local theologian, in which Charly Gurk is acclaimed as an example for all German youth to follow. "You are and will continue to be . . . ."

Heller learns that in his limited leisure time the great midfield strategist likes more than anything else playing with his two sons and three daughters; he can drive for hours in his car without getting tired; in addition to his own home he owns two apartment houses, four gas stations, and several tobacconists which accept betting slips. His favorite drink has always been: Milk. Asked what profession he has studied for, he replies: Traveler.

Now the radio producers are talking about Charly Gurk too, he's being chosen as the first celebrity for a hare-and-hounds chase through Hamburg; listeners are to pursue him happily through the town, following the trail of his typical characteristics; the number and value of the prizes hasn't yet been decided. Is it that late? It seems to be, for one of them hastily turns on the television set high on the wall, they arrange their chairs, call for Edith—so she's called Edith—and take the precaution of ordering another round; and then there appears on the screen something that is taking place only a couple of blocks away—Charly Gurk's farewell performance.

Heller watches a bloated, bandy-legged woman in a herringbone coat waddling across the front garden, pulling a key ring out of her pocket as she goes, to open the door of the house. Immediately afterward fluorescent lights flash on behind the frosted-glass windows. He can guess what she is doing from the movements of her shadow. Like himself, an old man with an apathetic child is looking at the doctor's office.

On the screen an homage to Charly is being presented with a wild outburst of cowbells, sirens, and rattles which render the commentator superfluous; however, he won't give up and offers a mutilated and incomprehensible commentary on the ceremony taking place on the field, in which Charly is being awarded a variety of honors by gentlemen dressed in black suits: honorary life captaincy, for instance, and a position as adviser to the Foreign Minister of the German Football Association, if that sounds possible.

The waitress sets down his drink without looking at him, carefully transports her precarious hairdo over to the radio producers, and allows one of them to place his arm on her unnaturally protuberant hipbone as he orders another round.

Why not him, in fact, thinks Heller to himself, why don't we make someone like him into our exemplary person, since a theologian has already provided him with a testimonial for the job? Why should I boggle at the very idea of considering Charly Gurk? He's just being presented with a "cup for good sportsmanship," designed specially for him: doesn't that represent a good starting point as a theme for our anthology?

And now, cutting ahead of the shuffling old man, a tall redhead disappears into the house; she too opens the door with a key and appears shortly afterward behind the frosted window.

There's a roar, a persistent, deep-throated, menacing roar booming out from distant lungs: they've kicked off and Charly immediately shows his quality with one of his masterly chopped passes, over forty yards long, which, for his family's sake, he will no longer be booting after today. Everyone wishes he himself could kick the ball like that and a bellow of enthusiasm begins, swells up suddenly in anticipation, and subsides as the ball goes out. Presumably he's an unsuitable candidate for inclusion as an exemplary character in an anthology, thinks Heller, because there's hardly anything of a really problematical nature in his life, there's hardly a trace of any sort of contradiction that's universally valid. The only things that can be illustrated in his life, after all, are nothing more than "metaphorical" problems, I mean, and they're not applicable to actual life.

That must be them in the heavy dark two-seater which is bumping up over the curb and parking on the sidewalk, between those two trees whose bark has been scraped off, and over the rim of his glass Heller can see Charlotte emerge with a practiced twist of her hips and then the good-humored athlete himself, who has to bend down a second time into the low car in order to fish out a small, flat, metal-bound box. Both of them look toward the lighted frosted windows as they saunter across the front garden, chatting as they go; she naturally lets him unlock the door and it is she who also asks him to hold the door open for the old man and the child, who want to be first in.

Heller makes a sign to the waitress and orders a piece of cheesecake, which is then dumped unenthusiastically under his nose.

An angry voice, a voice of fury and frustration from the television strikes his ear just as he's taking his first bite, because their idol has been brought down, someone has left his leg sticking out and Charly Gurk falls over it, as anyone would have, and even after rolling a couple of times on the slushy turf he can't seem to get to his feet. The radio producers explain to each other what they've just seen, in their indignation they reach for their glasses, and one of them looks suspiciously over at Heller, almost in rebuke, presumably because at a moment like this he has managed to carry a forkful of cheesecake to his lips. Now will Charly Gurk also "leave his leg sticking out" if the occasion offers? Heller wonders, and lingers for a moment on the idea, with the portrait of an "exemplary man" in mind; but he immediately discards it as being too restricted in its context. He now wants to pay his bill and since the amount isn't so much told him directly as breathed at him in dying tones, he slams his coins down onto the table, not without satisfaction, and counts as loudly and clearly as he can while she gives him his change, and then reaches past the ash-blond superstructure for his coat, sweeps all his change into his pocket, and, without a word, skips his way to the revolving door.

Anyone leaping like that down the stone steps, anyone greeting the gas-station attendant so debonairly as he passes, anyone crossing the grimy, slippery Rothenbaumchaussee the way he does, is surely confessing that he either has just done or else is about to do something which justifies this high-spirited method of progression. Heller vaults sharply over the low garden gate, his open waterproof coat making a hissing sound. The outer door is now held open by a small bag of sand; according to the arrow, the office is that way, and the bell's here. Someone in his state naturally has to ring several times; nor, when the buzzer sounds, does he walk in timorously like a patient but eagerly, certain of his welcome, like a man bringing glad tidings.

And there, surrounded by filing cabinets, commanding the corridor and keeping guard over the long varnished doors which lead out of it, Charlotte, dressed in a white coat, is sitting at her command post, swiveling around in her revolving chair and

335

checking medical records. On the walls the "Lovers of Vitebsk" are proving their ability to walk in the air in Chagall's conception of them, in green on a blue background; beside them, Buffet's "Tristesse" has taken over a few free spaces. "It's the first door along the corridor," Charlotte is saying as she swings around and looks at Heller—as aghast as if he had come in carrying his own head under his arm.

"But it's not possible—it can't really be you." Utter amazement gives way to resentment and then to faltering protest: "Why have you come? Why are you doing this to me? We'd arranged to meet this evening." Heller makes his apologies. With a shrug of his shoulders he ignores her objections, pleas, and disbelieving questions; he has the impression, he says, no doubt as a result of his sedentary occupation, that he is due for a thorough medical examination. Charlotte refuses to believe him; speaking in a rapid, offended voice, she expresses her suspicion that he's only come to embarrass her and stir up trouble. She's forced to change her tone to welcome newly arrived patients and ask them to wait, and then, when they're alone again: "Please spare us that, Janpeter, and if you really need a doctor, find another one."

But Heller feels like being a private patient, he insists on his right of free choice, and since he's heard how good Dr. Thormählen is, he would like to take advantage of his skill himself. "So be a nice girl, Charlotte, and put me on one of your index cards."

"You know the understanding between us," says Charlotte, "I mean, between Gerhard and me."

"That's just it," says Heller, "that's why I expect particularly sympathetic treatment from him."

She shuts her eyes and leans back in her chair, her lips quivering, and then she pulls out a green index card and begins to fill it in, laboriously, it's true, but never once hesitating over the personal details; while he twists his body and with ironical admiration reads as she writes, taking each entry as an homage to himself: Look at that, how much you still remember. Staring at the ornamental butterfly clip which holds her hair back, Heller expresses his hope that her present husband will receive from her future husband the attention which is his right. But it's Heller himself, not Charlotte, who feels that this demonstration of superiority seems rather overdone, as does the bow with which he acknowledges her request not to smoke in the waiting room.

"Is this the way to the waiting room for private patients?"

"We don't make any distinctions," Charlotte says in a flat voice, "we've only got one waiting room."

Even before he shuts the door, he can see Charlotte slipping off her chair and hurriedly grabbing the receiver, and he laughs at the thought that at this moment she's warning him, alerting him, agreeing to adopt a certain attitude: Look out, there's a wolf at the gate, we shouldn't, now we must . . .

With rather too hearty a "good evening," Heller introduces himself into the waiting room so loudly that some of the older patients—of whom there are more than he had expected, including two tired old-age pensioners—sit up sharply and break off their reading—mainly professional medical reviews but also tattered copies of the *Property Owners' Journal*—which suggests that the doctor's a property owner himself. While Heller is still hesitating over where to sit, a boy crouches behind his back—narrow-eyed, snorting, and in a burgundy-colored pullover like himself—springs up, and smashes a dirty fist between his shoulder blades, so unexpectedly that Heller gives a grunt, spins around, and instinctively raises his fists but then drops them and gives a sour smile as the boy retreats toward a very young delicate-looking woman, vigorously thrusts himself between her thighs, and puts his head on her chest, as though wanting to listen to her heartbeat. The boy peers at him malevolently out of one eye, the woman raises a slender scratched hand toward him to express her helplessness and her apologies.

Heller wouldn't be Heller if he didn't now sit down beside her, with a placatory nod, and put his hand on the boy's shoulder: "That was a pretty good surprise attack." The very young woman, whose sweater is covered with cat's hairs, points to a blighted geranium and makes a gesture with her head toward a chessboard on which the chessmen are lying, laid low as though after a direct hit—the net result of their waiting thus far. And Heller, dismissively: "That's nothing, that can all be set right; if you aren't going to be halfhearted about a permissive upbringing, then you have to be prepared to accept the damage." And he lands a good-humored dig in the boy's ribs, who, constricted by polyps, proceeds to emit a series of squeaks.

"Herr Heller?" He stands up uncertainly, he can't believe that having been the last person in, he should be the first one to be called, but the bandy-legged woman makes a sign to him, no, not into the office but into a room opposite, into the lab, as she says, and as he assumes that Charlotte has inoculated her with the appropriate information, he looks for confirmation in the attitude of the woman as she takes him gently by the sleeve and leads him along with her, equally gently. She quietly pushes him down onto a chair; his index card is lying on the table over there, in front of the test tubes and small bottles.

How silently and nonchalantly she sits down beside him, without a word draws some blood out of his earlobe, and then a few cubic centimeters from a vein. She is taking his blood from him so unobtrusively and painlessly that Heller has the feeling she is turning into a plant which is gently sucking it out of him. What can he say? "If you were to pump me dry, I wouldn't notice it the way you do it."

The woman shrugs her shoulders, walks over to the table, and, with her face averted, says, "After I'd done that, you wouldn't find it very easy to go about your business, Herr Heller." Then, with a very steady hand, she holds out a little bottle to him. "Now if you wouldn't mind letting me have a sample of your urine, if that's possible—the toilet's next to the dressing room there." Heller assesses the size of the neck of the bottle, waits undecidedly, expecting the woman to repeat her request, because he would like to show her how cheerfully he's prepared to cooperate and with what aplomb he will comply with it and thus complete this ritual examination, but the woman avoids meeting his eye.

While he's trying to pee into the neck of the bottle, he can see himself standing there, bent forward, screwing his head sideways

338

and concentrating hard, worried in case the urine might spurt out unevenly and miss the bottle; he imagines to himself what impression he would be making on himself seen from the middle distance, in this attitude of humble and doubtless suppliant expectation, hesitating with an asinine look on his face, and he has to laugh and put the bottle down. For his next attempt, he first pulls the chain to prime himself and this time he manages it and, smugly triumphant, hands back the warmed-up bottle to the woman in the lab.

Even now she has nothing to say to him, merely sticking a label on the bottle, then taking him once again by the sleeve and piloting him across a corridor into a windowless room, where he is greeted with a smile from the biggest mouth he has ever seen, set beneath a head of shining red hair. "This is Herr Heller." He's handed over, delivered, the woman from the lab says good-bye, good luck, and then he's left alone with the tall assistant, in the light of a standard lamp. What now?

"And now, Herr Heller, let's do a nice little"—she actually says "nice little"—"EKG, so that we can all put our minds at rest." Her gangling, overgrown limbs, the way she dashes about, her high-pitched, relentlessly cheerful voice, like that of the eternal nursery-school teacher, and last but not least, her general appearance—all these things might have silenced any patient taken unawares or perhaps even given him qualms. Not so Heller; he undresses as requested, puts his clothes to one side, cheerfully does the obligatory knee bends, which the giantess counts with him, and then stretches out on the cool couch, legs apart. Electric plugs click into their appropriate sockets. Multicolored wires are disentangled and arranged in order, contact plates lie snugly on his skin, and the graph paper awaits in the apparatus ready to register the confused shorthand of his heart. The giantess sits on the edge of the bed and regards him with a satisfied look—Heller thinks: like her prey tethered down with wires—and he imagines that with controlled electric shocks she will now shrink him to a manageable size and take him home in her shopping bag.

"Well," she says, "now let's see what naughty things the heart's been up to." Heller stares at the apparatus, in which black cylinders are rotating and spidery needles start moving in jerks, as it now begins to squeeze a wide flowing strip of paper out of itself, like something it had digested. "There you are," says the giantess, "here it comes." And Heller says, "Just a novelette, I suppose, nothing much more than that." "Anyway," says the giantess, "you're sure of having at least two readers." She switches the wires around and for a moment follows the line traced by the pointer, which is lashing out quite regularly and not very excitedly. The coded message is received with satisfaction and as if the result concerned not only Heller but herself, she says, "That's very good, that's what we like to see." Heller is allowed to get off the couch and dress; he would like to know the details of what she's learned—after all, one can never know too much about oneself—but the giantess shakes her head; she neither may nor will say anything, the whole story will be passed on to him in a minute, by the doctor himself. Will he follow her, please?

Back to the lab, past a veranda, and then in front of a door standing ajar the woman shakes him by the hand as she says goodbye with an encouraging smile. Heller pushes open the door and finds himself in a special waiting room. With their jackets on their knees and the shirt sleeves on their left arms rolled up to an identical height, the two old-age pensioners are looking at him from the window seat opposite: their greeting is slow and as though rehearsed. With a grin, they draw Heller's attention to the fact that they're each pressing a wad of cotton on a tiny prick in the bend of their arm. "I suppose you're both suffering from the same thing?" It's Heller's turn next.

The hard dry hand—oarsman? expert gymnast?—wraps itself around his, draws him into the office, and does not release him until they have reached the desk, on which, arranged fanwise on a blotting pad, there are approximately seven hundred rectangular slips of paper to remind its user of appointments, dates, and deadlines.

"How do you do, Herr Heller. I am happy to have this opportunity to make your acquaintance. Charlotte has told me so much about you, as you may imagine." "How do you do." Pause. Silent appraisal on both sides. For the first time they can view each other at close range. Mutual assessment of their personas: If a film were made on Sauerbruch he would certainly be suitable for the part of the second assistant, not a speaking part of course. . . . The beard is presumably intended not only to disguise a receding chin but as a deliberate expression of protest. . . . So that's the man. . . . So that's what my predecessor looks like.

"I knew, Herr Heller, that you were in town, of course. Charlotte tells me that you're taking part in a teachers' conference."

Heller, with an air of superiority, passing his thumb over his mouth, replies, "Charlotte is always getting ideas into her head and her reports are always larger than life. It's not a teachers' conference but just a modest committee meeting, to edit an anthology, the three of us."

"Oh, I see."

"Yes. If you deduct one whole size—purely as a precaution— then you get the actual measurement."

The long, starched doctor's coat, which emphasizes his waist and makes Thormählen look even slimmer than he is, crackles as it straightens up behind the desk, and its wearer is now about to deliver himself of a statement, a declaration of principle—to avoid any misunderstanding, Herr Heller—but it doesn't eventuate because the young schoolmaster points out genially, rather than with any ulterior motive, that where any relationship with his wife was concerned, he could teach the other a thing or two, since, after all, he had been given the opportunity of accumulating a certain amount of experience.

"To avoid any misunderstanding, Herr Heller," the doctor says, "I hope that you haven't come to my office to discuss Charlotte with me."

Heller gives a smirk, leans back in his chair, and puts on an expression of familiarity which seems to irritate the doctor. He knows that it is going to sound like blackmail but still he makes the remark: "Meanwhile, Charlotte happens to be my wife."

"I'm not unaware of that fact, Herr Heller; nevertheless, I see no reason to discuss that topic with you, today or at any other time. And since you seem to think it necessary to remind me of the existence of your marriage, I won't bother to point out to you what sort of marriage yours has been over the last few years. If you are anxious to be treated as a patient . . ."

"But of course," Heller interrupts, "that's why I'm here, after all"; and with what conviction he can muster, he puts on a show of submission to his fate and willingness to cooperate in the rest of his examination.

"Then will you please remove your clothes down to the waist?"

"Only down to the waist?"

"That will be quite sufficient for us."

While Heller removes his clothes with relish, he notices his index card on the desk and stapled to it one yellow and one white sheet of paper, as well as a packet of flimsy graph paper. The doctor is reading as Heller's round shoulders make their appearance, a hairless, flabby rather than muscular chest, a skin patterned with stripes and spots like a map, and since he's never regarded nudity as something which automatically exposes your weaknesses or which may even arouse pity, he stands with his legs apart and waits for the doctor imperturbably, confident of victory.

Twice Dr. Thormählen ignores the ringing of the telephone, and then, still reading, he lifts the receiver, absentmindedly murmurs "Hello," and slowly raises his head; his gaze wanders over Heller and slowly comes down and fastens on a photograph of an old doctor. He lowers the receiver, although the man at the other end is still talking—a posture that reminds Heller of several films he has seen and which is intended to register agitation, if not violent, inexpressible emotion. In slow motion he replaces the receiver, shakes his head, places his opened fingers over his eyes. Then he gropes for the handle of a drawer and pulls it open. Then he places a pack of cigarettes on the table and lights a cigarette, so hurriedly and clumsily as to make it plain that he is not a regular smoker. Then he stares at the telephone, smoking, squaring his shoulders as though not wanting to move.

Heller wants to draw attention to the fact that he is not only present and waiting but stripped to the waist; he asks: "Bad news?" and follows it immediately with: "Is there something wrong?"

Thormählen gives a nod; merely stubbing his cigarette out won't suffice, he presses on it until it bursts and then crushes it. "My apologies, Herr Heller, I wasn't expecting that."

"Something can always go wrong," says Heller in an understanding voice.

The doctor, taking the blood-pressure gauge out of a drawer, says, "We can never know enough, and if we once forget that, it doesn't take long for something to remind us of it." In a matter-of-fact voice he asks Heller to hold out his arm, wraps a gray-green piece of canvas around his elbow, and fastens it.

"I hope it wasn't personal?"

"It depends what you mean; it was the hospital informing me of the death of one of my patients."

The doctor is pumping air into the canvas tube, the pressure on Heller's arm increases; his arm is seized in a cool grip.

"Ah well," says Heller, "in Germany nowadays there's no obligation to hang out a red lamp in front of your office if someone has died on your hands." Then he realizes, too late, that his remark was in poor taste and that he might well have refrained from making it. Thormählen hasn't understood and even if he has he doesn't show it; perhaps he wants Heller to realize from the start, from the rigorous objectivity of his attitude, that his office is used for one purpose only.

He pumps the tube up tightly, the pressure increases, and Heller now thinks he can overhear his pulse beating, a tiny mechanical gong in the dungeons of his body.

How she used to fuss, thinks Heller, how she arranged to have at least two diagnoses for every illness, because she believed that every doctor might now and again make a mistake and especially where her family was concerned; she needed this double guarantee so badly; and he says, "If I understand Charlotte correctly, she would never be satisfied with one diagnosis."

"Your blood pressure is normal," says Thormählen, "and now

will you please breathe in and out deeply, with your mouth open."

"The fact is," says Heller, "that if Charlotte is faced with two alternatives, she will always assume that the worse one is more likely to happen, and she'll act accordingly."

"You're forgetting to breathe, Herr Heller."

The stethoscope is roaming over Heller's flabby back listening to his inner signals and suddenly seems to have discovered some extra sounds, for it lingers noticeably under the left shoulder blade. "It's remarkable that experience can't be handed on, bequeathed; it's just as if we insist on never learning from other people's mistakes. Don't you think so too, Doctor?"

"Please stretch your arms out and breathe regularly, that's better."

Has the metal got stuck to his back? "You see, as far as knowing Charlotte is concerned, I've got a big head start on everybody, and not only am I able to hand it on, free, gratis, and for nothing, but I'm very willing to do so."

"I don't suppose it's anything, Herr Heller," says the doctor, "but I think you ought to have an X ray, just to be sure. I'll give you the address of a colleague of mine."

"To hear you talk," says Heller, "or rather, to hear you not talking, it's tempting to detect Charlotte's influence; even Stefanie knows now what questions not to answer on principle."

"You may get dressed now, Herr Heller." Thormählen goes back to his desk, jots down a note to himself on a slip of paper, which he half pushes under his blotting pad, while Heller pulls his sweater over his head with a grimly sardonic smile. "Please sit down."

So here come the disclosures, the sifting of the results that have been gleaned, a recapitulation, but beforehand and first of all, after a quick run-through, a few general soothing words: Let him say right away, all in all, Herr Heller can be reassured. Heller is neither surprised nor relieved, he's always assumed that to be the case and he's only sitting here, one supposes, in order to come to the topic that interests him. But the doctor gives him no opportu-

344

nity and compels him to listen while he presents the information on Heller which has just been garnered and mentions the reasons why the two of them, doctor and patient, may be reassured. How carefully he releases his words, Heller thinks, he's pouring the whole diagnosis out over you like some epic saga, steadily and imperturbably, and when Heller tries to say something, he follows up once again with his warning, the advice to have an X-ray check, a warning which he delivers this time not from behind his desk but when he's already on his way to the door, so that Heller automatically stands up and also moves in that direction. But he casts out one more hook, behind the doctor's back: "Since you're so pleased with me, Doctor, I suppose you wouldn't mind certifying me as legally fit to marry, or can't you?"

Thormählen turns around, eyes him with an expression that might be considered a look of pity, and then, standing beside the door, says, "Of course, you'll be receiving a written copy of the result." Heller's not prepared for an ending like this; he feels as if his mouth were filling with tobacco juice, bitter and astringent, and ignoring the hand which the doctor is offering with no great conviction, just in case, he bows stiffly from the hips, a gesture which immediately reminds him an exchange of greetings between two men "each supposing the other to be of high rank."

He finds himself out in the corridor so abruptly and unexpectedly that for a moment he can find nothing to say to Charlotte, sitting at her command post and pretending to be concerned, to the exclusion of everything else, with her index cards and portable typewriter. His coat, first of all; he ought to pick up his coat from the waiting room, where he now sees not a single empty seat, they all look at him searchingly and inquiringly, no doubt hoping to read encouragement for their own ills in his face.

"So you see, Charlotte, everything went quite painlessly," says Heller, "and now at least I'm reassured." He feels a different man from the one who first came in, smaller and inferior, while she on the other hand seems even more unattainable at her command post and from the refuge of her desk she can allow herself an unconscionably long delay in answering.

345

"But you don't seem very pleased," she says with a quick upward glance.

"Me? I've been completely reassured, I'm as fit as a fiddle, I'm even going to get a written report, you might even say I'm to be congratulated." He comes closer and stands beside the raised, box-shaped desk and watches Charlotte's efforts to take refuge in frantic activity with an amused look on his face, rolling his head back and forth like someone watching a game of tennis.

"Can't you see you're making me nervous?" says Charlotte.

"Me?" says Heller, assuming an innocent air. "I'm just admiring your brain cells at work, your mechanical brain if I may use the phrase."

"Don't try to be so superior, Janpeter, I know what you think of my work. Aren't you satisfied with having come here? At breaking in here just to embarrass me?" She says goodbye to an old man in a friendly voice and wishes him a rapid recovery.

"Listen," says Heller, "I'd like to make you a proposition: Put all those cards away, put your coat on, and come with me. Come away with me, Charlotte."

Showing no sign of surprise, the woman looks up and eyes him with a sad, contemptuous expression of wonder, as though she had been expecting, if not this, at least some similar sort of proposition, an offer which, she senses, was not in his mind when he came into the office. "What's the point?" she asks quietly. "Just to go on talking and talking? And what about my work here?"

"Anyone could do that," says Heller, buttoning his coat. "You don't think that you're indispensable?"

"No, but I do know what I have to do for the present."

Heller is listening to something behind one of the doors, where he can hear a sound of intermittent cheerful protest, probably a ticklish patient, he thinks to himself. And now he places both hands on the impregnable desk and repeats his invitation; the woman, bending over her work, shakes her head. He stands back and asks for confirmation that their arrangement for meeting later that evening still stands, and the woman, after an initial indecisive shrug of her shoulders, immediately corrects herself and points out that they've now met and so there's no further point. And then, not excessively disappointed, he inquires when he would be most likely to reach her at home, and Charlotte seems to ponder for a long time before informing him that for the next few days there were no absolutely certain times. Heller has anticipated this, but he still waits until she returns his parting words. "I said: 'See you' . . . Shall we?" He turns up his collar and walks out quickly.

Anyone watching Heller on his way out and trying to size up this man as he leaves the office with a sheepish rather than a malicious look, trudging along rapt in thought, would no doubt assume the obvious: there goes a man who has just been diagnosed as suffering from some unsuspected disease and who is going to have to observe a strict regimen. Seen from behind, his gait was that of a man bearing a heavy load, the gait of a man afflicted, someone on whom life has imposed too heavy a burden. Damp is working its way up his suede shoes—how can anyone be wearing suede shoes in this kind of weather? Are those needles that a gust of wind is driving into his face, needles applying a hot, savage massage which makes his blood begin to tingle?

Two youths blunder past carrying a half-rolled banner which the wind is trying to entice out of their grasp; the canvas is billowing and blowing about high above their heads as they hurry along to the nearby stadium, because Charly Gurk must be informed that the Hamburg Electricity Board wishes to offer him their greetings on this day. Heller shakes his head, Heller comes to a halt and listens to a sound which, on this slippery November day, has just been borne to his ears by the wind, snatches of a Christmas carol—and there it is again—shepherds wa-a-atched their flocks by night—sung by children, obviously the children's choir of the North German Radio, rehearsing in an empty studio.

Still bending forward, Heller quickens his step and doesn't slow down until he reaches the Mittelweg at the end of the North German Radio block. Walking on the black remains of old leaves, past gleaming puddles, he is trying to find his way to the Hotel-

347

Pension Klöver. He is unperturbed by car horns, nor do the flashing lights of a car make him move with any greater alacrity, muffled as he is in his clothes. He even walks unconcernedly past the clumsy, arrogant building of the Garrison Headquarters, past the gloomy Archives, which must have his name on record, too.

He's right: the Hotel-Pension Klöver also has a back entrance, a staircase leads down to it between two walls; in this vague gloom Heller has the impression that the stairs are leading him onto the roof and from there into the bowels of the house. Here's the mailbox, chock-full; it is trying to spew out the mail which has been forcibly stuffed into it. Heller takes it upon himself to empty it, fishes out newspapers and letters, looks through them, and takes them over to the reception desk.

There under her white cap sits Magda, counting the receipts with her thick fingers, sitting on the strings of her white apron, struggling with figures, and she is about to get them all wrong again when the clammy mail thuds down on the table. Heller receives a reproachful look for disturbing her and his key his handed over with a marked coldness. Has Herr Pundt come in yet? he would like to know. Herr Pundt was expected to be in, yes, he'd ordered tea for himself, but he hasn't yet put in an appearance, there's his key still hanging up there. Would she please take Herr Pundt's tea up to Heller? To the conference room? No, up to Heller's room. "If you can wait a moment, I'll bring the tea up to your room," Magda says, and puts the two piles of receipts on top of one another again. Heller goes up to his room, shrugs off his coat, pulls the curtains closed with a throwing-stick, and then, without bending down, slips off his battered wet shoes and flings himself down onto his bed. He crosses his hands behind his neck, stares, dazzled but persistently, at the light, apparently sorting out and assessing his recent experiences, without, however, reaching any decision, for suddenly, as though blowing against a hot potato, Heller expels air through his pursed lips, lifts a pack of photocopied sheets from the bedside table, and places them on his stomach. He lifts one leg amazingly high in the air and waggles his toes in his socks, which are too thin. With his foot he writes a word in the air, it might be "shit."

Is that Magda already? Her morose look betrays the fact that once again the receipts have failed to work out the way she hoped and that simply to get rid of Heller's order for tea she has just now decided to bring it up. "Well, here's your tea, Herr Heller."

"I hope it's warmer than the radiator."

"Isn't it warm enough for you here?"

"Some people refuse to come to Hamburg in the winter merely because the heating is so unreliable here."

"They must feel cold even in summer, then!"

"Well, I suppose your room is warm enough, anyway."

"I haven't even got a radiator, only a tiny electric heater."

"Nobody else?"

"What do you mean?"

"Perhaps a cuddly little hot-water bottle?"

"You must drink your tea before it gets cold."

"Your room is over the private rooms, isn't it?"

"That's none of your business."

"It's in case there's a sudden cold spell; I'm not to be despised as a hot-water bottle actually."

"Watch what you're saying, Herr Heller."

"Well?"

"Drink your tea." Magda taps the empty plywood tray against her thigh as she walks with a smile toward the door, and when she reaches it, she asks Heller, still lying down, relaxed, "I'd like to know what you're really discussing, honestly," and then she stands with one hand on the door handle and seems to be expecting an answer on the spot.

"What we're discussing?" Heller hesitates, reflects, thinks he knows, realizes that he doesn't, and then says, "We're trying to find somebody, some figure, a type, a personality—if you get me —a man or woman who could walk dry-footed through the sea and by doing that could help the greatest possible number of people to walk dry-footed to the Promised Land as well."

"Now you're pulling my leg, Herr Heller."

"Then let me put it like this: we're looking for a model person, an idol, someone who has behaved in such an exemplary way— if you can follow what I mean—that he makes a lot of other people want to imitate him."

"So you're kind of advertising, then?" asks Magda.

After an enjoyable pause for reflection, Heller says, "Yes, in a way we're advertising something. I'll tell you about it in detail later on when I bring you the hot-water bottle."

Magda shuts the door. Heller heaves himself over onto his side and places the photocopied sheets in the light of the bedside lamp. Propped up on his elbow, he begins to turn over the pages and reads: "The Unsuccessful Interview," turns over some more, and then turns back again and settles down to read properly.

BURNING QUESTIONS, an interview on BURNING QUESTIONS of the day conducted by the reporter Hermann Count Katulla, on the forty-fourth day of Lucy Beerbaum's voluntary captivity. Although Lucy had set the time of the interview herself, she had to be wakened by Irene because she had fallen into an exhausted sleep on her couch, and it was also the stolid bulky girl with her knee socks continually slipping down to her ankles who opened the door for Katulla and his male stenographer and asked them to wait in the hall. On the second floor, a diffident tape recorder was running; a burst of laughter was quickly stifled, as though frightened by its own sound. The reporter, scenting a contrasting effect that might be useful for his story, exchanged glances with the stenographer and they both looked upstairs, where a giggling girl's voice continued to make fun of everything.

"My aunt can see you now," said the girl dreamily, causing them to bring their gaze down from upstairs and prompting Katulla to inquire: "Aunt?" "My sister and I call her our aunt." The reporter, who, presumably because he knew too much, had adopted an air of permanent resignation, now inquired whether they were, in fact, related in any way, to which Irene replied that yes, they were, but so indirectly that it was practically impossible to work it out. Since Katulla's face seemed familiar to her, she was looking at him thoughtfully but only in order to judge to what extent he resembled his photographs; the symmetrical lips, held together as if by a zipper; the narrow nose, somewhat off course; the almost sorrowful expression of certainty of being proved right in the end, of always being right every time. "Let me show you the way," said Irene, "it's the housekeeper's day off."

Lucy was lying on her couch and it was from there that she held out her hand to greet the two men, gaily pointing out that to the best of her belief BURNING QUESTIONS had never objected to the position which the person being interviewed was in and anyway he was not unfamiliar with horizontal positions and wouldn't find it an obstacle to conversation. Accustomed to being met with compliments and respectful suspicion, Katulla took these words, too, merely as a form of appreciation and, having asked permission to smoke, he recalled that in the olden days decisions were, he thought, always reached by discussions between people who were recumbent, the Roman baths were surely nothing but an unofficial annex of the Senate. The two men, the reporter and the stenographer, accepted with thanks the coffee which Irene had prepared for them and silently spread out the tools of their trade: handwritten notes, newspaper clippings, a shorthand pad.

Lucy was lying motionless and silent on her back, a blanket over her legs; only her lips were quivering: what was it that was warning her that all their questioning could strip you naked to the bone? She could hear the men muttering together, making whispered arrangements like people preparing a trap: Irene asked shyly whether she might stay and listen and the reporter said he could see no objection. Then the final formal statement, addressed to Lucy in a matter-of-fact and almost flat tone of voice: the entire conversation with all its digressions and byways . . . in view of the special type of reader, there were private aspects which must also . . . her biography will be kept in a special box . . . the final condensed version would under no circumstances be published without the agreement . . . incidentally the date of publication had not yet . . .

Lucy turned her head, looking for Irene standing in the background in the semi-darkness, winked at her, and snapped her fingers. Katulla was looking at her challengingly with the professional consideration of a man who has up to now been able to overcome every disappointment or disaster by means of his stylistic gifts.

QUESTION: Professor Beerbaum, for the last forty-four days you've been a source of astonishment to all of us. What did you have in mind in going into voluntary captivity?

ANSWER: As you know, on April 21 the Army took control in Greece. Among the large number of people arrested were friends and colleagues of mine. I want to draw attention to their plight.

Q.: This gesture which you have felt it necessary to make here in your house in suburban Hamburg—are you making it as a protest, to show solidarity, or is it a demonstration? How would you define your action?

A.: I want to protest by showing my sympathy.

Q.: Sympathy with whom?

A.: Sympathy with my innocent friends.

Q.: And you're protesting against what?

A.: I'm protesting against those who have seized power under a pretext.

Q.: Can you explain to us more precisely what form your sympathy takes in practice?

A.: I allow myself only the things that they are allowed: the same amount of living space, the same rations, the same living conditions. In this way, I can remain in contact with them.

Q.: How did you learn about the rations and the living conditions under which your friends are detained?

A.: From letters. From reports and letters.

Q.: Your friends under detention are up against substantial opposition: twenty officers, a hundred and fifty tanks, and three

352

thousand soldiers. That factor determines the nature and duration of their detention. Whom would you describe as *your* opponents, *your* judges, *your* guards?

A.: My imagination. That suffices to put me into a situation similar to that of my friends.

Q.: Are you saying, then, that for you there's no real difference between an imaginary and a real captivity?

A.: Possibly there are differences of an external nature.

Q.: Professor Beerbaum, as things are, we can describe you as a prisoner with a housekeeper. You have the power to determine the length of your captivity yourself. And if we're not mistaken, you are surrounded by solicitous members of your family. Don't you think that in these circumstances you may be devaluing your friends' captivity by comparing yourself to them?

A.: In my experience, imaginary suffering can affect you at least as much as suffering arising from external causes.

Q.: One of your imprisoned compatriots, Georgios Mangakis, succeeded in smuggling a letter out of jail. In it he makes this confession: "In the hell I suffered during my interrogations I lost all personal human dignity and in its place there only remained pain." You're not required to suffer either interrogation or physical pain. Are you still of the opinion that your captivity can be compared with that of your friends?

A.: Take a prison with a hundred cells: in each of those cells there's an individual kind of captivity and yet a captivity that is the same for all.

Q.: Have you any information about whether your voluntary captivity has become known in your native land?

A.: Some people know of it.

Q.: In positions of importance?

A.: I don't keep that kind of record.

Q.: Suppose you were to be told that someone in a position of importance, having heard of your protest, shrugs his shoulders and ignores it—will you still go on making it?

A.: Yes.

Q.: For how long?

A.: Until the plight of my friends changes for the better.

Q.: Are we right in thinking that by protesting as you are you're pursuing a question of principle? That your protest is directed against injustice in general?

A.: What I want to demonstrate is my sympathy with the plight of those innocent people.

Q.: Even when those innocent people were arrested in the name of a new order, of a revolution?

A.: Nothing can ever justify the sufferings of innocent people.

Q.: Professor Beerbaum, we've been told that you have a special relationship with one of the internees—with your Greek colleague Victor Gaitanides. He has the reputation of being a very good biochemist. Could it be that your decision to act as you have is particularly affected by the fact that Professor Gaitanides is one of the detainees?

A.: Professor Gaitanides is one of the prisoners, certainly.

Q.: We merely wanted to ascertain whether it was a personal relationship that finally decided you to make your gesture.

A.: A decision such as I've taken always has more than one motive.

Q.: The *coup d'état* took place within the framework of the Prometheus setup of NATO and it was this that helped the new regime to succeed. Among other things, they have shown how confident they feel by releasing a good number of the detainees. So if your colleague Victor Gaitanides is allowed to return home in the near future—would you automatically call off your voluntary captivity?

A.: I'm afraid I can't answer that question.

Q.: Would you care to explain why you can't?

A.: I would hope that you might realize at what point insinuations become improper. And your question contains an insinuation.

Q.: Don't you think that when a scientist of your standing decides to take a step like this, everything becomes a matter of interest, even her private relationships?

354

A.: You won't be able to persuade me that the public is naturally interested in my private affairs. It's you who are inciting the public to take such an interest.

Q.: We know that Professor Gaitanides and you were friends in your youth. We also know that your scientific careers have followed a similar course. Let's suppose that Professor Gaitanides had been the only scientist arrested and detained by the instigators of the *coup d'état:* Would that have been a sufficient reason for you to take your present action?

A.: Yes, that would have been enough.

Q.: In such a case, whom would your sympathy have been mainly for, the friend of your youth or the scientific colleague working, as we know, in the same field?

A.: You're asking me hypothetical questions and expecting a concrete justification. I don't think I'm required to justify my decision to you.

Q.: But you do admit that we're trying to throw light on the background and helping people to understand your action?

A.: By background you obviously mean exposing the person you're interviewing; your preference for certain types of questions proves that to me.

Q.: Does that mean that you deny our readers the right to know everything?

A.: Your readers aren't told everything. You only pretend to tell them everything by exposing your interviewee or getting him to expose himself. Just consider the questions you've been asking: what are they based on? Weary condescension and the attempt to cast doubt on a decision.

Q.: We're sorry if we've given you that impression. So you don't share our view that the reader has a right to know more than appears on the surface?

A.: I wonder whether your readers do learn more when from the start you not only disparage my personal decision but also arouse suspicions in your readers: Just look at that, that's what lies behind it all, now you can all work it out for yourselves. You're trying to uncover vague connections, to

355

hint at equivocal relationships. All your questions contain prejudiced judgments; don't you realize that or have you reached the point where you can't realize it any more? Anything that can't be condemned or exposed or laughed at, anything that's not scandalous, seems to you not worth taking into account.

Q.: Do you agree that we should break off the interview? Or postpone it?

A.: It would interest me to know what your own attitude is; that is, if your condescension allows you to adopt an attitude at all.

Q.: What do you mean exactly?

A.: I'm not aiming at exposing you to other people's malicious pleasure. I'm simply interested in knowing where your sympathies lie; with the respected traditions of parliamentary government or with the pigheaded saviors of the country who saw Greece as being threatened?

Q.: Between those two alternatives, do you think we could give any other answer than yours?

A.: No, of course not. And now I must ask you to excuse me.

Q.: Professor Beerbaum, do you consider it would be advisable for us to come back as soon as you're feeling better?

A.: Oh, I think I . . . that I'm still capable of coping with your questions. So go on asking.

Q.: We've just been to Greece. We've learned that your protest is known, at least in university circles. Some of our press colleagues are also aware of it—of course, they're not allowed to write anything about it. However, would you explain the fact that Professor Gaitanides has admitted to knowing you only in the period when you were both students? That he denies any further connection with you? And that he describes your protest as a senseless gesture that won't help anybody?

COUNTER-QUESTION: What was his state of mind? I mean, what kind of impression did he make on you?

A.: We didn't have the impression that he had been tortured.

356

Would you like to make a comment on Professor Gaitanides' attitude?

A.: In his situation—anyone in his situation has the right to be treated as an exception.

Q.: And even now, you yourself wish to refrain from saying anything concerning your relationship?

A.: Yes, I must refrain from doing that.

Q.: Then don't you share our view that it would be better, under these circumstances, to cut short our interview?

A.: Since for your purposes I'm not very productive, as far as I'm concerned we can stop now.

Q.: But despite that may we still thank you for this conversation?

Lucy's deprecatory gesture was taken by the reporter as an apology for her inadequacy, and then in gloomy silence they collected their gear together. Katulla and his stenographer stood for a moment undecided, as if trying to agree on a formula for taking their leave: "All the best" would hardly meet with Lucy's approval, nor would "Good luck" or "Have a nice weekend"; finally the reporter admitted to having found it enjoyable despite everything—and the stenographer was obviously of the same opinion. However, he still did not want to leave, but, instead, twisting his head slightly sideways, was listening to the sounds from upstairs, where the tape recorder was no longer running modestly on half throttle but so loudly that "Oh, Happy Days" was dominating the whole house and could not fail to be heard; and since no one supplied an answer to his inquiring gesture, he turned to Irene with the remark that music was always a compensation and presumably always would be. "It's my sister's birthday," said Irene coldly. "Shall I show you out?"

Oblivious to the outer world, as stiff as a board although her eyes were open, Lucy made no reply to the two men's second, vague farewell, nor did she follow them with her eyes. And she said nothing to Irene when she sat down beside her and tried to give further reasons for Lucy's protest or her reluctance to talk by referring to specific questions which she had noted during the interview; and as the girl had never seen her like this before—so remote, so unresponsive, so lost in thought over something that was paralyzing her breathing—she was suddenly seized by anxiety and, wide-eyed with fear, retreated backward toward the door and ran upstairs.

There she disturbed a game; and put an end to it: sitting opposite each other on the couch and on chairs in a position not only acrobatic but positively painful, Ilse had pressed her mouth against Udo's and Vera against Armin's; the two couples were locked in a loose embrace, their mouths open far wider than necessary and, as it were, sewn together while their suspicious glance never left their opponents, on the lookout to detect any sign of cheating. The winner had not yet been decided, they were still sucking away and they would have perhaps continued with their competition if the frightened Irene had not burst in. She switched off the tape recorder. Whom should she speak to when all the faces were so close together? "Excuse me for butting in—Ilse, can you listen to me for a moment?"

Her sister swung her legs off the couch, pouting—presumably because they'd broken off the mouth-to-mouth breathing too abruptly—and not until she had struck herself several times on the chest did she ask, "What's up? I thought you were having an interview? And incidentally, can't you knock?"

"The interview's been postponed," Irene said slowly, and then suddenly to the others: "Please go now, please."

"It's my birthday," said Ilse in a gently threatening voice, "and these are my friends; they're going to stay," and, lean and restless, she made for the tape recorder, pressed the start button, but turned the sound down.

"It's Aunt Lucy," said Irene, "please understand, you must go now."

The friends were lolling about straightening their sweaters and trying to stand up; they looked uncertainly toward Ilse, who made no sign, but simply said, "We'll all stay here because Aunt Lucy herself . . . yes, it was Aunt Lucy who insisted that we celebrate my birthday, you know that perfectly well because you

358

were there. And didn't she say more or less that she didn't want any special consideration or attention? You see! So, you're staying."

"And *I'm* asking you to go because Aunt Lucy isn't well"; and then to her sister: "Just because she doesn't ask for consideration, it doesn't mean that we needn't show her any, does it? You just go down and take a look at her."

"I went down to see her this morning," said Ilse, "and do you know what Aunt Lucy said to me when I left?"

"Of course," said Irene, "she advised you to behave as if it concerned her alone. But do you really believe that? Does it satisfy you? Sooner or later doesn't something like this begin to concern us?"

The friends stood up grumpily, clearly finding the atmosphere chilly; in any case, their exchange of glances showed that the party was certainly over.

"Don't go on like that, Irene, why not just say you've suddenly begun to understand Aunt Lucy or perhaps you're even going to join in with her?"

"Just go down," said Irene, "the way she's lying there . . ."

"So what? When I was with her, we were both laughing together." She dashed over to her friends, stooped down, and holding out her hands, said, "No, please stay, it's my birthday." But the two youths took hold of her shoulders and heaved her to one side: they'd decided that the birthday was over. A hand casually slipped over the shoulder, a gentle biff on the chin, a tap on the cheek as they said goodbye—"So long, old girl; we'll have an extra birthday party to make up"—while Irene stood watching them go without moving from the spot and taking care not to reply except with an imperious shake of her head as they gave her a tap or brushed her an indulgent kiss as they passed.

Ilse flung herself down on the couch, drew up her legs, and sat there, sniveling but dry-eyed, until her three friends had made their exit; but as soon as the door had slammed she raised her head. "Now you've succeeded, you've spoiled my birthday."

"I think we must take care of Aunt Lucy," said Irene, "something's wrong with her."

"Aunt Lucy gave her approval," said Ilse, "and let me tell you once and for all, what she's doing doesn't concern me one little bit. It's old-fashioned, unnecessary, and useless. It's becoming impossible to live in this house. So now you know and as far as I'm concerned you can tell Aunt Lucy what I think about it all."

Irene looked at her sister without hostility or surprise and there was no reproach in her voice as she said, "Let me tell you what *I* think then. Nobody can do more than Aunt Lucy's doing. You call it old-fashioned, but I think it could become new-fashioned if a lot of people did it, perhaps everybody. For me she's an example people ought to follow."

"Sympathy galore as part of the duty of every citizen?"

"No, Ilse: protesting by participating—that's what Aunt Lucy calls it." Having delivered herself of this view, which she had just adopted, she left and she didn't need to eavesdrop at the door, she knew that after a few dry-eyed snivels, her sister would sit down to write to her diary and, as always when she had been frustrated, would furiously scribble down all her woes until she had more or less worked her anger out of her system.

That must be Magda's voice, thinks Janpeter Heller, who else but Magda would be answering the calm, inevitable questions which an obvious Mr. Grouser in person was asking, first in the corridor and then in Pundt's room; and raising his head, he feels the compulsion to interpret the sounds in Pundt's room—the steps, the clicks, the groaning of cupboard doors which were never oiled—until the conviction is involuntarily forced upon him that something unusual is taking place next door. Is that a suitcase being opened? Is one of Pundt's research rivals plundering his knowledge of the origins of the alphabet? His feet grope for his shoes and slop about inside them, he's off the bed, and after further fruitless listening, gently, gently he goes into the corridor, he's just getting ready to launch his shock attack to nail the unknown visitor in Pundt's room when the door, which is only ajar, is flung open from inside and he stands there dazzled and himself taken aback.

He's greeted by two cops, and before he can gather his wits, Magda is telling him the reason for their visit: Awful, Herr Pundt's been assaulted and they tried to drown him, he drifted out into the Alster in a boat. Heller nods to the fuzz and considers it unnecessary for them to introduce themselves as CID; without being invited, he walks into his colleague's room.

"Are you a colleague of the victim?" asks one cop.

Heller in turn asks, "So something has happened to Herr Pundt?"

"You can say that again. By chance our colleagues from the river police happened to be around and purely by chance they discovered the drifting boat and it was only by chance that they were able to rescue the man, who was unconscious."

Heller gropes for a chair which is standing helpfully behind him and, having sat down, he listens to a more detailed account of how chance came to Pundt's aid that night on the choppy Alster. And the longer he listens, the less horrified he becomes, indeed is compelled to become, for the language they use turns the assault into a banality, recorded in matter-of-fact officialese, typed with two fingers: in view of this, attempted robbery cannot be automatically assumed . . . evidence as to the exact time . . . the results of the medical analysis . . . in view of the absence of eyewitnesses . . . And now they must, they intend to, they can only submit all the data that might lead to a clarification of the affair to careful investigation. What does someone like Heller ask after this exhausting briefing? He asks, "Do you know if Herr Pundt is able to talk after his experience?"

And one of the cops replies, "The victim of the assault is in a condition to answer questions only to a limited extent, if that's what you mean."

20

A<small>ND</small> Rita Süssfeldt jumps up from the breakfast table with her yellow tobacco-stained teeth firmly clamped on half a buttered roll; with no explanation except that she's late, she dashes to her study, snatches up her leather briefcase, empties its contents out onto the floor, and, still with her roll protruding from her mouth like some animal which she has bitten to death, she quickly gathers together the notes which she will be using to justify her proposal; they include leaflets from her heaped-up desk.

And Janpeter Heller, with his briefcase propped up against a table leg, is assuring Magda the maid for the second time that he'll transmit her best wishes for a speedy recovery to Herr Pundt, meanwhile not raising his eyes from his newspaper, which, in bold headlines, is still telling its readers about Charly Gurk, mentioning, among other things, that the athlete has refused an offer of six hundred thousand marks to go to Italy because he felt that his place was with his old teammates, with whom he had shared so many victories and defeats.

And after attempting to light her roll with a match, Dr. Süssfeldt first boldly underlines single sentences in red and then covers page after page with exclamation marks, but she finds even that inadequate and looks around for a green pencil, and in the course of her fruitless search manages to acquire a run in her other stocking as well without realizing it.

When the young schoolmaster is informed that his taxi is

362

waiting, he picks up his briefcase, humming the while, and before leaving the room makes a detour, silently hems Magda in against the corner table, and silently runs a practiced forefinger over her comfortable bosom, at which, as if this were just a new way of saying goodbye, she merely says, "Well, see you later then."

And now once more Rita Süssfeldt makes her inevitable dash for her car with her coat flying, drives off jerkily, and turning right and then right again in accordance with a fixed plan, speeds on her way to the newly opened central hospital, where she parks under a sign forbidding even ambulances to stop. As a result, she has merely to duck under a barrier in order to get to the tube-shaped fruit shop, where—since Heller will presumably be bringing flowers—she buys a small basketful of grapes, bananas, and apples.

And Heller doesn't even bother to answer the pleasantries with which he is bombarded by a relentlessly cheerful driver; he can't even manage a smile when the driver confesses to him that sometimes he would like to be a snake because then he wouldn't have to wash under his armpits with cold water. On the assumption that Rita will be bringing flowers, he stops for a few seconds in front of a fruit shop to choose some apples, bananas, and grapes as well as two rustling paper bags of mixed dried fruit.

And Rita Süssfeldt stumps her way over the stone floor of the vast unadorned lobby, and since the porter seems to have fled from the five telephones all ringing at once, she addresses a student nurse, obviously Siamese: if there was a single gentleman—if there were other lobbies, and finally what was Herr Pundt's room number, Pundt, spelled d-t. The student nurse lifts her arms, spreads her hands, and with lively fingers evokes the calyxes of flowers in their dialogue with the sun, and affably shakes her head.

And from the swinging door as he comes out of the toilet, Janpeter Heller is spotted from behind; he hears a short cry of joy from the porter's desk and shuffles, grinning, toward Dr. Süssfeldt, who is gabbling excuses even before she has time to shake hands, while he turns his paper bag around so that she can see the same words as appear on her own offering: "Apples are good for you. If that doesn't help . . ."

"Well, our patient is in room 403," says Heller, "and is said to be getting on nicely. Excited?"

"A little."

They are borne smoothly aloft by an elevator which greets every floor with a cheerful ring of its bell; they are accompanied by an auxiliary male nurse, a giant black man, possibly a Masai tribesman, who on being asked the whereabouts of room 403 replies, "Thank you, thank you," several times, in English. At the same time he bows, holding his plastic box containing a number of razors. This must be the fourth floor: a totally deserted corridor, sound-absorbing floor, and on the walls framed water colors of medicinal plants: St.-John's-wort, eyebright, sloe, and camomile. Room 403 is empty, the casement windows are swinging, leaving the curtains flapping, sinisterly albeit decoratively—has Pundt thrown himself out of them? No, we mustn't assume that, perhaps we ought to ask the ward sister.

She's been called away, of course, but there's a student nurse on duty, sitting among her teacups and steaming teapots. "Monsieur Poundt? Yes, 'e's 'ere, we 'ave 'ad to move 'eem because 'e complained about ze 'eating." And now there's no further justification for delay, Valentin Pundt is in room 417. "Will you knock or shall I?" Together they push open the door, it's Pundt, there he is. In spite of the compress they can recognize him, Valentin Pundt, his face swollen, green, blue, and yellow; his hands folded over the blanket, brooding, as though resting after work. A limp gesture expressing both helplessness and pleasure. You certainly hadn't expected that; I didn't expect it myself either.

As they unpack their offerings, they shower him with questions. How did it, how was it, and why you especially? That kind of thing really shouldn't be possible in the center of a town and they find it hard to find adequate expression for their amazement and incredulous indignation. He's not going to be allowed to escape, he must tell them all about it, although they don't pay that

364

much attention to what he says; settling themselves on either side of his bed, they insist on hearing more than just the main points, and they are not content merely with what Pundt knows. The background, the hidden motives—as if you could always assume such things. "Well," says Pundt, "it happened as simply as this: I heard cries for help, I went to their assistance; you can see the results." He plucks at his blanket, looks at their offerings, smiles when he notices the dried fruit, expresses his thanks, and confesses that at this point a gulp of his Great Lüneburg Cock-a-doodle-do, even if it didn't put him on his feet, would help him along.

And then as if in collusion, they make encouraging noises, they console him by pointing out how much worse it might have been, they move on to express belief, hope, trust: will certainly soon, can't fail to, sooner or later we shall once again, because the proverbial ill winds, etc., etc. And as they sit by the sick man's bed, it's Heller who first brings the conversation around to their subject. "Well, you know, Herr Pundt, the longer I think about it and endeavor to assess exactly what happened to you, the more I'm forced to this conclusion: Shouldn't it be you? Why shouldn't what you did be considered an example of the kind of behavior to be imitated? The moral: Anyone who offers his help must be prepared for a slap in the face—wouldn't that be rather good?" Pundt solemnly protests, and cuts off the idea with a stiff gesture of his hand: No, my dear colleague, you surely won't do that to me, and Rita Süssfeldt supports him by pointing out that it would be necessary to write it all up. The remark has the effect of a loosening-up exercise. They realize that their perches on the edge of the bed are not very comfortable, so they slip off onto two chairs, bouncing tubular chairs which entice you to rock back and forth.

Have they their briefcases handy with the documents in them? What is that expression on Pundt's face? In view of their colleague's present plight, is it right for them to embark on a decision here and now? Or ought they, indeed, quite definitely do so? Is there the remotest likelihood that he has decided in favor of a passage? That he can give reasons for his choice? But how should they, how can they introduce the subject when Pundt is lying there with such a blank look in his eye, so sunk in his own thoughts?

While they are watching him, while they are delicately wondering how to begin, Pundt is thinking to himself: Yes, I'll re-write it, using the yellow tables and the same division into chapters; so that will be "The Mother of Alphabets," from the Phoenician through to the Aramaic. The major migrations of the alphabet: how the Mongolian alphabet proceeds from the later Syrian. Hieroglyphics, quipu, picture writing: I'll write the history of all of them again as soon as they let me go home.

He draws himself up. His massive torso swells and seems to increase in stature, ready to make a weighty pronouncement; a gruff authority suddenly emanates from his whole being and, addressing the end of his bed, with no expression of regret, the old headmaster states his intention of withdrawing from their enterprise: here and now. He has given the matter careful consideration, he is fully aware of the consequences, his decision is irrevocable.

Yes, if it turns out to be definitely the case—and it already seems almost certain—that the manuscript is lost, then I'll write it again.

After Pundt's announcement, it's hardly possible to remain seated, they walk around the bed, they ask if they may smoke, they look at Pundt out of the corners of their eyes; his announcement has obviously weakened him and he stretches out his legs. And it's Rita Süssfeldt who is the first to respond to his decision. "That can't be your last word," she says, "when we're just about to reach our goal. If I see it correctly, after all the work we've invested in it, what's left is only a formality; we make our choice and forget all our difficulties." And she also says, "We entirely understand, dear Herr Pundt, that your decision has been brought about by your present condition and for that reason we feel sure you'll want to withdraw it as soon as you're better. You can always rely on us to understand your position."

366

The old headmaster gives a nod, in fact a grateful nod, and their silence is an obvious invitation for him to give them his reasons for withdrawing.

"You'll be surprised," says Heller, "how quickly we shall be able to agree if circumstances make it necessary. Since we've got our suggestions all ready, shouldn't we at least make the attempt?"

There must still be a copy of the chapter on hieroglyphics at home, thinks Pundt, and I can even remember where I can lay my hands on it . . .

"You must believe me when I say that my decision has nothing to do with my present state," he says.

The origins of syllabic and phonetic script must still be in my suitcase in my room in the hotel . . .

"No, nothing to do with these temporary aches and pains. My decision is more fundamental: I've realized that I'm not the right man to recommend exemplary people to others. If you prefer, I'm not qualified to do it."

"And how about us?" asks Heller. "Are we any more qualified? Have *we* got any special qualification for such a job?"

"I must leave it to you to make up your own minds as to that," says Pundt; "in my case, my personal experience runs counter to it."

"What You Can Learn from a Tally Stick"—that was the title of the introduction and I'll use it again, thinks Pundt.

Does Heller really believe that he can still influence Pundt? He reminds him of his previous statements, he recalls that he had agreed that there will always be exemplary actions, and he hints that it was Pundt himself who had finally convinced the wavering Heller of the usefulness of the project. And now this sudden volte-face? Deserting the sinking ship? Sending back the contract just when they've almost completed it? Pundt seems to be finding these questions rather too blunt, he protests: "You must give me some credit; let's not misunderstand each other, I'm still convinced that it's part of a teacher's job to draw attention to exemplary actions but I'm equally convinced that I can't bring myself to recommend one specific exemplary act. I just lack the right to recommend."

"To recommend what?" asks Heller.

Thoughtfully and bitterly, the ex-headmaster replies, "Doctors and schoolteachers are supposed to be allowed only one mistake, and that mistake may be one too many. In any case, my mistakes have reached the permissible level and I still don't know how I will be able to cope even with their present consequences. Now do you understand why I don't want to run the risk of making any further recommendations?"

But who'll be able to prepare the tables for me as accurately as Harald did, because he seemed to understand the development of the letters almost instinctively—at least in their older forms in the West and the East . . .

"So we can pack up," says Rita Süssfeldt, "and all our rummaging around in Lucy Beerbaum's life has turned into a dog's dinner—unless you're generous enough to let us use your name, Herr Pundt, and if you do, of course, you may be certain that we'll choose something that goes halfway to meet your ideas. After all, we three are the official editors and it was we who received the commission."

Pundt shakes his head, he seems to have expected this suggestion, and he shuts his eyes in refusal when Heller suggests that after making their choice they would come to see him so that he would have the chance of giving his blessing to the example they had agreed on. "No," says Pundt, "there's no possibility of half measures any more. Even if you were to decide in favor of one of my proposals, I wouldn't feel in a position to lend my name to it."

There are no claims on my time now. "The Carolingian Minuscule, or the Mastery of the Flourish" has been printed in advance already, yes, writing it up again will be easier.

What now? First of all, the student nurse appears with tea and a friendly admonition to Monsieur Poundt, puffs up his pillows, counts out three lumps of sugar in front of his eyes, points to the large sturdy watch on her wrist: "Monsieur Poundt, 'e needs repose, pleece. Per'aps you are Monsieur Poundt's family?"

368

"Certainly," says Heller, "a sort of family related by fate, if you see what I mean."

So what now? Give up, chuck it away, go their separate paths? Send the publisher—and that means their eager taskmaster Dr. Dunkhase—a telegram: "Exemplary Lives a failure, contract returned with thanks"? Send a second telegram to Dr. Kock of the Ministry of Education subcommittee: "Have stopped work on anthology. Unable discover any thoroughly recommendable exemplary life"? What else remains to be done since Valentin Pundt has withdrawn his collaboration once and for all?

"I hope it's not a quarter past ten yet?" asks Rita Süssfeldt suddenly, and when Heller laconically tells her that it's already twenty-five minutes past, she stages a panic departure: at half past, in fact, the Züllenkoop prize is going to be awarded and she is, in fact, a member of the panel and since her candidate, in fact, is going to get it, she really ought to, she really can't do anything but be present. "You must excuse me, dear Herr Pundt, I do hope you'll soon be better and we'll be keeping in touch, somehow or other."

Pundt has no objection, he eagerly waves his assent, not only to her but to Heller, who hasn't yet mentioned his intentions at all but is looking with a rather puzzled expression from one to the other; and all he can say is: "And how about me?" Dr. Süssfeldt knows what he can do, he can, in fact he must, come along with her, since the two of them must now find a solution. "So say goodbye to Herr Pundt and come along." Heller is still showing signs of surprise as he shakes hands with Pundt, presumably he would have worked on the old headmaster a little longer to try to get him to change his mind, but Dr. Süssfeldt is urging him to come, and so as he takes his leave he says to Pundt, "Anyway, you did manage to surprise us."

How inhibited and awkward they feel as they wave to him once again from the door. As they're already falling over each other's feet, neither of them notices Pundt's grim drawn mouth, his arms stretched out limply beside his body, his vacant eyes staring into space. What now?

In the corridor, in the elevator, in the lobby, in fact all the way,

Heller keeps asking what Pundt's real reasons were for throwing in the sponge. "Can we really accept his reasons? Shouldn't we make him tell us everything?"

"There aren't any other reasons, Herr Heller, come along, now we shall have to finish it by ourselves," Rita Süssfeldt keeps saying, and leads him to her car, where she calmly plucks a traffic ticket from behind the windshield wiper and without reading it stuffs it into her coat pocket. "Get in, Herr Heller, I never lock my car and that's why it's never been stolen."

A brief general staff discussion as to the route and they begin their painless approach—right and then right again—to the Kunsthalle, in whose small lecture hall the Züllenkoop prize is about to be awarded. "As far as I'm concerned," says Rita Süssfeldt, "there's one thing I'm certain of, and that is that after all these preliminaries I'm not going to give up our commission; what's more, I've got my proposal in my pocket."

Heller has also made his choice; he's settled on something and has provided himself with arguments to support his choice, although he feels rather strange now that Pundt has withdrawn. "It's odd, as long as he was in with us, he seemed to me a kind of personal obstacle—and now I miss him."

"If you need an obstacle as much as that," says Dr. Süssfeldt, "perhaps I can manage to replace Herr Pundt in that capacity."

"So we'll go ahead?"

"I'll inform Dr. Dunkhase."

"And I'll break the news to Dr. Kock."

"So the anthology is going to have only two editors?"

"Is there likely to be any objection?"

"I can't see why there should be. We can begin right away. But first we must go through with this ceremony."

Rita Süssfeldt can't quite drive as far as the checkroom, but she does drive gaily up over the curb and manages to land one wheel on the first step of the side entrance. "We can stop here, don't you think?" Heller can leave everything in the car, his briefcase and coat, there's no need to worry, she'll take the precaution of not locking the car. "Come on! It must have started already."

Here we are and now let's hope the door doesn't creak for once. They attract neither disapproving nor hostile glances from the apathetic audience, the speaker doesn't break off to admonish them with pained silence; on the contrary, they slip almost unnoticed into the badly lit room, creep down to the first row, which has, as so often, been reserved for umpteen guests of honor, many of whom haven't shown up. They find a couple of seats side by side off the center aisle, at the foot of the speaker's desk.

At the moment, the speaker's desk is giving tongue: the voice is old, a bleating falsetto, highly pleased with itself, every sentence is a crow, an outcry, a cheerful whiplash. There is talk of a great, a deep-rooted tradition, of virtues that can flourish only in red and white, that is to say, in the colors of the Hanseatic League, and their special quality is made plain, in the confident words of the desk—alias a bald, frail old man who can now be discerned standing beside it—if you consider his grandfather, who, in addition to the customary dash and flair of Hamburg businessmen, had a typical motto, which was: "Give and take!" "That's old Züllenkoop in person," Rita Süssfeldt whispers to Heller, "he's the one who founded the prize. A dashing soybean dealer himself, like his father and his grandfather before him, the tradition-obsessed old man one day had the idea that he should publicly reward daring outstanding performances in other fields, and so he founded no less than fourteen awards; they include a prize for the best work in the field of research on illnesses connected with the common cold as well as one for skill in parliamentary debate."

Hamburg not only has tradition; Hamburg *is* tradition, he proclaims triumphantly, and, I say, its very own traditions; and to prevent this tradition from being overshadowed and diluted, he had put up this prize to reward the virtues of this great city; and, I say, its proven virtues must not fall into oblivion, because even today—and an anemic-looking arm shoots emphatically into the air—they can provide standards of value.

"Do you notice something?" whispers Heller, and Rita Süssfeldt, bending toward him, says, "Not much!" Heller turns around and runs his eye over the hall, there are fewer faces than he'd expected and it's not local daring but resigned acquiescence that they're registering—the audience is revealing an encouraging lack of spirit. Old Züllenkoop is greeted with warm but subdued applause; it sounds as though people are clapping with only one hand, Heller thinks, and is about to offer his services to help the gay little man off the dais, but it's already being attended to, two thickset sons-in-law have grasped him under the armpits and are hoisting him down.

Some music? Some Brahms, perhaps? Or that favorite composer of interludes, Handel? Music is not included because Züllenkoop diverted the money intended for an award to a musician to a prize for the best work on problems of the environment. "That's Anker Kallesen," whispers Rita Süssfeldt, "the chairman of our panel," and this worthy—hollow-backed, spotty-faced, in red vest, doubtless an exponent of higher horsemanship by inclination—allows himself to be carried onto the dais by, presumably, some old nag and makes a report on the work of the panel. Our task, as you know, was to try to discover which was the best of the one hundred and twenty-two manuscripts received on the subject of the Hamburg Tradition. One—he actually says "one" —had tackled the task with extraordinary conscientiousness, applying the strictest standards, and had been amazed at the high level of talent, which suggests to one how greatly sought after the prize had become. After a preliminary sifting, there still remained fifteen, and then with a fine-tooth comb one had reduced these to three, and out of these the subsequent ballot had produced the prizewinner, whose work deals with anonymous donations in Hamburg. The panel considers that this work admirably reflects the purpose of the topic that had been set, by discovering and describing a virtue that is real Hamburg, through and through: giving without any expectation of recognition, helping by stealth, doing good anonymously.

The Hamburg audience approves, they clap, in moderation, all except Heller, who is too preoccupied with trying to discover the reason for Rita Süssfeldt's growing unrest and, above all, to find out the recipient of the surreptitious conspiratorial gestures which she is distributing with a loosely flapping hand, directed toward one particular spot all the time. It can't be Züllenkoop's thickset sons-in-law, it must be the man they're covering. But at this moment Anker Kallesen thinks the time has come to inform those who do not yet know it of the name of the prizewinner, not an unknown name, just the opposite: highly regarded in professional circles as the author of a widely known book: . . . *And the Ark Floated*—well known, indeed, to a wider public—the new prizewinner, Heino Merkel, is far from being an unknown quantity. And now might he ask Heino Merkel to come forward and say a few words, if he would care to do so?

"Heino Merkel?" says Heller in amazement, but, busily applauding with both hands, Rita Süssfeldt ignores his question, jumps to her feet, and not only claps but obviously wishes to be seen clapping by the prizewinner. Not everybody but almost everybody has stood up to applaud Heino Merkel as he walks toward the platform, giving two quick amateurish bows as he makes his reluctant way to the desk, where he plays with some loose sheets of paper, sorting them out and shuffling them together, so that everyone—including his enemy in the second row—recognizes that he is not enjoying but enduring the occasion. He would like to launch out at once and plunge straight into the safe haven of his text in order to avoid the sharply glinting questions of a hundred specially polished spectacles, but first he has to submit while the panel's flattering recommendation is read out, has to receive his certificate and check and repeat the congratulatory handshake for the photographers. "Aren't you a member of the panel, too?" asks Heller, and Rita Süssfeldt replies, "Yes, why do you ask, hadn't I told you? Listen to what he's going to say."

Heino Merkel now thanks the panel, thanks the donor, and, without looking at them, thanks the audience for coming. He admits that he had written his work without any idea that it might receive an award. He had undertaken his research into the nature of anonymous donations in Hamburg, not in the public interest, but rather because of private suspicions and for himself; he was pleased that the result of his work has been honored by etc., etc.

"It's the first prize he's ever won," whispers Rita Süssfeldt, "and he really has deserved it." The stick belonging to the querulous old gentleman in the second row who has been griping about something for the last few minutes—he seems to Heller to be an enemy of the prizewinner—slips and falls with a clatter on the wooden floor. The general silent disapproval has no effect on him; he continues his disparaging running commentary. The prizewinner has no need to corroborate his words: his pleasure, his emotion, and his reserve are obvious to everyone. Since people have been kind enough to honor his work in this way, perhaps he might be allowed to make one or two confessions concerning the subject he had chosen; in particular he would like to devote a word or two to the question of a kind of sensibility that belonged specifically to the citizens of Hamburg. How did this reveal itself? Well, even in other parts of the world, people earned money—and sometimes a great deal of money—but nowhere else had people developed to so fine a degree the awareness of the point at which earning money begins to become indecent. And that meant, in his view, that there existed in this city a tradition of realizing when it became a matter of obvious duty to pay a ransom for excessive gains.

There's a protest, the enemy in the second row is protesting, but Heino Merkel doesn't hear him and, encouraged by some timid laughter, ventures to make one or two more confessions. Sharks, he says, are a widespread phenomenon, but nowhere are they so eager to obtain absolution for their spoils as here in Hamburg. How do they do it? They make donations. And so that they won't be identified, their donations are made anonymously.

"Scandalous," exclaims the enemy in the second row, his stick banging angrily on the floor, and then, somewhat louder, he shouts, "We're Protestants in this town!"

Heino Merkel registers amused approval. He's completely relaxed now and he remarks that good deeds are performed elsewhere, etc.—in America, for example, where every successful sausage maker decides to make a donation on his sixtieth birthday. And that donation is like some bellying mainsail bearing the name of the donor during the whole of its existence, and as it swells out, visible from afar, the good deed brings the good man good repute as well, doesn't it? But meanwhile he would like to know what inferences we are to draw with regard to the good deed which remains in the dark.

"Modesty," interjects the enemy loudly, "discretion which does them credit, if you really want to know." Heino Merkel has heard this outburst; he hesitates, smiles uncertainly, takes it up, considers it, and then asserts: "Yes, on the one hand, it is modesty and a praiseworthy sense of discretion. But on the other hand, doesn't the good deed done by stealth arouse the suspicion that someone is trying to salve his conscience and would thus prefer to remain unknown? Adopting the motto that gratitude won't help profits? In fact," the speaker concludes, "a helping hand which remains unknown can never be bitten, and thus it surely seems justified to assume that anonymous donations spring from an ulterior motive: not to be bitten."

Heino Merkel's enemy finds this conclusion "scandalous," and indeed he shouts, "Scandalous!" several times as he shuffles out of the hall, as ostentatiously as possible, accompanied by applause condemning his wrathful exit: he leaves amidst laughter.

"What a touchy old enemy," whispers Heller, and Rita Süssfeldt dismisses him: "It's only Wilhelm Wanderkluth, he's a well-known Hamburg character; he thinks he has a monopoly in local history." And then she waves to Mareth, who is sitting in the center of the room; Mareth looks severe and cautious, you might detect a warning in her eyes. Is the warning intended for Rita Süssfeldt? Because of her over-impetuous, uninhibited applause? Or perhaps because of her blatant enthusiasm? She continues to show restraint, barely acknowledges her sister's wave, and immediately returns her attention to Heino Merkel, who is continuing his speech without raising his voice and indulging in some revelations which, to his embarrassment, arouse moderate ap-

375

plause. Maybe it's because of this that his voice becomes quieter and quieter, for every exposure produces new outbursts of hilarity; Heller even detects in him an increasing despondency and thinks that he is skipping whole sentences of his speech, because now and then he turns the pages over so quickly.

"And that is why I believe that anonymous donations may be regarded as a specialty of Hamburg; let us be glad that there is a place where a successful looting expedition automatically reminds people of their imperative duty toward the community, let us applaud a town where it is traditional for heavy consciences to unburden themselves, even if they do so by stealth."

Heino Merkel bows, gathers his papers together, and leaves the platform while the audience is still leaning back, comfortably enjoying being reprimanded and unprepared for his abrupt departure. The prizewinner is not required to face the final applause unaided, he's already surrounded by well-wishers, donors, and members of his family.

Heller would like to congratulate him as well, he eases his way through the throng and hears old Züllenkoop thanking him for making a speech that was exactly the kind of thing he liked. "Wonderful, the way you let us have it, the most delightful dressing down we've had in a long time." The prizewinner is invited to join Züllenkoop in an Austrian hunting lodge to shoot grouse, or, failing that, to do some trout fishing in water guaranteed unpolluted. "But we'll discuss that in detail over lunch." Now Heller forces his arm between two black-clothed bodies, opens his hand, feels it being gripped before Merkel sees who it is, but then the prizewinner recognizes him, draws him toward him, and although it's really his occasion for the moment, he asks in a low voice, "How goes our exemplary life? Made a decision yet?"

Heller slowly shakes his head. "More difficulties," he says, "Pundt has bowed out, so we're going to see what the two of us can do."

"Is Lucy Beerbaum still in the running, as it were?"

"Still there," says Heller, "and she's well in the lead. Anyway, we're settling it this evening."

376

Unexpectedly, Heino Merkel suddenly walks over to Anker Kallesen, the chairman of the panel, has a quiet word with him, looking several times toward Heller as he does so, appears to reach agreement, and with a smile of satisfaction comes back to Heller and invites him to attend the official luncheon. "I may perhaps be able to help you in your decision, Herr Heller, because there's still something else, or there might be something else, and since it was I who suggested Lucy Beerbaum, I feel it's my duty to tell you everything. So will you do me the honor?"

"And what about Dr. Süssfeldt?" asks Heller.

"She'll be there of course," says Heino Merkel.

21

In the conference room, there are just the two of them addressing each other across the expanse of rosewood table; face to face, in a dignified posture which discourages any passion—and, moreover, sitting beneath the panoply of exotic weapons—they feel somewhat like an English Governor General and his spouse, seated so far apart that the only conversational possibility is to inquire after each other's health.

So Heller suggests settling their business in his own room, which, although not exceedingly warm, is uncommonly cozy and that is a definite help to concentration.

And so they clump their way up to Heller's room, apparently unnoticed, hang up their wet coats on the room's one hanger, empty their briefcases on the diminutive tabletop that can barely hold the lamp, and sit down as best they can: Rita Süssfeldt on the only chair, Heller on the edge of the bed. A tiny enamel ashtray, extolling the qualities of one of Hamburg's beers, stands ready. So as not to be disturbed by the gymnastics of roof tiles, Heller draws the curtains, then turns on the light. So far agreement has been rapid. Who's going to be the first to let the cat out of the bag?

They haven't yet lit their first cigarette to "loosen their tongues" when there's a somewhat imperious knock on the door. Without waiting for an answer Magda pushes it open and, looking impenetrably at Heller and at him alone, takes her time producing her question: would any tea be required, possibly? No

tea would be required. One might, continues Heller imperson-
ally, one might be ordering tea once their work was over but for
the moment all that was needed was to be left undisturbed for a
while. After such a remark, can the maid do anything but leave
in an offended silence?

"Anyway," says Rita Süssfeldt, "they seem to be very concerned about you here."

"No wonder," says Heller, "apart from me, the only people
staying in the hotel just now are some urologists."

How then will they begin, make their suggestions, attach their
price tags to what they are going to propose? They're both smiling, each assures the other that they're excited, they think it's not
impossible that in the end they may both even decide on the same
chapter. Would you like to . . . ? As far as I'm concerned, you're
very welcome to start.

There's another knock on the door, rather a limp one this time,
and spaced out, and on Heller's irritated invitation to come in,
there's a deliberate pause before the door opens. "Oh, it's you,
Frau Klöver?"

It's the proprietress of the hotel, puffing slightly, as always, her
dewlaps quivering with her every movement. Her bored expression nevertheless betrays a certain embarrassment, her apology
is somewhat grudging. "Excuse me, Herr Heller, if I'm disturbing you in your work, but . . ." But what? Her weighty bracelets
clang together as her hand swings in an arc that covers the whole
room from wall to wall. "Well, the position is," she says, "in this
hotel it's not usual for two people to go up to a room together,
because there is the conference room if you want to work. I'm
sorry but that's how it is." Her remark doesn't prevent her from
wishing Rita Süssfeldt "Good afternoon" in a mournful, not
unfriendly voice, and offering Heller her fleshy hand, which he
takes, looking perplexed.

He pretends not to have heard properly, he inquires incredulously, "Does that mean that you object to our working in my
room?"

"It's not usual, Herr Heller."

Crossly the man flings back the curtains, flicks off the light, and glares at his papers. He says, "Frau Klöver, have you any idea at all what we are producing here?"

"We've always worked on that system," the woman says in a tired voice.

"An anthology," says Heller, "an anthology for young people that's intended to show them what kind of world they're living in."

"My husband thought the same," says the woman; "for certain types of work the conference room is available." She apologizes again, wishes them a thoroughly polite "Good afternoon," and withdraws, confident of having made her meaning quite plain. What now?

"Let's humor her," says Rita Süssfeldt, "let's make *her* our model and go downstairs."

Grumpily they gather their papers and notebooks, and take their coats and their irritation downstairs into the familiar conference room and spread themselves out around the rosewood table, where an invisible Pundt sits between them. "Everybody's safer here," says Heller grimly. "You from me, I from you, and Frau Klöver from the external vigilance of public opinion. What would people think? Most people's idea of danger is, I suppose, a bed."

"Sometimes they've been proved right, too," says Rita Süssfeldt. "Now perhaps some tea with rum?"

"No, nothing, thank you; the drinks at the luncheon party were enough for me."

"Well, here we are again."

"Yes, the wheel's come around full circle."

They set out their papers, with their proposals on top and handwritten notes underneath: so now what's left, what's been caught in the educational dragnet? Rita Süssfeldt is now waiting, ready to start, but Heller is still hesitating, looking questioningly at his notes as he twirls a few hairs in his already curly beard, and suddenly requests a short postponement, for reasons which he immediately explains. He hadn't yet read the last chapter on

380

Lucy Beerbaum and he had just been told, during lunch, that it might contain what they were looking for. "Then we will have absolutely nothing to reproach ourselves for," he says. "When we've assessed the last chapter—and Herr Merkel strongly advised me to do so—no one can accuse us of not having done Lucy Beerbaum justice. We owe it to her and to ourselves as well, after all the trouble we've taken." Is Dr. Süssfeldt willing to suspend judgment until they've done this? Rita Süssfeldt is willing, and Heller turns to the last chapter, wets his lips, and reads:

On the eighty-second day of her confinement, her temperature rose again and Johanna overcame all her objections and scruples and telephoned Dr. Paustian. He promised to come right away. Then Johanna went into the kitchen, took the last of the waffles out of the waffle iron, spread them with jam, and, together with the news that the doctor was on his way, took them in to Lucy, who was lying on her couch, shivering with fever. Too weak to protest, she had to accept an eiderdown. Johanna was bringing her something which she had, in fact, finally said she would like: waffles and jam; she had gently refused all other suggestions because, she said, she couldn't face any other kind of food, and even now, as Johanna offered her the plate containing the waffles and broke up the heart-shaped patterns with a fork, Lucy looked at them for a long time, as though still undecided, before finally allowing herself to be persuaded. She lifted the fork to her mouth just once, chewed with some effort, and then pushed the plate away. "It's no good, Johanna, I'm sorry, but I just can't eat them."

"But you said yourself that waffles were your favorite food, even when you were a child."

"I'll come back to them again, one day."

No reproaches as in the early days; now only a kind of mechanical moaning sound: that was how Johanna registered Lucy's decision and, still moaning, she began preparing the room for the doctor's visit. Lucy's forehead had to be wiped, her neck and her upper lip, on which little bubbles were forming. Her hair? She didn't dare pass a comb through Lucy's damp hair, she contented herself with stroking it with her hand and straightening her disarranged parting. What else? She shook up the eiderdown. Finally she took the unused cutlery back to the kitchen and then got herself ready to meet Dr. Paustian: she took off her apron, changed her shoes, rearranged her hairpins, still with the taciturn doctor in mind, and with a clean handkerchief tucked in the cuff of her sleeve, she felt properly dressed for his visit.

Sitting with her hands clasped in front of her, she still had the feeling that Lucy had not yet accepted the need for Dr. Paustian's visit; so she went over her reasons again. Although Dr. Paustian hadn't called for some months now, Johanna thought she could recognize him by the way he rang the bell: it was short and sharp, impossible to ignore—the ring of someone accustomed to being expected. As on previous occasions, Johanna couldn't understand his greeting this time either, and her attempt to detain him, to close a veil of conspiracy around them, was promptly thwarted as he strode past her with a blank look toward the hall closet, where he took off his coat and hung it up on a hanger himself.

Nor, of course, did he wait for Johanna to show him the way to the sickbed, preferring to open every door himself; and he nodded his head reproachfully at the sick woman, as though the illness were a personal affront to him. Is this really necessary? he seemed to be saying, and what have we been up to this time?—so that the patient felt guilt-stricken. Shaking his head, he steered his way toward the bed, dropped his bag, hauled Lucy's hand from under the blanket, and patted it with his hands. Lucy now started smiling, which was exactly what he had wanted, and, interpreting his look, there was little else she could say but: "I'm sorry that we had to trouble you, Henry, but . . ."

Dr. Paustian was nodding his head, not at all, no trouble, it happens all the time, why shouldn't it be you? Stroking Lucy's hand, he looked around at the area of her voluntary captivity, objectively and without surprise; apparently he'd imagined it like that. Not a word concerning the blacked-out windows or the heap of unopened letters and telegrams. "I do hope I'm not causing you unnecessary concern," said Lucy, and the doctor replied,

"We'll soon discover, my dear." Now he did not want to be interrupted and when Lucy inquired whether and how she could help him—"Do you want me sitting up or lying down, Henry?"—he murmured, addressing himself rather than the patient: "Loss of strength resulting from undernourishment, presumably anorexia."

Standing beside the table and following the examination, Johanna reacted to his first diagnosis with a moan.

"What's your temperature, Lucy?"

"A hundred and three point five, an hour ago."

"Then we'll listen to your heart and lungs, if you don't mind." He bent over her frail body, letting his stethoscope roam here and there over it, listening hard, tapped her chest and discovered something, but didn't say anything about it. "Pain when you breathe, Lucy?"

"Yes."

"Feeling hot and thirsty all the time? Brownish sputum? Short of breath? Temperature going up?"

Lucy said yes to all the doctor's questions, and then Dr. Paustian said, "Well, we've got a nice case of pneumonia on our hands." While he was preparing an injection, he reminded Lucy of her two previous attacks of pleurisy. "They often leave a chronic thickening of the lung tissue."

Behind the doctor's back, Johanna gave a sigh and a cough, and Dr. Paustian looked at her, startled. "Not you too, Johanna?"

"No, not me."

Lucy managed to sit up unaided, gathered her nightgown in her hands, and, pulling it up, watched the needle sink into her flesh. "I think you know what my position is, Henry."

"First and foremost, you're sick," said the doctor, "and that means that you can't go on with your plan; a different kind of protest has priority now."

Lucy put her hand on his arm. "I know," she said, "if you had your way, everything would be left to the healthy persons of this world: anyone who wants the right to protest must first pass a medical examination."

"It's not that, Lucy. I'm concerned about something else."

"Will you tell me what it is?"

He fumbled in his bag, fished out various medicines, seemed unable to find what he was looking for, and on his lap wrote out some prescriptions, which he handed to Johanna without looking up. In an admonitory voice, he listed the foods, meat broths above all, which he was not merely recommending but positively prescribing.

For her part, feeling blameless, Johanna reinforced the doctor's warnings with a knowing look: now you make a note of that, Professor, take heed and do what the doctor advises, like I've been telling you all along.

"I want to say something to you, Lucy: if someone is prepared to sacrifice himself, then the sacrifice must have a meaning or at least a commensurate effect. I mean that such a drastic step must be justified. And when one sees that it is completely out of proportion with the effect it produces, it becomes clear how irresponsible and wasteful such a supreme sacrifice is, and one can only feel angry or sorry—or both. Believe me, people should be extremely cautious about risking their lives. Don't expect anyone to lose any sleep over it; nowadays nothing is ever more than news for a day, not even the greatest sacrifice."

Lucy edged away from beneath his hand and lay there staring into space. Then she turned to him. "Henry," she suddenly whispered, "what happens with pneumonia, if the worst happens?"

"Why do you want to know that?" asked Dr. Paustian. "Isn't is enough that you have it?"

"It will relieve me considerably," said Lucy. "It will simplify things and give me relief, so please tell me."

"You won't be any better off if I tell you," said the doctor.

But Lucy persisted. "I've never been put out by knowing something, Henry, only by things that I don't know or only half know —that's the kind of thing that makes me restless."

Dr. Paustian avoided her eyes; he stood up and in a strained voice, trying to be casual, offered a few vague generalities: "In the broadest sense, it's an illness . . . in the narrower sense, you assume . . . that is to say, an inflammation or a thickening of the connective lung tissue—or rather an inflammatory exudation in the lung vesicles." He broke off and, with his lips pressed tightly together, he stood looking at Lucy; then suddenly he went on with his description, more coherently and easily than he had begun. "All right, Lucy, then listen to me. After a certain stage of blood starvation in the blood vessels, exudation takes place into the lung vesicles. It's fluid but it then coagulates, more or less. It expels the air and makes the affected section as tough as leather, we call it hepatization. The greater the hepatization, the greater the difficulty in breathing. In the extreme stages of hepatization, when the air has been driven out of too large a section of the lungs, death can ensue."

The doctor was showing how exasperated one can get with oneself; especially because he could not retract what he had said. A grumpy farewell. Instructions about what to do, delivered without looking at her. Over his shoulder, he said, "I'll be back soon, Lucy, sometime today, late this afternoon; I hope what I've told you helps the cure."

He didn't wish to be shown out, but snatched up his bag and —it must be said—hurried out of the room, not even troubling to close the door carefully behind him.

Johanna sat down on the stool and tried to catch Lucy's eye. "So now you can see, Professor, that I wasn't the only one to be worried and unhappy. Dr. Paustian was, too." Since Lucy didn't stir but merely kept staring at the split rafters in the ceiling, Johanna went into the kitchen, heated up some beef tea, chopped some parsley into it, and stirred in a few slivers of butter until they melted without a trace, then she tasted it, put some in a bowl, and brought it into Lucy. "Here you are, you can't get out of it now." Expecting her to decline it with her usual muttered refusal, Johanna lifted the bowl into Lucy's field of vision, determined not to allow herself to be ignored this time, but to her surprise Lucy nodded, heaved herself up with an effort, smoothed the towel flat over the bedcovers, and picked up the spoon as though it were a matter of course.

"Now you must eat, too, Professor."

"Yes, certainly."

With Johanna's assistance, the sick woman ate, moaning gently, stopping frequently with her hand pressed against her body, occasionally closing her eyes in disgust. No trace of satisfaction or sign of benefit, even after emptying the bowl, nothing but an expression of disgust, and when, after praising her lavishly, Johanna offered to get some more, Lucy made a gesture of refusal. "I think that's probably enough for the first time."

Johanna realized that here was her chance and, not wishing to let it pass, pressed her point: "And now perhaps a newspaper or a book, or shall I open a few letters for you?"

"Nothing, Johanna." That sounded a trifle disapproving, once again you could detect willfulness and self-consciousness, and from her dismissive attitude Johanna knew that she wanted to be left alone, with the curtains drawn. She did not stir as Johanna shut out the daylight—jerkily, because she had trouble with the mechanism for letting down one of the blinds—but just as she was going to the door, Lucy lifted her hand: "Just a moment, Johanna, please"; and Johanna turned back, the bowl still in her hands.

And for the first time Lucy took her by the wrist, drew her toward her, and asked uncertainly whether everything hadn't now become pointless and didn't matter any more. Johanna demurred: "How could that be?" And Lucy said she was really asking herself whether it wasn't illogical, and like abandoning something before it was finished, for her to accept, in the difficult situation she was in, care and solicitude which would never be given to the people whose plight she was trying to bring to the attention of the public. And Johanna maintained that it wasn't illogical for someone to try to get well. And determined not to spare herself, Lucy went on to ask what was the value of her action if she allowed herself more than the others, who would not dare ask for any concessions. Wouldn't it be a breach of solidarity if she claimed the right to special treatment? And Johanna replied, "In order to do the kind of thing that you're doing, Professor, surely you need to be in good health." Nor could she imagine how anyone would be helped by someone else's illness. And Lucy inquired doubtfully if after her recovery it could still be the same kind of protest as it had been at the beginning. To which Johanna replied, "If it has to be like that, then I can't see any difference."

"Hm," says Heller, breaking off, "that's not the end of the chapter, there are still a good half dozen pages on the so-called peaceful death, which took place five days later, almost as if providing concrete proof of the general rule." But he thinks they can take the ending as read because it can't be compared with the chapter which he has chosen himself. "What do you think—can we spare ourselves that?"

Rita Süssfeldt would have agreed with him but for the fact that shortly before her death Lucy asks Johanna to come to her bedside and not only discusses everything that has be settled but makes her review all her instructions and arrangements—a scene that had impressed her by its exemplary objectivity; this is what she imagines dying ought to be like in the world of today. Heller didn't deny this, but he does question whether this exemplary quality really had to be depicted by such a general—and also senseless—phenomenon as dying, particularly in an educational work. What was the educational purpose in that? Surely not to recommend learning first how to die before having come to grips with the rough and tumble of life itself? Rita Süssfeldt says, "That's a somewhat wild interpretation; everything needs to be seen as a whole—Lucy's decision, her protest on grounds of sympathy, then her unexpected illness, and the final settlement of her affairs at the end." This is how she prefers to understand and interpret the scene: but Rita Süssfeldt wants to keep an open mind, she won't dig in her heels, because she has known for some time what she is going to propose. But in spite of all this, wouldn't Heller like to read the conclusion, perhaps just the last page and a half, because there were certain things there, too, which were picked up and brought into focus and which might throw further light on the subject. That's all right by him—so:

. . . and first unloaded his bags and bottles and parcels in the kitchen before going into Lucy's room and introducing himself to the doctor, who was sitting at the end of the sick woman's bed. Then Professor Pietsch took Lucy's hand, bent forward to bring his face down to hers, confident of the reassuring effect that his appearance produced on every occasion, and waited like that until Lucy stirred and raised her eyes to look at him. "Good news, Lucy," he said; her lips quivered and her body seemed to shrink away in sudden fear. He could feel her fingers close convulsively in his hand and then she reached out to his arm and gave a slight tug as if she wanted to pull it away. Pietsch gently brushed her hand away and placed it back on the coverlet as though it were a separate, unattached object, gave the doctor a perplexed glance, and then looked back at Lucy. Lucy was collecting her strength to try to sit up, but she couldn't make it. The windows were blacked out, the only light came from a table lamp on the secretary behind the half-open sliding door in front of which Johanna was standing. In a quieter voice, Professor Pietsch said, "It's to welcome you back, Lucy, the whole Institute wants to welcome you back"; and as she made no reply, the statement sounded so shabby and insincere that the man moved uncomfortably away from the bed and looked questioningly at the doctor, as though hoping for his support. The doctor plunged his face wearily into his hands, and said nothing. Pietsch gave him a tap on his bent back, the doctor looked up; "What is it?" A brief resigned gesture from the other man: "Nothing, excuse me." He was about to go past Johanna without saying goodbye, but before reaching the door he noticed the rocking chair through the half-open door of the next room and, as though this had been his intention from the start, he walked over to it, gave it a tentative push, and then sat down. He brought out his leather cigar case, tapped it lightly against his knee, after a short pause opened it, pulled out a cigar and licked it. He passed the unlighted cigar from one corner of his mouth to the other. As he fumbled for matches, he watched Johanna and the doctor intently; they did not stir, even when the matchbox fell to the floor. But when, after a short pause, he struck a match—screening it behind his hand but nevertheless unable to prevent the match's scratching and spluttering from echoing so loudly in the silence that he himself was unnerved—and just as he was raising the lighted match to his cigar, the pair of them, Johanna and the doctor, looked toward him, not in fact reprovingly but in amazement, and Dr. Paustian stood up, patted his breast pocket, and, after a moment's hesitation, walked over toward him.

Relieved, Professor Pietsch hastened to proffer his cigar case, but with a gesture of his hand the doctor refused, drew him away toward the large blacked-out window full of flowers and climbing plants, and by the very persistence of his silence left Pietsch in no doubt at all as to what was happening. Despite this, Professor Pietsch said, "But I've news for Lucy."

"Senseless," said the doctor, "it was utterly magnificent and utterly senseless."

"It's our work," said Pietsch, "our joint work at the Institute; we've just made a breakthrough."

"There's no need for you to concern yourself any more," said the doctor, making his way back to the stool. "It's all been useless, a completely useless sacrifice. You're not going to change anything now with your news. What has anyone been able to do? What's been changed? Can anyone tell me what's been achieved by all this?"

"No," said Heller, tossing the book onto the table, "we're not going to find our model here, not out of this last chapter; because even if our Lucy's death is impressive, surely we can't recommend that people imitate it. As far as I'm concerned, I'd like to stick to my proposal."

Rita Süssfeldt, after a moment's halfhearted reflection, decides that she would like to do the same. "Okay. Then let's put our cards on the table."

Hesitation, reluctance, cheerful willingness to let the other person go first—they both seem to have expected this and even now each of them seems anxious to let the other begin, it might almost be thought that neither would raise any objection to postponing making their statements. But there's nothing to be done: even though Heller once again tries to gain time by recapitulating their method, there's no way out of it, sooner or later you have to show your true colors. So Rita Süssfeldt makes her own declaration: "Well, my first and last proposal is the conversation between Lucy Beerbaum and Professor Pietsch, on his first visit, and the title would be, roughly, 'The Wasted Sacrifice.' The chapter must illustrate exemplary behavior. The example itself has to be presented in the form of a dilemma. There ought to be at least two possible interpretations. My view is that this chapter meets all the requirements. The conflict between external obligation and personal sympathy is obvious; the various points of view are clearly differentiated, the question as to the usefulness of the sacrifice is posed, but left open. The fact that the situation is a topical one should work in its favor. A young person can imagine himself in this situation and look for reasons to behave in one way or the other. The dialogue is a kind of confession. If we think it is important that exemplary behavior should not act as a palliative but should arouse doubt in someone's mind, this chapter is a good example for us. What's your view, Herr Heller?"

The young schoolmaster purses his lips, nods, and makes a light smacking sound—which is, if not an exaggerated, at least a thoughtful acknowledgment: Yes, certainly there's something there. But now it's his turn to let the cat out of the bag, and with a twinkle in his eye, he makes a surprising announcement: "You'll be amazed to see how close we are, because my proposal is the interview with the reporter of BURNING QUESTIONS; as the title I'd like to suggest: 'The Unsuccessful Interview.' As you can see, this is a critical examination of Lucy's example, too, her action has been going on for some weeks by this time. The torch of protest is not burning quite so brightly, her arguments have lost some of their force—we're introduced to the conflict at a moment when there's a stocktaking. The central point, as in your example, is the question of the usefulness of her sacrifice; its sense or its senselessness is discussed, but the issue is not definitively decided. So far our proposals are in agreement. But what makes this suggestion of mine seem particularly suitable is that the problem is taken up directly by the two girls, they illustrate the rift which has opened up as a result of Lucy's action, and they suggest a possible decision by their opposing attitudes. Anyway, after all our proposals, there seems to me nothing so suitable for our anthology as that chapter."

Rita Süssfeldt breathes a sigh of relief. "We really aren't so very far apart. That is a good sign." From eye level she drops an earring onto her cigarette pack and flicks it over to Heller, who catches it and deliberately rolls it back. "All the same, Herr Heller, I wouldn't want to withdraw my proposal yet. An exemplary person should be shown with her contradictions, so a crisis can only make her more credible, and in my passage this crisis will be obvious to everyone; while Lucy is establishing one kind of solidarity, with her defenseless friends, she is prejudicing another kind, with her colleagues at the Institute, on whose work a great deal depends. I mean that in this way her action works on more than one level and offers an extra challenge to anyone who would interpret it."

Heller would like to issue a caveat; too many possible interpretations might obscure the general issue, in a typical, heavy, German, conceptual fog. He could already sense a certain temptation to over-interpret, in any case. For a certain age group, it was better to start from concrete, intelligible contradictions. Incidentally, he knew people who were perfectly capable of understanding life as long as they weren't faced by too many interpretations of it. His chief anxiety was for Lucy's conflict not to be seen purely in isolation but to be communicated to others, to arouse an echo in them, thus proving its viability.

Well, what should they do? Should they take a short break? Order some tea with rum or some apple juice? Since it's not possible to take a vote and since neither of them can face the prospect of a new search for an exemplary life, should they spread their wings and take leave of each other until another opportunity happened to bring them together again? Heller pointed to the collection of weapons on the wall. "Why not do this: you take the blowpipe, I'll take the little bow, we'll darken the room, and the survivor's proposal is automatically adopted."

Rita Süssfeldt doesn't smile; it is to be assumed that she hasn't in fact understood the invitation, since she is shuffling and collating pages of manuscript, hastily comparing texts and sheets of paper, looking here for connections and transitions, trying out an elision there, and it is only from watching her face slowly change from being taut and serious to becoming relaxed and content that Heller realizes that he is witnessing the birth, examination, and confirmation of an idea. "Well?" he asks. "Have we still got a chance? Shall I give a smoke signal that will finally release a charmed and expectant public from their uncertainty as to the kind of exemplary life that we're going to dish up to them?"

"Listen to this," says Rita Süssfeldt, "we'll combine the two suggestions. Just a question of making a few snips here and there; the two girls whose attitudes illustrate the conflict won't be shown at the end of the unsuccessful interview but after Professor Pietsch's visit. We don't need to write anything new to join the two parts: we can do all that is required with scissors and paste. Would you like to look over the text again?"

Skeptically Heller pulls the papers toward him, compares them, turns them around, isolates certain sentences, and links separate events together without once looking up. Will he agree? Can anyone like him ever be convinced?

And now, abruptly, he stands up, walks toward the raised doorway with an inscrutable expression on his face, and presses the knob of the bell so energetically that its high-pitched tone can be heard throughout the house. Then he turns around. Then, across the whole expanse of the room, he holds out a congratulatory hand toward Rita Süssfeldt. Then he listens for the unobtrusive footsteps of the maid. Then he skips down the steps, comes back to the table with a portentous demeanor, and in reply to Rita's question: "Will it do then or not? It can be done, can't it?" he gently shakes his head. "Not only can it be done," says Heller, "but I think that it's the example I've been looking for myself. It's an example we needn't be ashamed of. Let's have a drink on it."

"That's that, then," Rita Süssfeldt says, gathering up her papers, books, and notebooks. "I'll get the whole passage ready. Dr. Dunkhase will be able to read it this very day. Shall we leave the title as is?"

"Too highfalutin," says Heller, "too ambitious and too full of pathos. I suggest: 'Controversial Decision.' "

"Doesn't that make you think of football?"

"Yes, it does," says Heller, "and it makes you think of lots of other things and that's exactly why I'd like to suggest it."

The maid arrives; before Heller can give his order, Rita Süssfeldt says, "Anyway, the next chapter promises to be more relaxing. Do you know what the title is?"

"It's either 'Man and Beast' or 'Justice and Injustice.' "

22

Someone absolutely has to be told about it, someone must be made to stop and listen to how they've finally reached their tricky decision, after all their sifting and weeding and the effort involved in producing their third chapter; so this is why Rita Süssfeldt brakes harder than usual, doesn't wait to switch off her headlights, slams the car door with her heel, and rushes across the front garden; the light is on, the tiny so-called "burglar" light, which Mareth confidently expects to provide adequate protection; the doors are closed. With her coat unbuttoned, she sweeps through the rooms, switches on the main light, and from the landing, calls out her sister's name and Heino Merkel's as well, briskly at first, as though calling the roll, and then more and more quietly, disappointed at finding herself alone. In the kitchen, brownish star-shaped pieces of pastry are lying cut out on the floury table: cinnamon cakes; beside the baking pan, already greased, an unfinished cup of coffee is swimming in a puddle. A grayish-white worm of cigarette ash is lying stretched out on a saucer, only its heavy-headed filter has been bent off. Over there, beside a chair leg, Mareth's grimy apron is lying in a crumpled heap. The preheated oven is still giving off a perceptible heat.

Rita Süssfeldt goes into her study and flings her briefcase down onto the desk—or rather, halfway through her swing she stops short, seized by a sudden suspicion, and walks up to the desk, as anyone would have if someone had carelessly dumped a pigskin document holder onto a crowded blotting pad and put the torn shreds of a check on top of it. In a film you would now witness roughly the following sequence of images: a groping hand reaches out for the torn scraps of check; the close-up reveals an incomplete figure, written in a flowing hand, let's say "Fiv . . . sand"; the pigskin case is lifted, revealing a stained document, just beginning to curl up at the edges; gray-green scraps of paper flutter down onto the document from medium height; another close-up, this time of Rita's face, with pursed lips and pensive look; her expression visibly sharpens in the apprehension of disaster. Suspicion is aroused. Fingertips drum excitedly on the document. Misgivings focus on something and a conclusion is reached.

And then from the position in which she is standing, Rita Süssfeldt leaps toward the door and charges upstairs; Heino Merkel's room confirms what she had feared: a slow pan shot over gaping drawers, cupboards torn open, a carelessly abandoned chaos which bears witness to a definitive departure. No need to touch or examine anything closely: the large suitcase is no longer lying on top of the wardrobe and the tray containing the notes and newspaper clippings has disappeared from the desk. Perhaps there's a letter? A note? Not on the desk, anyway, nor on the chair, which Rita walks hesitantly around before going to the window and looking down onto the street for a moment. Two black umbrellas are struggling by and immediately behind them two nuns sail noiselessly past in line abreast and turn off into the gloomy garden of the Elizabeth Church—beating superbly into the wind, as Günter Grass had taught them, once and for all, in a course on dry land.

Rita tightens her headband, leaves the room, and without turning off the lights hurries out of the house with a purposeful look; she drives at a brisk speed down the Rothenbaumchaussee in the direction of the Dammtor railway station, pursued by a decrepit car plastered with pink clover leaves, which pulls up beside her at the traffic light, very close, as though wanting to make contact. Young men wave to her and spread their arms out wide. A cyclist in the uniform of the Hamburg police force—his flashlight dangling from his leather chest—gives them a piece of his mind at the light. From force of habit Rita Süssfeldt parks in front of America House.

There's the Dammtor station, a gloomy art nouveau mosque dedicated to tourist traffic, that's where Mareth and Rita always left from and came back to when they took the train, and Heino Merkel as well: it's *their* railway station.

Rita Süssfeldt thrusts her way over a zebra crossing in the midst of a bunch of students, pushing through clouds of vapor emitted by Afghan coats, steering around people who are comfortably shuffling along, until there's a sudden obstruction and she finds herself in front of a loose gathering of men and women. "Can I get by? Please let me through." They move aside to let her pass, sulkily because they're anxious to hear the next selection by the police band, which is bringing its week of good relations with the public to a close with a performance of popular tunes. Our uniformed friends and helpers seem extremely fed up, even their acrobatic conductor; they're all playing with morose concentration and stiff fingers and anyone so inclined can hear plaintive protest in their solemn-sounding version of "Down by the Riverside." Past them, past everybody: past the lines in front of the ticket offices, past the hungry travelers slouching around the newsstand vacantly taking bites out of steaming sausages, past a group of reservists howling their delight beneath their straw hats, on and on and up the steps to the main-line platform.

November mist hovering over brightly polished tracks, neckless passengers waiting buried in their coats, regularly falling drops forming a pattern in the damp dust and exposing tiny circles of originally clean concrete.

Where and which one could he be? Rita makes a quick check as she scouts once up and once down the platform, examining the waiting travelers, peering, to their surprise, at frosty faces so suddenly and closely that she occasionally has to apologize; she even puts her hand on the padded shoulder of a dark-blue coat that could certainly have been his. But suppose he's taking the suburban line to the central railway station?

Over there, on the suburban platform, in the constant comings and goings of the throng of passengers there are just as many people resembling him in gait and posture, he could just as well be standing at the newsstand as next to the departure platform where a man in a red cap is giving the signal for a train to leave. Isn't that Mareth over there?

With her coat loose, elbowing her way through the crowd, looking all around her, and standing exhausted beside the stairs to watch the passengers as they emerge or scurry off, that must be Mareth, searching like herself as she now looks in her direction without noticing either Rita or the exaggerated signals she is giving.

I'll come over, Mareth, wait for me there—this is what Rita Süssfeldt is signaling to her sister, and she leaps down the steps leading from the main-line platform and once again hurries across the main hall. Hands reach out to catch her, she brushes them aside, someone places his hand on her behind as though sizing it up, but still she presses on without turning around. Going up the stairs is too slow, far too slow, as she finds herself wedged into a disgruntled line of people who react with irritation to any attempt to speed them up. Where's Mareth? She's no longer to be seen on the platform, she must have gone out through the other exit, the one behind the newsstand, perhaps she's taken the suburban line to the central railway station. High up in the domed ceiling, a blowtorch is showering sparklers. Where should she go now? Her aching temples, those butterflies in her stomach, which make her slightly unsteady on her feet: uncertainly Rita moves toward the edge of the platform, looking first in front and then behind and then only at the train as it comes boisterously in, as though she were trying to work out the most favorable or safest moment to jump.

She doesn't get in. Caught in the undertow, she allows herself to be carried down into the main hall, where she checks on the lines at the ticket offices and the people telephoning in the telephone booths. The band is playing "Anchors Aweigh," making it sound like a farewell to a ship about to be towed away to the scrapyard. A newspaper vendor is attracting customers with the offer of a railway accident.

That might be Mareth, that woman hurrying out of the station in the direction of the Stephansplatz—but why is she showing such a lack of interest in all the people coming toward her? Rita Süssfeldt follows and tries to catch up to her, even calling to her in a restrained voice, but then she disappears in the heaving mass by the Memorial. Something's happening at this unwieldy monument to those who fell in the war, something's causing the passers-by to stop and utter threats or cries of encouragement, there's something happening over there which is forcing people to react, in any event there is a hammer at work and presumably a chisel as well. Isn't that Mareth over there? Rita Süssfeldt forces her way through the bystanders, pushing and shoving until she reaches the front. She's mistaken. She must go back; she must go home.

Hardly has she driven off when a car's headlights start flashing behind her, someone's following her and signaling, keeping a constant distance behind her; and as she swings right and then right again, someone is trying, without danger to himself, to come up level with her. He won't pass, he won't let himself be shaken off either, probably one of those idiots who insist on following you, thinks Rita to herself, putting her hand over her rearview mirror.

She passes an elderly cyclist without incident, brakes in front of a man with a dog as a precautionary measure, manages, by swift evasive action, not to remove a careless old-age pensioner from the bosom of his family: everything's going well today, even to avoiding a collision with a vehicle riding without lights—thus does she pursue her course and very soon turns into the Hoheluftchaussee and now into Innocentiastrasse.

Is he still there? Yes, he's still there. As if moved by the same desire or propelled by the same mechanism, he slows down and, like Rita Süssfeldt, drives one of his wheels with a bump up onto the pavement and ends up in front of the streetlamp.

If that isn't Matthiessen! Matthiessen, the publisher's reader,

Dr. Dunkhase's assistant, who is clambering out of his car some-what more rapidly than she is, and now ambling toward her. All he wants to know is how their work's going. And whether she'd care to go out for a bite to eat with him. "Yes," she says, "I mean no, or perhaps you wouldn't mind waiting and taking the work away with you right now."

"Take your time," he says, "I'm good at waiting, I don't easily get tired of my own company."

Rita Süssfeldt does not have to say goodbye to him for the moment, so she turns away and goes toward the house, which is more brightly lit than the neighboring houses, climbs the steps, and suddenly turns to wave toward the car down below—not that it was expected of her, but to release an unaccustomed tension.

The doors are either open or ajar, there's been no change since she left the house. The document and the torn-up check are still on her desk, the star-shaped pieces of pastry on the kitchen table are still waiting to be put into the oven. However, Mareth's coat is hanging up in the closet, carelessly flung over a hanger.

"Mareth? Mareth, where are you?" Although her sister makes no reply, Rita knows where to find her, and she goes upstairs, noisily and taking her time as though wanting to announce her arrival well in advance. In Heino Merkel's room, where she's clearing up the traces of his departure, Mareth doesn't look up or reply to Rita's greeting; even when Rita walks into the room, her sister refuses to take any notice of her, but merely goes grimly on, brooding to herself, working away in a manner which immediately suggests protest and rejection. Obviously she'll have to stand in her way in order to be noticed at all, probably best of all in front of the open cupboard or the stripped bookshelf. From the way she's holding up a pair of shoes, turning them around, putting them away with their toes facing outward, and then giving them a little dab, you could almost imagine that she was trying to bring them to life or God knows what.

"You might answer me when I speak to you, Mareth." A short pause, a brief hesitation, and then her sister continues with her task. "What's happened, Mareth? Is this how we're supposed to treat each other from now on?" This time at least Mareth does throw her a glance, a contemptuous, dismissive glance from where she is squatting. "Why won't you tell me what's happened? Why did you run away from me at the Dammtor station?" And now merely a curt peremptory gesture: stop asking silly questions, there's no point now. A red, a blue, and a white scarf are folded one after the other, smoothed out, and put away.

"If you're accusing me of something, Mareth, at least you might tell me what it is." Even if she doesn't admit it, the elder sister seems to have been waiting for just such an opportunity, just such a provocation, to allow her to spew out the reproaches that she had kept bottled up, and with a puzzled look, as though it would have been all right to ask her anything except to question her motives, Mareth turns toward her and tugs so energetically at each end of a folded leather belt that it makes a sharp crack.

"You really don't know what's happened? You still don't know?"

She is obviously too agitated to talk directly to her sister, she has to go back to her task in order to work off her accumulated burden of reproaches and disappointment. "Now you've managed to do it, Rita; because of you he's learned what he's really worth, and if you ask me, if it'd been me, I'd have gone away, too."

Once again there's the ache in the temples and the tiny butterflies in the stomach that give her a queasy feeling. "I'm sorry, Mareth, I'll have to sit down."

"In the state he was in and sensitive as he was, you know very well, Rita, that he was suspicious of anything that suggested sympathy. There was only one thing that could help him: recognition from the outside, without fear or favor."

Rita Süssfeldt flips a cigarette out of the pack but forgets to light it. "But what have I got to do with all that, Mareth?"

"Heino knows who got him the prize, he's been told which member of the panel it was who gave him the vote he needed, don't you see? He's probably even read the minutes of your meeting."

Rita Süssfeldt watches the cigarette between her fingers begin to tremble; she quickly transfers it to her other hand but the trembling continues. "All right, Mareth, I wanted to help him, I admit it. We both know that what he needed in his situation was confirmation from the outside, some sign of recognition. I provided him with that but . . . I didn't allow for his suspicious nature, that's where I was to blame."

"Not only that, Rita, now you know all the harm you can do by showing careless sympathy."

"Did you talk to him again?" Rita asks.

"He telephoned and wanted to speak to you but you hadn't come back yet. He left behind for you all the things you had helped him to win—the check, the certificate, that damned prize. Yes, it was through you that he learned what he's worth: a castoff, dependent on charity, who was given the prize only because of his illness."

Silently, Rita protests, she raises her hand to defend herself and slowly lets it drop: it's impossible to decide whether Mareth is capable of understanding what she is saying or not. "But I thought it was the best work; I would never have intervened on Heino's behalf like that if I hadn't been absolutely certain that his work was better than that of the others. You do believe me when I say that, don't you, Mareth?"

Even now, nothing is finding its way back to drawers and shelves without due consideration, even the glass-and-brass weights move back into their old place. Mareth seems to find it easier to continue her accusations while busying herself like this and keeping her head averted; what she says seem colder, more definitive, as if it had been prepared long in advance. And her favorite turns of phrase to express her accusations? That's how you . . . now it's for you . . . it remains to be discovered . . .

And now Rita quietly asks where he has gone or where he was intending to go, and her sister replies vaguely, "He's gone away forever." And with the idea of concerting their efforts, Rita suggests telephoning his school friend who lives near Hannover, the remarkable pharmaceutical chemist, just in case, and Mareth ignores her suggestion because she alone knows that the chemist has died and so Heino can't go and live with him. And Rita Süssfeldt wonders what can possibly be done now, and Mareth says, "You can congratulate yourself on achieving what you wanted." Is that meant to be her last word? Is that intended to indicate the kind of life they'll be leading from now on? Is it putting an end to their life together? Oh, Mareth. Rita feels like saying something but then decides against it. She goes to the door and waits, surely Mareth would have to stop tidying up now and at least look her in the face; she does so and repeats: "Yes, you can congratulate yourself."

"Now listen, Mareth, listen to me and look at me," says Rita Süssfeldt. "You're trying hard to delude yourself, you think that it was only that business of the prize which caused him to go away—the prize I helped him to win. I'm telling you, Mareth, that was merely the final protest and a welcome one because he had already decided to leave some time ago when he realized how much his illness made him depend on you. He'd been finding it impossible to accept his lack of independence for a long time and it was for that reason more than any other that he needed a chance to prove himself."

How composed Rita remains under those narrow, hostile eyes, how calmly she replies to Mareth's question: Where did you get that idea from? "From Heino himself," she says, "and let me tell you this as well: he often had the feeling that the worst thing he could do, as far as you were concerned, was to get well, because he was afraid that if he did he would be devaluing the sacrifices which you had made for him during the period when he was ill; he told me so. Oh no, Mareth, he didn't leave because he was disappointed about the prize, but because he wanted to prove to himself that he can manage without your help."

"And he talked to you about it?"

"Yes," says Rita.

After that disclosure, surely almost anything might happen—

more violent accusations, for example or a refusal to believe, or renunciation—you might also think that the elder sister would walk out of the room in such a way as to leave no doubt that she was breaking off all relations; but Mareth reacts in a way Rita could never have foreseen: stiffly, but slightly deflated, she goes over to the monster of a chair, picks up the leather straps, places the buckles together, and snaps them shut. She doesn't test their efficiency, but just sits there, shackled and motionless as though she has settled down to stay for good, or else—and this is just as true—as though she had to accustom herself never to expect anything definite again.

Rita cannot now merely turn away and leave her sister to herself as she sits there not asking any more questions, not even trying to confirm what she has just been told. As always, when something has been gained, something else has to be lost. Now Mareth lifts her face and follows Rita with anxious eyes as she goes across the room—only to get some matches from the shelf —and when Rita comes and sits down opposite her, smoking, full of sympathy, she quickly drops her eyes again.

What's to be done now, Rita? What can we do? These are the questions she will be asking later on, when she has acknowledged her defeat. For the moment, however, she merely wants to snap open the catches and run to the door to discover who it is who is ringing yet again, not impatiently but rather timidly; however, Rita has already gone ahead and is on her way, so that all she can do is call after her, "Don't leave me here alone, not too long by myself."

Naturally, Matthiessen is uneasy, he doesn't want to intrude, he hopes he's not disturbing, he would just like to inquire how much longer they're likely to take with their editing; in addition, he would like to propose—if there were any problems—that they might give the text a final polish together, perhaps over a bottle of '64 St.-Emilion—how about it?

Rita Süssfeldt listens for any sounds from the house and then says, "I'm afraid I can't manage it today; I do hope you understand."

"But how about Dunkhase?" the man says. "He was to have the manuscript to read today."

"Wait here a minute."

And then Rita Süssfeldt goes into her study—through the open door he can see her hastily reading the first few sentences of manuscripts, thumbing through them, putting them to one side —and she comes back with two bundles of sheets fastened together and hands them to the man without looking him in the face.

Here they are, they're the two chapters that have to be amalgamated with each other. She asks the man to hand the passages on to Dunkhase, with her compliments, please, and if possible with the request that the two chapters be combined to form one new work: "Controversial Decision," or something like that, so that they will be read together, in combination. Could she ask him to do that for her? And can she rely on him to understand her position? And would he now please excuse her because something had happened which left her no choice but to stay here.

Matthiessen shrugs his shoulders, rolls the manuscripts up together, strikes them against his open palm, and then, softly, almost caressingly, against Rita's right shoulder. "I hope nothing like this happens when we're doing the final editing," he says, "because I'd like to do that with you."

"May I go now?" asks Rita.

"Of course. I'm only waiting so as to impress on my mind the way you walk, seen from behind—it reminds me of people who with the best intentions in the world always arrive late."

23

Aᴿᴹᴇᴅ with his indispensable favorite newspaper, Janpeter Heller is now slouching his way through the vestibule, dusting the morning's snow from his coat before going to the desk to pick up his keys. His bunch of keys is not hanging on the board; nevertheless, he tells Ida Klöver the number of his room, and while the woman ponderously starts looking for it, he waves at the maid, opening and shutting his fingers in a stiff scissors-like movement, all to no avail, however, because Magda merely looks up with a brief uncomprehending glance and then with perspiring upper lip returns to her football-pool coupons, a living witness to the toil and trouble you have to take to clinch your luck with ticks and crosses.

"Oh yes," says Ida Klöver, "we've already brought your luggage down—you're leaving today in any case, aren't you?—and someone's already moved into your room." Heller's suitcase is standing beside the concealed fireplace and his briefcase is balanced carefully on top. Now, who's responsible for the bill?

Heller will pay the bill himself. He inquires, "What's the damage?" and beneath Frau Klöver's gaze he counts onto the table the grubby bank notes which he has been keeping in his trouser pocket, held together with nothing but a paper clip. He's folding the receipt with one hand—as if he wanted to demonstrate to the old woman what he's capable of doing with only one hand—when with a sharp rustling sound Ida Klöver pushes another piece of paper toward him. "There's this, too. I almost forget."

"Surely not a charge for extra heating?"

"It's your wife, Herr Heller, she's already phoned you twice; here's the number where you can reach her."

That's not my number, it must be the number of the doctor's office, he thinks as he goes into the telephone booth. After dialing, he turns around and through the dusty glass he can see the two women talking together, the older one doubtfully wagging her head while the younger one points her pencil toward him with a grin.

"Charlotte?"

"Just a moment please."

Apparently she's put the receiver on the parapet of her command post so as to be free to receive an incoming patient or listen to a long-winded departing one. "Charlotte?"

"Yes, here I am, you must excuse me, we're terribly busy here this morning." He can sense the difficulty she has in starting the conversation and imagines her keeping an eye on the doors as she speaks to him in a rapid undertone; and he can tell immediately that she's not called merely to know whether he's still there. The tone of her voice warns him that something unusual has taken place or is about to take place, it's Charlotte's small, oracular voice, inviting you to adopt an attitude of solemn expectancy.

"Listen, Janpeter, I've decided to hand in my notice."

"You have?"

"I haven't done it yet, but I've been thinking about it ever since yesterday evening."

"Does he know?"

"If I do it, it'll be because of him." Charlotte stops talking, not because she's forced to, but because she's disappointed that Heller is not showing more eagerness or at least more involvement in his questions: in fact, she even has the impression that his interest is waning as she now proceeds to relate the lively dispute which had been sparked, of course, by his visit to the office: in the car, so he understands, there was merely harmless small talk about the events of the day; in the restaurant over dinner, he started making snide remarks, all of them directed

406

against Heller; driving home, after all that red wine, ironic references to the breakup of the marriage; and then finally at home— fortunately Stefanie was already in bed—he let loose a tirade of hatred and contempt. "You must admit one's bound to feel oneself under attack, too. Anyway, I'm all set to hand in my notice."

Heller sighs and looks wonderingly at the mouthpiece of the receiver as he assesses what he has just heard and estimates the consequences before he starts speaking: "If you're asking my advice, Charlotte . . . too hasty . . . too impulsive and exaggerated; after all, you should examine the other side and try to understand it, especially because many things sound different from the way they're intended."

He'd like to persuade her not to be in too great a hurry to hand in her notice, he'd like to warn her in general against too hasty decisions. "Charlotte? Are you still there?"

"Yes, I'm still here"; and then, after a pause, in an almost completely flat voice: "So you're advising me not to do it?"

"No, not that exactly," Heller says, "but for the moment, Charlotte, I'm advising you to wait and not take the bull by the horns immediately, because acting impulsively and spontaneously . . ."

Heller is listening carefully to himself as he talks, and the more words he uses, the more he feels uncertain whether they're being taken in and evoking any response. "That's the reason, Charlotte: I want to protect you from doing something that you might regret later on."

She can't go on listening to him any longer, the medley of voices coming from in front of her command post tells him that she's hard-pressed, that everyone's clamoring for her attention: why is he trying so hard to keep on talking? "Do you see what I mean, Charlotte?"

She has to hang up now, all she'd like to know is whether he can call her again, either here or at home. "Please call me again, Janpeter."

Heller is not quite certain. Heller will try. Through the glass in the telephone booth he recognizes Rita Süssfeldt, who is at this moment breaking off her conversation with the old woman and coming toward him, so, hastily, as though he was doing it merely to satisfy her, he says to Charlotte, "I'll try and do it, sometime." They both hang up without saying goodbye, she more quickly than he.

From the way he comes out of the telephone booth, Dr. Süss-feldt feels impelled to ask him if everything is all right, to which Heller replies, "Why shouldn't everything be all right?" A hearty handshake. As far as he was concerned, everything was fine, he'd seen to everything that needed seeing to, his luggage is already waiting over there, but he supposes that he still must say good-bye.

First he shakes hands with Frau Ida Klöver, and as he is immediately assured that he was a welcome guest, he finds it no longer possible to fulfill his original intention of expressing his barbed thanks for fairly good heating, fairly good breakfasts, and also fairly good service; instead, he gives the impression that he's been comfortable on the whole—it was quite bearable, anyway.

Then he shakes hands with Magda, surreptitiously runs his fingers over the flat depressions of her hand, and is not surprised when the maid abruptly cuts the handshake short and flings herself around in her revolving chair more violently than necessary, so that her betting coupons flutter onto the floor. Relief is clearly discernible in his voice as he calls across the room, "Bye-bye again." Cheerfully he picks up his baggage. Rita Süssfeldt opens both doors for him. And once outside?

Once outside he looks in vain for the friendly frog-green car and Rita Süssfeldt apologizes as she calmly announces that once a month the car goes on strike, that today happens to be the day, and there's nothing she can do about it. Even if she takes all the care in the world, the battery runs down once a month, she's got used to this little habit, not least because her car more than makes up for such behavior in so many other ways.

She suggests that, on this particular occasion, they take the bus into town. Heller is forced to agree. The bus is only half full, Heller is able to put the suitcase between his legs, his briefcase is resting against his thigh, in fact he's not inconveniencing any of the passengers with his luggage, unlike the old man with the tough-looking face who has actually brought along with him an antiquated baby carriage full of tools, a spirit level, a crowbar, and a compass saw wrapped in burlap.

The pair of them—Rita and Heller—have been eyeing each other for too long, someone has got to ask a question, and it's Heller who inquires, "Still feeling the same?"

"I think so," says Rita Süssfeldt. "The two chapters taken together ought to produce the right effect. Unfortunately I haven't been able to amalgamate them, presumably Dunkhase will be able to read them."

"Are you really crazy about Lucy?" Heller suddenly asks.

"No, I'm not—are you?"

"I'm not either, and that's what convinces me that she's suitable. A resplendent Lucy, a Lucy we're both inspired by, who fills us with blind admiration, wouldn't be an acceptable model at all. Someone whose life resists any single interpretation— that's what I had in mind. A heroine who can also be taken to task for her actions."

"There were many times," says Rita, "when I would have liked to come to the help of our paragon: great decisions certainly seem to leave you defenseless—or vulnerable in other directions—and that's exactly how she seemed to me sometimes: defenseless."

"And perhaps limited," Heller says, "but in the nobler sense of the word in which any model person is bound to be limited."

"We've been rooting around for this example," Rita says, "and when I think how many young people will find her getting on their nerves—well, I feel a bit apprehensive."

Two seats in front of them, a lively discussion is taking place, sparked, as always, of course, by a ticket inspector, who's trying to explain to the man with the portable workshop that it's still a good quarter of an hour too early to travel on his old-age pensioner's reduced-fare ticket, to which the old man replies in a threatening tone that his daughter's flat has been flooded since this morning. So the inspector would like to call attention to the conditions that are attached to the privilege—that is the word he uses—of traveling at a reduced fare; is it not the case that the use of public transportation is permitted only between certain hours? "You can tell that to the high tide," the old-age pensioner replies, and turns his back with an offended look.

One has to admire the way the pipsqueak of an inspector sticks to his guns undaunted, for he now endeavors to ask the pensioner whether he is in fact aware that he's using his special ticket a good fifteen minutes before the proper time. When the pensioner merely replies, laconically, "Shove it," the ticket inspector, for reasons known only to himself, requests him to repeat the expression.

At this point, inevitably, Heller has to butt in from where he is sitting. He calls out, "What's the matter? Why can't you leave the old man alone? If he has to pay extra, I'll pay it."

It's the pensioner, not the inspector, who answers: "Now don't you start throwing your weight around," he says, "what do you take me for?" And without a word but with an eager glint in his eye, the inspector pushes his way past the baby carriage and, as if this were his way of replying, requests Heller to hand over his ticket, which, with obvious relish, he checks for date and number, rubs between his fingers, and even holds up to the light. With the words "Lucky for you," he hands the ticket back and then turns his attention once more to the old man, a fish almost landed which only needs gaffing.

There we are and now everyone will have to work out the likely ending of this everyday dispute for himself, for Rita Süssfeldt informs Heller that this is where they get off. "It's that house over there, the old narrow one." Heller humps his luggage past the two men, who break off their argument for a few moments while the bus is at a stop.

"Shall I take something from you?"

"That's okay," says Heller, "I can manage."

A door that sticks, worn-out stone steps, a makeshift glass cage behind which a girl, businesslike to the point of rudeness, acts as receptionist and telephone operator: only now does Rita Süssfeldt ask whether, since he has brought all his luggage with him, Heller is going to leave Hamburg whatever the outcome may be. He thinks he'll have to leave, things have turned out like that. With his shin he eases his suitcase in little jerks up against the glass cage to the exact position indicated by the girl with a blink of her eyelids, and then they're allowed to find their way to Dr. Dunkhase: "Second floor, just keep following the sign with the three boats."

Winding corridors, but above all stale, stagnant air . . . yes, Dr. Süssfeldt is convinced that it's the air in the corridor which is troubling her vision and causing her painfully throbbing headache. She stumbles, wipes her eyes, and furtively rubs her temples, but when Heller looks at her questioningly she gives a reassuring nod: I can manage. One last corner and there is a glass-paneled door with the silhouette of three stylized boats stuck onto it, floating on a few, but nonetheless decorative, waves.

So these boats are sailing home with their cargo of eternal Spirit, Beauty, and Absolute Truth, at the moment under the captaincy of Dr. Dunkhase. "Is this where we knock?"

Although their knock elicits no reply, they go in, step apart, and take up their positions beside the doorposts, like doorkeepers, simply because there's nothing else they can do in a room whose floor and walls, tables and radiators and shelves are covered with large-size photographs. And over there by the window, as it were on a small surviving headland, is Dr. Dunkhase with his carefully casual Roman emperor's haircut and a thick teacup in his hand, glumly eyeing the photographs lying on the floor, like a flood that, disappointingly, isn't going to yield anything very much.

Heller's first thought is: he could easily be one of my class. On Dunkhase's left, with a checked sports cap on the back of his head, a photographer, late middle age, looking embarrassed; on his right, pale and thin-cheeked, with an American sergeant's stripes on her upper arm, the photographer's daughter, obviously part of the business.

Greetings are exchanged across the photos; a few words, a vague gesture or two, and then immediate withdrawal into gloomy contemplation. Apparently all these photos are for a picture book, titled *Faces of Germany*, and what seems to be making him so glum is the fact that the pictures provide no sort of information about Germany or at least they don't seem to be illustrating the country he has in mind. His foot twitches as he uses it to push the photos cautiously to one side, scrapes out a kind of ford, and appraises the photos from another angle—with the same melancholy result, because now he's shaking his head disgustedly and sighing as he explains to the photographers the reason for his dissatisfaction: "Those barges on the Rhine—as soon as I see that glittering triangle in the water with a decorative mist veiling the cliffs and naturally with the inevitable ruined castle on top—okay, it's charming, all the charm of a graveyard, just the thing perhaps for a restaurant car on German Railways, but no, not for us. Or this one: North German shrimp fishermen photographed through a hanging net—a picture of unalloyed contentment after work; all you need is a gold frame and then no one will ever know of the godawful life that shrimp fishermen actually have. And those cheerful coal miners taking a shower at the end of their shift—I can't imagine that they've ever even heard of such a thing as pneumoconiosis. Pretty pictures, peaceful, carefully selected pictures of Germans at work—with a lovely matte finish—for crying out loud, that's exactly what we didn't want."

Dr. Dunkhase knocks back his tea, looks over to Heller and Rita Süssfeldt for support, notices that they are without cups, and calls out to an adjoining room, "Olga, some more tea and two more cups." He roams disconcertedly among the landscapes, past town fountains and brilliantly lit factories, irritably taking in the all too familiar Sunday-supplement pictures—an old wine-grower in the Mosel; altar boys at Rottach on the Inn; Hamburg longshoremen—while the girl begins, almost soundlessly, to gather up the photographs.

And now here's Olga bringing in the tea, a frightened-looking woman bearing the cups at arm's length across the sea of photos, half-filled cups, and then she pours some more tea for Dunkhase out of a bottle.

"Your very good health."

"Good God," Rita says, "it's straight whiskey."

"We call it tea," Dunkhase says casually, "and it's just as good for us as tea."

A sweep of the arm: "Now, what are we going to do with all these appallingly good photos? What's your opinion, Paul? I can't help it: everything you point your camera at is transformed into a treasure chest, even our own country. You see grapes as riper, snow as whiter, faces more open and honest, and even mist becomes part of your composition. If only you two weren't so perfect! If you could hold on to your love of stillness and yet come to terms with action as well! You even show nasty situations bathed in sunlight. When do you ever hint at signs of unrest? What were you doing with your camera during those protests against the Shah? Why are you idle when the police are clubbing people? Why didn't you photograph those young squatters who took over that empty house on the Alster?"

He breaks off and looks toward the door, which is being opened cautiously. It's Matthiessen, the publisher's reader, who seems to wish to avoid attention as he strides storklike to his desk, apparently to look through his mail, which he now, however, pushes to one side as he sits down next to the telephone. "Olga? Tea, please."

Before Olga can oblige, he pulls a manuscript out of his breast pocket and holds it out toward Dunkhase with the words: "Agreed. There's nothing there." Dunkhase gives a nod as though he has been waiting for this information. He glances toward Heller and Rita Süssfeldt and for the first time apologizes for not being able to offer them a seat and then he asks them when they would like to discuss the matter. "No preference? Well, no time like the present!"

In any case, further discussion is needed on the pictures; actually, they could probably agree on a few of them—a long gulp;

a brief meditation. The supple leap from one scene to the next. The new stage sets are already in place. "Well now, my dear colleagues."

This opening bodes little good. Dr. Dunkhase weighs the manuscript in his hand, makes a play of recognizing what it is, then points to Matthiessen and then to himself. "We've both read this third chapter, or rather what is intended to form the third chapter, and our opinion is: an interesting suggestion. The conflict: arguable; the political background: enlightening. The exemplary heroine herself, Lucy Beerbaum: a very worthwhile person, at any rate. And we do see the advantage of combining the two episodes."

"In other words," Heller says, "you appreciate our proposal but consider it unsuitable for the anthology."

Dunkhase doesn't want his statement to be interpreted in such black-and-white terms as that, he had in fact been interested in the proposed text; what is more, he insists on giving the reasons for his judgments. He manages to squeeze himself onto the windowsill, crosses his legs, takes a nip from his cup, and is about to expound his general principles, but Rita Süssfeldt doesn't give him the chance. She asks, "You've heard of this unusual woman, haven't you, and know what she did?"

"Very well," Dunkhase replies, "I was friendly with one of her assistants for quite a while, Rainer Brachvogel. Perhaps you know him?"

And he would like to say, too, that even if it was stimulating in itself, the work would not be acceptable in a German anthology. Unless he's completely mistaken, they were supposed to find an exemplary life, a model for our times: that was what the original commission had said and they had agreed on that.

"Well, tell us if you know of a better one," says Rita Süssfeldt. Dunkhase's tight jeans seem to be pinching him in the crotch, he tugs playfully at the region of his genitals and gingerly uncrosses his legs. "It's not a question of the best example," says Dunkhase, "it's rather that we're looking for a model that is appropriate for us today, one that corresponds to our way of life in these latitudes."

414

"Doesn't Lucy do that, then?" asks Rita Süssfeldt abruptly, and she gives Heller a nudge in the ribs to encourage him to counter-attack at once.

But Heller is listening in an attitude of dispassionate attention, as if he knows in advance what will be said and is staying on merely to hear his fears confirmed one after the other. And so he gives a quick nod of approval when Dunkhase describes Lucy's action as an example of passive resistance, undoubtedly a splendid and idealistic demonstration but apart from that completely ineffective. Moreover, the model they're setting up for the young people of today was an old woman, or at least she was getting on in years; he himself is still young enough to regard this as a challenge to the spirit of his generation. Mistrust is bound to arise from the very nature of the thing. And doubts. And reluctance to accept any lesson that such a heroine might have to teach.

"I must be hearing things,' says Rita Süssfeldt.

Dunkhase, who seems to be reading the words from a neon sign, goes on: "I feel even greater qualms when I think of the kind of action that is being put forward as exemplary. A protest against illegal violence—that's all well and good. But it's a private protest. Contemplative, meditated. Elegiac. A humble rebellion. No education oriented toward emancipation can be satisfied with that kind of thing: a protest that involves no action and as a result achieves nothing. And I find it equally impossible to imagine our young people being satisfied with any model who is remarkable primarily because she suffers and because she feels for the suffering of others."

"That's precisely it," Heller says, "and that's why the only qualified exemplary life is one which is either a call to action or an embodiment of it, anything else is just raspberry-flavored ambrosia."

Dunkhase ignores Heller's sarcastic comment, but then accepts it as though he had uttered it himself. He goes on: "Ultimately both the theory and the practice of political struggle show that changes are brought about only by being active. In any case, the revolutionary potential in the schools must be aroused in a different way: by people *acting* in exemplary ways."

"People acting for the sake of action," Heller adds, "because they look upon compromise as a disaster. Action as a new type of solution, as a religion regardless of where the congregation ends up. The solution is merely the situation which you happen to land in each time, the Promised Land is wherever the train happens to stop."

Momentarily at a loss, Dunkhase says, "I don't quite see what you're getting at."

Heller kindly spells it out: "I merely wanted to draw your attention to a new variety of arrogance—action for its own sake."

"I see," Dunkhase says. "Well, that aspect of it seems to have escaped my notice, but that's yet a third objection against your heroine, and if you're agreed . . ."

"Would you be referring to the futility of her sacrifice?" asks Rita Süssfeldt.

"No, it's something else: it's her tiresome predilection for self-justification. We're expected to show too much understanding. Just think how much time your heroine spends asking for indulgence. Pleading her own case. You surely can't imagine our young people of today having any truck with that? We don't think that an exemplary life needs self-justification. Its actions are justified by the circumstances of the time. I'm sorry, Herr Heller, no doubt at your age a Lucy Beerbaum may seem a model worth following; but for us she gives the impression of someone who's discovered Gandhi rather late in life! . . . Olga? Tea!"

And Olga whisks out of the side room like a little mouse forever willing to oblige and pours some more special tea out of a bottle, not for Heller nor indeed for Rita Süssfeldt, though the photographer seems to be in particular need of it and allows his cup to be filled to the brim.

"As you see, Paul," says Dunkhase to the photographer, "we all have our problems, similar problems"; and then addressing Heller and Rita Süssfeldt: "Well now, you two, no hard feelings, but the third chapter really is worth another try. If you like, you can have till tomorrow, but drop any idea of people like Lucy

416

Beerbaum, such lotus blossoms of nonviolent resistance. Nowadays we know that every relationship is based on force, and in order to face up to that, any hero for our times must act. Don't aim so high or look so far afield: a rent strike, a sit-in, an untoward incident in the administration of a school, that sort of thing offers plenty of scope for exemplary action. Or am I wrong, Lothar?"

Matthiessen, who even when seated looks like a human question mark, lifts his index finger and wags it back and forth, clicking like a metronome the while: any possibility of error is definitely excluded. However, once having testified to this, he would like to make a further comment: if there's a shortage of material or examples, being an anonymous instigator of such things, he has a whole stock of letters of thanks, and if called upon he would be happy to offer his assistance in the matter, and so on. Dunkhase smiles. So may he now hand back the manuscript for them to use as they like? Can he definitely rely on receiving a new proposal, perhaps even by tomorrow afternoon? And will they excuse him, he has a lot of work on his desk and he hopes he needn't feel that he's stepped on too many feet?

To Rita Süssfeldt's surprise, for she is breathing fire and brimstone and breaks two matches as she hastily tries to light a cigarette, Heller turns up his coat collar, shrugs his shoulders, and then nonchalantly catches the manuscript which Dunkhase tosses to him across the photographer. "Okay, let's go." Rita Süssfeldt refuses and pushes Heller's hand away from her arm; she's not going to go quietly, because even if there is no appeal against the judgment, she'd still like to get one or two things off her chest.

"Have you any idea," she asks, "of the time the three of us spent on this project before we decided on this particular example? The mass of material we read and assessed and discarded? Can you imagine how exhausting and boring a job it was to reach agreement?"

Having assumed that his judgment and its consequences were now a thing of the past, Dunkhase puts on a show of bewilderment followed by irritation. "Excuse me," he says, "surely you must be aware that it's not the trouble you may have had in coming to an agreement which we're discussing, but merely the result of your deliberations: that's the only thing we have to consider."

"He's right," says Heller, reaching out determinedly for Rita's arm in order to drag her away. "And the longer you defend yourself, the more certain it is that he's right. Anyway, you've just heard: exemplary lives don't need self-justification." In taking his leave, Heller disguises his contempt under elaborate formulas of politeness, whereas Rita Süssfeldt gives notice that, as far as she is concerned, this isn't the end of the matter, she still has a few remarks and comments up her sleeve, you could be sure, because she refuses to accept defeat until she's compelled to —or words to that effect.

And then they go out in single file and along the winding corridor, and since Heller is leading the way it's not surprising that all of a sudden he feels a prickling, burning sensation on his neck, a tingling between his shoulder blades, a buzzing in the back of his head, and an itch behind his knees, and as things are becoming increasingly uncomfortable the longer they walk in silence one behind the other, he lets Rita Süssfeldt catch up with him, takes her by the elbows, turns her angry face toward the light, and says, emphasizing every word, "If you don't stop fuming like that, you're going to set fire to my coat. I can feel it singeing already." An attempt to free herself, a groan, a dismissive gesture. "Oh, let's forget about it, Herr Heller."

They set off again down the corridor, with Heller explaining to her over his shoulder why she is so enraged: she's doubly disappointed, first at the rejection of their proposed text and then, on top of that, at his failure to put up any sort of resistance. "You're furious because I didn't stand up for myself, that's the reason, isn't it? Because I didn't set him straight, didn't contradict him, didn't finish him off. Anyway, you'd have felt better if I'd spoken out strongly in support of our chapter instead of taking refuge in sarcasm."

The only reply is the regular thud of her feet, and after a pause,

418

Heller continues: "Perhaps you're even blaming me for being disloyal to our work by being so ready to accept defeat. If you really think that, then I must tell you something. Even if I haven't learned very much, there's one thing I can recognize immediately: whether it's worth trying to persuade someone or not. And Dunkhase is the sort of person who is unpersuadable; for him anybody else's opinion is always suspect because it represents an unknown power. Such people can never understand our belief in ambiguity. The only satisfaction you can get in such cases is the satisfaction of not wasting your breath."

Rita makes no reply and they reach the reception area in silence; Heller picks up his luggage and lets Rita go ahead into the street.

Cold, wind, discomfort; you have to catch your breath. The wind is blowing fine mortar dust from the demolition site across the way, where a perfectly habitable house is being torn down and gutted, a spacious old hulk that is submitting more or less calculatingly to the calculated onslaught.

Now what? Is this the moment to take their leave? "Yes," Rita Süssfeldt says, twisting her gloves around her fingers, "I did expect you to defend yourself better, a few sparks, some resistance, you know what I mean. After all, over this period we have become quite expert."

"Experts without any backing," Heller says, and is debating whether to put his luggage down in order to begin his goodbyes; but he doesn't have to decide, because Rita dashes past him into the street and snaps her fingers for a taxi. "Here we are, let's get you to the station."

He is only mildly surprised that she joins him in the back seat and tells the cab driver in her own peculiar way where to drive: "One-way trip to the central railway station, if that's possible." They sit quietly side by side, exposed to identical emotions and preoccupied with a foretaste of parting. There are still many things that need to be said; the drive would be more bearable if they were to speak, indeed a few words to express their inner thoughts might perhaps have relieved the sense of poignancy, but

419

they both decide against it, merely drawing each other's attention briefly to construction sites or to a couple of black limousines escorted by motorcycles for which they're forced to stop. Not until they draw up in front of the railway station does Rita start inquiring into the details of his journey, and Heller has to admit that he hasn't got a ticket and doesn't even know when the next trains for Diepholz are due to leave. And he has to admit, too, that he's not leaving in the best of moods, at least not in the mood he would have liked to be in. He carefully balls up the cellophane outer covering of a pack of cigarettes, which Rita then with supreme nonchalance throws onto the floor under the driver's seat of this painstakingly cared-for cab, whose floor mats, artificial wax flowers, and seat covers remind him of a nicely respectable German parlor. "We've still got one thing to do," says Rita Süssfeldt. What's that? "In a minute, inside the station: we've got to decide what we're going to do next."

The woman goes on ahead, threading her way between groups of palavering foreign workers and schoolchildren from the provinces who've just been on a tour of the harbor and are explaining to each other what they've seen, already preparing for the inevitable essay. She pilots them around the mound of luggage belonging to two Turks who are living proof that you can travel with a complete electric kitchen and, further on, around sailors, bystanders, and strapping railway policemen until they reach a board displaying departure times. "In any case, it's the Bremen line we want, isn't it?" Heller gives a nod, Heller has made up his mind, all he wants now is a ticket. Rita Süssfeldt also has something she wishes to do, so they part company and arrange to meet again shortly, in the milk bar, at a corner table if possible.

And while the man is telling a ticket clerk his destination, the woman fights her way to a kiosk and waits until the revolving display tower of postcards is free. And having obtained his ticket, Heller does not make for their meeting place ʋut walks over to the line of besieged telephone booths. And turning the tower around, Rita Süssfeldt examines colored views of Hamburg, summer harbor scenes with honest Fritz in the foreground, swans on the Alster, St. Pauli by night, and decides on a photograph of a divers' boat beside which the pilothouse of a wrecked barge is clearly recognizable: "The Salvage." And finally established in an empty booth, Heller firmly dials a number, lets it ring five times, dials a second number and lets it ring only four times, and then leaves the booth with the expression of a man who has just received his best news of the day. With what élan he's swinging his briefcase! And despite its weight, how well he manages to maintain this sprightly gait until he reaches the milk bar.

Rita Süssfeldt has managed to appropriate a corner table and has already ordered a raspberry shake for him—"and don't you dare tell me you don't like raspberries!"—and now she draws his attention to the postcard on the table and the address written in block letters. Pundt? "Yes," says Rita Süssfeldt in a warning voice, "Valentin Pundt, and now try and think what we're going to write to him." Heller cheerfully suggests informing their old collaborator of the departure time of the Bremen train—with their best wishes for a good recovery, of course. But Rita Süssfeldt dismisses the proposal with a reproachful look, stares at the card, looks up as though she had had an inspiration, and then rejects it without saying a word.

Well, what about it? And where do they go from here? Heller draws the card along the table toward him, turns it over, contemplates the salvage boat, and then with a preliminary smack of the lips: "Why not tell him about our shipwreck? Why shouldn't Pundt be informed that our project struck a reef called Dunkhase?"

"In the first place," says Rita Süssfeldt, "we must show consideration toward someone who is still convalescent, and secondly I don't at all feel that we've run aground: certainly Dunkhase will find himself having to read a new proposal—or better still, two proposals—very soon. If not tomorrow, then in the course of the next few days. It's up to you, too, Herr Heller, to show how quick we can be—and how determined we are—to offer him something else."

Heller stirs his raspberry shake with a plastic spoon, vigorously producing bubbles, then shakes the cardboard cup and can't bring himself to lift it to his mouth. "Mm . . ." The long-drawn-out sound reveals his uncertainty or at least his reluctance: "Just between us, I feel the way a high jumper feels when they keep raising the bar higher and higher—far higher than his experience tells him he can clear."

"Even if that is the case," Rita says, "we can't quit in the middle of the competition."

"But suppose the height is becoming completely unnerving?"

"So you're giving up too?"

Heller makes an evasive gesture, he can't and doesn't want to say anything definite, not at this particular moment, not here and now, but he'll get in touch, he promises as much, and she'll get his definite decision in good time, whatever happens. Rita Süss-feldt ponders his words; neither disappointed nor bitter, she seems to accept the situation and then pushes the postcard toward him with her ball-point pen and asks him to write on it; she closes her eyes and drinks.

"Well, we'd got as far as 'Dear Herr Pundt,' what next?" Rita Süssfeldt stares at his hand and at the ball-point pen, held at the ready, which suddenly poises itself and begins to describe erratic circles in the air while seeming restrained by some obstacle from making contact with the postcard. What is there really worth communicating, after all? What news can we expect to interest him?

" 'Dear Herr Pundt,' at least there's no doubt about that." The woman beside him has no difficulty keeping silent, entirely absorbed in patient expectation. Is he to be amused, angered, offended, or merely sent their good wishes? And how interested may one assume him still to be? " 'Dear Herr Pundt,' okay"; and suddenly Heller puts pen to paper, presses his lips together, hesitates, as though making sure, and then writes, reading each word out loud as he does so: " 'Shortly before I left we even managed to discover a model for our times: it's a windmill, still intact, and when there's enough breeze, it beats the air with all four sails for everyone to see. I confide this discovery to you with

422

every good wish for a speedy recovery and a raspberry milk shake at my elbow. Janpeter Heller.' "

He flings the ball-point onto the table and with the tips of his fingers pushes the postcard over to her. And what does Rita Süssfeldt do? She doesn't bother to look over what he has written but quickly squeezes her signature into the margin, then shakes herself and shudders as if she suddenly felt chilly and hastily makes her way through the swinging door, pausing only to wish Heller a good journey. He looks at the postcard flapping in her hand and wonders what he has done to warrant such an abrupt farewell.